FREUD
AND HIS
FATHER

FREUD AND HIS FATHER

MARIANNE KRÜLL

TRANSLATED BY ARNOLD J. POMERANS

PREFACE BY HELM STIERLIN

W·W·NORTON & COMPANY

New York   *London*

The text of this book is composed in Times Roman, with display type set in
Albertus. Compositon and manufacturing by the Haddon Craftsmen, Inc.
Book design by Jacques Chazaud.

First Edition

Library of Congress Cataloing-in-Publication Data

Krüll, Marianne.
  Freud and his father.

  Translation of: Freud und sein Vater.
  Includes index.
  1. Freud, Sigmund, 1856–1939. 2. Psychoanalysts—
Austria—Biography. 3. Freud, Sigmund, 1856–1939
—Childhood and youth. 4. Freud, Sigmund, 1856–1939—
Family. 5. Freud, Jacob, 1815–1896. 6. Fathers and
sons. 7. Psychoanalysis—History. I. Title.
BF173.F85K7313 1986   150.19′52   85–26027

ISBN 0-393-01854-7

W. W. Norton & Company, Inc., 500 Fifth Avenue, New York, N.Y. 10110

W. W. Norton & Company Ltd., 37 Great Russell Street, London WC1B 3NU

1 2 3 4 5 6 7 8 9 0

"It is true that the biographer does not want to depose his hero, but he does want to bring him nearer to us. That means, however, reducing the distance that separates him from us: it still tends in effect towards degradation. And it is unavoidable that if we learn more about a great man's life we shall also hear of occasions on which he has in fact done no better than we, has in fact come near to us as a human being. Nevertheless, I think we may declare the efforts of biography to be legitimate. Our attitude to fathers and teachers is, after all, an ambivalent one since our reverence for them regularly conceals a component of hostile rebellion. That is a psychological fatality; it cannot be altered without forcible suppression of the truth and is bound to extend to our relations with the great men whose life histories we wish to investigate" (Freud, 1930e, 211f.).

Contents

LIST OF FIGURES   *x*

LIST OF TABLES   *xi*

PREFACE BY HELM STIERLIN   *xiii*

FOREWORD TO THE AMERICAN EDITION   *xv*

FOREWORD   *xix*

1. THE CRISIS IN FREUD'S LIFE AND THOUGHT   *1*

1. Before the Crisis (1885–96)   5

The emergence of a theory of hysteria. Jean-Martin Charcot,   5
Josef Breuer

From the "sexual theory" to the "seduction theory." The Fliess   8
Period Wilhelm Fliess . . . The sexual theory of actual
neuroses . . . The Emma-Irma-Anna episodes . . . Seduction
theory . . . Explaining the neuroses of defense by the seduction theory

2. The Acute Phase of the Crisis (Summer 1896–Autumn   40
1897)

The death of Jacob Freud   40

The struggle to save the seduction theory   43

Self-analysis   50

The renunciation of the seduction theory   54

3. After the Crisis (Winter 1897–Autumn 1899)   58

From the seduction theory to the Oedipus theory   58

The Interpretation of Dreams   64

4. Conclusions: The Significance of the Rejection of the   *68*
   Seduction Theory

2. PREHISTORY: KALLAMON JACOB FREUD   *71*

1. Political and Intellectual Currents in the History of   *72*
   Galician Jewry

2. Life in the Galician Shtetl   *78*

3. Tysmenitz   *85*

4. Jacob Freud's Childhood and His First Marriage to   *88*
   Sally Kanner in Tysmenitz

5. The Break with Tradition   *91*
   Jacob Freud, the wandering Jew   *91*
   Jacob's marriage to Rebekka   *96*
   Jacob's marriage to Amalie Nathansohn   *97*
   The death of Schlomo Freud   *99*

6. Conclusions: The "Old Man's" Secret   *100*

3. THE TRAUMA:
SIGMUND FREUD'S CHILDHOOD AND YOUTH   *103*

1. The Web of Relationships in Freiberg   *103*
   Jacob, the father   *108*
   Amalie, the mother   *115*
   Freud's nursemaid, Resi Wittek   *119*
   Freud's half-brother Emanuel   *122*
   Maria, Emanuel's wife   *123*
   Freud's half-brother Philipp   *124*
   Freud's nephew Johannes (John)   *128*
   Freud's niece Pauline   *130*
   Freud's sister Anna   *134*
   Freud's brother Julius   *135*

Rebekka, Jacob's second wife   *135*

Other contacts in Freiberg   *138*

Relatives of Freud's father in Tysmenitz, Jassy, Breslau,   *138*
Vienna, and elsewhere

Relatives of Freud's Mother   *139*

2. The Departure from Freiberg   *140*

3. The Early Years in Vienna   *147*

The Freuds' material circumstances   *147*

Sigmund Freud's early years in Vienna   *151*

Learning with his father   *156*

The counterfeit money affair   *164*

Freud's brother Alexander   *166*

At the *Gymnasium*   *168*

4. Visits to Freiberg   *169*

5. Freud's Half-Brothers in England   *172*

6. Conclusions: Jacob Freud's Mandate and the Crisis   *176*
of 1896–97

4. THE FULFILLMENT OF THE MANDATE   *181*

1. Sigmund Freud and the *Moses* of Michelangelo   *184*

Sigmund Freud, the son of Moses   *187*

Sigmund Freud, patriarch in the primal horde   *188*

The "sons": Adler, Stekel, Jung . . . Totem and Taboo   *189*

2. Sigmund Freud, the Man Moses   *194*

3. Conclusions: Reckoning Up   *208*

CHRONOLOGY   *213*

TABLES   *233*

NOTES   *247*

BIBLIOGRAPHY   *273*

INDEX   *287*

List of Figures

 1. Sigmund Freud in August 1890   3
 2. Jacob Freud at about 1895   3
 3. Detail from a Map of the Austrian Empire   73
 4. Part of Market Square in Tysmenitz   87
 5. The Interior of the Great Synagogue in Tysmenitz   87
 6. Detail from a Map of Freiberg   105
 7. Panorama of Freiberg   105
 8. The Vicinity of Freiberg   106
 9. The Market Square of Freiberg at about 1890   106
10. The House in which Sigmund Freud Was Born in Freiberg   107
11. The Staircase in the House in which Sigmund Freud Was Born   107
12. Josef Pur, Municipal Medical Doctor in Freiberg   137
13. Detail from a Map of Leopoldstadt, Vienna, in 1863   149
14. Leopoldstadt, Vienna: Jacob Nathansohn's House in 1851   150
15. "Coppersmith-House" in Leopoldstadt, Vienna   150
16. Jacob Freud and Sigmund Freud at about 1862   152
17. Amalie Freud with Sigmund, Rosa and Dolfi in 1864   153
18. Title Page of Philippson's Bible   157
19. Egyptian Gods in Philippson's Bible   158
20. Egyptian Temple in Philippson's Bible   159
21. Egyptian Funeral Ferry in Philippson's Bible   159
22. Egyptian Funeral Bier in Philippson's Bible   159
23. Moses in Philippson's Bible   185
24. The *Moses* of Michelangelo in S. Pietro in Vincoli, Rome   185
25. Sigmund Freud's Study at 19, Berggasse, Vienna, in 1938   209
26. Sigmund Freud's Desk at 19, Berggasse, Vienna, in 1938   209
27. Sigmund Freud at His Desk in 19, Berggasse, Vienna, in 1938   210

List of Tables

1. Freud's Theory of the Neuroses in about 1896   38
2. Facsimile of a Freud Family Tree by Hellreich (probably 1914)   233
3. Jacob Freud Family Tree   234
4. Facsimile of the "Register of Jews Resident in Freiberg" of 1852   236
5. Facsimile of Entry in Passport Register   237
6. "List of Articles Imported and Weighed In by Freiberg Merchants in the Years 1852–54"   238
7. Facsimile of Marriage Certificate of Jacob and Amalie Freud, Dated 1855   239
8. Facsimile of the Birth Entries of Sigmund and Pauline Freud and of Emil Fluss in Freiberg, 1856   240
9. Facsimile of the Birth Entries of Anna and Bertha Freud in Freiberg, 1858 and 1859   240
10. Facsimile of the Death Entry of Julius Freud in Freiberg, 1858   241
11. The Network of Sigmund Freud's Relationships in the Summer of 1859   104
12. Report in the Vienna Neue Freie Presse of the Trial of Josef Freud in 1866   242
13. Facsimile of Entry in Roznau Register of Spa Visitors for 5 June 1857   244
14. Facsimile of Postcard Sent by Philipp Freud to his Half-Sister Marie, 12 March 1902   245

Preface

by Helm Stierlin

This book is not just about Freud's relationship with his father and family; it is primarily about psychoanalysis—its sources, foundations, development, and limits.

A theory formulates principles linking observed phenomena. It resembles a telescope: it brings certain aspects of reality closer and fades out others, so determining what questions are asked, what answers can be found, what is essential and what is irrelevant. These criteria may also be applied to the psychoanalytical theory created by Freud's genius. As W. H. Auden pointed out, that theory has changed the intellectual climate of the Western world, creating a new self-understanding, a new psychological reality. However, it has also kept the critics busy and has forced us to ask: what did the psychoanalytical lens fail to take in, what did it distort, and what did it shut out?

The new paradigm of family therapy, in particular, has encouraged the asking of such questions, for it insists on reconciling the essentially individual-centered psychoanalytical view—which focuses attention on the identification of intrapsychic phenomena—with the increasingly complex family or systems approach, or else on delimiting the two. In addition, Freud's own work has had to be reviewed in the light of this new approach. It is that task Marianne Krüll has tackled in the present book. To that end, she has examined Freud's parental origins and above all the delegations, mandates, conflicts, and invisible loyalties embedded in his relationship with his father.

No pioneering theory, we should remember, develops in a straight line. It necessarily proceeds by a series of advances and retreats, of innovations and revisions. This is true of Freud's work no less than that of such other original thinkers as Darwin and Einstein. However, there are two factors that distinguish the psychoanalytical theory created by Freud: the close connection of its history with its author's personal conflicts and, following on from this, the dramatic renunciation of the centerpiece of psychoanalytical theory in 1897.

That centerpiece was the so-called seduction theory of neurosis. Freud had believed—and argued in his writings—that his patients' neuroses were the direct result of specific sexual traumas: their seduction by parents or other primary caretakers. Now he denied the pathogenic power of such traumas and instead stressed the pathogenic significance of intrapsychic, and especially sexual, fantasies and conflicts, no matter whether caused by seductive family interference or not.

This theoretical change was to have a profound effect on the theory and practice of successive generations of analysts and has left its mark on the way in which modern society has come to understand and to treat mental illness.

It is on this event that Marianne Krüll's book hinges. She demonstrates its links with another crucial happening—the death of Freud's father, an event that Freud himself has called "the most poignant loss in a man's life." In uncovering these links, Marianne Krüll also rewrites the history of the Freud family. She scrutinizes all Freud's writings, and especially his letters and dreams, for their autobiographical import, and reexamines the contributions of earlier Freud biographers. Above all, however, she pursues her own far-reaching historical studies, which have led her *inter alia* to a reconstruction of Jewish life in Tysmenitz, Galicia, the birthplace of Jacob Freud; have taken her to Freiberg (Příbor) in Moravia, where the infant Sigmund lived until he was three; and involved her closely in late nineteenth-century Vienna, where Freud spent his youth. In so doing, she opens up a panorama of cultural and social influences, and reveals a tissue of complex and often conflictual relations, which cast fresh light on the development not only of Freud but also of psychoanalysis.

No doubt the author's psycho-historical method has certain limitations: time and again gaps appear, time and again several explanations suggest themselves for one and the same fact. Of these limitations Marianne Krüll herself is perfectly aware, and for that reason she repeatedly stresses the conjectural character of many of her interpretations and assumptions. At the same time she carefully eschews all forms of sensationalism, in the face of what are often sensational discoveries or conclusions—and in this I see a special merit of her book.

Despite these reservations, largely acknowledged by the author herself, I find the overall conclusion of her book highly plausible. Above all, I consider the questions raised and the perspectives opened up so important that I would like to see this book in the hands of everyone who is interested in the development of psychoanalysis, in the formation and history of scientific theories, in the mainsprings of human creativity, and in psychology or psychotherapy in general.

Foreword to
the American Edition

I am very happy to see my book finally published in America, where many people have been eagerly awaiting its appearance in English.

My special thanks go to Arno Pomerans, whose brilliant translation is a pleasure to the eye and to the ear. I only wish he had also been the translator of Freud's works, letters, etc., in which case he would have saved us so much of the trouble we had to take in retranslating the Standard Edition in all those instances where my arguments would otherwise have been totally incomprehensible to the English-speaking reader not familiar with the German original.

This English edition of my book is essentially identical to the original German edition of 1979. Apart from a few minor corrections in the text, I have incorporated additions to the family tree, discovered and kindly provided by Peter J. Swales. His research in Czechoslovakia, undertaken in collaboration with Josef Sajner, has revealed among other things that Sigmund Freud's nursemaid was most probably not Monika Zajíc, as I had assumed in the first German edition of my book, but Resi Wittek. As a result of Peter J. Swales's research it is now certain, too, that Freud's patient Emma was not Anna Lichtheim, as I had thought, but Emma Eckstein (1865–1925). Further additions regarding Freud's visit to England in 1875 were made possible by virtue of a letter he wrote to Eduard Siberstein published in Ronald Clark's biography of Freud. And finally I was able to include a number of details about Sigmund Freud's family of origin from Anna Freud Bernays's little-known autobiography of 1930 (*Erlebtes,* Vienna, Kommissionsverlag der Buchhandlung Heller) which Sophie Freud Loewenstein kindly let me have. I want to thank all of these people for their generous help. I am of course pleased that the incorporation of this new material did not necessitate any revisions in my basic conclusions.

I am sorry that Jeffrey M. Masson's book, *The Assault on Truth—Freud's Suppression of the Seduction Theory,* came out in America before mine. The unnecessary sensationalism that has now entered the discussion of Freud's seduction theory might otherwise have been avoided. Although I agree with Masson's essential thesis regarding the value of Freud's early theory, I regret that in many important instances Masson did not apply careful scientific scrutiny to the matter and jumped instead to hasty and oversimplified conclusions. Since Masson knew my book, I find it surprising that he neglected to mention alternative explanations for Freud's abandonment of the seduction theory, no doubt the better to press his—to my mind—quite absurd idea that Freud was little more than a liar craving fame.

I would like to add a personal remark. Through my book, Sophie Freud Loewenstein, professor at Simmons School of Social Work in Boston, has become one of my best and most intimate friends. It was her wonderful review of the German edition of this book that started our friendship. She wrote: "As a granddaughter of Sigmund Freud I cannot be objective about a book that has deep personal meaning for me. It gave me the exhilarating opportunity to explore my own roots in eighteenth-century Polish Jewry. It confronted me with my own life-long conflicts of delegation, loyalty to, and betrayal of the Freud family tradition. I believe, however, that others too will find personal meaning in this book" (*Family Process,* 1980, vol. 19, p. 312). I feel that throughout the few years of our intensive exchange of ideas and feelings, our mutual attempts to understand each other's roots has given us both a most enriching and stimulating experience which has borne fruit in many ways. It has been an exploration in the spirit of Sophie's grandfather, although he might not have approved of everything we said or did . . . !

It was through Sophie's influence that feminism became the essential aspect of my living and thinking it now is, when at the time of writing my book it had been quite a remote idea for me. But now I would say that my book clearly reflects a woman's perspective. By turning to Freud's early theory of seduction, for example, I unconsciously took a woman's stand against the extremely patriarchal Oedipal theory. I also believe that my picturing Freud as a frightened and bewildered, yet courageous and curious, little boy is a view not easily reached by most men, and also not by those women who accept their subordinate role in our male society.

All this was unconscious, but I remember that, when writing my book, I did from time to time become consciously aware of the tremendous difference between my working condition and Freud's: I was in a far less favorable position than he was when he wrote or developed his thought. While he was working in his rooms, he did not have to bother at all about what went on in the "women's and children's" part of his home on the other side of the staircase. Nobody was permitted to disturb him, yet all he had to do was to cross over whenever it was time for his meals, for relaxation, or for going to bed. The rest was taken care of by his wife, Martha, and her sister, Minna. My situation was quite different: I had to take care of a family as a mother, wife, and housekeeper, and lend emotional support to two adolescent girls with all the time- and energy-consuming activities involved, in addition to holding a full-time job as a university teacher. Although my husband and I shared the household and child-rearing chores, this was not at all comparable with Freud's ideal situation. When writing, I constantly had the feeling that I was stealing time from my other, "true" obligations as a woman, and was always ready to leave my desk when the family called me. And I have since learned that this is by no means a personal, individual experience of mine, but that it is the "normal" situation of all professional women: We are either totally overburdened with work and family or must renounce marrying and having children in order to pursue a career. Men, on the other hand, are in the best position to advance their career when they are married, because they can then rely on their wife's taking care of their earthly needs and feel free to invest all their time and energy in spiritual matters, for which they earn social recognition, and are even granted a license to look down on their non-intellectual wives!

I thank you, Sophie, for helping to open my eyes to the feminist cause. I am sure I would have written this book differently today, but I hope that even in its present form the sensitive reader will be able to hear a woman's voice speaking.

Bonn, November 1984

Foreword

This work was planned originally as a short study, in which the intellectual, political, social, and economic background of Sigmund Freud was to be linked with the elaboration of psychoanalytical theory. My attempt to establish the sociohistorical foundations of that theory on the very sketchy material we have of Freud's own life, however, quickly forced me to extend the scope of my original project. In particular, to obtain satisfactory answers to my many questions, I had to do a large amount of field work: I traveled to Vienna and to Czechoslovakia, initiated searches in London and Manchester, and corresponded with many people who were kind enough to provide me with additional information.

As a result, not only did the intended framework of this book expand considerably but the focus of the investigation gradually shifted: from being a socio-epistemological study of the origins of psychoanalysis, it turned increasingly into a biography of Sigmund Freud and of his father, Jacob. The detailed presentation of the biographical material I had collected often seemed as important to me as the discussion of the original sociological problem.

This widening of scope also reflected my personal involvement with Freud and his ideas. Like so many others, I first came across his work when seeking explanations for my own conflicts and contradictions. The help I obtained from reading a number of Freud's writings explained my original enthusiasm for psychoanalysis. Yet I very soon came to question some parts of his theory because they were patently self-contradictory. My fascination turned into its opposite, rejection and criticism. Only years later, once I had begun to delve into my own biography, did I return to Freud. The fascination revived—this time, however, not so much with the work as with the man, Freud, its author. The achievements and failures of the work appeared to be so many reflections of the greatness and the weaknesses of its creator.

A special problem for me, as a German and a Gentile, was coming to grips with Freud's Jewishness. This effort led me ineluctably to a confrontation with the horrible fate meted out to Jews in Hitler's Germany. It became impossible for me to remain unaffected by the material I had to assimilate. To that extent, this book is also a part of my own confrontation with this dark chapter in

German history, a chapter that had exercised my mind ever since I started to think consciously, that has stamped my political views, that led me years ago on a study trip to Israel, and that, not least, has determined my academic career and stamped my personal life.

This book thus became a challenge to me in more than one respect. Whether I have succeeded in presenting my case objectively despite my own emotions, despite my deep personal involvement, is something the reader will have to decide for himself.

ACKNOWLEDGMENTS

Professor Helm Stierlin (Heidelberg) may be called the moving force of this book. His work on Hitler (Stierlin, 1975b) inspired me to return to my earlier idea of writing a study of Freud, and his personal encouragement helped me to turn that idea into a reality. Professor Josef Sajner (Brno, ČSSR) has earned my special gratitude for his kindness in putting at my disposal his entire collection of documents on the stay of the Freud family in Freiberg, which he gathered together with the help of Professor Renée Gicklhorn, and, in addition, for providing me, at great cost in time, with further material from Czechoslovak archives that were inaccessible to me. I am also grateful to Professor Sajner for the hospitality he extended to me in his home and for accompanying me to Příbor. Professor Gicklhorn (Vienna) gave me many valuable suggestions during my researches in Vienna. Szlomo Blond (Holon, Israel) has supplied me with invaluable information about his native Tysmenitz in Galicia and about the life of its Jewish people. To Tamar Somogyi (Bonn), I am indebted for important details on the Jewish religion and on Galician Jewry. I am also most grateful to her for the translation of several Hebrew, Yiddish, and Polish texts. Anna Freud has kindly provided me with a family tree from the Sigmund Freud Archives, New York. Dr. Kurt R. Eissler, Director of the Archives in New York, and Pat Marsden of Sigmund Freud Copyrights, Ltd., Colchester, England, helped me greatly in procuring documents, photographs, and other data. Elke Kuhne (Berlin) made searches for me in London and Manchester. I was given valuable information and practical help by Bill Williams and Fran Shepherd (Manchester), Dr. Avner Falk and Professor Ernst Simon (Jerusalem), Dr. Reinhard Sieder (Vienna), and many others, to all of whom I express my cordial thanks.

The book also owes a great deal to Dr. Christa Knirim (Bonn) for her constructive criticism of earlier drafts, and for her untiring assistance in drawing up the chronology, compiling the index, and reading the proofs. Professor Helm Stierlin, Professor Justin Stagl (Bonn), Eva Hermann (Zürich), and Helmut Krüll also read the manuscript and helped with critical observations. The benevolent interest of Professor Richard Martinus Emge (Bonn) has aided the work considerably. I would also like to thank those students at the University of Bonn who, during the winter semester of 1977, participated in my class on Psychoanalysis and Sociology, and who made so many useful suggestions in papers and discussions. Special thanks are due to C. H. Beck, my German publishers, and to Dr. Günther Schiwy in particular, for their readiness to change earlier plans and to include much more comprehensive tables and chronology than were originally envisaged.

Last but not least, I want to thank Juliane, Sibylle, and Helmut Krüll for having brought so much tolerance and sympathy to bear on the Freudomania of their mother and wife, partly under protest, partly with resignation, but ultimately with patient understanding.

Despite all the care I have taken, errors of fact or interpretation are bound to have crept into this book. I shall be most grateful to readers who bring these to my attention.

Bonn, December 1978 Marianne Krüll

FREUD
AND HIS
FATHER

1. The Crisis in Freud's Life and Thought

In what follows, I shall be examining a period in Freud's development that proved to be a turning point both in his scientific thought and in his personal life. It was a period during which he moved from the neurophysiological studies of his student years to psychology, during which he was transformed from a tempestuous young man out to conquer the world into a self-possessed *pater familias*. In Ernest Jones's words: "The end of all that labour and suffering was the last and final phase in the evolution of Freud's personality. There emerged the serene and benign Freud, henceforth free to pursue his work in imperturbable composure" (1953, I, 320). In the scientific field, the result of this change was psychoanalysis both as a doctrine and as a movement.

Such change did not occur without conflict; on the contrary, it marked a fundamental crisis in Freud's life. To what extent personal experiences were involved, how much of psychoanalytical theory sprang from Freud's scrutiny of his own psyche, will be shown in what follows.

In his scientific outlook, the crisis was preceded by a reorientation lasting several years, the beginning of which can be dated in various ways. It is possible to consider Freud's "On the Psychical Mechanism of Hysterical Phenomena: Preliminary Communication," which he wrote with Breuer (1893a),[1] as the first herald of psychoanalysis. One can go even further back and consider Freud's visit to Charcot in Paris in 1885 (1956a) as the beginning of his reorientation. Or it would be equally justifiable to start earlier still, and to consider Josef Breuer's successful treatment of Anna O. in 1880–82, in which Freud took a lively interest (Jones, 1953, I, 223ff.), as the real starting point of psychoanalysis.

But while this pre-psychoanalytical phase can be dated in different ways, all of Freud's biographers are agreed on the time when his crisis came to a head: it occurred in September 1897, and was marked by Freud's renunciation of his so-called seduction theory, first enunciated in 1893. Freud himself has described the change as follows:

... a mistaken idea had to be overcome which might have been almost fatal to the young science. Influenced by Charcot's view of the traumatic origin of hysteria, one was readily inclined to accept as true and aetiologically significant the statements made by patients in which they ascribed their symptoms to passive sexual experiences in the first years of childhood—to put it bluntly, to *seduction*. When this aetiology broke down under the weight of its own improbability and contradiction in definitely ascertainable circumstances, the result at first was helpless bewilderment. Analysis had led back to these infantile sexual traumas by the right path, and yet they were not true. The firm ground of reality was gone. At that time I would gladly have given up the whole work, just as my esteemed predecessor, Breuer, had done when he made his unwelcome discovery.* Perhaps I persevered only because I no longer had any choice and could not then begin again at anything else. At last came the reflection that, after all, one had no right to despair because one has been deceived in one's expectations; one must revise those expectations. If hysterical subjects trace back their symptoms to traumas that are fictitious, then the new fact which emerges is precisely that they create such scenes in *phantasy,* and this psychical reality requires to be taken into account alongside practical reality. This reflection was soon followed by the discovery that these phantasies were intended to cover up the auto-erotic activity of the first years of childhood, to embellish it and raise it to a higher plane. And now, from behind the phantasies, the whole range of a child's sexual life came to light (1914d, 17f., italics added).

A later account is perhaps clearer still:

Under the influence of the technical procedure which I used at that time, the majority of my patients reproduced from their childhood scenes in which they were sexually seduced by some grown-up person. With female patients the part of seducer was almost always assigned to their father. I believed these stories, and consequently supposed that I had discovered the roots of the subsequent neurosis in these experiences of sexual seduction in childhood. My confidence was strengthened by a few cases in which relations of this kind with a father, uncle or elder brother had continued up to an age at which memory was to be trusted. . . . When, however, I was at last obliged to recognize that these scenes of seduction had never taken place, and that they were only phantasies which my patients had made up or which I myself had perhaps forced on them, I was for some time completely at a loss. My confidence alike in my technique and in its results suffered a severe blow; it could not be disputed that I had arrived at these scenes by a technical method which I considered correct and their subject-matter was unquestionably related to the symptoms from which my investigation had started. When I had pulled myself together, I was able to draw the right conclusions from my discovery: namely, that the neurotic symptoms were not related directly to actual events but to wishful phantasies, and that as far as the neurosis was concerned psychical reality was of more importance than material reality. I do not believe even now that I forced the seduction-phantasies on my patients, that I "suggested" them. I had in fact stumbled for the first time upon the *Oedipus complex,* which was later to assume such an overwhelming importance, but which I did not recognize as yet in its disguise of phantasy (1925d, 33f; cf. the brief comments on the role of the seduction theory in 1905d, 190f., I and 1906a, 274f.).

Without exception, Freud's biographers[2] agree with him that the renuncia-tion of the seduction theory was his great achievement, facilitating the discov-ery of the Oedipus complex, of infantile sexuality, and hence of psychoanalysis.

* See pp. 5ff. below—M.K.

FIGURE 1 Sigmund Freud in August 1890 (aged thirty-four) *(Sigmund Freud Copyrights Ltd., Colchester, England)*

FIGURE 2 Jacob Freud at about 1895 (about eighty years old) *(Sigmund Freud Copyrights Ltd., Colchester, England)*

And indeed there appeared, immediately after this "renunciation," what Freud himself considered the most important of his writings: *The Interpretation of Dreams* (1900a), a work that paved the way for the breakthrough of psychoanalysis.

That this turning point in his intellectual outlook was closely associated with certain events in his personal life was something Freud does not seem to have appreciated until 1908, when he wrote the preface to the second edition of *The Interpretation of Dreams.* It includes this telling passage: "For this book had a further subjective significance for me personally—a significance which I only grasped after I had completed it. It was, I found, a portion of my own self-analysis, my reaction to my father's death—that is to say, to the most important event, the most poignant loss, of a man's life" (1900a, xxvi).

When his father died at the age of eighty-one, Freud himself was forty years old and married, with six children. Is it not strange that at that age he should still have described his father's death as "the most poignant loss of a man's life"? Did Freud genuinely believe that the death of an aging father is the most important event in the life of an adult? Why should the death of a father be more poignant than the loss of a mother, a wife, or a child, losses which, though he had not yet suffered them, he must surely have been able to imagine?

This strange phrase, in fact, bears witness to Freud's strong emotional ties to his father, of which there are numerous other examples in *The Interpretation of Dreams.* Many authors have examined Freud's—incidentally most ambivalent—father relationship, one of the most impressive attempts in recent times being that of M. Robert (1975). The writers all seem to agree that the discoveries Freud published in this, his first book, and of which he later said that they were the most valuable of his life,[3] were the result of confrontations with his recently deceased father.

If it is true that Freud was forced by his father's death to examine their ambivalent relationship, and that *The Interpretation of Dreams* was the upshot of that examination, then it seems reasonable to suppose that Freud's entire scientific reorientation, whose outcome was psychoanalysis, was connected with his father. It is this supposition I shall be scrutinizing in what follows, first trying to assess the scientific import of Freud's reorientation, and then looking at that reorientation against the background of his ties to his father.

It seems that Freud himself preferred to leave his readers completely in the dark about these ties. He liked to keep his emotional and personal life secret, and on several occasions destroyed his private notes and letters so as to keep them from posterity. The fact that Freud made the remorseless search of the most intimate spheres in the lives of his patients the cornerstone of psychoanalytical therapy, while failing to apply this principle to himself—indeed, refusing adamantly to discuss his private life in front of outsiders, let alone in public—has been called a strange contradiction (see particularly Grubrich-Simitis, 1971).

In the case of his own personal and scientific crisis, however, Freud's hide-and-seek stratagem was unsuccessful. We have a precisely dated account in

Freud's own hand, one that he himself would never have released for publication, but that was nevertheless published after his death: the letters he wrote to his friend and Berlin colleague Wilhelm Fliess, in 1887–1902 (1950a). The other part of that correspondence, Fliess's letters to Freud, were destroyed by the addressee.[4]

In that correspondence, Freud's personal crisis is documented in such a way that the sequence of events can be reconstructed with a fair measure of accuracy.

This crisis, which lasted from the summer of 1896 (the beginning of Jacob Freud's fatal illness) until the autumn of 1897 (Freud's declaration that he had renounced his seduction theory), was the climax of a protracted upheaval in Freud's life and thought. I shall try to describe this preliminary phase, the crisis itself, and the subsequent period ending with the completion of *The Interpretation of Dreams* in 1899. In so doing, I shall pay special attention to links between Freud's personal experiences and his theoretical arguments; in other words, to the ways in which his personal problems were reflected in the contents of his theory.

1.1 Before the Crisis (1885-96)

1.1.1 THE EMERGENCE OF A THEORY OF HYSTERIA. JEAN-MARTIN CHARCOT, JOSEF BREUER

While still a student, Freud distinguished himself by various neurological research projects in Ernst Brücke's Physiological Institute, and even after taking his M.D. degree in 1881 he still thought of following an academic career in neurophysiology. However, Brücke advised him against it. Freud himself has put it as follows: "The turning-point came in 1882, when my teacher, for whom I felt the highest possible esteem, corrected my father's generous improvidence by strongly advising me, in view of my bad financial position, to abandon my theoretical career" (1925d, 10).

In this connection it should be recalled that Freud became engaged to Martha Bernays on 17 June 1882, and was anxious to gain financial independence as soon as possible in order to marry her. He accordingly decided to open a general practice after training in the General Hospital of Vienna, where he worked in several departments, including the psychiatric section. At the same time he continued his laboratory work with an eye to qualifying as a lecturer in the Faculty of Medicine; and with several papers on the anatomy of the human brain and on coca to his credit, he was duly appointed a *Privatdozent* (Lecturer) in Neuropathology (Jones, 1953, I, 73, 1925d, 12).

In the summer of 1883 his fiancée moved, with her mother and sister, from

Vienna to Hamburg, so that the couple were separated. During the four and a quarter years of their engagement, Freud wrote Martha more than nine hundred letters, of which only a fraction has been published (1960a).

In 1885, the year in which he was appointed lecturer, Freud applied successfully for a traveling scholarship to pursue his neuropathological studies under Jean-Martin Charcot at the Salpêtrière in Paris (October 1885–February 1886). There he at first continued his anatomical research of the brain, but soon abandoned this work because Charcot's treatment of neurotic patients, and especially of so-called hysterics, interested him far more. In Vienna and in other medical centers, it was commonly believed at the time that hysteria was not a "proper" illness.[5] As Freud put it in his "Report on My Studies in Paris and Berlin": "During the last few decades an hysterical woman would have been almost as certain to be treated as a malingerer, as in earlier centuries she would have been certain to be judged and condemned as a witch or as possessed of the devil" (1956a, 11).

Charcot, by contrast, considered hysteria a neurotic disturbance "with a connection to the genital system." Moreover, he also diagnosed it in males— again in complete defiance of the prevailing medical opinion. His method of treatment, hypnosis, was as unorthodox, and generally frowned upon by medical circles. Under hypnosis, he would suggest to his patients the disappearance —and for purposes of demonstration, also the appearance—of symptoms that would actually vanish, albeit only for a short time. Freud was so taken with the results that "he left the Salpêtrière Charcot's unqualified admirer" (1956a, 10; cf. Chertok, 1973).

The reason why Freud was so impressed was, no doubt, that four years earlier his older friend and colleague Josef Breuer, whom he had met at Brücke's Institute (Jones, 1953, I, 223) and who had a prosperous practice in Vienna, had told him about an hysterical patient with whom he had had very similar experiences. At the time, Freud had made detailed enquiries about this patient, the now notorious Anna O.; her real name was Bertha Pappenheim, and she later became one of the leaders of the Jewish women's movement (see Freeman, 1972).

Anna O. had suffered from severe disturbances of vision, from paresis of the muscles at the front of her neck "so that finally the patient could only move her head by pressing it backwards between her raised shoulders and moving her whole back," from lack of sensation in the legs, and so on (Breuer, 1895, 23). In addition, she alternated between two distinct states of consciousness: in one, she seemed relatively normal, although anxious and melancholic; in the other, she hallucinated and was highly excited.

To his own surprise, Breuer then hit upon a method of treatment that rid the patient completely of her symptoms: he made her remember their first appearance, and as soon as she was able to recall this, together with all the associated emotions, the symptoms disappeared. To accelerate the process, Breuer had used hypnosis. He called his new method "catharsis."

However, Breuer quickly dissociated himself from his own successes, because his ministrations to Anna O. ended in disaster. At the insistence of his wife, who had followed her husband's personal involvement with the twenty-one-year-old girl with obvious feelings of jealousy, Breuer broke off the treatment, the more readily as the patient seemed to have improved. But that same evening Anna O. had a relapse, and shocked Breuer by a phantom pregnancy and hysterical childbirth, claiming that he was the father. Up to that point, the patient had appeared to him "to be an asexual being" and had made no allusion to such forbidden topics. Breuer was suddenly forced to realize that Anna O. desired him sexually. So surprised was he that he fled from her, presumably because he became aware of feelings toward her that he had not admitted to himself (Freeman, 1972; Jones, 1953, I, 224f.).

These experiences of his friend with Anna O. in 1880–82 had prepared Freud for Charcot's method of treatment, even though Charcot used hypnosis as a direct means of removing symptoms by suggestion and showed no interest in the "cathartic" technique, in which hypnosis is merely used to prod the patient's memory. Charcot's discovery that hysterical symptoms could be influenced by hypnosis, and Breuer's findings that they could be traced back to early experiences and hence eliminated, had turned Freud into a staunch advocate of a new theory of hysteria—one that his teachers and colleagues in Vienna utterly rejected. His report on his studies in Paris (1956a [1886]), in which he argued passionately in favor of hypnosis, together with several other publications on the same theme, thus gradually turned him into an outsider.

On 14 September 1886, shortly after Freud's return from Paris, he and Martha Bernays were married. During the years that followed they had six children.[6] To support his growing family, Freud was forced to concentrate on his general practice, the more so since he had to support his parents and brothers and sisters as well, as he had done even during his studies (1960a, 101f.).[7]

Under the circumstances, it took a great deal of courage to cling obstinately to Charcot's view of hysteria, a view so unpopular among his colleagues. His chief, Theodor Meynert, professor of psychiatry at the University of Vienna, who before the Paris trip had proposed to hand over to Freud his lecturing work on the anatomy of the brain (Jones, 1953, I, 207), now disowned him for holding opinions that seemed so patently false.

In May 1889, Freud began treating Emmy von N. (1895d, 48ff.) and used Breuer's cathartic method for the first time. He suggested to her the disappearance of her symptoms under hypnosis, and tried at the same time to make her recall their first appearance.

During his treatment of this patient, and of others as well, Freud took note of the sexual material that kept peeping through from behind the symptoms. He now realized that Anna O.'s sexual acting out, which had so shocked Breuer, had been no exception: "Thus, starting out from Breuer's method, I found myself engaged in a consideration of the aetiology and mechanism of the neuroses in general. . . . In the first place, I was obliged to recognize that, in so far as one can speak of determining causes which lead to the *acquisition* of neuroses, their aetiology is to be looked for in *sexual* factors" (1895d, 25f.).

With that, Freud had taken a further step on the road to alienating his colleagues. In particular, his friendship with Breuer came to an end, and for the next ten years or so he would be forced to develop his theoretical ideas in almost complete isolation—except for his correspondence with his friend Wilhelm Fliess from Berlin. It was a true intellectual *moratorium* in Erikson's sense, of the kind so many great people have to undergo before emerging: "a span of time . . . before their deeds and works count toward a future identity," and "one possible way of postponing the decision as to what one is and is going to be" (Erikson, 1958, 40).[8]

1.1.2   FROM THE "SEXUAL THEORY" TO THE "SEDUCTION THEORY." THE FLIESS PERIOD

1.1.2.1   Wilhelm Fliess

Freud's friendship with Fliess, an ear, nose, and throat specialist from Berlin, went back to the year 1887, when Fliess, in Vienna for purposes of professional study, attended Freud's lectures (1950a, 75, 10 July 1893; Kris, 1954, 8). A close friendship only developed, however, after Freud had broken with his friend and patron Josef Breuer in about 1892. Fliess, who was Jewish, married an acquaintance of Freud's in 1892; she had been Breuer's patient, so that in that respect, too, the two men had close links. They met several times a year, and exchanged ideas either in their homes or—as they called it—at "congresses" in other cities.

Unlike Breuer, Fliess was not put off by the sexual theory of neurosis. On the contrary, he was highly attracted to it, having himself tried to develop a similar theory (see Kris, 1950).

In particular, Fliess believed that there was a close connection between the nose and the genital organs, and that certain neurotic symptoms could be traced not only to sexual but also to nasal disorders. Freud helped him to publish an essay on nasal reflex neuroses (1950a, 63, 4 October 1892). Fliess's main work on this subject was a paper entitled "The Relations Between the Nose and the Female Sex Organs from the Biological Aspect" (Kris, 1950, 6). Idiosyncratic though this theory now sounds, Freud backed it for a long time, and several of his papers contain references to it. However, his correspondence with Fliess reveals early signs of skepticism, and Freud never incorporated the nasal theory into his own theoretical framework.

But another of Fliess's ideas did leave its mark on Freud for a long time: the theory of periodicity. Starting with the twenty-eight-day female menstrual cycle, Fliess developed the idea that males too had a cycle, although of only twenty-three days' duration. The numbers 28 and 23 and their various combinations then helped him to elaborate a quasi-mystical method of predicting events in people's lives, particularly illness and death.

Freud obviously believed in the method, on several occasions predicting that he would die on a given date. In 1894, shortly before his birthday, he mentioned his "death deliria" which, however, he did not admit to his wife (Schur, 1972, 47, Letter of 19 April 1894); and in 1896 he expected to die on his fortieth birthday, May 6. Since the Fliess correspondence has unfortunately not been published in full, we cannot tell with what degree of seriousness Freud treated his successive death expectations. Max Schur, who in Freud's late years became his personal physician, tending him until his death, and who wrote a very sensitive biography about his famous patient, has included several previously unpublished letters of Freud's to Fliess. From there it appears that Freud was truly convinced he knew the date of his death. "As far as I am concerned," he wrote, "I note migraines, nasal secretion and attacks of fear of death, such as today, for example, although Tilgner's* cardiac death is probably more responsible for that than the *time period*" (Schur, 1972, 97, Letter of 16 April 1896, italics added). "I am as isolated as you would wish me to be . . . because a void is forming round me. So far I bear it with equanimity" (1950a, 162, 4 May 1896, omission by the editors).

Schur also mentions an unpublished letter of 17 May 1896, in which Freud says that he has passed the critical date (of his birthday) but adds that he has no more vital energy (Schur, 1972, 104). Later, Freud became convinced that he would die at the age of fifty-one or fifty-two. He arrived at the first figure by adding Fliess's two periodic numbers. Later still, he believed that he was destined to live until the age of sixty-one or sixty-two. When this date too had passed, he finally expected to die at eighty-one and a half, the age his father and his stepbrother Emanuel had reached (Schur, 1972, 159; Jones, 1957, III, Chap. 14). He survived that date as well, dying on 23 September 1939, at the age of eighty-three. It is, incidentally, very strange that Freud should have based his computation on an error: his father was just under eighty-one, not eighty-one and a half, when he died (cf. Table 3). Freud had probably used Jacob's fictitious birth date (see p. 95, note 34, below) when making this last calculation. Nevertheless, it is odd that he should have done so, and that Jacob Freud's gravestone, too, should state that he had died in his eighty-second year (E. Freud, 1978, 161).

Freud did not merely think that the date of his death was predestined. Both he and Fliess firmly believed that other misfortunes could be predicted with the help of the periodic theory. Thus when Freud's father fell fatally ill in 1896, shortly before the date on which Freud expected his own death, he wrote to Fliess: "You know that I do not laugh at phantasies such as those about historical periods, and that is so because I do not see any grounds for it. There is something to such ideas; it is the symbolic presentiment of unknown realities, with which they have something in common. Since then not even the organs are the same, one can no longer evade the acknowledgement of heavenly influences. I bow before you as honorary astrologer" (Schur, 1972, 107, Letter of 9 October 1896).

Schur's explanation of Freud's interest in number mysticism, though it does

---

* A well-known Viennese sculptor—M.K.

not fit our picture of Freud the great realist and atheist, goes straight to the heart of something with which this book is deeply concerned: Freud's Jewishness. Freud's superstition was connected with a mystical tradition particularly widespread among Jews with an East European background—from which Freud's parents too had sprung (see 2.1 and 2.2 below). These Jews consider the number 52, one of the dates on which Freud expected to die, an unlucky number, while they consider the number 17, for which Freud had a special affection because he became engaged to Martha Bernays on the seventeenth day of the month, as lucky (Jones, 1957, III, 379; Schur, 1972, 25).

Freud appreciated the "specifically Jewish nature" of his "mysticism," as we can tell from a letter he wrote to Jung in April 1909, in which he speaks openly of his conviction that he would die between the ages of sixty-one and sixty-two (Freud/Jung, 1974, 219f.). True, he had yet another, purely psychological explanation for this superstition. A footnote he added in 1904 to the second edition of *The Psychopathology of Everyday Life* reads: "My own superstition has its roots in suppressed ambition (immortality) and in my case takes the place of that anxiety about death which springs from the normal uncertainty of life. . . ." (1901b, 260).[9]

At times the relationship between Freud and Fliess was extraordinarily close. Originally, Freud seems to have considered himself to be at the receiving end of that friendship, as one who looked to the other for help in solving a question that bothered him greatly: the connection between physiological and psychological phenomena in the genesis of pathological behavior. When he did not succeed in applying Fliess's theories to his problems, and instead found his own answers to the questions that occupied him, their relationship began to wear thin, particularly after personal differences were added. In 1904, Fliess broke off the friendship, claiming that Freud had cheated on a question of priority (Jones, 1953, I, 314f.; Fliess, 1906).

Freud's correspondence with Fliess contains, in addition to the actual letters, a series of drafts, including the important "Project for a Scientific Psychology" (1895). Besides the books and papers Freud published at that time, his work is of crucial significance to the present account of Freud's theoretical development.

1.1.2.2 *The sexual theory of the actual neuroses*

The starting point of Freud's sexual theory of the neuroses was his observation that many hysterical patients can be made to remember sexual experiences by the cathartic method, and that these experiences were responsible for their neurotic symptoms.

Now, Freud did not at first apply his recently developed sexual theory to hysteria. He had merely, as he put it, taken a "momentous step": "to investigate the sexual life of the so-called neurasthenics who used to visit me in numbers during my consultation hours" (1925d, 24). Among "genuine" neurasthenic symptoms, Freud included intracranial pressures; spinal irritation, feebleness, and dyspepsia with flatulence and constipation; and nervous irritation (1895b, 90; 1895g). In addition, he combined certain symptoms, which were subsumed under neurasthenia in his day, into a special syndrome, which he called "anxiety neurosis," and which included the following clinical symptoms: disturbances of the heart action (palpitation, arrhythmia, pseudo-angina pectoris); disturbances of respiration (nervous dyspnoea, attacks resembling asthma); and attacks of sweating, of tremor and shivering, of ravenous hunger, of diarrhea, of locomotor vertigo, and of what are known as congestions, as well as paresthesias (morbid sensations, such as numbness, pins-and-needles) (1895b, 94f.; see Table 1).

As early as the winter of 1892, Freud's ideas about the sexual etiology of the "actual neuroses"—as he later termed neurasthenia plus anxiety neurosis —had become consolidated into a theory, as witness two of the drafts he sent to Fliess (Draft A, written at the end of 1892, and Draft B, written on 8 February 1893; cf. 1950a, 64ff.). Neurasthenia in males, he wrote in Draft B, is acquired at the age of puberty and becomes manifest in the patient's twenties:

Its source is masturbation, the frequency of which runs completely parallel with the frequency of neurasthenia in men. One can regularly observe in the circle of one's acquaintances that (at least in urban populations) men who have been seduced by women at an early age escape neurasthenia. When this noxa is long-continued and intense, it turns the subject into a sexual neurasthenic and his potency is also impaired; and a sufficiently intense cause will correspond to a life-long persistence of the condition. . . . A second noxa, affecting men at a later age, is brought to bear on a nervous system which is either intact or predisposed to neurasthenia owing to masturbation. . . . This second noxa is *onanismus conjugalis*—incomplete copulation in order to prevent conception. . . . Where the subject has a strong predisposition or suffers from chronic neurasthenia even normal intercourse cannot be tolerated; and intolerance is exhibited (in an ascending degree) against the use of the condom, of extra-vaginal coitus and of *coitus interruptus*. A healthy man will tolerate any of these for a considerable length of time but not indefinitely. In the long run he behaves in the same way as a predisposed subject. His only advantage over the masturbator is a more extended period of latency or the fact that he requires the occurrence in every case of precipitating causes. *Coitus interruptus* is found to be the most severe noxa, and produces its characteristic effects even in non-predisposed subjects (1950a, 68f.).

In women, the etiology of neurasthenia was said to take a different form. In their case, masturbation could clearly not be a causal factor since Freud considered girls to be "healthy," i.e., not "spoiled" by masturbation:

Girls are normally healthy and not neurasthenic; and the same is true of young married women in spite of all the sexual traumas to which they are subject at that age. Neurasthenia occurs comparatively rarely in its pure form in married women and older girls and must then be regarded as having arisen spontaneously and in the same manner [as in men]. Far more often neurasthenia in a married woman is derived from neurasthenia in a man or produced simultaneously. There is then almost always an admixture of hysteria, and this constitutes the common mixed neurosis of women. The *mixed neurosis* of women is derived from neurasthenia in men in all those not infrequent cases in which the man, being neurasthenic, has lost some of his potency. The admixture of hysteria is an immediate result of the withholding of the excitation of the sexual act. The less the man's potency, the more prominent is the woman's hysteria; so that a sexually neurasthenic man makes his wife not so much neurasthenic as hysterical (1950a, 69).

In Freud's opinion, therefore, neurasthenia was the result either of masturbation or of contraceptive practices by the married male. The woman suffers from the male's reduced potency in the wake of masturbation and, like him, from contraceptive practices. She develops either neurasthenia or else a mixed neurosis.

Anxiety neurosis, by contrast, was said to be the result of such "abnormal" sexual practices as *coitus interruptus,* and as frequently of sexual abstinence. In this case too Freud postulated different causal factors for men and women respectively. In men there was the anxiety of the "intentionally abstinent" and the anxiety of "unconsummated excitation," for instance, "during the period of engagement before marriage"; in older men there was, additionally, the fear of decreasing potency "at the time of increasing libido." Men who are accustomed to masturbation can fall victim to anxiety neurosis as soon as they give up the practice. Such people are "particularly incapable of tolerating abstinence."

Anxiety in women, he contended, could take the form of "virginal anxiety" and "anxiety in the newly-married," which occurs especially in young married women "who have remained anaesthetic during their first cohabitations." Anxiety neurosis is most common among those women whose husbands "suffer from *ejaculatio praecox* or from markedly impaired potency," and "whose husbands practise *coitus interruptus* or *reservatus."* Anxiety neurosis also occurs as anxiety in widows and in intentionally abstinent women (1895b, 99–101; cf. 1950a, 88ff. Draft E, June 1894). Freud added:

> I may note here, as being important for an understanding of anxiety neurosis, that any pronounced development of that affection only occurs among men who have remained potent and women who are not anaesthetic. Among neurotics whose potency has already been severely damaged by masturbation, the anxiety neurosis resulting from abstinence is very slight and is mostly restricted to hypochondria and mild chronic vertigo. The majority of women, indeed, are to be regarded as "potent"; a really impotent—i.e., a really anaesthetic—woman is in a similar way little susceptible to anxiety neurosis, and she tolerates the noxae I have described remarkably well (1895b, 102).

The symptoms of anxiety neurosis, he argued, were in a sense *surrogates* of the omitted coitus, in which too there is accelerated breathing, palpitation, sweating, congestion, and so on (1895b, 111; cf. 1950a, 93, Draft E, June 1894).

Freud believed that both types of actual neurosis could only be cured if those concerned put an end to the "abuse" of the normal "sexual regime," and replaced it with "normal sexual activity," because "the symptoms of these patients are not mentally determined or removable by analysis" but "must be regarded as direct toxic consequences of disturbed sexual chemical processes"

(1925d, 25f.; cf. 1916–17, 385ff.). In Draft B, which he sent to Fliess at the beginning of 1893, he also claimed:

> It follows from what I have said that the neuroses can be completely prevented but are completely *incurable.* The physician's task is thus wholly concentrated on prophylaxis. The first part of this task, the prevention of the sexual noxa of the first period [i.e., the period before marriage, M.K.], coincides with prophylaxis against syphilis and gonorrhoea, for these are the noxae which threaten anyone who gives up masturbation. The only alternative would be free sexual intercourse between young males and respectable girls; but this could only be resorted to if there were innocuous preventive methods. Otherwise the alternatives are: masturbation, with neurasthenia in males and hysteroneurasthenia in females, or syphilis in males, with syphilis in the next generation, or gonorrhoea in males, with gonorrhoea and sterility in females. The same problem—how to find an innocuous method of preventing conception—is set by the sexual noxa of the second period, for the condom provides neither a safe solution nor one which is tolerable to anyone who is already neurasthenic. In the absence of such a solution society seems doomed to fall a victim to *incurable* neuroses which reduce the enjoyment of life to a minimum, destroy the marriage relation and bring hereditary ruin on the whole coming generation. (1950a, 71f., italics added).

Neurasthenia and anxiety neurosis, according to Freud, could only be avoided if young men were allowed to have premarital heterosexual intercourse. If society did not permit that, or if sexual intercourse was only possible with prostitutes—who should be shunned because of the threat of veneral diseases—then neurasthenia and anxiety neurosis were inevitable. Nor were they curable, for even when sexual intercourse takes place after marriage, the earlier damage caused by masturbation leads to reduced potency in the male, which in turn leads to neurasthenia or anxiety neurosis in both sexes. In addition, the need to practice birth control gives a fresh impetus to neurasthenia and anxiety neurosis.

The basic premise of Freud's theory of actual neurosis was therefore the belief that only heterosexual intercourse without the then customary birth-control practices could prevent the appearance of neurasthenic symptoms in the male, and that abstinence or masturbation, as well as all forms of contraception, were bound to produce neurotic illnesses.

It is remarkable that Freud should not have mentioned homosexuality or other forms of sexual activity in this context. I shall try below (p. 19) to give reasons for this strange omission.

Quite apart from the fact that Freud's ideas about the harmfulness of masturbation or the difference between male and female sexual behavior are no longer accepted, it is odd that he should have developed a theory based on a fundamentally different premise from that of his theory of hysteria conceived at the same time (see 1.1.2.4 and 1.1.2.5 below). Thus, while he attributed hysteria to traumatic childhood experiences of a sexual kind, he blamed neurasthenia and anxiety neurosis exclusively on current ("actual") sexual practices. Why did he fail to trace the latter back to childhood experiences as well, when it would have been so easy for him to do so?

Recent studies have shown that the symptoms of Freud's "anxiety neurosis" agree with those of "cardiac neurosis," which Richter and Beckmann (1969), for instance, have traced back to psychic causes. These authors have shown, in particular, that patients suffering from neurotic heart symptoms had an unusually close and clinging relationship to one of their parents, generally their mother, and this usually because separation from her in early childhood gave them a profound lack of self-assurance. The anxiety associated with their cardiac symptoms is thus not the effect but the cause of these symptoms. Cardiac neurosis is generally triggered off by threatened or actual separation either from parents or from parent surrogates. To people unsure of themselves, such separations constitute so many ego defects; they are acutely anxiety-producing precisely because they pose existential threats. If that response cannot be expressed overtly—as happens invariably when early childhood traumas are not accessible to consciousness—then cardiac neurosis is an alternative means of expressing the underlying anxiety (Richter/Beckmann, 1969, 63ff.).

Had Freud searched for that connection he would surely have found it, much as, in the case of hysteria, he uncovered early childhood dreams as soon as he made his patients recall the past.

It is also remarkable that though he stressed that the symptoms of hysteria, neurasthenia, and anxiety neurosis overlap, and though he observed transitional and mixed forms, he should nevertheless have retained his etiological distinctions.[10]

Freud did not change his views on the actual neuroses until very late in life. In 1924, he could still write: "Since that time I have had no opportunity of returning to the investigation of the 'actual neuroses'; nor has this part of my work been continued by anyone else. If I look back today at my early findings, they strike me as being the first rough outlines of what is probably a far more complicated subject. But on the whole they seem to me still to hold good" (1925d, 25f.).

Only much later (1933a, 93f.; see Editor's Introduction to 1926d) did Freud revise his views on anxiety neurosis, asserting that it too had psychic causes. However, at no time does he seem to have altered his belief that masturbation —to which he later added the castration complex—was the ultimate cause of neurasthenic and anxiety-neurotic symptoms.[11]

Why did Freud not renounce these assumptions about the actual neuroses when he saw fit to renounce his seduction theory (see 1.2 below)? Why did he not jib at the contradiction between these assumptions and his other theoretical constructions? And why did these two particular types of neurosis strike him as differing so radically from the rest?

The search for an answer leads us inexorably to Freud's private life. From his letters to Fliess, we gather that he himself suffered from the symptoms he described as neurasthenia and anxiety neurosis. His personal life was thus deeply involved in this particular theory, since with its help he was trying to interpret and solve his own problems.

Freud had discovered that the roots of his own neurasthenia lay far in the past, for in a letter to his fiancée, he declared that not only he but also his half-brother Emanuel and his sister Rosa had "a nicely developed tendency towards neurasthenia" (1960a, 223 and 213).[12] What he called "anxiety neurosis" must have attacked him first in 1889; in a letter to Fliess, Freud stated that his arrhythmia "occurred rather suddenly in 1889 after my attack of influenza" (1950a, 82).

During the autumn of 1893 he complained to Fliess about heart trouble, for which Fliess blamed Freud's heavy smoking. From several letters written that year, it appears that Fliess advised him to give up cigars. Freud made vain attempts to take this advice, but his nicotine addiction—he usually smoked twenty cigars a day (Jones, 1953, I, 309)—always got the better of him. Only during phases of acute heart trouble was he able to give up smoking for a short time; as soon as his physical health improved, he would take it up again, declaring, for instance: "I am not obeying your smoking prohibitions; do you really consider it such a great boon to live a great many years in misery?" (Schur, 1972, 42, Letter of 17 November 1893).

In April 1894, Freud had a violent heart attack, though he had not smoked for three weeks. He reported the incident to Fliess on 19 April 1894:

Then suddenly there came a severe cardiac oppression, greater than I had before giving up smoking. I had violent arrhythmia, with constant tension, pressure and burning in the heart region, burning pains down the left arm, some dyspnea—suspiciously moderate, as though organic—all occurring in attacks lasting continuously for two-thirds of the day, accompanied by depression which took the form of visions of death and departure in place of the normal frenzy of activity. The organic discomforts have lessened during the past two days, but the hypomanic mood persists, having the courtesy, though, to let up suddenly (as it did last evening and at noon today), leaving behind a human being who looks forward confidently again to a long life and undiminished pleasure in smoking (1950a, 82, with corrections by Schur, 1972, 43).

Schur was able to show that the original letter contrasts with Freud's otherwise extremely precise language structure and choice of words. It contains some highly unusual expressions (the words *Pressung* and *Brennung,* which have been rendered as "pressure" and "burning," do not exist in the German language); clumsy sentences ("all occurring in attacks lasting continuously for two-thirds of the day") together with two slips: *Rauflust* (pugnacity) instead of *Rauchlust* (pleasure in smoking),[13] and hypomaniac instead of depressive. Schur considers these faults and slips as an expression of Freud's highly ambivalent feelings toward his illness and toward himself (1972, 46ff.), something Freud himself voiced in the next paragraph of the same letter: "It is embarrassing for a medical man, who spends all the hours of the day struggling to gain an understanding of the neuroses, not to know whether he is himself suffering from a reasonable or a hypochondriacal depression" (1950a, 82; partially retranslated from the German).

Freud then consulted his friend Breuer, who did not rule out genuine heart trouble (chronic myocarditis). This opinion, as Freud confessed to Fliess, gave him a measure of satisfaction. However, Freud balked at Breuer's request that he should have himself examined, on the grounds that "these examinations generally do not result in anything being found" *(ibid.)*.

He went on to address a fervent plea to Fliess, begging to be told the whole truth:

> I am suspicious of you this time, because this heart trouble of mine is the first occasion on which I have ever heard you contradict yourself. Last time you explained it as nasal, and said the percussive signs of a nicotine heart were absent; this time you show great concern over me and forbid me to smoke. I can only explain the inconsistency by assuming that you wish to conceal the true state of affairs from me, and I appeal to you not to do that. If you can tell me anything definite, please do so. I have no exaggerated opinion either of my responsibilities or my indispensability, and I should endure with dignity the uncertainty and the shortened expectation of life to be inferred from a diagnosis of myocarditis; indeed, I might perhaps draw benefit from it in arranging the remainder of my life, and enjoy to the full what is left to me (1950a, 82ff.).

Freud called off a trip to the mountains and was unable to work for three weeks. Although Breuer failed to detect any organic impairment, he prescribed digitalis (used in the treatment of heart diseases), which rekindled Freud's fears that Breuer was keeping something from him:

> If . . . I ask what it actually is, I get the answer: "Nothing; in any event something that is already over." Moreover, he does not pay any attention to me at all, does not see me for 2 weeks at a stretch. I do not know whether this is policy, genuine indifference or fully justified. On the whole I notice that I am being treated evasively and dishonestly as a patient instead of having my mind set at rest by being told everything there is to tell in a situation of this kind, namely, whatever is known (Schur, 1972, 52, Letter of 22 June 1894).

In the study by Richter and Beckmann mentioned earlier, the behavior of patients with neurotic heart conditions is described in a way that tallies with Freud's opinion of his own symptoms.[14] Such patients try not to smoke, fear physical exertion even during sexual intercourse, feel generally debilitated, are unable to work, are in a depressed mood, live in the constant expectation that something terrible is about to happen, continually check their heart and other bodily functions, and so on. They do not believe their doctor and think he is merely trying to protect them. Above all, they have no specific organic abnormalities detectable by even the most up-to-date diagnostic techniques (Richter/Beckmann, 1969, 14ff.).

From Freud's own description of his symptoms, and above all from his attitude toward them, we must, I believe, conclude that he suffered from cardiac neurosis and not, as Schur claims, from "attacks of paroxysmal tachycardia with anginal pains and signs of left ventricular failure." Schur goes on to explain that "these attacks reached their peak during April, 1894, at which point he suffered an organic myocardial lesion, most likely a coronary thrombosis in a small artery, or perhaps a postinfectious myocarditis, with temporarily increased nicotine sensitivity" (1972, 62).

It may be thought most presumptuous of a medical layman to argue with Freud's personal physician, but then Schur himself seems rather vague about his findings, which he based exclusively on Freud's letters to Fliess.[15] The finding of cardiac neurosis, however, agrees with Freud's own diagnosis, upon comparison of his description of his own symptoms in his letter of 19 April 1894[16] with his essay "On the Grounds for Detaching a Particular Syndrome from Neurasthenia under the Description 'Anxiety Neurosis' " (1895b).

During, or shortly after, his major heart attack in 1894, Freud also developed a theory about the origins of anxiety, as we gather from Draft E, which he apparently sent to Fliess at the beginning of June. I take the view that the arguments advanced in it were based on personal experience, that Freud too was a "neurasthenic" who had been "diverted from masturbation by intellectual occupations without compensating for this by intercourse," a man "whose potency is beginning to decline and who abstain[s] from intercourse in marriage on account of [unpleasant] sensations *post coitum.*" In other words, I believe that all Freud's descriptions of the sexual background of neurasthenia and anxiety neurosis were signs of his own sexual difficulties in marriage, that he himself was one of those "men who practise *coitus interruptus*" and "who excite their sexual feelings in various ways but do not employ their erections for intercourse" (1950a, 90, 89).

This view is borne out by a series of Freud's remarks on the problems of married life. Thus in the essay on neurasthenia and anxiety neurosis, he stated:

In the anamneses of many cases of anxiety neurosis we find, both in men and women, a striking oscillation in the intensity of its manifestations, and, indeed, in the coming and going of the whole condition. . . . If we enquire into the number and sequence of the children and compare this record of the marriage with the peculiar history of the neurosis, we arrive at the simple solution that the periods of improvements or good health coincided with the wife's pregnancies, during which, of course, the need for preventive intercourse was no longer present (1895b, 104).

If we look at the births of Freud's own children in connection with his anxiety neurosis, we discover that Sophie, the fifth child, was born on 12 April 1893; he first wrote about his heart condition in a letter dated 18 October 1893, from which however it emerges that he had been suffering from that condition for some time (Schur, 1972, 41). The acute phase came, as I said earlier, in 1894. During the spring of 1895, he felt *"very* well," claiming "no more heart condition, just the 'treatment' through nicotine" (*ibid.,* 84, Letter of 27 April 1895). If we recall that Anna Freud was born on 3 December 1895, then Freud's phase of well-being must have coincided with his wife's last pregnancy.[17]

In his paper on anxiety neurosis, Freud also recommended the separation of the married couple as a means of avoiding "unnatural" sexual practices. "A chance absence of the husband from home, or a holiday in the mountains which necessitates the separation of the couple, has a good effect" (1895b, 103). Freud himself traveled a great deal and as a result was frequently separated from his wife (Jones, 1953, I, 300ff.).

In 1908, in his " 'Civilized' Sexual Morality and Modern Nervous Illness," Freud bitterly deplored the sexual plight of married couples during the present, third, stage of civilization, "in which only *legitimate* reproduction is allowed as a sexual aim." Before marriage, young people were expected to practice sexual abstinence, which predisposed them to neurosis early in life. And within marriage, they could attain sexual satisfaction for at most five years before reasons of contraception forced them to revert to pathogenic sexual practices or to abstinence:

> Fear of the consequences of sexual intercourse first brings the married couple's physical affection to an end; and then, as a remoter result, it usually puts a stop as well to the mental sympathy between them, which should have been the successor to their original passionate love. The spiritual disillusionment and bodily deprivation to which most marriages are thus doomed puts both partners back in the state they were in before their marriage, except for being the poorer by the loss of an illusion, and they must once more have recourse to their fortitude in mastering and deflecting their sexual instinct. We need not enquire how far men, by then in their maturer years, succeed in this task. Experience shows that they very frequently avail themselves of the degree of sexual freedom which is allowed them—although only with reluctance and under a veil of silence—by even the strictest sexual code. This "double" sexual morality which is valid for men in our society is the plainest admission that society itself does not believe in the possibility of enforcing the precepts which it itself has laid down (1908d, 194f.).

In the published section of the Fliess correspondence, Freud makes no overt reference to his own sexual problems. I believe, however, that it provides indirect evidence of the fact that his marriage was clouded by these very problems, particularly at the period under consideration. It is biologically most unusual and hence most unlikely that at the age of thirty-five[18] Martha should already have had her menopause—as one of Freud's daughters-in-law told Paul Roazen (Roazen, 1975, 52)—thus obviating the need for contraception in their marriage.

Freud and his wife must therefore have practiced contraception in one form or another unless they had abandoned sexual intercourse altogether. From the bitter, accusing tone of the above quotation, one might infer that the latter was indeed the case. Corroboration may also be found in several more or less overt remarks in Freud's correspondence, for instance: "Sexual excitation is of no more use to a person like me" (1950a, 227, Letter to Fliess, 31 October 1897); or, "I have finished with begetting children" (1950a, 312, 11 March 1900); or later still, "You said then that your marriage had long been 'amortized,' now there was nothing more to do except—die" (Letter from Emma Jung, 1911, in Freud/Jung, 1974, 456). In his sensitive *Sigmund Freud, the Jew,* Ernst Simon attributes what he too believes to have been Freud's sexual abstinence to his Jewish background, remarking that Freud acted like any Orthodox Jew anxious to observe the religious commandments but unwilling to bring any more children into the world (1957, 293).

Did Freud allow himself the "double morality" mentioned above? Roazen considers that his remark in a letter written in 1915—"I stand for an infinitely freer sexual life, although I myself have made very little use of such freedom. *Only so far as I believed myself to stay within the limits of what is allowed"* (1960a, 314, italics added; retranslated from the German)—invites "appropriate caution" (Roazen, 1976, 49). But in the lengthy passage quoted earlier (1908d, 194f.), Freud seems to be justifying the double standard.[19]

We may also take it that Freud must have felt an urge to masturbate, which at a time of renewed abstinence must have been particularly distressing for him. Here too we have no hard evidence, but Freud's general comments on masturbation suggest that he thought it harmful. It was the "primary addiction," and he believed that the other addictions (alcohol, morphine, tobacco, etc.) merely "enter into life as a substitute and replacement for it" (1950a, 239). As I said earlier (p. 10), Freud also thought that masturbation was the real cause of neurasthenia. He believed that, when practiced in youth, it rendered men impotent, and he advised breaking the habit with medical help. "To break the patient of the habit of masturbating is only one of the new therapeutic tasks which are imposed on the physician who takes the sexual aetiology of the neurosis into account; and it seems that precisely this task, like the cure of any other addiction, can only be carried out in an institution and under medical supervision. Left to himself, the masturbator is accustomed, whenever something happens that depresses him, to return to his convenient form of satisfaction." Medical treatment should aim at leading the neurasthenic, once he had recovered his strength, back to normal sexual intercourse. "For sexual need, when once it has been aroused and has been satisfied for any length of time, can no longer be silenced; it can only be displaced along another path" (1898a, 275f.).[20]

If Freud himself masturbated, then he clearly used his theory of neurasthenia and anxiety neurosis to explain his own neurotic symptoms. More than that: his case must have seemed hopeless because—as I assume—he abstained from sexual intercourse with his wife so that he was left with no other form of morally defensible sexual activity. If Freud believed that his neurasthenia and anxiety neurosis were the result of unsatisfactory sexual practices, then he simply had to bow to his fate and accept that his condition could not be alleviated, that he had to live with his neurosis. Unlike the so-called neuroses of defense (hysteria, paranoia, obsessions) (see Table I and 1.1.2.4 and 1.1.2.5 below), which he attributed to the repression of sexual experience in early childhood, and which he believed could be cured by psychotherapy, his own neurotic symptoms were incurable. We shall see, however, that Freud suddenly found himself forced to describe his own neurosis as a form of hysteria, a step that was to have far-reaching consequences for him.

The extension of his sexual theory to other symptoms, too, was connected with his own condition. In 1895, he published "Obsessions and Phobias" (1895c), which originally appeared in French and in which he described certain phobias as the "psychical expression" of anxiety neurosis, that is, as direct consequences of actual sexual practices. Such phobias were said to be "contingent"—that is, fears about special conditions that inspired no fear in the "normal man," for instance, "agoraphobia," and "phobias of locomotion" (1895h, 1895c, 80).[21] In this connection it is worth pointing out that Freud himself suffered from a "phobia of locomotion" in the form of a fear of railways, which at times must have been very strong, as witness some of his remarks to Fliess (1950a, 306, 21 December 1899; 219, 3 October 1897; 237, 3 December 1897; see 3.2 below).[22]

Freud also included melancholia among the actual neuroses and claimed that it occurred in women as a result of "anaesthesia" (i.e., frigidity) and in men as an "intensification of neurasthenia as a result of masturbation" (1950a, 102, Draft G, 29 August 1894; cf. 1950a, 90, Draft E, June 1894). Melancholia, Freud believed, "consists in mourning over loss of libido," and occurs predominantly in impotent people, while "potent individuals easily acquire anxiety neuroses" (1950a, 102 and 107). Melancholia, too, was a condition he had discovered in himself in connection with his death fantasies.

In March 1895, Freud sent Fliess a manuscript in which he also explained migraine by means of his sexual theory, as a direct consequence of "abnormal" sexual practices. He maintained that "migraine represents a toxic effect produced by the stimulus of the sexual substance when this cannot find adequate discharge" (1950a, 117, Draft I, 4 March 1895). Migraine, again, was an ailment about which Freud himself often complained (Schur, 1972, 98ff.).

In other words, Freud looked upon his own neurasthenic symptoms, his railway phobia, his depressions and fears of death, his migraine attacks, and so on, as symptoms of actual neurosis, that is, he assumed they were caused by current sexual practices.[23]

Freud's theory of actual neurosis is thus a theory of his own neurotic symptoms. I believe that this is the reason why he did not include any other forms of deviation from heterosexual intercourse in his theory—he was solely concerned with such "deviations" as affected him personally. In other words, it was for his own symptoms that he developed the sexual theory which holds current sexual practices, not psychical causes, responsible for various disorders.

Freud thus felt that he had attained theoretical mastery over the actual neuroses. His essay on neurasthenia and anxiety neurosis appeared in January 1895, and its critical reception persuaded him to write a reply (1895f) that contains a particularly telling account of his sexual theory. He then dropped the entire subject, no doubt because he believed he had solved it once and for all. As we saw earlier (p. 13), he remained convinced of that fact until late in life. He did not revise his ideas about the causes of anxiety until 1930, and even that revision involved no basic reformulation of his sexual theory.

In particular, this theory helped him to explain his own neurotic symptoms, albeit not holding out the promise of a cure.

1.1.2.3 The Emma–Irma–Anna episode

At the beginning of 1895, at the very time when Freud had found a satisfactory explanation of his own anxiety neurosis with the help of his sexual theory, his relationship to Fliess changed. This change cannot be reconstructed in detail since none of the letters he wrote to Fliess between August 1894 and March 1895 have been published. It is however clear that in the spring of 1895 Freud's need for his friend's opinions about his cardiac symptoms, which he expressed so clearly in the letters he wrote earlier in 1894, had made way for what can only be called a negative attitude. Thus he explained on 20 April 1895: "What I would like most is for you to agree to want to know nothing more about the topic heart" (Schur, 1972, 83). Freud had taken exception to Fliess's remonstrations about his smoking; nevertheless, he gave up smoking for fourteen months—until June of that year (1950a, 121, 12 June 1895).[24]

This loosening of Freud's emotional ties to Fliess was probably triggered off by an incident connected with Fliess's views on the links between the nose and female sexuality.

Freud had an hysterical patient whom he called "Emma" in his letters to Fliess. According to P. Swales, she was Emma Eckstein, a thirty-two-year-old spinster with strong feminist views (Swales, 1982b, 9), and not Anna Lichtheim-Hammerschlag as I assumed in the first German edition of my book. In Freud's famous "Irma dream," the first of his own dreams that he subjected to a systematic analysis (see p. 00 below; 1900a, 107ff., 292ff; and Schur, 1966), Emma Eckstein and Anna Lichtheim were fused into a single person.

Anna Lichtheim was the daughter of Samuel Hammerschlag, Freud's Hebrew teacher at high school. Anna, like Irma, was a young widow (1900a, 117); like Irma (*ibid.,* 106), she was a friend of the family, and Freud also observed that Irma's surname reminded one of the word "Ananas" (*ibid.,* 115). Now, Anzieu (1959, 29) has pointed out that one need only put "first name" for "surname" to identify Irma as Anna. In a letter to Karl Abraham, Freud himself mentioned that Mathilde (the wife of Josef Breuer), Sophie (Paneth, a nice of Samuel Hammerschlag), and Anna (Lichtheim) were the three women of the Irma dream (Freud/Abraham, 1965, 20; cf. Jones, 1953, I, 163). He did not mention Emma Eckstein.

Emma Eckstein was not only a patient of Freud's but also a friend of his family. During his treatment of her hysteria, Freud had advised her to ask Fliess to perform a nasal operation on her. She took his advice, and Fliess duly came to Vienna at the end of February 1895 to perform the operation. On 4 March 1895 (Schur, 1966),[25] Freud wrote to him that the operation had obviously been a failure, because the patient had had massive hemorrhages and purulent secretions. Two days later her condition became so serious that Freud brought in a Viennese ear, nose, and throat specialist, who drained the wound. In a letter to Fliess, Freud wrote:

R. cleaned the area surrounding the opening, removed some blood clots which were sticking to the surface, and suddenly pulled at something like a thread. He kept right on pulling, and before either of us had time to think, at least half a meter of gauze had been removed from the cavity. The next moment came a flood of blood. The patient turned white, her eyes bulged, and her pulse was no longer palpable. However, immediately after this he packed the cavity with fresh iodoform gauze, and the hemmorhage stopped. It had lasted about half a minute, but this was enough to make the poor creature, who[m] by then we had lying quite flat, unrecognizable. In the meantime, or actually afterwards, something else happened. At the moment the foreign body came out, and everything had become obvious to me, immediately after which I was confronted with the sight of the patient, I felt sick. After she had been packed I fled to the next room, drank a bottle of water, and felt rather miserable. The brave Frau Doktor* then brought me a small glass of cognac, and I felt like myself again. . . . She [Emma, M.K.] had not lost consciousness during the severe hemmorhage scene, and when I returned to the room somewhat shaky, she greeted me with the condescending remark: "This is the strong sex."

I don't think I had been overwhelmed by the blood; affects were welling up in me at that moment. So we had done her an injustice. She had not been abnormal at all, but a piece of iodoform gauze had gotten torn off when you removed the rest, and stayed in for fourteen days, interfering with the healing process, after which it had torn away and provoked the bleeding. The fact that this mishap should have happened to you, how you would react when you learned about it, what others would make of it, how wrong I had been to press you to operate in a foreign city where you couldn't handle the aftercare, how my intention of getting the best for the poor girl was insidiously thwarted, with the resultant danger to her life—all this came over me simultaneously. I have worked it off by now (Schur, 1966, 56f., Letter of 8 March 1895).

Freud must have had a terrible shock. Because he had trusted his friend, a close friend of his family had been brought to death's door. Characteristically, he did not tell Fliess about the incident there and then, but waited for two days. The patient eventually recovered, but only after several relapses, so that Freud felt impelled to write on April 11: "I'm really quite shaken that such a misfortune can have arisen from this operation which was depicted as quite harmless" (ibid., 65f.).

After a careful analysis of Freud's letters to Fliess, Schur concluded that Freud nevertheless tried to exonerate his friend by shifting the responsibility onto others, first her family doctor, and then even onto the patient herself, whose hemorrhages he now claimed were "hysterical": "Concerning Emma . . . I know so far that she was bleeding out of longing. She had been a bleeder all along, whenever she cut herself, etc. As a child she suffered from severe nosebleeds. . . . When she became aware of my deep emotion during her first haemorrhage while in the hands of R., she experienced the realization of an old wish to be loved in her sickness, and during the next few hours, despite her danger, felt happy as never before" (ibid., 81, Letter of 4 May 1896).

Schur too was astonished by what lengths Freud went in his attempts to exonerate Fliess—Freud did not so much as mention the iodoform gauze. Shortly after the happy ending of this episode, Freud dreamed his Irma dream (on the night of 23 July 1895). If one reads it with the Emma episode in mind,

* Perhaps Emma's mother, because Schur states that the operation was performed in Emma's apartment—M.K.

then the reality content of the dream images is obvious. This is how the dream went:

A large hall—numerous guests, whom we were receiving.—Among them was Irma. I at once took her on one side, as though to answer her letter and to reproach her for not having accepted my "solution" yet. I said to her: "If you still get pains, it's really only your fault." She replied: "If you only knew what pains I've got now in my throat and stomach and abdomen—it's choking me."—I was alarmed and looked at her. She looked pale and puffy. I thought to myself that after all I must be missing some organic trouble. I took her to the window and looked down her throat, and she showed signs of recalcitrance, like women with artificial dentures. I thought to myself that there was really no need for her to do that.—She then opened her mouth properly and on the right I found a big white patch; at another place I saw extensive whitish grey scabs upon some remarkable curly structures which were evidently modelled on the turbinal bones of the nose.—I at once called in Dr. M., and he repeated the examination and confirmed it. . . . Dr. M. looked quite different from usual; he was very pale, he walked with a limp and his chin was clean-shaven. . . . My friend Otto was now standing beside her as well, and my friend Leopold was percussing her through her bodice and saying: "She has a dull area low down on the left." He also indicated that a portion of the skin on the left shoulder was infiltrated. (I noticed this, just as he did, in spite of her dress.) . . . M. said: "There's no doubt it's an infection, but no matter; dysentery will supervene and the toxin will be eliminated." . . . We were directly aware, too, of the origin of the infection. Not long before, when she was feeling unwell, my friend Otto had given her an injection of a preparation of propyl, propyls . . . propionic acid . . . trimethylamin (and I saw before me the formula for this printed in heavy type). . . . Injections of that sort ought not to be made so thoughtlessly. . . . And probably the syringe had not been clean (1900a, 107).

Freud interpreted this dream at length, calling it a "specimen dream." For many psychoanalysts, it is *the* model dream of psychoanalysis, and its analysis an exemplary case of dream interpretation. Before the publication of the Emma letters, however, all examinations of this dream (Erickson, 1954; Anzieu, 1959, 24ff.) were bound to miss the point, because they were written at a time when nothing was known about the important subject of Freud's grievance against Fliess.[26] Moreover, their authors were also unable to trace the Irma dream back to Freud's childhood, something that is easily done once we know about the Emma episode. For the Irma dream really links up with a scene in Freud's early childhood mentioned in "Screen Memories" (1899a). At that time, another admired friend had misled him into "examining" a little girl, a lapse for which both boys had been punished (see 3.1.8 below). The two events—the Emma episode and the childhood experience—bear a close structural resemblance to each other, so much so that I feel justified in speaking of a repetition.[27]

His gradual estrangement from Fliess helped Freud to achieve greater theoretical independence. Though Fliess continued to be his sole interlocutor, the only person to whom he could impart his ideas, Freud now began to advance his own views much more freely, often in opposition to his friend's. He still agreed with Fliess on the causes of the actual neuroses—and this despite the fact that Fliess's sexual theory differed from his own in many important respects—but the gulf between their respective interpretations of the neuroses of defense gradually widened until it became unbridgeable. Whether the Emma episode was directly responsible must remain an open question. All we can say is that this episode marked a turning point both in Freud's relationship to Fliess and in his own theoretical development. For from the spring of 1895, he began to neglect the sexual theory of neurosis and to devote himself almost exclusively to the psychological study of what he called the "neuroses of defence."

1.1.2.4 The seduction theory

At the time when Freud was still concentrating on the problem of the actual neuroses and believed that he had solved it satisfactorily in the framework of sexual theory, he also continued to take an interest in the theoretical interpretation of hysteria and obsessional neurosis, to which he referred as "neuroses of defence." Freud had begun to treat hysterical patients with Breuer's "cathartic method" at the end of the eighties. His main concern was the theoretical interpretation of the resulting therapeutic successes. If the symptoms of hysteria or obsession disappeared once the patient could be helped to remember an incident in his distant past, then the origins of the symptoms must clearly be related to that event. The interpretation of the etiology of hysteria seemed to be within Freud's reach.

In order to follow the ideas on the etiology of the neuroses of defense which Freud developed at this time, the reader must remember what exactly it was that Freud subsumed under the headings of hysteria and obsessive neurosis (see Table 1).[28]

1. *Hysteria.* According to Freud, hysteria comprised aches of the most various kind without organic cause; split consciousness; hallucinations; motor hyperactivity or rigidity; anesthesia; neuralgia; visual disturbances; epileptiform convulsions; contortions; paralyses; tics; and so on. All these symptoms generally appeared during hysterical attacks (1893a, *passim;* 1894a, *passim;* and 1888b, 37ff., 58f.).

2. *Obsessive Neuroses.* These comprised phobic fears of animals and compulsive keeping at a distance from them; fear of pollution and compulsive washing; avoidance of infection; compulsive urination; compulsive reproaches; compulsive impulses; compulsive brooding; compulsive doubting; compulsive counting; compulsive collecting; and so on (1894a, 54f.; cf. 1896b, *passim*).

In December 1892, Freud and Josef Breuer wrote a paper entitled "On the Psychical Mechanism of Hysterical Phenomena: Preliminary Communication," which was published in January 1893. In this paper, and also in a lecture delivered at the beginning of 1893 (1893h), Freud described hysteria as what he later came to call a "neurosis of defence" (neuropsychosis of defense, psychoneurosis). Hysterical symptoms, he believed, served to ward off certain memories that for a great variety of reasons must not be allowed to enter consciousness. What was being defended, and why? And why did the defense take the form it did? According to Freud, the connection between symptom and cause was perfectly obvious in some cases:

We may take as a very commonplace instance a painful emotion arising during a meal but suppressed at the time, and then producing nausea and vomiting which persists for months in the form of hysterical vomiting. A girl, watching beside a sick-bed in a torment of anxiety, fell into a twilight state and had a terrifying hallucination, while her right arm, which was hanging over the back of her chair, went to sleep; from this there developed a paresis of the same arm accompanied by contracture and anaesthesia. She tried to pray but could find no words; at length she succeeded in repeating a children's prayer in English. When subsequently a severe and highly complicated hysteria developed, she could only speak, write and understand English, while her native language remained unintelligible to her for eighteen months (1893a, 4f.).[29]

In other cases, the connection appeared to be much less obvious. In particular, Freud was struck by the fact that though these patients were not conscious of the cause of the original event, they could be helped to recall it to memory and to relive it with all the emotions that accompanied it at the time: ". . . these experiences are completely absent from the patients' memory when they are in a normal psychical state, or are only present in a highly summary form. Not until they have been questioned under hypnosis do these memories emerge with the undiminished vividness of a recent event" (*ibid.,* 9).

The reason why these memories are not accessible to the conscious memory is that they "correspond to traumas that have not been sufficiently abreacted" (*ibid.,* 10), and this because "the nature of the trauma excluded a reaction . . . or because it was a question of things which the patient wished to forget, and therefore intentionally repressed from his conscious thought and inhibited and suppressed. It is precisely distressing things of this kind that, under hypnosis, we find are the basis of hysterical phenomena (e.g., hysterical deliria in saints and nuns, continent women and well-brought-up children)" (*ibid.,* 10f.).

This quotation suggests that in his assumptions about hysteria, Freud had already begun to suspect that the experience warded off by the defense mechanism was usually of a sexual kind. Breuer refused to follow him in this and offered an alternative explanation, the attribution of the emergence of hysterical symptoms to what he called a "specific hypnoid state." Freud, for his part, rejected this solution. These two conflicting views of the etiology of hysteria were both incorporated in the "Preliminary Communication," in which Freud, however, was rather reticent about his own hypothesis.[30]

But we know from a note he wrote to Josef Breuer in 1892 (included in Freud's posthumous writings) that by the time he drafted the "Preliminary Communication" he had already made up his mind that hysterical symptoms had sexual origins: "Sexual life is especially well suited to provide the content [of such traumas] owing to the very great contrast it presents to the rest of the personality and to its ideas being impossible to react to" (1941b, 150).

Freud's first explicit mention of the sexual etiology of hysteria can be found in his essay on "The Neuro-Psychoses of Defence," which appeared in January 1894, and therefore preceded his work on anxiety neurosis and neurasthenia. In it he stressed that "in females, incompatible ideas of this sort arise chiefly on the soil of sexual experience and sensation; and the patients can recollect . . . their efforts at a defence, their intention of 'pushing the thing away,' of not thinking of it, of suppressing it" (1894a, 47).

In 1894 he was working on the *Studies on Hysteria,* which he wrote with Breuer and which was published in 1895. That book contains an account of Freud's treatment of four female patients and of Breuer's treatment of Anna O., together with a theoretical study by Breuer in which he again propounded his theory of the "hypnoid" state, and a contribution by Freud on the psychotherapeutic treatment of hysteria in which he stressed the sexual etiology.[31]

Freud held that, in contrast to what happens in the actual neuroses, *current* sexual practices were not responsible for the neuroses of defense. These were all due to *past* sexual experiences. Hysterical symptoms, he believed, were not created by direct "sexual tension," as happened with neuroasthenia and anxiety neurosis, but by a psychic process—the warding off of a memory of the earlier sexual experience.

Admittedly, Freud was keen to trace even this psychic process back to chemical processes. To that end, he put forward the working hypothesis that in mental functions it was possible to distinguish a "sum of excitation" resembling "an electric charge" spread over the "memory traces of ideas" (1894a, 60). In hysteria, the sum of excitation accompanying unacceptable ideas is converted into physical symptoms. "By this means the ego succeeds in freeing itself from the contradiction; but instead it has burdened itself with a mnemic symbol, which finds a lodgement in consciousness, like a sort of parasite, either in the form of an unresolvable motor innervation or as a constantly recurring hallucinatory sensation, and which persists until a conversion in the opposite direction takes place" (*ibid.,* 49).

Bernfeld has shown that this approach was in keeping with the ideas of Helmholtz and his school, championed in Vienna by Brücke. According to that school, all expressions of life could be reduced to the effects of physical forces (Bernfeld, 1949, 172ff.). Applying Helmholtz's principle of the conservation of energy, Freud considered chemical and physiochemical processes as the ultimate causes of neurotic disturbances. P. Ricoeur has made the resulting conflict in Freud's thinking, that is, the conflict between "energetics" and "hermeneutics," the subject of a detailed analysis (1974).

In the case of the defensive neurosis, however, Freud's efforts to produce a physiochemical explanation met with great difficulties. It was hard to conceive of an "economics of nerve-force" (1950a, 120, 25 May 1895), according to which sexual experiences could be conserved over the years as a quantitively expressible "sum of excitation" that eventually produces neurotic symptoms.

Freud's main problem was to explain the defensive process, that is, repression. What force, he wondered, could produce the suppression of a memory and its conversion into a symptom? In August 1895 he thought he had the answer, for he told Fliess that "after prolonged thought I believe that I have found my way to the understanding of pathological defence . . . I hope it is not 'dream gold' " (*ibid.,* 122, 6 August 1895). It *was* dream gold; only ten days later he wrote to Fliess:

Soon after I proclaimed my alarming news to you, raising your expectations and calling for your congratulations, I came up against new difficulties; I had surmounted the first foothills, but had no breath left for further toil. So, quickly composing myself, I threw the whole thing aside and persuaded myself that I took no interest in it at all. . . . All I was trying to do was to explain defence, but I found myself explaining something from the very heart of nature. I found myself wrestling with the problems of quality, sleep, memory—in short, the whole of psychology. Now I want to hear no more of it (*ibid.,* 123, 16 August 1895).

In other words, Freud believed that his explanation of defense was untenable. What had happened? The answer becomes clear when we look at the "Project for a Scientific Psychology" on which he worked from late September to early October 1895 in a veritable burst of productivity. In September he had visited Fliess in Berlin, and on the return journey he had already begun to draft the paper. In the end, he never finished it—we shall see at what point he broke it off. He did however incorporate some of the ideas expressed in that paper into his *Interpretation of Dreams* (1900a, Chap. VII, 588–609). The "Project" was published posthumously together with the letters to Fliess (1950a, 355–445).

In this manuscript, Freud intended to explain neurotic disturbances with the help of certain assumptions about neurophysiological processes, the better to bring out the nature of psychic normality. He himself put it as follows:

The intention of this project is to furnish us with a psychology which shall be a natural science: its aim, that is, is to represent psychical processes as quantitatively determined states of specifiable material particles. . . . The first part of this project included what could, as it were, be inferred *a priori* from its basic hypothesis. . . . [The] second part seeks by an analysis of pathological processes to determine further features of the system founded on the basic hypothesis. A third part, based on the two earlier ones, will endeavour to construct the characteristics of the course of normal psychological events (1950a, 355 and 405).

In the first part, Freud advanced a general theory of such mental processes as a perception, memory, sleep, and dreaming, completely in accordance with the Helmholtz doctrine (Ricoeur, 1974, 85). His basic assumption was the flow of currents from the "φ-neurones," which serve the function of perception, to the "ψ-neurones," which are "the vehicles of memory and presumably, therefore, of psychical processes in general" (1950a, 360). The structure of the ψ-system, in this view, was based on pathways established through primary stimulation by φ-neurones and stabilized when the same perceptions are repeated. The building of pathways depends "on the quantity which passes through a neurone in the excitatory process and on the number of repetitions of that process" (*ibid.,* 361).[32]

However, according to Ricoeur, Freud failed in his attempt to establish a link between organic brain processes and psychical processes, let alone to derive the latter from the former: "The 'Project' [seems to have been] Freud's most determined attempt to assemble a mass of psychological detail in a quantitative theory, and an *ad absurdum* demonstration of the fact that the content explodes the framework. . . . For that reason we are fully entitled to say that nothing is so antiquated as the explanatory approach of this 'Project' (1974, 86).

Freud came to realize this himself when he wrote that "every endeavour to think of ideas as stored up in nerve-cells and of excitations as travelling along nerve-fibres, has miscarried completely" (1915e, 174).

The second part of the "Project," on the other hand, contains an idea that is highly relevant to the present study. In that part, Freud tried to interpret his clinical experiences without any reference to the neurone theory. In particular, he was concerned to clarify the link between the original sexual experience and the later appearance of the symptom. This link, he felt, must turn out to be a reversal of the therapeutic process which, after all, caused the symptom to disappear once the patient could be made to remember the original experience and to relive it with full emotional intensity. In this connection, Freud wrote:

The result of analysis is, in general terms, as follows. *Before* the analysis, A is an excessively intense idea, which forces its way into consciousness too often, and each time it does so leads to tears. The subject does not know why A makes him weep and regards it as absurd; but he cannot prevent it. *After* the analysis, it has been discovered that there is an idea B which rightly leads to tears and which rightly recurs often until a certain complicated piece of psychical work directed against it has been completed by the subject. The effect of B is not absurd, is comprehensible to the subject and can even be fought against by him. B stands in a particular relation to A. For there has been an event which consisted of $B + A$. A was a subsidiary circumstance, while B was well calculated to produce a lasting effect. The production of this event in memory now occurs as though A had taken B's place. A has become a substitute, a "symbol" for B. Hence the incongruity; for A is accompanied by consequences which it does not seem to deserve, which are not appropriate to it (1950a, 406f.).

Freud was clearly taken aback by the discovery that the displaced idea B had not been forgotten and could be remembered.

If we investigate the condition of the repressed [idea] B, we find that this idea can be easily be found and brought into consciousness. This is surprising, for we might well have supposed that B was really forgotten and that no trace of it remained in ψ. But no; B is a memory-image like any other. It is not extinguished; but if, as is usually the case, B is a complex of cathexes, then an uncommonly strong *resistance*, and one that cannot easily be eliminated, opposes any activity of thought in relation to B. This resistance to B can at once be recognized as a measure of the *compulsion* exercised by A, and we can conclude that the force which originally repressed B is at work once more in the resistance. And at the same time we learn something else. We had only known so far that B could not become *conscious;* we knew nothing of B's behaviour in regard to thought-cathexis. But we now find that the resistance is directed against any occupation of one's thoughts with *B,* even though it has already been made partly conscious. So that instead of "excluded from consciousness," we can say "excluded from thought-processes" (*ibid.,* 408f.).

Freud now had to determine what were the peculiar properties of *B,* why a particular memory of or mental occupation with *B* was forbidden, and why it had to be repressed. His answer was that what was involved here was a set of ideas awakening a "painful affect" or unpleasure, and invariably having a sexual basis. Here, admittedly, he was immediately led to an impasse: he could not understand why sexual ideas should be connected with unpleasure: "It is out of the question to suppose that disagreeable sexual affects so greatly exceed all other unpleasurable affects in intensity. There must be some other attribute of sexual ideas to explain why they alone are subject to repression. . . . Accordingly, the process of repression remains the core of the riddle" (*ibid.,* 409f.).

It is at this point in the "Project" that Freud makes the point which concerns us here and which was to prove of such great importance in the emergence of his seduction theory. For Freud described a symptom that he had observed in "Emma," the main character of the Emma episode and of the Irma dream (see 1.1.2.3 above). Emma was unable to enter shops alone; and using the cathartic method, Freud discovered that when she was twelve, she had had to rush out of a shop in a fright. It was possible to elicit the idea that she had done so because two male shop assistants had been laughing at her clothes and one of them had attracted her sexually. Here, therefore, was a symptom (fear of entering a shop) that could be traced back to an event in early puberty. However, that event was so unremarkable that it was hard to understand why a symptom should have developed from it. Freud accordingly probed further and discovered a second memory: as a child of eight, Emma had gone alone into a shop to buy candy and the shopkeeper had "grabbed at her genitals through her clothes." Despite this experience she had gone there a second time, and later reproached herself for having gone back as if to provoke another assault. Laughter became an associative link between the two events, for the shopkeeper had grinned throughout the episode. When, at the age of twelve, the laughing shop assistants reminded her of the original event in a similar setting, she became filled with anxiety and hence developed her symptom (*ibid.,* 410ff.).

In the "Project," Freud tried to interpret the origins of this symptom with the help of his neurophysiological theory—in my view, unsuccessfully. The account, however, already contained all the elements of the future seduction theory: sexual seduction in prepubertal childhood, repression of the incident due to guilt, recall of the incident with the onset of puberty, repression of the memory by means of a newly created symptom associated with an unessential aspect of the first and also the second scene (not entering shops alone).

Nevertheless, in the "Project" Freud had not yet managed to formulate the seduction theory, which states that the childhood experience repressed from memory is invariably one of sexual seduction by parents or guardians. This failure was possibly due to his fixed concentration on neurophysiological problems, to his determination to trace back psychic to physiological processes.

Similarly, Freud had to admit defeat in the third part of his "Project," in which he tried once again to explain normal psychic processes with the help of his neurophysiological assumptions. Again the stumbling block was the problem of repression. With the last pages of the manuscript, he enclosed the following note to Fliess:

I have a third notebook, dealing with the psychopathology of repression, which I am not ready to send you yet, because it only takes the subject to a certain point. From that point I had to start from scratch again, and I have been alternately proud and happy and abashed and miserable, until now, after an excess of mental torment, I just apathetically tell myself that *it does not hang together yet and perhaps never will.* What does not hang together yet is not the mechanism—I could be patient about that—but *the explanation of repression,* clinical knowledge of which has incidentally made great strides (*ibid.,* 125f., 8 October 1895, italics added).

In other words, Freud's "Project" fell short in two ways: firstly, it failed to explain psychic in terms of physiological processes; and secondly, it failed to explain repression. Freud could not understand why sexual memories should be so unpleasurable as to demand repression.

The first, physiological problem, admittedly came to concern him less and less in the following years, although he made further attempts to resolve it (cf. *ibid.,* 129, 20 October 1895; 143, 1 January 1896; 162, 4 May 1896). Instead, his attention was increasingly focused on the explanation of problems that appeared in his clinical practice and that eventually led to the formulation of his seduction theory.

In the same letter to Fliess in which he expressed his fears that the ideas on neurophysiology contained in the "Project" might perhaps never "hang together," Freud also developed a new theory of repression. He had discovered that in his patients the repressed sexual experience was either accompanied by feelings of pleasure or by feelings of unpleasure. "Among other things I suspect the following: that hysteria is conditioned by a primary sexual experience (before puberty) accompanied by revulsion and fright; and that obsessional neurosis is conditioned by the same accompanied by pleasure" (*ibid.,* 126, 8 October 1895). This idea occupied him for some time: "I am practically sure I have solved the riddle of hysteria and obsessional neurosis with the formula of infantile sexual shock and sexual pleasure, and I am just as sure that both neuroses are radically curable now—not just the individual symptoms but the neurotic disposition itself" (*ibid.,* 128, 16 October 1895).

Later in October 1895, he repeated in a lecture before the Viennese College of Physicians the view he had first expressed on October 8, that repressions leading to hysteria could not have originated after puberty: "After puberty [repressions] seem to be totally impossible. If new symptoms appear in later life, then they are associated with the earlier repressed memories" (1895g, 697, last of three lectures held on October 14, 21, and 28).

Only too quickly, however, his excitement about the new discovery became stifled in doubt. As early as October 31 he announced that he had had second thoughts about the pleasure–pain explanation of hysteria and of obsessional neurosis "which I announced with such enthusiasm" (1950a, 131). On November 8 he wrote that he had "bundled the psychological drafts into a drawer." By way of explanation, he added that he had had new insights, which called for revision of his ideas, and that he had neither the time nor the strength for that task. Moreover, he was "fully occupied with [a commissioned article on] children's paralyses, in which I am not in the least interested. Since putting the psychology aside I have felt depressed and disillusioned" (*ibid.,* 134, 8 November 1895).

One month later, on 3 December 1895, Anna Freud was born. Now, Schur has established a remarkable connection between the Emma episode and Anna's conception, for he claims that Anna was conceived "immediately before the Emma episode" (1972, 85). Whether Freud himself expressed an opinion on this coincidence in a letter or whether Schur merely assumed a connection will only become clear once the entire Fliess correspondence has been published, without cuts.

Anna was named after Anna Hammerschlag-Lichtheim (Jones, 1953, I, 163, 223). Did Freud, by giving her that name, merely express his affection for a friend of the family? Or was he trying subconsciously to tie down his daughter —who was the only one of his children to continue his work, who never left him, and who eventually became his "Antigone" (Freud/Zweig, 1968, 66, 25 February 1934; 106, 2 May 1935)—even before her birth, by naming her after Anna–Irma–Emma, toward whom he felt guilty? Had the child been a boy, he explained, he would have called him Wilhelm after Wilhelm Fliess (1950a, 136), his "comrade in crime" (see 3.1.7 below).

Freud attributed a change of fortune in his medical practice to Anna's birth, although no one can really be sure whether the following remark was meant seriously or ironically: "We like to think that the baby had brought a doubling of my practice. I have trouble in fitting everything in, and I can pick and choose and begin to dictate my fees. I am getting confident in the diagnosis and treatment of the two neuroses, and I think the town is gradually beginning, to realize that something is to be had from me" (*ibid.,* 8 December 1895).

1.1.2.5 *Explaining the neuroses of defense by the seduction theory*

This newly gained assurance was reflected in Freud's theoretical work. On New Year's Day, 1896, he sent Fliess Draft K, which he called "a Christmas fairy tale." It was an outline of the seduction theory, listing its most important concepts.

Freud started from the assumption that the neuroses of defense (among which he now included not only hysteria and obsessional neurosis but also paranoia and "acute hallucinatory amentia"; see Table 1) were all due to sexual experiences before puberty. An innovation was his claim that the repressive forces were shame and morality, although he was still unable to determine the origins of these forces. The course of the illness, he claimed, was the same in all defensive neuroses:

1. A sexual experience (or series of experiences) which is premature and traumatic and has to be repressed; 2. the repression of this experience on some later occasion which recalls it to memory, and the consequent formation of a primary symptom; 3. a stage of successful defence, which resembles health, except for the existence of the primary symptom; and 4. a stage in which the repressed ideas return and in which, during the struggle between them and the ego, fresh symptoms are constructed, which constitute the illness proper: that is, a stage either of coming to terms or of being overwhelmed, or of recovery accompanied by a malformation (1950a, 148, Draft K).

This sequence had emerged during the analysis of Emma's fear of entering a shop. It was formulated here as a general principle for the first time, and so was the idea of sexual shock and sexual pleasure: pleasure accompanying sexual seduction in childhood gave rise to obsessional neurosis; unpleasure accompanying sexual seduction gave rise to hysteria. Because sexual pleasure elicits feelings of guilt, the main affect in obsessional neurosis is self-reproach, which the patient tries to assuage by his various obsessional acts. In hysteria, by contrast, the patient tries to avoid the fear he experienced during the primary sexual experience. Freud believed that this led to displacement, to conversion into, for instance, motor or hallucinatory symptoms (*ibid.,* 151f., 154f.).

Characteristically, Fliess thought little of these ideas (*ibid.,* 155f., 6 February 1896), which did not however worry Freud nearly as much as it would have done in the past. Indeed, he wrote two essays on the subject and sent them to his publishers on 6 February 1896. These, as he informed Fliess, were his "Further Remarks on the Neuro-Psychoses of Defence" (1866), which appeared in March in the *Neurologisches Zentralblatt;* and a "general essay," "L'hérédité et l'étiologie des névroses" (1896a), which he sent to the *Revue neurologique.* The French essay, incidentally, was never translated into German.

Ten weeks later, on April 21, he delivered a lecture that was published in a series of articles in the *Wiener klinische Rundschau,* beginning on May 31, under the title "Aetiology of Hysteria" (1896c). These three papers comprise Freud's entire published work on the seduction theory; the ideas he developed later within the framework of that theory have only come down to us through the Fliess letters.

The French paper was in fact a "general presentation" of his views. Since Freud wrote it for French readers who could not be expected to be familiar with his work on neurasthenia and anxiety neurosis, he began with an account of his theory of actual neuroses as described above (see 1.1.1.2), and then went on to show how hysteria and obsessional neurosis could be treated by the new psychoanalytical methods, which he still attributed to Josef Breuer.

Hysteria, he claimed, could invariably be traced to an unconscious memory of a sexual incident, of a "precocious experience of sexual relations with actual excitement of the genitals resulting from sexual abuse committed by another person." The period of life at which this fatal event takes place is "earliest youth—the years up to the age of eight to ten, before the child has reached sexual maturity." "A passive sexual experience in puberty" was therefore the "specific aetiology of hysteria" (1896a, 152; cf. 1896b, 163f.). The thirteen cases of hysteria Freud had treated included seven cases of sexual relations between "blameless children," in general between brothers and sisters, the male seducer having frequently been seduced first by an adult of the female sex. "The boy would repeat the same practices with a little girl over and over again and without alteration—practices to which he himself had been subjected by some female servant or governess" (1896a, 152; cf. 1896b, 164). Freud explained that in several cases the original seduction occurred as early as the second year of life; in most cases, however, it occurred between the ages of four and five.

Admittedly, Freud did not manage even in these papers to elucidate the mechanism of repression. With an almost absurd lack of logic, he claimed that the precocious sexual excitement had little or no effect on the child, and that for that very reason a psychic trace of it was preserved in the unconscious (1896a, 154). Elsewhere he wrote:

A psychological theory of repression . . . might start out from the following indications. It is known that having ideas with a sexual content produces excitatory processes in the genitals which are similar to those produced by sexual experience itself. We may assume that this somatic excitation becomes transposed into the psychical sphere. As a rule the effect in question is much stronger in the case of the experience than in the case of the memory. *But if the sexual experience occurs during the period of sexual immaturity* and the memory of it is aroused during or after maturity, *then the memory will have a far stronger excitatory effect than the experience did at the time it happened;* and this is because in the meantime puberty has immensely increased the capacity of the sexual apparatus for reaction. An inverted relation of this sort between real experience and memory seems to contain the psychological precondition for the occurrence of a repression. Sexual life affords—through the retardation of pubertal maturity as compared with the psychical functions—the only possibility that occurs for this inversion of relative effectiveness. The traumas of childhood operate in a deferred fashion as though they were fresh experiences; but they do so unconsciously (1896b, 166f., note 2, italics added).

Why did Freud use this illogical argument? He might just as well have argued that the experience had to be repressed precisely because it was so intensely exciting and hence disturbing to the child, the disturbing factor perhaps being less the actual physical sensation than the feeling toward the seducer, whose own excitement suddenly transformed him from a familiar person into a strange and threatening one. I believe that Freud did not arrive at this much more obvious idea because he would not allow his theoretical attempts to stray from the physiological model. In other words, his determination to uncover the physiological processes underlying the facilitation of memory traces still prevented him from basing his theory on purely psychological premises. A few weeks later all that was to change.

Despite his continued reluctance to rid himself completely of neurophysiological conceptions, Freud had already taken one further step away from this earlier attempts to adduce an organic explanation. In particular, he had turned against the purely hereditary theory of hysteria propounded by Charcot's French disciples:

As regards nervous heredity, I am far from being able to estimate correctly its influence in the aetiology of the psychoneuroses. I admit that its presence is indispensable for severe cases; I doubt if it is necessary for slight ones; but I am convinced that nervous heredity by itself is unable to produce psychoneuroses if their specific aetiology, precocious sexual excitation, is missing. I even believe that the decision as to which of the neuroses, hysteria or obsessions, will develop in a given case, is not decided by heredity but [by] a special characteristic of the sexual event in earliest childhood (1896a, 156).

Freud had thus come to think that heredity had only a slight influence, if any, on the development of neuroses. For purposes of analysis, at all events, he thought the assumption of the hereditary factor superfluous, since in any case sexual seduction in childhood was needed to produce the neurotic symptoms. Bringing the act of seduction back to consciousness and discussing it sufficed for removing the symptoms.

In his "Further Remarks on the Neuro-Psychoses of Defence" (1896b), Freud examined obsessional neurosis and paranoia at greater length than he had done in the French article. He again attributed obsessional neurosis to pleasurable sexual seduction in childhood, and argued that the patients felt they had to assuage the associated guilt feelings with the obsessional acts. In the course of this explanation, Freud mentioned a remarkable link with the actual neuroses. It is possible, he claimed, that not only the sexual experience was repressed but also the resulting self-reproach. This was done by the conversion of self-reproach into a different feeling, for instance, into "hypochondriacal anxiety (fear of the physical injuries resulting from the act involving the self-reproach), into social anxiety (fear of being punished by society for the misdeed), into religious anxiety, into delusions of being noticed (fear of betraying the act to other people) or into fear of temptation (a justified mistrust) of one's own moral powers of resistance) and so on" (1896b, 171). Freud went on to say: "Many cases which, on a superficial examination, seem to be common (neurasthenic) hypochondria belong to this group of obsessional effects; what is known as 'periodic *neurasthenia*' or 'periodic *melancholia*' seems in particular to resolve itself with unexpected frequency into obsessional affects and obsessional ideas—a discovery which is not a matter of indifference therapeutically" (*ibid.,* italics added).

Only a few months earlier, neurasthenia and melancholia had been declared neuroses resulting from actual sexual practices and hence not open to therapy (see 1.1.2.2. above). Now both were subsumed under the title of obsessional neurosis, whose cause is traumatization in early childhood, and could accordingly lend themselves to psychotherapeutic treatment. Freud had therefore begun to extend the seduction theory to the so-called actual neuroses. The distinction between actual neurosis and defensive neurosis had become blurred, and the earlier etiological assumptions and views of the therapeutical consequences could no longer be maintained.

In this paper (1896b), Freud also treated paranoia as a neurosis of defense. In an earlier essay he had already extended his system to embrace the psychoses, propounding the view "that the ego has fended off the incompatible idea through a flight into psychosis. . . . The ego breaks away from the incompatible idea; but the latter is inseparably connected with a piece of reality so that, in so far as the ego achieves this result, it, too, has detached itself wholly or in part from reality. In my opinion this latter event is the condition under which the subject's ideas receive the vividness of hallucinations" (1894a, 59f.).

Now, two years later, he contended that paranoia was a defensive psychosis (1896b, 177) and that it developed in the same way as obsessive neurosis, namely, through self-reproaches. True, in contrast to what happens in obsessive neurosis, the patient himself does not consider these reproaches justified, and hence does not perform compulsive acts as a form of expiation. In paranoia, the self-reproach is repressed "in a manner which may be described as projection. It is repressed by erecting the defensive symptom of distrust of other people. In this way the subject withdraws his acknowledgement of the self-reproach; and, as if to make up for this, he is deprived of a protection against the self-reproaches which return in his delusional ideas" (*ibid.,* 184). The hearing of "voices," a typical symptom of paranoia, was due to "self-reproaches about experiencess that were analagous to a childhood trauma" (*ibid.,* 182), and visual hallucinations were repressed images seen in childhood.

Taking the case of a patient, Frau P., Freud demonstrated that all her symptoms could be interpreted as visual or acoustic projections of incidents directly connected with past sexual scenes—between the ages of six and ten the patient had had a sexual relationship with her brother. Frau P. experienced constant visual hallucinations of the lower part of a woman's abdomen. In analysis, it appeared that at the beginning of her illness she had in fact been upset by seeing women in a hydropathic establishment, but that this scene had merely helped her to mask the memory of sexual games with her brother and the associated guilt feelings.[33]

Freud's extension of his theory of neurosis to the psychoses provoked much the same criticism from the psychiatric establishment of his day as the "sociogenetic theory" of psychosis elicits nowadays (cf. Krüll, 1977a). His views of paranoia were dismissed as "gruesome, horrible, old wives' psychiatry" by one Dr. Rieger of Würzburg (1950a, 171, 2 November 1896).

In Vienna, his lecture on "The Aetiology of Hysteria," delivered at the end
of April 1896 before the Society of Psychiatry and Neurology, received "an
icy reception," one of the leading psychiatrists, Professor Krafft-Ebing, opin-
ing that "it sounds like a scientific fairy tale." Yet Freud was seemingly
undeterred by these attacks, for he described his audience as asses, incapable
of appreciating the importance of "the solution to a more than thousand-year-
old problem—a 'source of the Nile' " (Schur, 1972, 104, Letter to Fliess of 28
April 1896).[34]

This lecture contained the same ideas on hysteria as the two papers cited
above, except that the scenes of sexual seduction were now set out in more
concrete form:

> In all eighteen cases . . . I have . . . come to learn of sexual experiences of this kind
> in childhood. I can divide my cases into three groups, according to the origin of the
> sexual stimulation. In the first group it is a question of assaults—of single, or at any
> rate isolated instances of abuse, mostly practised on female children, by adults who
> were strangers, and who, incidentally, knew how to avoid inflicting gross, mechanical
> injury. In these assaults there was no question of the child's consent, and the first effect
> of the experience was preponderantly one of fright. The second group consists of the
> much more numerous cases in which some adult looking after the child—a nursery
> maid or governess or tutor, or, unhappily all too often, a close relative—has initiated
> the child into sexual intercourse and has maintained a regular love relationship with
> it—a love relationship, moreover, with its mental side developed—which has often
> lasted for years. The third group, finally, contains child-relationships proper—sexual
> relations between two children of different sexes, mostly a brother and sister, which are
> often prolonged beyond puberty and which have the most far-reaching consequences
> for the pair. . . . Where there had been a relation between two children I was sometimes
> able to prove that the boy—who, here too, played the part of the aggressor—had
> previously been seduced by an adult of the female sex. . . . In view of this, I am inclined
> to suppose that children cannot find their way to acts of sexual aggression unless they
> have been seduced previously (1896c, 207f.).

It was always adults who seduced the children originally, often violating
them rather brutally: "For the idea of these infantile sexual scenes is very
repellant to the feelings of a sexually normal individual; they include all the
abuses known to debauched and impotent persons, among whom the buccal
cavity and the rectum are misused for sexual purposes. . . . People who have
no hesitation in satisfying their sexual desires upon children cannot be expected to jib at finer shades in the methods of obtaining that satisfaction" (ibid.,
214).

Nevertheless, as Freud went on to stress, a defensive neurosis does not
necessarily appear after even the worst sexual abuses. For that to happen, the
experience must also be repressed, expunged from memory. People who have
conscious memories of infantile sexual experiences do not turn into hysterics.
"The scenes must be present as *unconscious memories;* only so long as, and
in so far as, they are unconscious are they able to create and maintain hysteri-

cal symptoms. But what decides whether those experiences produce conscious or unconscious memories—whether that is conditioned by the content of the experiences, or by the time at which they occur, or by later influences—that is a fresh problem, which we shall prudently avoid" (*ibid.,* 211).

The last sentence shows that Freud had still not solved the problem of repression, although in the same lecture he came very close to a solution when he described the link between the sexually abused child and the seducing adult in the following words:

> . . . the adult who . . . is . . . armed with complete authority and the right to punish, and can exchange the one role for the other to the uninhibited satisfaction of his moods, and on the other hand the child, who in his helplessness is at the mercy of this arbitrary will, who is prematurely aroused to every kind of sensibility and exposed to every sort of disappointment, and whose performance of the sexual activities assigned to him is often interrupted by his imperfect control of his natural needs—all these grotesque and yet tragic incongruities reveal themselves as stamped upon the later development of the individual and of his neurosis, in countless permanent effects which deserve to be traced in the greatest detail. Where the relation is between two children, the character of the sexual scenes is none the less of the same repulsive sort, since every such relationship between children postulates a previous seduction of one of them by an adult. The psychical consequences of these child-relations are quite extraordinarily far-reaching; the two individuals remain linked by an invisible bond throughout the whole of their lives (*ibid.,* 215).

Freud thus maintained that repression is based in the authoritarian relationship between the superior adult and the completely dependent child or, in the case of two children, between the stronger and the weaker. The child has no one in whom he (or she) can confide his experience; the adult demands silence and has complete control over the child. Moreover, the child will consider the adult's demand for silence an order he must obey, albeit unwillingly, like so many other unpleasant orders. The result—Freud could easily have concluded —is repression, that is, the erasure of the relevant incidents from consciousness.[35]

The reason why Freud did not arrive at this apparently obvious conclusion was probably connected with the same personal problems that drove him a few months later to renounce his seduction theory (cf. 1.2 below).

It should also be stressed that in this context, too, Freud was thinking of one type of sexual seduction only, that by someone of the opposite sex. Homosexual relations were something he simply glossed over.

The seduction theory had thus been rounded off. In a letter to Fliess he added a few more details about determining the time of the primary sexual scene (1950a, 163, 30 May 1896). No essential changes were made until Freud later undertook his own analysis and began to recall his own childhood.

He believed that this theory had finally removed all the obstacles that still stood in the way of his theoretical edifice. This explains his extraordinary burst of activity and euphoria in the spring of 1896. He planned a "noble" work,

Table 1: Freud's Theory of the Neuroses in about 1896

		Neurasthenia	Anxiety Neurosis	(Melancholia) (called "actual neurosis" in the Fliess letters only)	(Migraine)
Symptons (according to Freud)		Intracranial pressure, spinal irritation, fatigue, dyspesia, nervous irritation, etc. In women: often connected with hysterical symptoms.	Disturbances of the heart action, disturbances of respiration, attacks of sweating, attacks of tremor and shivering, attacks of locomotive vertigo, attacks of parasthesias. Associated with phobias: agoraphobia, phobias relating to locomotion (trains, travel, etc.) (But see phobias under "obsessional neurosis.")	Depression, fear of death	Neuralgias (headaches, and nervous affections)
Etiology (Freud's causal assumptions): "sexual theory"	General	Cause of actual neurosis: current "abnormal" sexual behavior. "Normal" = heterosexual intercourse without contraceptive measures. The "sexual chemistry" produces poisons if sexuality is not expressed "normally."			
	Special	Masturbation, forms of "abnormal" sexual behavior. In men: masturbation during puberty which predisposes the subject to later "abnormal" sexual behavior. In women: lack of potency in the male during coitus.	Sexual abstinence. In men: frustrated sexual excitation, for instance, through coitus interruptus or diminished potency. In women: virginal anxiety, fear of "abnormal" sexual intercourse.	In men: melancholia as increase of neurasthenia due to masturbation or mourning lost potency. In women: frigidity	Disturbed sexual release through "abnormal" sexual intercourse.
Therapy (Freud's therapeutic suggestions)		Incurable; cannot be influenced by psychoanalysis. Actual neuroses only disappear if "normal" sexual behavior can be restored. Prophylaxis or possible prevention: greater sexual liberty in youth so as not to damage the health of adult males by masturbation.			
Bearing on Freud's personal life		Freud had symptoms of all these types of actual neurosis.			

(Neuropsychoses of defense, psychoneuroses, later transfer neuroses)

		Hysteria	Obsessional Neurosis	Paranoia	(hallucinatory acute amentia)
Symptoms (according to Freud)		"Conversion Symptoms": pains without discernible organic basis, splitting of consciousness, hallucinations, motor hyperactivity or rigidity, anaesthesia neuralgia, visual disturbances, convulsions, contractures, paralyses, tics and twitches, etc., in paroxysms	Phobias of various kinds, fear of infection, fear of pollution, compulsive washing, compulsive impulses (for instance, to kill oneself or others), compulsive brooding, compulsive doubting, compulsive reproaches, compulsive hoarding, compulsive watching, etc. (See phobias under "anxiety neuroses".)	Delusions of persecution; hallucinations, hypochondria, etc.	*(mentioned in the Fliess letters only)* *(not specified)*
Etiology (Freud's causal assumptions: "seduction theory")	General	All neuroses of defense result from sexual, coitus-like seduction in childhood (before the age of eight) by adults or by sexually abused children. During puberty, the memory of this primary experience is rekindled but has to be repressed. The resulting symptom becomes associated with the affect, and serves to ward off that affect felt during the primary experience. Heredity, or a predisposition toward neurotic illness plays a minimum role. Freud was unable to determine the "sexual chemistry" of the neuroses of defense.			
	Special	Experience of the primary seduction was passive and anxious (hence hysteria more common in women). Affect: anxiety, which is warded off by conversion into body sensations.	Experience of the primary seduction was active and pleasurable. Affect: feeling of guilt and shame that are treated as self-reproach Defense by substitution of guilt which is transferred to other spheres.	Experience of the primary seduction was pleasurable. Affect: feelings of guilt and shame which are not accepted but are projected onto the outside. Defense through projection.	Affect: mourning (not specified in greater detail)
Therapy (Freud's therapeutic suggestions)		Psychoanalysis. By helping to bring the primary experience and the associated affect back into consciousness, the therapist helps to eradicate the symptoms.			
Bearing on Freud's personal life		Before his self-analysis, Freud believed that he did not suffer from any of the above-mentioned symptoms of defensive neurosis. (However, shortly before he renounced seduction theory in 1897, he had come to the belief that his symptoms were hysterical.)			

to be entitled *The Psychology and Psychotherapy of the Neuroses of Defence,* into which he proposed to put his "whole soul" (1950a, 1960, 16 March 1896). He was certain that he would not have to retract any of his findings, and had the feeling that he had found "a lump of ore containing an unknown amount of precious metal." He added that he was met with hostility, and lived in such isolation that "one might suppose I had discovered the greatest truths" *(ibid.).* Freud's youthful longing for philosophical knowledge seemed about to be satisfied "now that I am going over from medicine to psychology. I have become a therapist against my will. I am convinced that . . . I can definitely cure hysteria and obsessional neurosis" *(ibid.,* 162, 2 April 1896).

In Table I, the reader will find a schematic outline of the development of Freud's ideas as I have presented them so far.

1.2 The Acute Phase of the Crisis
(Summer 1896–Autumn 1897)

1.2.1 THE DEATH OF JACOB FREUD

In the summer of 1896 Freud received news that his father had fallen ill,[36] and it did not take him long to realize that the illness was fatal.[37] On 15 July 1896, he wrote to Fliess: "The old man has a paralysis of the bladder and rectum, his nutrition is failing, and at the same time he is mentally overalert and euphoric. I really think that these are his last days, but I do not know his final day [term]. . . ." (Schur, 1972, 105, 15 July 1896).

Freud's reactions were inconsistent. He called off a planned meeting with Fliess with the following explanation: "I . . . do not dare to leave, least of all for two days and for a pleasure which I would like to indulge in fully. To meet you in Berlin . . . and then suddenly have to rush back during the day or night because of news which might turn out merely to have been a false alarm—that is something I would like to avoid. . . ." *(ibid.).* Yet, soon afterwards, he felt free to go on a fairly long journey that took him even further afield. In August, he traveled first of all to Aussee in Styria, some 150 miles from Vienna, where his family had been on holiday for several weeks. It would have been possible to return to Vienna very quickly from there. However, he then took his brother Alexander to Italy, where an urgent message could not have reached him easily and from where he could not, in any case, have returned to Vienna within a few hours. Jones claims that this holiday was the longest Freud had ever taken (1953, I, 333). Altogether he was away from Vienna for two months—while his father was on his deathbed.

On 15 July 1896, before he set out on this journey, he wrote to Fliess in a tone that suggested he had already taken leave of his father: "By the way, the old man's condition does not depress me. I do not begrudge him the well-deserved rest, as he himself desires it. He *was* an interesting human being, intrinsically very happy. He is suffering very little now, and is fading with decency and dignity. I do not wish him a prolonged illness, nor [do I wish that for] my unmarried sister who is nursing him and suffering while doing so" (Schur, 1972, 105f., 15 July 1896, italics added). After returning from his journey, he wrote to Fliess: "My father lies on his death bed. He is at times confused and is steadily shrinking toward pneumonia and a fateful date" (*ibid.,* 106, 29 September 1896). Jacob Freud died less than a month later.

On October 26, Freud wrote to Fliess: "The old man died on the night of the 23rd, and we buried him yesterday. He bore himself bravely up to the end, like the remarkable man he was. He must have had meningeal haemorrhage at the last; there were stuporous attacks and inexplicable temperatures, hyperaesthesia and muscular spasms, from which he would awake without temperature. The last attack ended with an oedema of the lungs, and he had an easy death. It all happened in my critical period, and I am really down over it" (1950a, 170).

How shaken Freud was by his father's death becomes clearer from a letter dated November 2: "By one of the obscure routes behind the official conscious-ness the old man's death affected me deeply. I valued him highly and under-stood him very well indeed, and with his peculiar mixture of deep wisdom and imaginative light-heartedness he meant a great deal in my life. By the time he died his life had long been over, but at a death the whole past stirs within one" *(ibid.).*

In the same letter he related a dream he had had on the night of the funeral, the true importance of which he failed to appreciate for, as M. Robert (1974) has stressed, he called it "a very pretty dream":

I must tell you about a very pretty dream I had on the night *after* the funeral. I found myself in a shop where there was a notice up saying:

You are requested
to close the eyes.

I recognized the place as the barber's to which I go every day. On the day of the funeral I was kept waiting, and therefore arrived at the house of mourning rather late. The family were displeased with me, because I had arranged for the funeral to be quiet and simple, which they later agreed was the best thing. They also took my lateness in rather bad part. The phrase on the notice-board has a double meaning. It means "one should do one's duty towards the dead" in two senses—an apology, as though I had not done my duty and my conduct needed overlooking, and the actual duty itself. The dream was thus an outlet for the feeling of self-reproach which a death generally leaves among the survivors (1950a, 171, 2 November 1896, italics added).

In my view, this dream holds the key to the important crisis in Freud's life with which we are concerned here: It was plainly an expression of the guilt feelings he entertained toward his father. Now it seems highly improbable that he should have felt guilty about the simple funeral arrangements, since his relatives later approved of these. However, M. Robert has argued that the simple arrangements may have meant cutting the Jewish ritual to a minimum, and that this economy might have explained his guilt feelings.

In any case, Freud felt guilty about his lack of punctuality. But why could he not have asked his barber, whose regular client he was and who must have known about the funeral as well, to serve him first so that he did not arrive late at the Grüne Thorgasse? Was there perhaps an unconscious flight impulse, similar to the one that had previously driven him from his father's deathbed?

It seems to me, moreover, that Freud failed to mention a much deeper and more fundamental significance of this dream, either deliberately or else because he was unable to appreciate it for reasons we have still to discuss. When he retold the same dream in *The Interpretation of Dreams,* he changed a few details, a fact that would have escaped us without the Fliess letters. These changes, in my opinion, point to the deeper significance the dream had for Freud. In *The Interpretation of Dreams,* we read:

> During the night *before* my father's funeral I had a dream of a printed notice, placard or poster—rather like the notices forbidding one to smoke in railway waiting-rooms —on which appeared either:
>   "You are requested to close the eyes"
> or,
>   "You are requested to close an eye."
> I usually write this in the form:
>   "You are requested to close $^{the}_{an}$ eye(s)."
> Each of these two versions had a meaning of its own and led in a different direction when the dream was interpreted. I had chosen the simplest possible ritual for the funeral, for I knew my father's own views on such ceremonies. But some other members of the family were not sympathetic to such puritanical simplicity and thought we should be disgraced in the eyes of those who attended the funeral. Hence one of the versions: "You are requested to close an eye," i.e., to "wink at" or "overlook." Here it is particularly easy to see the meaning of the vagueness expressed by the "either-or." The dream-work failed to establish a unified wording for the dream-thoughts which could at the same time be ambiguous, and the two main lines of thought consequently began to diverge even in the manifest content of the dream (1900a, 317f., italics added).

By changing the original version and claiming that he had dreamed this dream before, and not after, the funeral, Freud was able to dissociate his lateness from his impulse to flee the scene and his consequent guilt feelings. He could accordingly relate the "winking at" requested in the dream to the trappings of the funeral, even adding that the simplest ritual would have been in accordance with his father's wishes. The "winking at" his lack of filial piety was conveniently forgotten.

The change in the wording of the notice strikes me as being significant as well. In *The Interpretation of Dreams,* Freud explained that there were two possible versions. To close the eyes of a dead person meant rendering him a last service, taking one's leave of him. But Freud clearly preferred the second version, "to close an eye." In so doing, he altered the original report of the dream: if one "closes an eye," one can still tell what is happening, and only holds back the truth out of consideration for others; whereas if one closes both eyes, one sees nothing at all and remains totally in the dark.[38]

In my view, these modifications of the original dream can only mean one thing: Freud felt that his father wished him not only to render him a last service but also to shut his eyes to certain facts. In other words, this dream must have reminded Freud of an unspoken taboo Jacob had passed on to him in early childhood, namely, not to delve into his, Jacob's, past. I believe that the crisis in Freud's life which followed his father's death and lasted for nearly a year was the direct result of his wrestling with just that taboo. Several months later he found it was more than he could cope with, and he renounced his seduction theory.

1.2.2 THE STRUGGLE TO SAVE THE SEDUCTION THEORY

His father's death thus had direct repercussions on Freud's view of the defensive neuroses. Since the Fliess correspondence has been published in fragmentary form only, we cannot follow these effects in detail. It is however clear that Freud's interest shifted to the "seducers" and to the reasons for their abuse of the trust of dependent children. Before entering into his deliberations on this subject in greater detail, I must first draw attention to another of Freud's ideas that emerged at this point and that would have had wide theoretical implications had he pursued it further. On 6 December 1896 he wrote to Fliess: "As you know, I am working on the assumption that our psychical mechanism has come about by a process of stratification: the material present in the shape of memory-traces is from time to time subjected to a rearrangement in accordance with fresh circumstances—is, as it were, transcribed. Thus what is essentially new in my theory is the thesis that memory is present not once but several times over, that it is registered in various species of 'signs' " (1950a, 173).

Repression now struck him as an imperfect system of "signs," an inadequate "translation." "A failure of translation is what we know clinically as 'repression.' . . . Within one and the same psychical phase and among transcriptions of one and the same species there can appear a *normal* kind of defence against the generation of unpleasure. *Pathological* defence is directed only against memory traces from an *earlier* phase which have not yet been translated" (*ibid.,* 175f.)

Freud was not entirely satisfied with this purely linguistic explanation, however, and in subsequent passages of the letter he tried to revert to an energetic interpretation. Memories of sexual experiences in early childhood, he claimed, had such intense effects because the "magnitude of excitation" increases as time passes, i.e., as sexual development takes place. His purely hermeneutic approach, which dispensed with all biochemical assumptions, thus remained exceedingly short-lived (Ricoeur, 1974; Lorenzer, 1973a, 1973b, 1976; and Lorenzer, *et al.,* 1971).[39]

The letter of December 6 also contained the first reference to the seducer's "perversions":

It seems to me more and more that the essential point of hysteria is that it is a result of perversion on the part of the seducer; and that heredity is seduction by the father. Thus a change occurs between the generations—1st generation: Perversion. 2nd generation: Hysteria, and consequent sterility. Incidentally there is a metamorphosis within the individual: he is perverse during the age of his strength and then, after a period of anxiety, becomes hysterical. Thus hysteria is in fact not repudiated *sexuality* but rather repudiated *perversion* (1950a, 179f.; cf. 182, 17 December 1896).

Here the father's perversion is mentioned for the first time as the real cause of the child's seduction. Freud was not yet thinking of his father, because he still believed that his own symptoms were due not to hysteria but to an actual neurosis. With his multigeneration theory of hysteria, he would, however, have been forced to delve into his own "prehistory," in other words, the history of his father, just as soon as he realized that his own neurosis too was defensive, was a form of hysteria.

Freud's "psychical excavations" have often been linked with his interest in archeology, not least because he himself mentioned the connection several times. In my view, both alike are rooted in his—most probably unconscious —desire to explore his father's past.[40]

At the beginning of 1897, Freud took stock of his achievements and expressed the certain hope that he would make even greater discoveries in the future:

We shall not be shipwrecked. Instead of the passage we are seeking, we may find oceans, to be fully explored by those who come after us; but, if we are not prematurely capsized, if our constitutions can stand it,[41] We shall make it. *Nous y arriverons.* Give me another ten years and I shall finish the neuroses and the new psychology. . . . In spite of the complaints you refer to, no previous New Year has been so rich with promise for both of us. When I am not afraid I can take on all the devils in hell, and you know no fear at all (1950a, 182f., 3 January 1897).

This passage reflects Freud's certain belief that his theory of neurosis would make him famous one day. The first sentence, moreover, seems to contain a "Freudian slip" and sheds fresh light on his ambitions. For where he speaks of leaving the exploration of the oceans to those who come after us, he uses the word *erübrigen* (to render unnecessary) when he obviously wanted to say *überlassen* (to bequeath), as if he wished—in his unconscious, and flying in the face of the overt meaning of the words—not only to cover new oceans but also to reserve them for himself, in other words, to leave nothing to his successors. It seems to me that it was this very ambition, of which he himself was unaware, that later led him to clash with so many of his followers.

During the next few weeks he narrowed his view about the age at which the seductions occur: "Everything now points more and more to the first three years of life" *(ibid.)*. In the case of psychosis, work with his patients had shown him that seduction must have taken place even earlier, "from 1¼ to 1½ years of age" *(ibid.,* 185, 11 January 1897).

His patients increasingly provided unequivocal proof of the reality of childhood seductions. One male hysteric who had originally been seduced by an uncle went on to have relations with his little sister, who had witnessed the original scenes of seduction and who later became a psychotic. The patient's own children from two marriages had a variety of neurotic complaints. Freud concluded: "This will show you how it comes about that a neurosis increases into a psychosis in the following generation. . . . " *(ibid.)*. In April, he told Fliess about a woman patient who had confessed that her father had taken her to bed regularly between her eighth and twelfth years to practice "external ejaculation," and that she had felt very anxious. The same thing had happened to one of her sisters, and she knew that a cousin had had to "resist the advances of her grandfather" *(ibid.,* 195f., 28 April 1897).

However, Freud also looked to quite different sources for confirmation of his assumptions. In particular, he scrutinized medieval theories of possession and exorcism, and thought that he could see a parallel between the confessions of witches or possessed persons and those of his patients. Both involved sexual seductions, and he wondered whether untoward childhood experiences might not have been responsible for both. The cruel punishments meted out to witches, moreover, seemed to bear a resemblance to the self-punishing tendencies of his patients—the hysterics among whom would quite often stick pins into themselves or have "their breasts cut open." These self-destructive tendencies could always be traced back to early seduction, and time and again patients[42] had been tortured with pins by those responsible. In the same vein, the inquisitors had often searched with needles "for diabolical stigmata, and in that similar situation the victims remember the old gruesome story. . . . Thus victim and torturer alike recall their earliest youth" *(ibid.,* 188, 17 January 1897; retranslated from the German). Seduction in childhood, Freud thus believed, also underlay medieval ideas of possession and of exorcism. For a closer investigation, he had bought a copy of *Malleus Maleficarum,* the fifteenth-century text on the identification of witches. "I am beginning to dream of an extremely primitive devil religion the rites of which continue to be performed secretly, and now I understand the stern therapy of the witches' judges. The links are abundant" *(ibid.,* 189, 24 January 1897).

Freud also looked to Jewish history for corroboration of his theory: "I am toying with the idea that in the perversions, of which hysteria is the negative, we may have the remnants of a primitive cult which in the Semitic East may once have been a religion (Moloch, Astarte)" *(ibid.)*. Schur has published the continuation of these lines, cut by the editors of the Fliess letters. They read: "Think of it; I have been given a scene about the circumcision of a girl, involving the cutting off of a piece of one of the labia minora[43] (which is shorter even now) and the sucking off of the blood, after which the child got to eat a piece of the skin. This child at the age of thirteen once claimed she could swallow a piece of an earthworm, which she actually did. And an operation once performed by you had to come to grief from a hemophilia based on all this" (Schur, 1966, 83f., 24 January 1897). Here Freud links—and I believe not by chance—perversion, a Semitic sex cult, castration, and the Emma episode (see 3.1.8 below and 1.1.2.3 above).[44]

Freud also considered studying the behavior of his own children, but found the obstacles too great: "Why do I not go to the nursery and . . . experiment? Because with twelve-and-a-half hours' work I have no time, and because the womenfolk do not back me in my investigations" (1950a, 192, 8 February 1897, omission by the publishers). Clearly, neither Martha Freud nor her sister Minna Bernays—who had moved in with the Freuds shortly after the birth of Anna, at about the beginning of 1896, and had become something of a second mother to Freud's children—had been initiated in, let alone converted to, Freud's theory of child sexuality (Roazen, 1975, 58). More generally, too, Freud seems to have been reluctant to use observations of children in support of his theory. Jones wrote in this connection: "It seems a curious thing to say of the very man who explored the child's mind to an extent that had never before been possible that he should nevertheless have retained some inhibitions about coming to too close quarters with it. It is as if some inner voice had said 'Thus far and no farther' " (1955, II, 261).

Instead, Freud turned his attention to his parental family, in an effort to determine to what extent his siblings' neurotic symptoms were due to parental seduction. Jones mentions an unpublished letter of 11 February 1897 in which Freud inferred from the existence of some hysterical symptoms in his brothers and several sisters (not himself) *that even his own father had to be incriminated,* though he immediately added that the frequency with which such occurrences were generally reported raised his suspicions (1953, I, 322, italics added). At the time, Freud still firmly believed that his own neurotic symptoms were the result of an actual, not a defensive, neurosis. But the examination of his own family had set a stone rolling, since only a few weeks later he could no longer exempt himself and felt impelled to begin his self-analysis.

In a wild passion for work, Freud was spending up to twelve hours a day looking after his patients and then continuing, with increasing enthusiasm, the work on his own theoretical contribution. At the end of April 1897, he met Fliess at yet another "congress" in Nuremberg. As always, their meeting gave him a fresh impetus. This time he went on to develop a new idea on the origins of fantasies, especially in cases of hysteria. In my view, this new idea constitutes an important extension of the seduction theory:

Everything points to the reproduction of scenes which in some cases can be arrived at directly and in others through a veil of intervening phantasy. The phantasies arise from things *heard* but only understood *later,* and all the material is of course genuine. They are defensive structures, sublimations and embellishments of the facts, and at the same time serve the purpose of self-exoneration. Their contingent origin is perhaps from masturbation phantasies. A second important insight is that the psychical structures which in hysteria are subjected to repression are not properly speaking memories, because no one sets his memory working without good cause, but impulses deriving from the primal scenes (1950a, 196, 2 May 1897).

With this letter Freud sent a manuscript in which he set out his new ideas about the origin of hysteria even more clearly:

> The aim seems to be to hark back to the primal scenes. This is achieved in some cases directly, but in others only in a roundabout way, *via* phantasies. For phantasies are psychical outworks constructed in order to bar the way to these memories. At the same time, phantasies serve the purpose of refining the memories, of sublimating them. They are built up out of things that have been *heard* about and then *subsequently* turned to account; thus they combine things that have been experienced and things that have been *heard* about past events (from the history of parents and ancestors) and things seen by the subject himself. They are related to things heard in the same way as dreams are related to things seen. For in dreams we hear nothing, but only see (*ibid.,* 197f., Draft L).

According to Freud, the child thus interprets "primal scenes,"[45] that is, the original seduction scenes, on the basis of what he hears. Now what the child hears are stories about parents and ancestors, and these the child associates with his own seduction. In that way, Freud believed, the child tries to explain an event for which no explanation could be obtained from others, let alone from the seducers. The outrage committed on the child is something he can only interpret with the help of the stories he has heard. True, such interpretations are fantasies, ideas that cannot be verified since verification would imply a realization of what actually happened. Since, however, the child constructs fantasies out of stories he has heard from members of the family, these fantasies cannot be so very far removed from reality. A child who has been sexually abused by an adult probably develops a very fine appreciation of the guilt and shame felt by his seducers. If he hears adults talk of things that are connected with the incident or that suggest, by the emotions they elicit in the adults, that they are or have been involved in it—which happens particularly during discussions of sexual topics—then, we may take it, the child will register the contents of such stories very attentively. His fantasies will revolve about such topics, the more so as they impinge on his own experiences.

Such fantasies, Freud believed, were sublimations, embellishments of the facts, but at the same time self-exonerations helping to ward off the memory of the terrifying event. As soon as the child has developed a fantasy that renders his seduction comprehensible, the seduction ceases to oppress and unsettle him to the same extent it did before—the child can now think of the fantasy and need no longer fret about the actual incident. The protection the fantasy "outwork" thus provides is evident.

On May 25 Freud developed this idea further in Draft M, in which he also set out the process by which traumatic experiences and fantasies are linked together:

Phantasies arise from an unconscious combination of things experienced and heard, constructed for particular purposes. These purposes aim at making inaccessible the memory from which symptoms have been generated or might be generated. Phantasies are constructed by a process of fusion and distortion analogous to the decomposition of a chemical body which is combined with another one. For the first kind of distortion consists in a falsification of memory by a process of fragmentation, which involves a disregard of chronological considerations. . . . A fragment of a visual scene is then joined up to a fragment of an auditory one and made into a phantasy, while the fragment left over is linked up with something else. This makes it impossible to trace their original connection. As a result of the construction of phantasies of this kind (in periods of excitation) the mnemic symptoms cease. But instead there are now unconscious fictions which have not succumbed to defence. If the intensity of such a phantasy increases to a point at which it would have to force its way into consciousness, it is repressed and a symptom is generated by a backward drive from the phantasy to its constituent memories (*ibid.,* 204, Draft M).

Freud believed that the traumatic incident becomes linked to the fantasy images derived from conversations with adults not by direct association but by a process of "fragmentation." Only fragments of the actual scene are connected with parts of what has been heard and so reconstructed into a fantasy. This process of fantasy formation by fragmentation makes the remembrance of the original incident even more difficult and hence offers complete protection against its recall.

However, the fantasies too become dangerous after some time and have to be repressed in their turn. The result—so Freud clearly thought—was the appearance of the symptom which referred back to the original scene, because that scene provides the material for its elaboration.

Repressed fantasies thus underlie the formation of symptoms directly connected with traumatic childhood experiences: "A romance of being a stranger (*e.g.,* in the family) (*cf.* paranoia) is found regularly, and serves as a means of bastardizing the relatives in question. Agoraphobia seems to depend on a romance of prostitution, which itself goes back to this same family romance. Thus a woman who will not go out by herself is asserting her mother's unfaithfulness" (*ibid.,* 205, Draft M). In other words, the horrifying seduction experience turns the child's closest relatives or guardians into strangers, and the child then tries to find some explanation for that strangeness in a "romance of being a stranger," i.e., in a fantasy. Paranoic alienation is therefore a symptom produced by the repression of that fantasy. In more specific terms, the child transforms the experience of his or her mother's unfaithfulness into a prostitution fantasy, which later causes the symptom of agoraphobia.[46]

It seems to me that with this idea Freud had taken the first step beyond his original, pure seduction theory. His very choice of a prostitution fantasy revolving about the "family romance" of the mother's unfaithfulness as a model shows that he now attributed the traumatic event not only to a concrete sexual experience, that is, to a genuine seduction scene in childhood, but also to apparently disconcerting or shocking incidents in the life of the child's primary caretakers. True, Freud did not pursue this idea further, but only because he renounced seduction theory as such soon afterward.

Had he not done so, he might well have stripped the theory of its extreme fixation on sexual traumas. Seduction in childhood—he might have continued the argument—need not necessarily have been sexual to produce a traumatic effect. A different form of seduction, of misleading the child, for instance by a mother who preaches morality while being "unfaithful," or by a parent whose strict sense of justice is a mere cloak for extreme brutality, or love that is nothing short of possessiveness and persecution, and many similar forms of hypocrisy could easily have been fitted into the frame of the seduction theory if Freud had really wanted to extend it in that direction.

That same month—May 1897—brought a spate of Freudian discoveries. "Inside me is a seething ferment," he wrote. "I have felt impelled to start writing about dreams, with which I feel on firm ground." He had read the literature on the subject and rejoiced that no one before him had had the slightest inkling of the truth: "I . . . feel like the Celtic imp: 'How glad I am that no man's eyes have pierced the veil of Puck's disguise.' No one has the slightest suspicion that dreams are not nonsense but wish-fulfilment" (*ibid.*, 200f., 16 May 1897). He had "an obscure feeling that very shortly something vital will have to be added," and that was why he could not yet bring himself to produce a preliminary summing up *(ibid.).*

There were also setbacks. One of his patients, a banker, "who had got furthest in his analysis, made off at a critical point, just before he should have produced the final scenes. This . . . has shown me that I do not yet know all the factors that are at work" *(ibid.).* The banker's action seems to have made a marked impression on Freud, for he gave it later as one of the reasons for renouncing the seduction theory (see 1.2.4).

Another disappointment was that Freud's application for the position of associate professor had been turned down again. In January 1897 he had written to Fliess: "I am left cold by the news that the board of professors have proposed my younger colleague in my speciality for the title of professor, thus passing me over. . . . It leaves me quite cold, but perhaps it will hasten my final breach with the university" (*ibid.,* 190, 24 January 1897). The repeated mention of the fact that it left him cold shows better than anything that he was far from indifferent to the slight. In May, the board of professors proposed him again, and again he was passed over. This last rejection must have been particularly galling, because he considered himself as good as being a professor already (*ibid.,* 210, 12 June 1897; according to Schur, the correct date of this letter is June 22). As it was, Freud had to wait for his appointment until 1902. The reasons have been discussed by various authors.[47] This is not the place to repeat their often controversial views; all that matters here is that this being passed over was certainly an additional burden for Freud during his critical period.

1.2.3 SELF-ANALYSIS

Though Freud himself was not aware of it, his theoretical reflections were leading him to the point where he had to analyze himself. On 31 May 1897, he sent Fliess another batch of notes (Draft N). He had discovered that children have hostile impulses against their parents, and argued that "in sons this death wish is directed against their father, and in daughters against their mother." Kris has called this phrase the first hint of the Oedipus complex (in 1950a, 207, note 3), which is doubtless correct as far as the content is concerned, but ignores one important difference, for in the Draft Freud also stressed that "the identification [with the parents, M.K.] which takes place here is, as we can see, merely a mode of thinking and *does not relieve us of the necessity for looking for the motive*" (1950a, 207, Draft N, italics added). Here the death wishes against the father are not—as later in the Oedipus complex —presented as a universal human condition, but are said to be in need of further elucidation. Psychologists and therapists were challenged to discover the underlying cause.

Freud also produced a new view of repression: "They [hostile impulses against parents] are repressed at periods in which pity for one's parents is active—at times of their illness or death. One of the manifestations of grief is then to reproach oneself for their death (*cf.* what are described as 'melancholias') or to punish oneself in a hysterical way by putting oneself into their position with an idea of retribution" *(ibid.).* Freud thus claimed that the child represses reproaches against his or her parents because he does not want to hurt them.[48]

In my view, this part of the Draft is of great importance. It contains an anticipatory interpretation of what Freud was to discover in himself during the next few weeks—something that was present in germ even while he wrote the above lines at the end of May 1897: that his own hostile impulses against his father had to be repressed because "the old man" had just died, and because his own feelings of grief were mixed with feelings of guilt.

It is very hard to see the connection between the last paragraph of Draft N and what went before; the apparent non sequitur takes one utterly by surprise. The last paragraph reads as follows:

Definition of "Holiness." "Holiness" is something that is based on the fact that, for the sake of the larger community, human beings have sacrificed some of their freedom to indulge in sexual perversions. The horror of incest (as something impious) is based on the fact that, as a result of a common sexual life (even in childhood), the members of a family hold together permanently and become incapable of contact with strangers. Thus incest is anti-social and civilization consists in a progressive denunciation of it. Contrariwise the "superman" *(ibid.,* 209f., Draft N., 31 May 1897).

But this mental leap may not have been as great as it seems to be. It may well be that Freud associated the idea of filial piety toward weak, ill, or dead parents with another form of piety, namely, piety toward the people of Israel, a people that also deserved pity—for being a persecuted minority. Now to pious Jews, holiness is tantamount to serving the community, the people of Israel. The reference to incest, one of the strictest taboos of Judaism, may be explained in the same way. It seems to me that Freud had grasped intuitively that his disinclination to expose his father was part and parcel of his affiliation to the Jewish people, by virtue of which Jacob's taboo became all the more binding on him.[49]

In the letter accompanying Draft N, Freud mentioned two dreams that throw further light on the impending climax of his personal crisis:

Not long ago I dreamt that I was feeling over-affectionately towards Mathilde [Freud's eldest daughter, M.K.], but her name was "Hella," and then I saw the word "Hella" in heavy type before me. The solution is that Hella is the name of an American niece whose photograph we have been sent. Mathilde may have been called Hella because she has been weeping so bitterly recently over the Greek defeats. She has a passion for the mythology of ancient Hellas, and naturally regards all Hellenes as heroes. The dream of course fulfils my wish *to pin down a father as the originator of neurosis* and put an end to my persistent doubts (*ibid.,* 206, italics added).

Here Freud expressed his aim very clearly: he wanted to expose a father as a seducer. But why did he feel entitled to deduce that wish from the dream thoughts? Were his "over-affectionate" feelings for his daughter a form of seduction, so that he had to consider himself the originator of a neurosis? Did he believe that Mathilde thought of him, too, as a hero, whose defeats she had to bewail? Or was he himself the child Hella, who wept for the unheroic father Jacob, the cause of his own neurosis? In any case, it seems rather unconvincing that this dream should have referred exclusively to his analytical doubts, as Freud obviously tried to suggest. Quite simply, he had not yet recognized his personal involvement.

The second dream was no less revealing. It was the now well-known "staircase dream":

Another time I dreamt that I was walking *up* a staircase with very few clothes on. I was walking up very briskly, as was emphasized in the dream (heart not affected!) when I suddenly *noticed* that a woman was coming up *behind* me, whereupon I found myself rooted to the spot, unable to move, overcome by that paralysis which is so common in dreams. The accompanying emotion was not anxiety but *erotic excitement.* So you see how the feeling of paralysis peculiar to sleep can be used for the fulfilment of an exhibitionistic wish. Earlier that night I had really climbed the stairs from the flat below, at any rate without a collar, and it had occurred to me that I might meet a neighbour (*ibid.,* 206f., 31 May 1897, italics added).

Like the dream about his father's funeral (see 1.2.1 above), Freud changed this dream when retelling it in *The Interpretation of Dreams:*

I was very incompletely dressed and was going upstairs from a flat on the ground floor to a higher story. I was going up three steps at a time and was delighted at my agility. Suddenly I *saw* a maid-servant coming *down* the stairs—*coming towards* me, that is. I felt ashamed and tried to hurry, and at this point the feeling of being inhibited set in: I was glued to the steps and unable to budge from the spot (1900a, 238, italics added).

With these omissions and alterations, Freud obviously meant to eliminate the sexual element from his dream. For not only the omission of the remark that his emotion was one of erotic excitement but also the reversal of the direction of the female on the stairs helps to rob the story of its sexual overtones: being surprised by a woman climbing up behind one is much more evocative of seduction by an active partner than just seeing a woman coming downstairs. Freud's correction of this dream, moreover, was made after he had learned that this scene was a genuine childhood memory of his nursemaid (see 1.3.1 and 3.1.3 below), who had been his "instructress in sexual matters" (1950a, 220; cf. 1900a, 247f.). When he reported this dream to Fliess, he had forgotten her existence. His unconscious had thus used the dream to remind him of the fact that he himself had been seduced in childhood.[50]

At the beginning of June 1897, during the Whitsun holiday, Freud took his family to Aussee, where he intended to have a complete rest "because I do not want to do any more work" (1950a, 206, 31 May 1897).[51] It was during this holiday or shortly afterwards that his phase of "intellectual paralysis" started, not to disappear again until he renounced his seduction theory. As late as May 31, he was still confident that he was "about to discover the source of morality." "Thus the whole thing grows in anticipation and gives me the greatest pleasure" *(ibid.).* But about three weeks later, he wrote to Fliess: "I have never yet imagined anything like my present spell of intellectual paralysis. Every line I write is torture. . . . Incidentally, I have been through some kind of a neurotic experience, with odd states of mind not intelligible to consciousness—cloudy thoughts and vague doubts, with barely here and there a ray of light. . . . I believe I am in a cocoon, and heaven knows what sort of creature will emerge from it" *(ibid.,* 210f., 12 June 1897).[52]

On July 7, he was still not certain about the cause of his intellectual paralysis: "I still do not know what has been happening to me. Something from the deepest depths of my own neurosis has ranged itself against my taking a further step in understanding of the neuroses, and you have somehow been involved. My inability to write seems to be aimed at hindering our intercourse. I have no proofs of this, but merely feelings of a very obscure nature" *(ibid.,* 212, 7 July 1897).

Freud's "inability to write" seems to have been not just a turn of phrase but a psychomotor disorder, for Jones quotes an unpublished letter of June 18 in which Freud said that his inhibition about writing was "really pathological" (1953, I, 235). Six weeks later he wrote that his handwriting "is more human again" (1950a, 214, 18 August 1897). His study of neuroses had brought him up against the wall of his own neurosis. Only on "neutral" territory, that of the theory of dreams, did he still feel sure of himself: "The firmest point seems to me to be the explanation of dreams; it is surrounded by huge and obstinate riddles" *(ibid.,* 212, 7 July 1897).

Freud called off a meeting with Fliess at Aussee, Freud's favorite holiday resort, on August 13. His explanation was:

> Things are fermenting inside me, but I have nothing ready; I am very satisfied with the psychology, tortured with grave doubts about the neuroses, very lazy, and have done nothing here to get the better of the turbulence of my thoughts and feelings; that must wait for Italy. After a spell of good spirits here I am now having a fit of gloom. The *chief patient* I am busy with *is myself. My little hysteria,* which was much intensified by work, has yielded one stage further. The rest sticks. That is the first reason for my mood. *This analysis is harder than any other.* It is also the thing that paralyses the power of writing down and communicating what so far I have learned. But I believe that it has got to be done and is a necessary stage in my work (*ibid.,* 213f., 14 August 1897, italics added).

The italicized parts are Freud's first published references to his self-analysis, but in an (unpublished) passage of an earlier letter dated May 2 he had already written: "My recovery can only come about through work in the unconscious; I cannot manage with conscious efforts alone." According to Jones, this was probably the first hint of Freud's perception that he had to pursue a personal psychoanalysis (Jones, 1953, I, 325). Elsewhere, Jones mentions that Freud had to make arrangements for his father's gravestone in the middle of July 1897, and that this was just when he was beginning his self-analysis (*ibid.,* 334). Whether that was coincidence or not is something that will only be known when the complete Fliess correspondence has been published.

Freud had dared to tackle the impossible:[53] he had started to interpret his own neurotic symptoms as hysteria. In other words, he had ceased to consider them signs of an actual neurosis (see 1.1.2.2 above) and was treating them as signs of a defensive neurosis and hence of seduction in early childhood. Was it then the recall of certain childhood experiences that had caused his intellectual paralysis? Had he uncovered misdemeanors of his primary caretakers toward himself? Was his paralysis the result of the paternal taboo that had appeared to him in symbolic form in the dream he had had after his father's funeral and that had warned him not to look any further?

At the end of August Freud went to Italy. It is not clear who accompanied him. On August 18 he wrote to Fliess that Martha was looking forward to the journey (1950a, 214). According to Jones (1953, I, 334), however, he traveled with his brother Alexander and with Dr. Gattl, a pupil from Berlin, who had been attending his lectures for some time and who was becoming very much "attached" to him and to his theories (1950a, 213, 7 July 1897). Possibly he set out with Martha—from August 25 to September 1 he gave Venice as his address to Fliess—and then continued with his brother and colleague on a tour that lasted until September 20 and took them, among other places, to Orvieto.[54]

His visit to Orvieto is particularly worth mentioning in this connection because Freud was greatly impressed by Signorelli's frescoes in the cathedral, claiming that *The Last Judgment* at Orvieto was "the finest I have seen" (1950a, 264, 22 September 1898). In a short essay (1898b), and more briefly in *The Psychology of Everyday Life* (1901b), he explained that it was the topic of "death and sexuality" that had drawn him to these frescoes:

> We must assume . . . that the topic itself was also intimately bound up with trains of thought . . . which, in spite of the intensity of the interest taken in them, were meeting with a resistance that was keeping them from being worked over by a particular psychical agency and thus from becoming conscious. That this was really true at that time of the topic of "death and sexuality" I have plenty of evidence . . . derived from my own self-investigation (1898b, 293f.).

Might Freud, under the impression of Signorelli's paintings in Orvieto, have been reminded of his father's taboo once again? Was it in Orvieto that he resolved to turn his back on the seduction theory? Death and sexuality were to remain the two great themes with which Freud was to concern himself his whole life long, and which more than twenty years later he described as the two general instincts of man. Was it these two topics that also forced him to disavow his seduction theory?[55]

1.2.4 THE RENUNCIATION OF THE
SEDUCTION THEORY

On 21 September 1897, one day after his return from Italy, Freud wrote the retraction letter which all biographers consider clear proof of a great theoretical transformation, the breakthrough to psychoanalytical theory.[56] I quote that letter at length, and have numbered its main arguments for the sake of greater clarity:

> Here I am again—returned yesterday morning—refreshed, cheerful, impoverished and without work for the time being, and I am writing to you as soon as I have settled in again. Let me tell you straight away the great secret which has been slowly dawning on me in recent months. I no longer believe in my neurotica. That is hardly intelligble without an explanation; you yourself found what I told you credible. So I shall start at the beginning and tell you the whole story of how the reasons for rejecting it arose. [1.1] The first group of factors were the continual disappointment of my attempts to bring my analysis to a real conclusion, [1.2] the running away of people who for a time had seemed my most favourably inclined patients, [1.3] the non-arrival of complete successes on which I had counted, and [1.4] the possibility of explaining my partial successes in other, ordinary ways. [2.1] Then there was the astonishing thing that in every case [2.2] *not excluding my own,* the father had to be accused of perversion, and [2.3] realization of the unexpected frequency of hysteria where the same condition would apply, though it was hardly credible that perverted acts against children were so general. (Perversion would have to be immeasurably more frequent than hysteria, as the illness can only arise where the events have accumulated and one of the factors which weaken defence is present.) [3] Thirdly, there was the definite realization that there is no indication of reality in the unconscious, so that it is impossible to distinguish between truth and emotionally-charged fiction. (This leaves open the possible explanation that sexual phantasy regularly makes use of the theme of the parents.) [4] Fourthly,

there was the consideration that even in the most deep-reaching psychoses the unconscious memory does not break through, so that the secret of infantile experiences is not revealed even in the most confused states of delirium. When one thus sees that the unconscious never overcomes the resistance of the conscious, one must abandon the expectation that in treatment the reverse process will take place to the extent that the conscious will fully dominate the unconscious.

So far was I influenced by these considerations that I was ready to abandon two things—[5.1] the complete solution of a neurosis and [5.2] sure understanding of its aetiology in infancy. Now I do not know where I am, as [5.3] I have failed to reach theoretical understanding of repression and its play of forces. It again seems arguable that [5.4] it is later experiences which give rise to phantasies which throw back to childhood; and with that the factor of [5.5] hereditary predisposition regains a sphere of influence from which I had made it my business to oust it—in the interests of fully explaining neurosis.

Were I depressed, jaded, unclear in my mind, such doubts might be taken for signs of weakness. [6.1] But as I am in just the opposite state, I must acknowledge them to be the result of honest and effective intellectual labour, and I am proud that after penetrating so far I am still capable of such criticism. Can these doubts be only an episode on the way to further knowledge?

It is curious that [6.2.] I feel not in the least disgraced, though the occasion might seem to require it. Certainly I shall not tell it in Dan, or publish it in Askalon, in the land of the Philistines—but between you and me [6.3] I have a feeling more of triumph than of defeat [6.4] (which cannot be right). . . .

I vary Hamlet's remark about ripeness—cheerfulness is all. [6.5] I might be feeling very discontented. The hope of eternal fame was so beautiful, and so was that of certain wealth, complete independence, travel, and removing the children from the severe worries which spoiled my own youth. All that depended on whether hysteria succeeded or not. [6.6] Now I can be quiet and modest again and go on worrying and saving, and one of the stories from my collection occurs to me: "Rebekka, you can take off your wedding-gown, you're not a *Kalle** any longer. . . ."

There is something else I must add. [6.7] In the general collapse only the psychology has retained its value. [7] The dreams still stand secure, and my beginnings in metapsychology have gone up in my estimation. It is a pity one cannot live on dream-interpretation, for instance . . . " (1950a, 215ff., italics and numbering added; partial retranslation from the German).

If we look at Freud's reasons for this recantation (1.1 to 4) more closely, we find that all except one, which concerns him personally (2.2), lack plausibility. In connection with point 1.1, it must be remembered that Freud had only been engaged in self-analysis for two to three months, and that in the case of his patients, he never counted on so speedy a "conclusion." Why then did he allow himself to become discouraged so quickly with his own analysis, which at the same time he considered so difficult? The reference in point 1.2 was probably to his banker patient, the termination of whose analysis he had mentioned to Fliess on May 16, adding that he himself had been responsible for its failure because he did not yet "know all the factors that are at work" (see p. 46 above). Why then the sudden despair at "the lack of the complete

* Freud uses the Hebrew word for bride—M.K.

success on which I had counted" (1.3), when he must have expected that outcome? In the past, such lack of success had never caused him to renounce his theories; on the contrary, obstacles had only spurred him on to look unfalteringly for new explanations, but always in the framework of the old (seduction) theory. And what did he mean by "other, ordinary, ways" of explaining therapeutic successes (1.4)? Did he want to disqualify his own psychoanalytical procedure?

The reasons for renouncing the seduction theory listed under point 2 seem to me to be much weightier. The assumption that the fathers of all hysterical patients must have been "perverse" (2.1) would indeed have been very hard to verify. However, Freud himself had already extended the theory to accommodate other primary caretakers in the child's life (mother, nurse, uncle, siblings, etc.) as seducers, so that even this objection was not altogether valid (see p. 45 above). As I said earlier, point 2.2 strikes me as being the real reason for Freud's rejection of the seduction theory. The passage I have italicized is not found in the 1950 edition of the Fliess letters[57]—it was added only in the 1975 edition. Hence it appears that the editors, including Anna, Freud's daughter, were trying to observe Jacob's taboo even after Freud's death! For had he retained the seduction theory, Freud would have had to assume that even his own father was a seducer and so "perverse." In other words, Freud had come up against the most crucial event in his self-analysis: he had reached the point where he had to hold his father responsible for his own neurotic symptoms, and further investigations would needs have led him to Jacob's own "prehistory." Jacob, however, had enjoined him in highly dramatic form "to close the eyes."

Neither before nor after the rejection of his seduction theory had Freud had a problem with explaining the frequency of hysteria by the pathogenic and repressive sexual morality of his day. Why then should that frequency have become a reason (2.3) for his recantation? Even the allegedly "definite realization" (3) that it is impossible to distinguish between truth and fiction in the unconscious was not really in conflict with his earlier view of repression; then he had always been able to uncover the experiences beneath the fantasies, the latter being so many "screen memories" covering the traumatic event. In conjunction with point 4, that conclusion amounted to the assertion that this type of neurosis was incurable. For if the therapist is incapable of bringing unconscious processes into consciousness, then the patient cannot, indeed, be helped, because he cannot distinguish fact from fiction, and because the unconscious cannot surface into consciousness by itself. But how did it come about that Freud arrived at so negative a view of all his previous work, when it was precisely with his old approach that he had been able to surmount the patient's resistances, and when, time and again, he himself had used that approach to render unconscious processes conscious?

Freud fully appreciated the consequences of the rejection of his seduction theory. Abandoning the attempt to uncover the effects of the seduction—or better, misleading—of children by their parents was tantamount to abandoning "the complete solution of a neurosis" (5.1). And since after his renunciation of the theory he could no longer consider childhood experiences as the actual cause of neurosis (5.2), the problem of the causal factors was thrown wide open again. Later experiences giving rise to "phantasies which throw back to childhood" might prove to be as traumatic as the early childhood experiences (5.4). Freud was to say so explicitly in his fantasy theory (see particularly 1899a and 1.3.1 below).

Furthermore, whereas he had previously considered seduction in early childhood the primary cause of neurotic symptoms, he was now forced once again to claim (5.5) that hereditary factors played an important part in the creation of these symptoms.[58]

Still, far from feeling disgraced (6.2) by his recantation, Freud felt a sense of triumph (6.3) and was proud of his "honest and effective intellectual labour" (6.1). However, he added that this feeling might not be justified (6.4), and that for that very reason he would not "tell it in Dan or publish it in Askalon, in the land of the Philistines." In my view, such conflicting feelings of regret and triumph are typical concomitants of all compromises. When one has tried to reconcil two conflicting goals by doing some pruning of both, one is glad to have found a solution, yet disappointed at having abandoned one's original objectives. Whereas his "pure" doctrine had held out the promise of eternal fame and wealth (6.5), the watered-down version seemed unlikely to earn him many laurels (6.6). According to Schur (1972, 191), the meaning of the Rebecca joke was obvious: "The wedding is off—take off your bridal gown" (see 3.1.11 below). Freud felt like a bride who had been cheated out of her wedding! There had been a "general collapse" of all values (6.7), and new priorities had to be set.

Freud could not have suspected that this compromise theory, of which he had so poor an opinion, would one day help to make his name and also bring him a fair measure of prosperity. Did he or Fliess realize that his arguments were spurious? He had renounced his objectives (5.1): solution of a neurosis; 5.2: reliance on its etiology in infancy; 5.3: theoretical understanding of repression); had surrendered his basic position (5.5: rejection of the factor of hereditary predisposition; and 5.4: assertion that later experiences could not give rise to psychic traumas); and believed that he had cut off every path to eternal fame (6.5, 6.6)—and all this without adducing a single sound argument against his former views. It all suggests that in some way he was still convinced of the value of the abandoned theory. Or did he himself know that his rejection of the seduction theory was irrational, that he was allowing himself to be led by his unconscious?

His views on dreams (7) admittedly still stood, and so did his "metapsychology," by which he probably meant the ideas contained in his "Project" of 1895 and also in the various drafts he had enclosed with his letters to Fliess. I might add that the sexual theory of actual neuroses was something he did not revise either (see 1.1.2.2 above). All that he had renounced, therefore, was his seduction theory. And he did this, as we saw, precisely at a time when his self-analysis could have forced him to accuse his own father of being a seducer, of being perverse.

1.3 After the Crisis
(Winter 1897–Autumn 1899)

1.3.1 FROM THE SEDUCTION THEORY
TO THE OEDIPUS THEORY

In the same week that he announced his renunciation of the seduction theory, Freud visited Fliess in Berlin, staying there from 26 to 29 September 1897. This is unfortunate, for had Freud continued to expound his views in letters, we might have had a clearer idea of the background to this whole development. On October 3 he again set down in writing the latest results of his self-analysis, which, he explained, was making progress through the interpretation of dreams. At that time, and in the next few weeks, he apparently had a spate of dreams about his early childhood in Freiberg. Unfortunately, his description of these was very sketchy:

I can only say that in my case my father played no active role, though I certainly projected on to him an analogy from myself; that my "primary originator" was an ugly, elderly but clever woman who told me a great deal about God and hell, and gave me a high opinion of my own capacities; that later (between the ages of two and two-and-a-half) libido towards matrem was aroused; the occasion must have been the journey with her from Leipzig to Vienna, during which we spent a night together, and I must have had the opportunity of seeing her nudam . . . [59] and that I welcomed my one-year-younger brother (who died within a few months) with ill wishes and real infantile jealousy, and that his death left the germ of guilt in me. I have long known that my companion in crime between the ages of one and two was a nephew of mine who is a year older than I am and now lives in Manchester; he visited us in Vienna when I was fourteen. We seem occasionally to have treated my niece, who was a year younger, shockingly. My nephew and younger brother determined, not only the neurotic side of all my friendships, but also their depth. My anxiety over travel you have seen yourself in full bloom.

I still have not got to the scenes which lie at the bottom of all this. If they emerge, and I succeed in resolving my hysteria, I shall have to thank the memory of the old woman who provided me at such an early age with the means for living and surviving. You see how the old liking breaks through again (1950a, 219f., 3 October 1897).

I shall be returning to these dreams and examining their reality content (see Part 3 below). Here all I want to show, by means of Freud's memories of his nursemaid, is what effects the renunciation of the seduction theory had on the interpretation of these dreams. When he wrote his letter, Freud did not yet know whether this nursemaid, whom he called his "primary originator," had really existed, any more than he had known it in May after the staircase dream. In a postscript added a day later, Freud reported another dream about the nursemaid, which he had had during the night of October 3:

She was my instructress in sexual matters, and chided me for being clumsy and not being able to do anything (that is always the way with neurotic impotence: anxiety over incapacity at school gets its sexual reinforcement in this way). I saw the skull of a small animal which I thought of as a "pig" in the dream, though it was associated in the dream with your wish of two years ago that I might find a skull on the Lido to enlighten me, as Goethe once did. But I did not find it. Thus it was "a little *Schafskopf*" [literally, "sheep's head"; figuratively, "blockhead" A.P.]. The whole dream was full of the most wounding references to my present uselessness as a therapist. Perhaps the origin of my tendency to believe in the incurability of hysteria should be sought here. Also she washed me in reddish water in which she had previously washed herself . . . and she encouraged me to steal "Zehners" (ten-Kreuzer pieces) to give to her. A long chain of association connects these first silver Zehners to the heap of paper ten-florin notes which I saw in the dream as Martha's housekeeping money. The dream can be summed up as "bad treatment." Just as the old woman got money from me for her bad treatment of me, so do I now get money for the bad treatment of my patients (*ibid.*, 220f., 4 October 1897).

Freud had no inkling, even after this revealing dream, who his "instructress in sexual matters" might have been, for at the end of the letter he added: "A severe critic might say that all this was phantasy projected into the past instead of being determined by the past. The experimenta crucis would decide the matter against him. The reddish water seems a point of this kind. Where do all patients derive the horrible perverse details which are often as alien to their experience as to their knowledge?" *(ibid.).*

It was in fact no fantasy projected into the past but a genuine memory of an incident in childhood, which influenced his adult life. Just a few days later he received confirmation of this fact from his mother:

I asked my mother whether she remembered my nurse. "Of course," she said, "an elderly woman, very shrewd indeed. She was always taking you to church. When you came home you used to preach and tell us all about how God conducted His affairs. At the time I was in bed when Anna was being born," (Anna is two-and-a-half years younger) "she turned out to be a thief, and all the shiny Kreuzers and Zehners and toys that had been given you were found among her things. Your brother Philipp went himself to fetch the policeman, and she got ten months." Now see how that confirms the conclusions from my dream interpretation (*ibid.*, 221f., 15 October 1897).

His mother had in fact given him confirmation of the seduction theory he had just discarded, for when she let it be known that his dream had been based on real events, she also made it seem likely that the other dream contents were no mere fantasies—but she did not confirm them, either because Freud had not asked her about them (reddish water, instructress in sexual matters) or else because she herself knew nothing about them. In his letter to Fliess, Freud did not enter into these details himself; he only mentioned an error he thought he might have made: "I have easily been able to explain the one possible mistake. I wrote to you that she got me to steal Zehners and give them to her. The dream really means that she stole herself. For the dream-picture was a memory that I took money from a doctor's mother, *i.e.* wrongfully. The real meaning is that the old woman stood for me, and that the doctor's mother was my mother. I was so far from being aware that the old woman was a thief that my interpretation went astray" (*ibid.,* 222, 15 October 1897).

In this commentary, Freud did not specify what for him personally was the much more important matter of sexual "seduction" by the nursemaid. The error which he tried to correct—whether he himself stole the money or she —strikes me as trivial by comparison.[60] Freud dreamed of a sexual seduction in childhood; instead of interpreting it as such, he preferred to dwell on details of secondary importance.

He might, incidentally, have considered the confirmation of his dream memory a refutation of one of the arguments he had adduced in his renunciation letter, namely, that it is impossible to distinguish between truth and fiction in the unconscious (point 3; see p. 51 above). The absent "indication of reality" had been supplied by his mother.

Freud continued with a report of a scene that had obviously impressed him even more, because he remembered it not only in the dream but also in the waking state. That memory apparently provided him with proof that the dream was a genuine, repressed memory of a childhood scene and not of a story about his nursemaid heard at a later stage of his life:

If the woman disappeared so suddenly, I said to myself, some impression of the event must have been left inside me. Where was it now? Then a scene occurred to me which for the last twenty-nine years [since the age of twelve, M.K.] has been turning up from time to time in my conscious memory without my understanding it. I was crying my heart out, because my mother was nowhere to be found. My brother Philipp (who is twenty years older than I) opened a cupboard [Kasten] for me, and when I found that mother was not there either, I cried still more, until she came through the door, looking slim and beautiful. What can that mean? Why should my brother open the cupboard for me when he knew that my mother was not inside and that opening it therefore could not quieten me? Now I suddenly understand. I must have begged him to open the cupboard. When I could not find my mother, I feared she must have vanished, like my nurse not long before. I must have heard that the old woman had been locked, or rather "boxed up" [eingekastelt], because my brother Philipp, who is now sixty-three, was fond of such humorous expressions, and still is to the present day. The fact that I turned to him shows that I was well aware of his part in my nurse's disappearance (*ibid.,* 222f., 15 October 1897).[61]

In a later section, I shall be examining at some length to what extent we are justified in interpreting this incident as yet another seduction scene, one in which the leading actors were admittedly not little Sigmund, but his mother Amalie and his half-brother Philipp (see 3.1.6 below). All I wish to stress here is that we can agree with Freud when he asserts that this memory too was a "genuine" memory of an actual event and not of a story he had picked up later.

In the same letter Freud also presented his famous compromise, or Oedipus, theory for the first time. Characteristically, he prefaced its formulation with a confession:

> I have found love of the mother and jealousy of the father in my own case too, and now believe it to be *a general phenomenon of early childhood,* even if it does not always occur so early as in children who have been made hysterics. . . . If that is the case, the gripping power of Oedipus Rex, in spite of all the rational objections to the inexorable fate that the story presupposes, becomes intelligible, and one can understand why later fate dramas were such failures . . . but the Greek myth seizes on a compulsion which everyone recognizes because he has felt traces of it in himself. *Every* member of the audience *was once a budding Oedipus in phantasy,* and this dream-fulfilment played out in reality causes everyone to recoil in horror, with the full measure of repression which separates his infantile from his present state (*ibid.,* 223f., 15 October 1897, italics added).

Clearly, the Oedipus theory was a complete reversal of the seduction theory. For Freud, *everyone* had once been in love with his mother and wanted to murder his father. Father and mother had been transformed into passive objects of such wishes; they were no longer active seducers. That is why he could openly confess his own Oedipus complex. Had he continued to adhere to his seduction theory, he would have had to ask what his parents had done to awaken "perverse" desires in him.

It seems that Freud did not remember the original Greek legend clearly when he made it the basis of his new theory, for a few months later, on 15 March 1898, when he was already engaged in writing *The Interpretation of Dreams,* he told Fliess that he would have to read more about the Oedipus legend but did not yet know what (*ibid.,* 248). We may however take it that he was familiar with the entire legend by the time he had finished *The Interpretation of Dreams.* Nevertheless, he stripped the legend of its "prehistory," as G. Devereux (1953) has shown.

In Gustav Schwab's *Sagen des klassischen Altertums (Myths of Classical Antiquity),* which was published in 1838–40, and with which Freud was probably familiar as a child, that prehistory is set out as follows. Laius, King of Thebes, lived with his wife, Jocasta, in childless marriage. The Oracle at Delphi informed him that a son would be born to him and that he would perish by that son's hand because Zeus had heard the curse of Pelops. "For Laius had been driven from his kingdom in youth and had been received at Pelops' court, but had repaid his benefactor's kindness with ingratitude, abducting Chrysippus, Pelops' beautiful son, at the Nemaean games. Knowing that he had done wrong, Laius believed the Oracle and for a long time lived apart from his wife" (Schwab, 1975 I, 231f.; translated from the German). When Jocasta nevertheless brought forth a son, Laius had the newborn boy thrown into the wild mountains of Cithaeron after three days, with pierced and bound feet. However, the shepherd who had been ordered to abandon the boy took pity on him and handed him to another shepherd, who took him to his master, King Polybus of Corinth. Because of his pierced feet, the child was called Oedipus, meaning "swollen foot." And now that part of the legend which Sophocles so artfully retells in his play begins. Oedipus grows up, hears rumors that Polybus is not his real father, consults the Delphic Oracle, and is informed that it is his destiny to murder his father and to marry his mother. In order to escape this fate he leaves Corinth, and then chances upon his real father, Laius. Schwab has described that encounter as follows:

Oedipus saw a chariot coming toward him . . . in which an old man was seated beside an arms bearer, a charioteer, and two servants. The charioteer and the old man haughtily ordered the young man to make way for them, whereupon Oedipus, hot-tempered by nature, struck the proud charioteer. The old man now aimed his double goad at the bold young man's head and delivered a sharp blow. Oedipus was beside himself, and for the first time in his life made use of the superhuman strength the gods had bestowed on him: he lifted up his walking stick and pushed the old man from his seat in the chariot. There was a contest: Oedipus had to ward off three assailants, but his youthful vigor won the day. He killed them all save for one who ran off, and then continued on his way (Schwab, 1971, I, 233f.; translated from the German).

Oedipus eventually reached Thebes, which was threatened with destruction by the Sphinx, a terrible monster. The monster set Oedipus a riddle: What animal walks upon four feet in the morning, upon two at noon, and upon three in the evening? The answer, correctly given by Oedipus, was man, who in the morning of life walks upon his hands and feet, during the years of manhood walks upon his two legs, and in the evening of life supports his old age with the assistance of a staff. Oedipus thus defeated the monster and relieved the city. As a reward he was given Jocasta, the king's widow and his own mother, as wife. She bore him four children, but later, when their true relationship was discovered, Jocasta took her life and Oedipus put out his eyes. Led by one of his daughters, Antigone, who remained loyal to him, he left Thebes.[62]

Devereux (1953) quotes other authorities according to whom Laius was the "inventor" of pederasty. Others again claimed that Oedipus was sacrificed to assuage Hera's anger at Laius' abduction of Chrysippus, Laius being blamed not so much for his seduction of the boy as for abducting him by force and so abusing Pelops' hospitality. Laius' character is not painted in favorable colors by any of them; he is depicted as brutal, violent, and hot-tempered, which is shown clearly in Schwab's account of his encounter with Oedipus, and also from the fact that he pierced the feet of his newly born son.[63]

According to the legend, Laius was thus a "perverse" person, an active homosexual with sadistic traits, the type of father who, in Freud's seduction theory, had to be considered the cause of his own children's neuroses. Oedipus, by contrast, was an innocent victim, who had to atone for the sins of his father.

The unabridged Oedipus legend might have served as a symbolic account of the seduction theory. The fact that Freud stripped it of the Laius prelude and then used it as a symbolic representation of his new fantasy theory is yet another pointer to his relationship with his own father: his father's past must remain a closed book at all costs.

In the same letter of October 15, Freud also wrote that the "idea has passed through my head" that Shakespeare might have written *Hamlet* because his own unconscious understood that of his hero:

How can one explain the hysteric Hamlet's phrase "So conscience doth make cowards of us all," and his hesitation to avenge his father by killing his uncle, when he himself so casually sends his courtiers to their death and despatches Laertes so quickly? How better than by the torment roused in him by the obscure memory *that he himself had meditated the same deed against his father because of passion for his mother*—"use every man after his desert, and who should 'scape whipping?" His conscience is his unconscious feeling of guilt. And are not his sexual coldness when talking to Ophelia, his rejection of the instinct to beget children, and finally his transference of the deed from his father to Ophelia, typically hysterical? And does he not finally succeed, in just the same remarkable way as my hysterics do, in bringing down his punishment on himself and suffering the same fate as his father, being poisoned by the same rival? (1950a, 224, 15 October 1897, italics added).

According to Freud, it was because Hamlet desired his mother in secret that he felt unable to heed his father's orders and eliminate the hated rival. I shall show later (see 3.1.6 below) that this situation—a son dwelling with impotent rage on the ruthlessness of his mother and his uncle—had parallels in Freud's own family. In my view, this is the very subject Freud had broached earlier in the letter in which he described his childhood memories of the cupboard. Here I wish merely to point out that Freud too had been given orders by his late father in a dream which, though the subject was not revenge, as in Hamlet's case, nevertheless caused the son comparable qualms of conscience. Another reason for Freud, in my view, to feel so drawn to the Hamlet theme.

Apart from the renunciation letter of 21 September 1897, this letter (of October 15) is probably the most important document in the entire Fliess correspondence. It enables us to resurrect the links between Freud's own childhood experiences and his theoretical ideas, links he himself was unable to recover once he had discarded the seduction theory. This explains his failure to appreciate that he had stripped the Oedipus legend of its prelude or that his own history resembled that of Hamlet.

In October, Freud was almost totally absorbed in his self-analysis. In the middle of November, he reported an interruption (*ibid.*, 234, 14 November 1897), but then seems to have returned to his preoccupation. Among other things, it became clear to him that his longing for Rome was "deeply neurotic," and this neurosis explained why during his last summer leave he had, like Hannibal, gone only as far as Lake Trasimene (*ibid.*, 236, 3 December 1897). He realized, too, that his anxiety about travel was connected with a childhood memory of a traumatic train journey from Freiberg to Leipzig (see 3.2. below). He again sent Fliess accounts of his dreams, which unfortunately have not come down to us (*ibid.*, 238, 12 December 1897).

1.3.2 THE INTERPRETATION OF DREAMS

At the end of 1897, Freud seems to have decided to implement his old idea of writing a book about dreams (1950a, 200, 16 May 1897; cf. p. 46 above, and Jones, 1953, I, 356). At Christmas, he met Fliess in Breslau and, as always, this new "congress" gave him fresh ideas. He now threw himself into his new project, and a few weeks later he was able to inform Fliess that he was "deep in the dream book" (1950a, 244, 9 February 1898), by which he undoubtedly meant that he had been working on it for some time. Directly after the "congress" he sent Fliess, in several consignments, the latest instalments of his "Drekkologie," so called because—as he had explained in an earlier letter— "I can hardly tell you how many things I (the new Midas) turn into—filth [*Dreck*]" (*ibid.,* 240, 22 December 1897, German added). Now he wrote: "I am sending you today No. 2 of the *Drekkologikal* reports, a very interesting periodical, published by me for a single reader. No. 1, which I have retained, contains wild dreams which would hardly be of interest to you; they are part of my self-analysis, which is still very much in the dark" (Schur, 1972, 140, 4 January 1898).

Time and again, Freud's dream associations led him to details too intimate to mention even to Fliess. On several occasions he quoted a line from Goethe's Faust: *"Das Beste, was Du wissen kannst, darfst Du den Buben doch nicht sagen"* (After all, the best of what you know may not be told to the boys) (1950a, 236, 245; cf. 1900a, 142, 453). Invariably, the forbidden subject was his own sexuality; for instance, in the dream whose "deeper meaning shuttles to and fro between my nurse (my mother) and my wife. . . ." (*ibid.,* 245, 9 February 1898, omission by the editors of the letters).

On 15 March 1898 he sent Fliess the first few manuscript pages of *The Interpretation of Dreams,* of which he obviously took a positive view (*ibid.,* 249, 15 and 24 March 1898). In this way, as each section was completed, the whole work was sent off in batches by Freud to his friend for comment. As Jones points out, Freud obviously needed a censor, a superego, to check up on him (1953, I, 298f.). However, Fliess does not seem to have been particularly interested in Freud's self-analysis—he did not become Freud's therapist, nor help him to a more rounded interpretation of his dreams and of the underlying childhood experiences. In other words, Fliess did not give Freud the kind of help that Freud tried to give his own patients. Fliess probably considered it his sole task to assist Freud in reading the proofs and toning down certain passages that struck him as being too candid. Thus he advised Freud not to include the "big" dream Freud had sent him toward the end of May. Freud replied:

I also thank you cordially for your criticism. I am aware of the fact that you have undertaken a very thankless task. I am reasonable enough to recognize that I need your critical help, because in this instance I myself have lost the feeling of shame required of an author. So this dream is condemned. However, now that the sentence has been passed I would like to shed a tear for it, and confess that I regret it and that I cannot hope to find a better one as a substitute. You must know that a beautiful dream and no indiscretion do not go together. At least write me to which topic you took exception, and where you feared an attack by a malicious critic. Was it *my anxiety,* or *Martha* or the *Dalles* [a Jewish word for poverty. Schur], or my *being without a fatherland?* [Please let me know] so I can omit the topic you designate in a substitute dream, because I can have dreams like that to order. . . . (Schur, 1966, 74f., 9 June 1898, italics added).

This "big" dream, which Freud later described as the only one he had "thoroughly analysed" (1950a, 269, 23 October 1898), was accordingly left out from *The Interpretation of Dreams.* Freud obviously regretted its exclusion, for as he explained to his friend: "My mourning for the lost dream is not yet over. As if in spite I recently had a substitute dream, in which a house constructed of building blocks collapsed (we had built a *staatliches* house) [the word *"staatliches"* is a pun combining the two words: *"stattlich"*—stately, imposing, grand; and *"staatlich"*—pertaining to the state, to public affairs, to politics. Schur]" (Schur, 1966, 75, 10 June 1898). Both these passages were cut out by the editors of the Fliess letters. However, some later references to the "big" dream did not fall victim to their censorship (1950a, 269, 23 October 1898; 262, 26 August 1891; 281, 28 May 1899; 288, 1 August 1899; and 292, 20 August 1899). Freud probably intended to build his entire *Interpretation of Dreams* on this dream; instead, he replaced it with a "small collection of dreams." It is most regrettable that Fliess should have advised him against the first course, for the section of the letter published by Schur makes it clear that the "big" dream contained highly revealing autobiographical material (Schur, 1966, 74ff.), and that the dream censored by Fliess was not the "Irma" dream, but one that was omitted in its entirety from *The Interpretation of Dreams.*

It is possible that "Screen Memories" contains at least a part of the big dream. That essay was published by Freud in May 1899, one year after his first mention of the big dream (1950a, 281, 28 May 1899). One can call its subject a "thoroughly analysed" example, for the associations to it range from the present through puberty back to early childhood. It involves the subject of poverty and indirectly of Freud's wife Martha, since it introduces the idea of marriage to another woman. Anxiety is mentioned in connection with a castration threat consequent upon masturbation. Only the "lack of a fatherland"— Freud was probably referring to his Jewishness—is not mentioned explicitly in "Screen Memories." Thus if "Screen Memories" is indeed based on the big dream, then Freud must have reproduced it there in somewhat shortened form. I shall be returning to this subject at greater length (see 3.1.8 below).

From a remark in *The Interpretation of Dreams* (1900a, 173) in which Freud, commenting on the dream of the "botanical monograph," refers to his "Screen Memories," Grinstein (1968) has concluded that this dream must have been similar to the one described in that paper. The dream of the botanical monograph covers the "Martha" theme in still greater detail; "poverty," too, is a central subject, and "anxiety" and "lack of a fatherland" are implied. According to Kris (1950a, 246, note 1; see 1900a, 172f.), the dream of the

botanical monograph occurred on or about 10 March 1899. This might be
considered further evidence that it was part of the big dream, for Freud must
have dreamed the latter at about the same time—we know that Fliess rejected
it at the beginning of June. Possibly the big dream has thus come down to us
after all, at least in part.

Freud's game of hide-and-seek in "Screen Memories" also suggests that he
was trying to unburden himself of his big dream. As Bernfeld (1946) has
shown, Freud clearly concealed his own identity behind the case he describes
in that essay: a thirty-eight-year-old man of university education [Freud himself was forty-three in 1899), who, "though his own profession lay in a different
field, has taken an interest in psychological questions ever since I was able to
relieve him of a slight phobia by means of psychoanalysis" (1899a, 309).
Incidentally, Freud omitted that essay from his *Collection of Shorter Writings
on the Theory of the Neuroses* published in 1906, though it dealt with a basic
concept of psychoanalysis for the first time (Bernfeld, 1946, 17; cf. Grubrich-
Simitis, 1971, 26; Jones, 1953, I, 32f.).

"Screen Memories" clearly reflects Freud's concern to defend the replacement of the seduction theory by his new compromise, the Oedipus theory.
According to the seduction theory, the childhood memory reported in the
essay (1899a, 310f.) would have had to be a "screen" for an actual seduction
scene that had been repressed by the dreamer. The screen memory takes its
place, evoking the same emotions. In his theoretical preamble, Freud explained
that screen memories are "incomplete" memories of childhood experiences in
which "what is important is suppressed and what is indifferent retained" (*ibid.,*
306; cf. 1895d, 122f.). Of his own childhood memory set out in the essay, he
claimed, by contrast, that it was not a screen for the important childhood
experience but for forbidden desires in the *present-day* life of the (adult)
dreamer. The dream, he asserted, simply seizes upon a childhood theme which
—no matter whether it was remembered rightly or wrongly—makes a suitable
screen for a current, impermissible dream. In plain contradiction to his theoretical deliberations in the preamble, he went on to state: "A recollection of
this kind, whose value lies in the fact that it represents in the memory *impres-
sions and thoughts of a later date* whose content is connected with its own by
symbolic or similar links, may appropriately be called a 'screen memory' "
(*ibid.,* 315f., italics added).[64]

Freud no longer asked what really happened on the dandelion-carpeted
meadow in Freiberg on which the childhood scene had taken place (see pp.
123ff. below), because he no longer considered it a "screen," a minor part of
the important scene to which the dream really pointed. He, so to speak,
allowed the screen memory to descend as a screen over the actual scene, and
indeed over several other scenes as well. In the essay, he hid his own identity
behind that of a patient, and he tried to "hide" the essay itself by not including
it in his *Shorter Writings.* As a result he provided us, not only in his writings
but also in his behavior, with an unexcelled example of the genesis of screen
memories.[65]

In July 1898, soon after Fliess's rejection of the "big" dream, Freud sent him a parcel about which not even the editors of the Fliess letters could say for certain whether it was another chapter of *The Interpretation of Dreams*. In his covering letter, Freud wrote:

Here it is. I found it very difficult to make up my mind to let it out of my hands. Personal intimacy would have been an insufficient justification for letting you have it, but our intellectual honesty to each other required it. *It was all written by the unconscious,* on the well-known principle of Itzig, the Sunday horseman. "Itzig, where are you going?" "Don't ask me, ask the horse!" At the beginning of a paragraph I never knew where I should end up. It was not written to be read, of course—any attempt at style was abandoned after the first two pages. In spite of all that I of course believe in the results. I have not the slightest idea yet of what form the contents will finally take (1950a, 257f., 7 July 1898, italics added).

Like the censored dream, these papers too must have dealt with deeply personal matters, possibly of a sexual nature. I have quoted the above passage to show Freud's probable attitude while writing long passages of *The Interpretation of Dreams*—he felt like a rider on a runaway horse.[66] The choice of the epigraph *Flectere is nequeo superos, Acheronta movebo* (If I cannot bend the Higher Powers, I will move the Infernal Regions) (1900a, 608) was significant as well. It was borrowed from Virgil's *Aeneid* (VII, 312) and the lines are spoken by Juno when Jupiter refuses to grant one of her wishes (Ellenberger, 1970, 452). True, Freud himself was thinking more of the powers of the dream derived from "repressed instinctual impulses," but the motto might equally well have served to characterize his own attitude to *The Interpretation of Dreams*. For a long time, he had vainly tried to bend the "higher powers," that is, his father; now he had succeeded in doing so with the help of the unconscious. Only after the conclusion of *The Interpretation of Dreams* did Freud become aware of the fact that his book, too, was an examination of his relationship with his father, precipitated by the latter's death (1900a, xxvi).

Once the book had been sent to the printers and set, except for a few pages, he wrote to Fliess: "You describe very aptly the painful feeling of parting with something that has been your very own. It must have been that which made this work so distasteful to me. Now I like it, certainly not much, but a lot better. In my case it must have been even more painful because what separated itself was not ideational possessions but my very own feelings" (Schur, 1972, 198, 4 October 1899).

To Freud, the dreams and dream associations recorded in his book were not just illustrations of his dream theory, but were rooted in his own childhood and hence had a dynamic emotional significance for him. But since he could only remember the underlying events as images that he could not fully comprehend, he felt that his dreams were governed by uncontrollable forces which, time and again, confronted him with fresh enigmas.

The other events and ideas that kept Freud busy until he finished *The Interpretation of Dreams* in September 1899[67] need not detain us here. In what follows, I shall merely try to show what effects the change from the seduction theory to the Oedipus theory had on his self-analysis, on the actual wording of *The Interpretation of Dreams,* and hence on the early history of psychoanalysis.

1.4 Conclusions: The Significance of the Rejection of the Seduction Theory

Why was it impossible for Freud to continue his self-analysis without discarding his seduction theory? Why was he as good as paralyzed when he began to realize that he too had been "seduced" in childhood? And why was it that his new fantasy theory—the Oedipus theory—allowed him to examine those very childhood memories he had shied away from and which now seemed to pour over him like a tidal wave?

According to the seduction theory, the parents or other primary caretakers in the child's life were to be considered active "seducers." Freud himself would accordingly have been forced to compromise his own parents, and above all his father, as soon as his self-analysis revealed that his own neurotic symptoms also served to ward off traumatic childhood memories.

According to the Oedipus theory, by contrast, the parents are not active seducers, but mere objects onto which the (male) child projects his own libidinous desires, the libido being a universal force directed at a single goal (destruction of the father in order to possess the mother). The replacement of the seduction with the Oedipus theory thus enabled Freud to examine his own childhood without having to blame his parents for his neurosis. According to the new theory, that neurosis was caused by his own forbidden desires. Nor did he have to blame himself for these desires, for they were universal.

The Oedipus theory exonerated Freud in more than one respect. It was a "creative solution" (Stierlin, 1970b, Chap. 3), by which he was able to reconcile the conflicting missions his father had given him: on the one hand to "close his eyes" to his father's transgression, and on the other hand nevertheless to solve the great enigma of (his) life. The Oedipus theory enabled him to do just that.

I believe that the flood of dreams and childhood memories Freud mentioned in his letters of 3 and 15 October 1897, shortly after renouncing his seduction theory, was a direct result of that renunciation. Before it, he could not dream about his childhood because every dream impinged on a taboo he dared not break. This explains his paralysis in June–July. But once he no longer had fears of "catching" his father in the act of seduction, he was able to dream freely about his childhood. I am convinced that in all his associations to his own dreams—even in those which he did not impart to us—Freud never reached his real childhood experiences. I believe that in none of these dreams did he reconstruct more than those fragments of the real scenes which the dream threw up in the form of screen memories. For I am convinced that otherwise he would not have been able to dream at all, that he could only remember dreams because the Oedipus theory provided him with an inner censor that blocked the forbidden discovery of the real incidents.

The rejection had other important consequences as well. As Freud himself stressed in his letter of 21 September 1897, the idea of a "hereditary disposition" had gained new weight as a causal factor of neurosis. Whereas he had previously believed that heredity played a much smaller part in the defensive neurosis than seduction, the Oedipus theory starts with the premise that the child projects desires onto his parents, and that these desires are not aroused by the parents' actions, but have sources within the child. *Why* these desires produce neuroses in some instances but not in others was left unexplained at first. For, unlike the seduction theory, which asserts that active seduction is the cause, the Oedipus theory could not account for this difference.

Freud accordingly extended the instinct concept, which he had never abandoned in his sexual theory of the actual neuroses, to embrace the defensive neuroses as well. True, even while he had still upheld the seduction theory, he had never given up his attempts to apply the idea of "sexual chemistry" to the defensive neuroses; but these attempts gained fresh impetus after he had renounced the seduction theory. The elaboration of the libido concept (1905d) and the theory of instincts with its phylogenetic extension show clearly that heredity had become of increasing importance to Freud's view of the etiology of all the neuroses.

This consequence too is the logical outcome of Freud's motives for rejecting the seduction theory. The idea that human behavior is inherited obviates any need for looking to the experiential context for the explanation of individual behavior (Krüll, 1977a, Chap. 3). As soon as we postulate that a certain form of behavior is inherited, or in any way based constitutionally on organic processes, we abandon the search for biographical, experiential explanations. And in my view that is what happened with Freud. Had he adhered to the seduction theory, he would have been forced to look for the experiential background of what he called the "libido." I am convinced that Freud used the instinct concept precisely where, after his rejection of the seduction theory, he dared not probe any further.

In contrast to most authors who have written about Freud's renunciation of the seduction theory, I do not believe that his Oedipus theory helped him to advance from neurological conceptions, from a medical theory based on natural science, to psychoanalysis (Lorenzer, 1973a, 40f.), or from energetics to hermeneutics (Ricoeur, 1974, especially 118ff.). In my view, Freud had developed a true psychoanalytical theory with his seduction theory—all he needed to do was to rid it of its extreme fixation on *sexual* seduction. Freud could easily have expanded his seduction theory into a "misguidance" theory: the child is misguided by his or her parents or primary caretakers and hence develops neurotic aberrations. That theory would, at one and the same time, have been a theory of "guidance" toward socially acceptable behavior. I believe that he missed this opportunity, and that with his Oedipus theory, which is based on instincts, far from making an advance, he took a step backward toward a mechanistic, biologistic model of human behavior.

I agree with Stierlin that as a result he had to forego many insights that an extended seduction theory would have provided, particularly the appreciation of the importance of the "family and the formative human influences expressed in it" (Stierlin, 1975c, 137; cf. Schatzman, 1973). The premises of his Oedipus theory forced him to ignore many important connections that seduction theory would have shown up. I have tried to demonstrate the results by the example of the screen memories and by his abridgment of the Oedipus legend. Other examples will be given below (see Part 4).

It must, however, be said that Freud never discarded his seduction theory altogether. In *The Interpretation of Dreams* and other early works written before 1910, he quite frequently based his arguments on it; and in his later writings we find quite a few references to the theory, for instance, in the remarks in the *Autobiographical Study* that "seduction during childhood retained a certain share, though a humbler one, in the aetiology of neuroses" (1925d, 34f.).[68]

But the seduction theory was never again allowed to be applied to Freud's own person. It can be shown that many of his often violent reactions to criticisms by his followers (Adler, Stekel, Jung, Tausk) occurred whenever he was asked, directly or indirectly, to be frank about himself, to interpret his own neurotic symptoms (see 4.1.2 below). Freud could not allow this to happen, for to do so he would have had to break Jacob's taboo.

2. Prehistory: Kallamon Jacob Freud[1]

Freud's crisis of 1897, as I have tried to show, was rooted in his childhood. For that reason, a biographer ought really to reconstruct his early life first, before going further back to his family background—that is, to the biography of Freud's parents. That sort of regressive analysis would have been "psycho-logically" correct. Unfortunately, such a presentation proved so intricate that I found myself forced instead to proceed in chronological order, beginning with the life of Jacob Freud and continuing with the childhood of his son, Sigmund (in Part 3).

Equally, it would have been desirable, in addition to Jacob's life, to reconstruct that of Freud's mother, but almost nothing is known about her childhood and youth before marriage. And although Amalie Freud survived her husband by thirty-four years, dying at the age of ninety-five just nine years before her son Sigmund, what information we do have about her later life is very sparse indeed. Almost nothing is known of her parents—of her mother, for instance, we know only her name. To what extent Amalie's strong emotional ties with her son Sigmund reflected her own childhood ties must therefore remain a secret. Possibly the hitherto unpublished family letters will throw fresh light on the matter.

More biographical details are known about Jacob Freud—particularly after the recent searches by J. Sajner and R. Gicklhorn in Czechoslovak archives —but that material too is scanty enough in all truth. Basically, therefore, all I can hope to do here is to describe the general environment in which Jacob Freud grew up, and to speculate on how the important political and spiritual movements of his day affected him.

Jacob lived at a time of great change which had particularly marked repercussions on East European Jewry. He was among the first Galician Jews to abandon the traditional ways and to build himself a new life, both intellectually and materially. As an aid to following this process, it seems helpful to give a brief outline of the history of Galician Jews at the period under review.

2.1 Political and Intellectual Currents in the History of Galician Jewry[2]

In 1772, just over forty years before the birth of Jacob Freud, Galicia became part of Austria. Until then it had been part of Poland, a country that had played a dominant role in East European politics since the fourteenth century.

In comparison with other feudal states, Poland was a liberal country and hence acted as a magnet on persecuted Western Jewry. Especially during the fifteenth and sixteenth centuries, Jews flocked to Poland, where they worked chiefly as artisans and merchants, and in addition performed a multitude of services for the nobility, such as tax collection, estate management, and inn-keeping. The Polish kings granted them a large measure of self-government, the Jewish community, or *kahal,* constituting an autonomous unit in all Polish towns inhabited by Jews. The Jewish newcomers were *Ashkenazim* (Hebrew for Germans) and carried their language—Middle-High German studded with Hebrew—with them to Poland. This language, called "Yiddish," also collected Slavonic elements in the course of time.

The golden age of Polish Jewry was under the Jagiellon dynasty, which came to an end with the reign of Sigismund II (1548–72).[3] Thereafter, the balancing and uniting power of the king was broken and no recognized authority was left to curb the centrifugal tendencies of the gentry *(szlachta).* For the Jews, this meant that they were left at the unpredictable mercy of the various princes.

Another consequence of the downfall of the Polish kingdom was a rebellious movement of the Russian Orthodox population, especially in southern Poland, against their Polish and Catholic oppressors. The Jews, many of whom were employed by the Polish (Catholic) princes, became the first victims of that rebellion. When Bogdan Chmielnicki struck in 1648 at the head of an army of Cossacks (armed peasants from the southeast) and unleashed a campaign of murder and pillage that took him from the Ukraine and Galicia to Warsaw, he massacred between 100,000 and 500,000 Jews (Dubnow, 1928, VII, 40).

As a result of these and other bloody acts, many Jews became deeply dispirited and demoralized. They asked themselves why God should punish His chosen people so cruelly, and wondered what sense there was in keeping the Law of Moses when the God of Moses had so patently abandoned them. This crisis of faith became fertile soil for a host of mystical or messianic movements whose effects lasted well into the nineteenth century and which could therefore have had some influence on the life of Jacob Freud.

Judaism has included a mystical strain since very ancient times, that of the Kabbalah (literally: "Tradition"). The Kabbalah holds that the Torah (the

Pentateuch) is the living incarnation of divine wisdom. For that reason the faithful have a duty to try to grasp the real meaning of the Word of God behind the letters, the better to reach an understanding of the divine essence (Scholem, 1969, 32ff.). Because each letter of the Hebrew alphabet also represents a number, Kabbalists believe that they can divine God's secret with the help of numerical combinations. Thus it was not rare for prophecies to be based on the fact that the letters of a divine promise added up to a number that could then be used to compute the date on which that promise would be fulfilled.[4]

During the bloody persecutions of the Jews in seventeenth-century Poland, this mystical tradition developed into a full-blown messianic movement known as Sabbateanism. Shabbetai Zevi, a Jew from Smyrna in Turkey, proclaimed himself the Messiah, promising the Jews that he would end their exile and lead them back to Jerusalem. Many Jews who had escaped the great massacres believed this promise, the more so as it seemed to make sense of the terrible carnage meted out to them by Chmielnicki—according to the mystical tradition, the arrival of the Messiah was preceded by a reign of horror. Shabbetai Zevi, however, was soon afterward unmasked as a false Messiah; imprisoned by the Turkish sultan, he adopted the Mohammedan faith in 1666 to save his life.

Just over a hundred years later, in 1775, another messianic sect caused a stir among Polish Jews. The new Messiah, Jacob Frank, led a movement that combined a modified form of Sabbateanism with a sexual mystery cult. Sanctity, Frank claimed, could be attained through ecstatic orgies. Having been

FIGURE 3 Detail from a map of the Austrian Empire by F. Fried, Vienna, 1855 *(Austrian State Archives, War Archives, Vienna; photograph, Hubmann)*

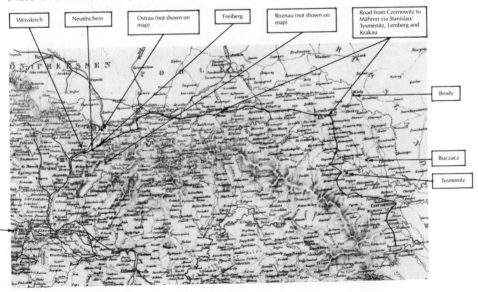

rejected by most Jews, Frank, like Shabbetai Zevi, became converted, not to Islam but to the Catholic Church.

However, Sabbateanism as well as Frankism continued to have Jewish adherents until well into the nineteenth century. To what extent Jacob Freud had contact with either movement is impossible to say; I find it hard to agree with Bakan that there are direct links between Sigmund Freud's interest in sexuality and Frankism, or between his preoccupation with the hidden side of human experience and Sabbateanism (Bakan, 1958, 109, 102). If such links ever existed they must, in any case, have been handed down to the founder of psychoanalysis by his father, since Freud himself had no direct contact with Galician currents.

More certain, by contrast, because it was mentioned by Sigmund Freud himself (1960a, 394), is the fact that his father came from a Hasidic background.[5] Hasidism—the word *hasid* means "devout" (Buber, 1947, 2)—was the third great mystical movement among East European Jews, and as such had many things in common with its two precursors, although it also differed from them in important respects. The main difference was that Hasidism made no messianic promises for the immediate future, and as a result was far less extreme in its expectations than either Sabbateanism or Frankism. Above all, none of the leading Hasids defected to other religions.

The founder of Hasidism was Israel ben Elizer, also known as the Baal Shem Tov, "Master of the Good Name" (Buber, 1947, 11), or Besht for short. He was born in about 1700, and first appeared as a healer through prayers, invocations, and amulets, but also promised to heal the sick with herbs and to cure spiritual ills. His unassuming piety put many people under his spell. Above all, the simple folk, faced with the betrayal of their messianic hopes and dulled by increasingly remote and dry rabbinical discussions, felt a strong need for a faith they could understand and embrace with heartfelt emotion. The Baal Shem Tov filled that need, and his doctrine soon became one of the most important spiritual currents in Judaism. His message to the people was that God loves men who love and revere Him, more than He loves even the most learned rabbis; that one can serve God in his daily life and not merely by studying the Torah; that everyone can merge with God through fervent prayer; and that God grants miraculous powers and the gift of prophecy to the *Zaddikim,* or Righteous Ones, among His people.

This belief that other men too could work miracles and become prophets helped Hasidism to spread far afield after the Besht's death in 1760. His successors looked upon themselves as his apostles and as miracle workers with the same power as the Besht had possessed. They also went some way toward reconciling mysticism with rabbinical Judaism, because not a few Talmudic scholars joined their ranks (Dubnow, 1928, VII, 221).

Even so, Orthodox Jews soon came to feel that the spread of Hasidism posed a serious threat to their form of Judaism. Whenever a Zaddik appeared in some district and attracted followers with his miracles or prophecies, credulous people flocked to him and began to neglect the traditional commandments.

The enemies of Hasidism accordingly demanded the expulsion of all such sectarians from the community. In some areas, above all in those parts of Poland that had come to Russia after the division of Poland—namely, the Ukraine, Podolia and Wolhynia—the Hasidim were in the majority. In Galicia, by contrast, and in Lemberg and Brody in particular, Rabbinism remained strong until well into the nineteenth century (Friedmann, 1929, 41f.). Only from 1840 onward did the Hasidic movement begin to make some headway in Galicia, after several Zaddikim had settled there. We shall see how these two movements clashed even in Tysmenitz, the birthplace of Jacob Freud (see 2.3 below).

These currents, as I have said, were not independent of political developments in the host nation, Poland. After the attack by the Cossacks under Chmielnicki, the power of the Polish princes was broken. As a result, Poland could no longer resist the claims of its neighbors. In the course of the first partition of Poland in 1772, Galicia was ceded to Austria. During the next two partitions, in 1793 and 1795, the rest of the old kingdom was shared out between Prussia, Russia, and Austria. Poland did not regain its national independence until after World War I. Until then Galicia remained part of Austria.

Before the first partition, only some 70,000 Jews had lived in Austria, and another 80,000 or so in Hungary. Following the annexation of Galicia by Austria in 1772, that number was swelled by more than 200,000 (Dubnow, 1928a, VIII, 31).[6] This was seen as sufficient reason by Maria Theresa (b. 1717, v. 1740–80) and her co-regent and later successor, Joseph II (1780–90), to apply the restrictive laws against Jews that had always obtained in Austria with particular severity to Galicia also. These laws were aimed above all at reducing the Jewish population. To that end, the poll tax for Jews was collected with remorseless severity; many people who could not pay up had to go into hiding and lived in constant fear of being expelled. An unduly high marriage tax was introduced in 1773, and since few could afford to pay it, many Jewish marriages had henceforth to be solemnized in secret.

In 1785, Jewish children were ordered to attend German schools, the so-called *Normalschulen,* of which only a few were ever set up. Attendance at such a school was nevertheless made another prerequisite for obtaining a marriage licence. In 1789, Joseph II extended these restrictions with his so-called *Toleranz-Patent* which, though ostensibly furthering the emancipation of Jews, actually meant the destruction of their social and cultural order. By virtue of this decree, Jews were granted the rights and privileges of all the king's other subjects and subjected to the national system of legislation and jurisdiction (Dubnow, 1928a, VIII, 294 ff; Adler, 1960, 46f.). At the same time, this meant that they had to give up their autonomous self-government of the *kahal,* which even during the most terrible pogroms had boosted their morale in the old Polish kingdom. Furthermore, the restrictions placed on the exercise by Jews of certain common occupations were tightened. Compulsory military service was instituted in 1788. Admittedly, Jews could buy themselves exemptions—the more so as the Austrians did not consider Jews to be trustworthy soldiers—but the so-called recruiting tax they had to pay was so high that few could afford it. It should also be mentioned that Joseph II decreed in 1789 that all Jews were to adopt family names, which was not then the custom among Jews. It was at this time that the Freud family took their name.

Despite their continuing anti-Jewish bias, these laws constituted a turning point in the attitude of the Austrian rulers and actually reflected the growing influence of the European Enlightenment movement. In Prussia, for instance, Moses Mendelssohn (1729–1786), one of the nation's leaders, had apparently been able to effect a change in the public attitude toward Jews and to eradicate many ancient prejudices.[7] His aim was the complete absorption of Jews into society, which meant giving up traditional Judaism. Mendelssohn abandoned many aspects of Orthodox Judaism; for example, he translated the Bible into German, which to many strictly Orthodox Jews was a grave sin (Adler, 1960, 37). Mendelssohn did not want the Jews to turn their backs on their own religion and become converts to Christianity. Rather, his aim was to render the Jewish religion less rigid, so that it would cease to be a bar to enlightened ideas or to the social integration of Jews into a society based on justice and reason (Dubnow, 1928a, VII, 370).

The Austrian rulers also were swayed by the ideas of the Enlightenment when they attempted to integrate the Jews in late eighteenth-century Austrian society. However, because of their latent or even explicit anti-Semitism,[8] and also because they underestimated the strength of the traditional ties of Galician Jewry, they made sad work of it.

In 1787, Joseph II charged Naphtali Herz Homberg, a pupil of Moses Mendelssohn, to open German-language Jewish schools in Galicia as envisaged in the *Toleranz-Patent.* Here the Bible would continue to be taught, but only in German; in addition, the children would be introduced to other subjects that could not be found in the syllabus of any *kheyder,* or rabbinical academy. The response of Galician Jewry was an almost total boycott of these schools, and bitter hatred of anyone who by means of such institutions, tried to turn their children from the Jewish religion. Herz Homberg failed miserably in his task. Most of the schools he opened had to be closed again at the beginning of the nineteenth century, although some continued to linger on in a few Galician towns and helped to prepare the advance of the Haskalah, the Jewish Enlightenment. Tysmenitz, the birthplace of Jacob Freud, housed one such school, and it is even possible that Jacob attended it (see 2.3 below).

The first contact of Galician Jews with the ideas of the Enlightenment therefore took place under an unfavorable star. Orthodox Jews of both the rabbinical and the Hasidic persuasion, put up a bitter resistance to all their new rulers' attempts to integrate them into Austrian society. They feared that with the extension of secular education, the abandonment of Hebrew, and the relaxation of the strict letter of the Law of Moses, their children would be robbed of their cultural heritage. While—by the beginning of the nineteenth century—those parts of the old Polish Empire held by the Russians, the Ukraine, Wolhynia and Podolia, were swept by the mystical movement of

Hasidism, and while at the same time Lithuania, also under Russian rule, remained under the domination of orthodox Rabbinism, Galicia had become a center of the Haskalah, the movement of Jewish Enlightenment. Enlightened ideas spread particularly to those towns in which Orthodox Rabbinism had dominated until then: Brody, the birthplace of Amalie Freud; Tarnopol; Lemberg; and—as we shall see—Tysmenitz as well (*Encyclopaedia Judaica,* Vol. 16, 1328; Gelber, 1924, 39ff.; and Friedmann, 1929, Chap. 3).

The Galician *maskilim,* as the followers of the Haskalah called themselves, were almost exclusively recruited from young Orthodox circles, upon whom the new movement exerted a particular attraction. Most of them had not had a European education but were, as Friedmann (1929, 45) has stressed, autodidacts, often with a very superficial knowledge of the world. They evinced a growing tendency to adopt German cultural patterns and the German language; the entire Jewish press in Galicia, for example, fell under the influence of the Haskalah.

The *maskilim* directed sharp attacks against the leaders of Orthodox Judaism, and in particular poured scorn and contempt on Hasidic "miracle-working" rabbis. The response of the Orthodox was to pronounce bans on them and to persecute them, the persecution being so vicious that in 1848 it led to murder of a Reform rabbi and his family in Lemberg in 1848 (Friedmann, 1929, 45ff.; Dubnow, 1928a, VIII, 304ff.).

At the beginning of the nineteenth century, when Jacob Freud was growing up, Galician Jewry was thus divided into two camps, the progressive and the conservative. Friedmann stresses that the result was an incessant war, "waged deep in the bosom of the family, in the form of the eternal fight between fathers and sons, and shattering the peace of the home" (1929, 51; translated from the German).

However, the relationship between rabbinical Judaism, Hasidism, and the Haskalah was not just one of conflict. The mystical movements, in particular, shared many ideas of the Haskalah. Indeed, mysticism may be said to have paved the way for the Haskalah and hence for assimilation, because it refused the unqualified adherence to the letter of the Law which rabbinical Judaism demanded. Whereas before the emergence of mystical mass movements it would have been unthinkable for a Polish Jew to seek salvation outside the strictest orthodoxy, new paths were no longer completely blocked to him now. It was upon the mystics' heretical attacks on traditional Rabbinism that the Reform movement could be built up at the end of the eighteenth and beginning of the nineteenth centuries.[9]

I must in any case agree with Bakan that it is impossible to describe the path of Jews from the medievally structured order of the East European ghettos and *shtetls* (small towns) into nineteenth-century bourgeois society as a straight line. Instead, there were many precursors in other movements which, in isolation, had nothing to do with the ideas of the Enlightenment, indeed were diametrically opposed to them, yet nevertheless paved the way for them (Bakan, 1958, 114).

For the purposes of this study it is also worth mentioning that at the turn of the eighteenth century these intellectual currents had a political dimension as well. The Haskalah in Galicia was not only used by the Austrian government to further the assimilation of Jews and to undermine Orthodox opposition; it also provided a link between Polish Jews and patriotic Poles, particularly during the Revolution of March 1848. Polish leaders proclaimed that the Jews were their allies in the struggle for freedom and national independence, and Jews declared that they and the Poles were allies with a common goal. There is some evidence that Tysmenitz, too, boasted a Jewish movement sympathetic to the Polish cause (see 2.3 below).

Hence there were two types of assimilation Galician Jews could adopt in about the middle of the nineteenth century: identification with the Austrian rulers, which was probably the safer path; or identification with the oppressed Polish minority, which was exceedingly perilous at the time because the Polish revolutionaries were being assailed from all sides—a Polish uprising in 1863 was beaten down remorselessly by the Russians (Friedmann, 1929, 210; *Encyclopaedia Judaica,* Vol. 16, 1330).

Jacob Freud thus grew up during a period of political upheaval and intellectual ferment in which the old traditions, and hence the organization of the Jewish community, were being fundamentally challenged, but during which the Jews were also being presented with unprecedented opportunities. Jacob Freud and his brothers decided to take the chance they were offered of abandoning the confinement of the Galician *shtetl* for a life that differed radically from that of their parents (see 2.5 below).

2.2 Life in the Galician *Shtetl*

To convey to the reader what this forsaking of the tradition might have meant for Jacob Freud, it is necessary to picture life in the *shtetl,* the small-town Jewish community of Eastern Europe.

Most impressive and detailed accounts can be found in Zborowski and Herzog (1952), Landes and Zborowski (1950), and Zborowski (1966), all of which are based on reports by American immigrants and may be said to constitute an ethnography of East European Jewry. Although these texts deal with Jewish life in general at the turn of the nineteenth century, making no special reference to Galicia, I feel they are representative of life in the Galician Jewish *shtetl* as well, since there were no basic differences in the everyday life of Jews throughout Eastern Europe. Most were miserably poor and shared the bitter lot of having to live amid hostile neighbors. Above all, the strong ties of religion tended to even out most regional differences.

The Jewish religion is a way of life; it fills the life of the faithful at every moment of the day. Judaism is not an individual affair but a form of "social" piety (Baeck, 1958, 370), and as such must be expressed in communal life. That explains why *shtetl* life was marked by an extraordinary feeling of cohesion, was based on togetherness, and why the community exerted so much control over the behavior of individuals. It was almost impossible to keep anything secret; to be withdrawn was considered un-Jewish. To the pious Jew, every sin was a crime against the family, against the community, against the people of Israel, and against God. Similarly, all acts pleasing to God fostered not only individual well-being but the welfare of the whole people of Israel, inasmuch as they hastened the coming of the Messiah and the end of the exile (Zborowski/Herzog, 1952, 225ff.).

The solidarity of *shtetl* Jews and their sense of obligation toward one another were a principal tenet of the Jewish religion, and at the same time served as protection against the hostile world of the *goyim,* the non-Jews, all around. True, relations with the local Polish and Ukrainian peasants were normally good—Jews bought the peasants' produce, either as middlemen or as direct consumers, and supplied them with nonagricultural products. Nevertheless, there were sporadic clashes in which the peasants' latent anti-Semitism flared up and in which memories of earlier horrors and pogroms were rekindled.

Despite the common poverty, however, there were marked social distinctions. In every *shtetl* there were *sheyneh yidn,* Jews who were a little richer than the rest. The majority, the *prosteh yidn,* were poor and not greatly respected; they eked out a living or else were *luftmenshen,* people without a steady occupation and hence forced to live on alms. But *yikhus,* or status, was something a Jew could achieve without riches, learning being considered much worthier of respect than wealth. Many a young Talmud student from a humble home was supported by the community or by a rich patron, and attained *yikhus atsmo,* i.e. *yikhus* by one's own efforts. In general, however, it was only the rich or their sons who could afford to study at a *yeshiva,* or rabbinical academy. The rich *talmud khokhem,* or scholar, who did not keep his wealth for himself but, without shaming those on whom he bestowed his largesse, shared it out, had the greatest *yikhus* of all. Furthermore, the *yikhus* of the individual was reflected in his whole family. Thus "*yikhus* letters," which carried the names of learned and otherwise highly honored ancestors, played an important role in matchmaking (Zborowski/Herzog, 1952, 74ff., 272ff.; Maier, 1973, 574).[10]

A good, "true" Jew was compassionate and charitable. Even if he was poor, he was expected to share what little he owned. It was a *mitsva,* a divine commandment, to give charity. Admittedly, being at the receiving end of that charity was considered something of a disgrace and detracted from one's *yikhus;* but at the same time it enabled the benefactor to do a good deed, which may explain why the *shnorrer* (beggar), that typical *shtetl* character, has figured so largely in Jewish folklore.

Another Jewish virtue is moderation. Children are expected to be self-controlled and to eschew all forms of excess. Fights, physical arguments, let alone bloodshed, were thought of as totally un-Jewish—one reason why Jews did not defend themselves against their enemies (Zborowski/Herzog, 1952, 344ff.).

Pious Jews had to spend their whole life trying to fulfill the 613 *mitsvos,* commandments, listed in the Torah (the Pentateuch) and commented upon and defined in the Talmud (M. Friedlaender, 1890). Specific duties and prayers are associated with certain parts of the day and with certain days; during the Sabbath, which lasts from Friday night to Saturday night, all forms of work and such activities as traveling, lighting fires, and counting money are strictly forbidden. The Sabbath is a day of prayer, of studying the Torah, of rest and of joy. The commandments to sanctify the Sabbath were particularly difficult to observe in a non-Jewish environment, amid people for whom Saturday was a normal working day. Again, the fact that Jews treated Sunday as a weekday often earned them the active dislike of their Christian neighbors.

Particularly arduous was the observance of the many dietary laws. A pious Jew is forbidden to eat certain types of meat, including pork. Animals whose flesh is *kosher,* or ritually fit to use, have to be slaughtered in a way that ensures that they have been fully bled. Meat cannot be eaten or handled with milk or milk products, so that the Orthodox Jewish housewife has to use two sets of crockery and cutlery, which must be kept strictly apart. Every breach of the dietary laws renders food *treyf,* impure, and hence inedible. In case of doubt the rabbi has to be consulted, and he can "re-kosher" the polluted kitchen utensils by ritual immersion (Zborowski and Herzog, 1952, 365ff.; Maier, 1973, 507ff.; M. Friedlaender, 1890).

These dietary laws were but one of the obstacles that rendered it impossible for Jews to eat in the homes of non-Jews, where even the cutlery was not *kosher.* The restrictions Jews had to impose upon themselves as a result were completely incomprehensible to their non-Jewish neighbors. Worse still, the prohibition against pork on the grounds that it was impure was considered a downright insult, pork being the staple animal food of most East Europeans.

The strict implementation of the dietary laws was the task of the Jewish housewife. It was considered unseemly for a woman to acquire Talmudic learning, a status-acquisitive activity reserved for men. Quite often it was the wife who carried on the family business or supported the family in other ways while the husband was in the *yeshiva,* studying the sacred texts under a learned rabbi. Whenever possible a man with sufficient *kop* (brains) was expected to devote himself entirely to the scholar's life, and his wife to maintain him, in part because it was believed that his piousness was procuring a better place in the beyond for her too—women could only reach Heaven through their husbands' exertions.

The high esteem in which education was held meant that little Jewish boys were expected to start attending *kheyder,* the elementary religious school, at the age of three or four. Here, under the supervision of the *melamed,* or Hebrew teacher, who was also entitled to mete out corporal punishment, they had to study the Torah for up to twelve hours a day, first learning to spell it out word for word in Hebrew and then reading it out loud. Orthodox Jewish boys had little leisure—all their interest was expected to be focused on their sacred studies. When they had finished the infant grade, they were promoted to the next highest class, where they were taught the Talmud and other commentaries on the Torah and had to follow the most intricate Talmudic arguments. If a boy turned out to be clever enough to become a *talmud khokhem,* a Talmud scholar, then everything was done to facilitate his entry into a *yeshiva.* If his family was poor, the community helped to keep him there, generally by arranging regular meals in the homes of more prosperous families. Those who did not manage to become *yeshiva bokhers, yeshiva* students, were expected to study at home or in the *besmedresh,* the synagogue, whenever they could. Torah study was a lifelong task for every pious Jew, his only true purpose in life (see Zborowski/Herzog, 1952, p. 88ff.; Zborowski, 1966).

In a sense, even marriage was subordinated to Torah study. Since a young *talmud khokhem* could so easily be diverted from his studies by sexual sensations and thoughts, he was encouraged to marry early so that once his physical needs had been satisfied, he could again devote himself wholeheartedly to the Word of God. Purity was not sought in seclusion but ensured by a form of immunization: " 'There is no such thing as a Jewish monastery,' says the proverb. The precautions taken are not against sex but against the intrusion of sex at the wrong time and in the wrong context" (Zborowski/Herzog, 1952, 136).

Early marriage was customary not only among Talmud scholars but among East European Jews in general. The reason was rarely premarital intercourse and pregnancy, the chastity of Jewish girls being an absolute requirement and the intimacy of the *shtetl* ensuring near-total social control over the individual's behavior. But parents were in general opposed to love matches, because love was not considered a guarantee of a durable partnership. The ideal was a marriage by which two similar families were drawn even closer together. Such marriages were thought to lead automatically to love between the partners, as expressed by the *shtetl* saying: "First marry, then love" (Zborowski, 1950, 462). Marriages were accordingly arranged without consultation of the prospective partners, the *shadkhen,* or marriage broker, negotiating the marriage contract with the parents. It was not at all unusual to sign a marriage contract for twelve-year-old children, who were then considered to be engaged, often marrying at the ages of sixteen or seventeen. The *shadkhen* generally made sure that there were no great discrepancies between the two partners— no glaring differences in age, *yikhus,* or wealth—although the bridegroom could offset poverty with exceptional scholarship (Landes/Zborowski, 1950, 449; Zborowski/Herzog, 1952, 273).

As a result of poor living conditions the young couple were often forced to move in with the parents, generally those of the bride. In that case, the son-in-law was said to be living *"in kest."* The resulting relationship between father-in-law and son-in-law was considered to be particularly close, while that between father and son often lacked emotional warmth, being largely based on respect. If, alternatively, the son moved his bride into his father's house, then it was said that tension was inevitable, not only between father and son but above all between bride and mother-in-law, for the mother–son relationship could not admit of a third party, the mother being the unquestioned authority in all household matters.

Here the reader must try to imagine living conditions in an East European *shtetl:* very few families occupied more than two rooms, yet most families comprised large numbers of children. Many households had just one room in which their entire family drama was played out. If a daughter married and brought her husband to live in such cramped quarters, a new room was often created by hanging a curtain to form a partition, thus providing a modicum of privacy (Zborowski/Herzog, 1952, 362).

In marriage, a number of special commandments had to be kept. According to the Torah, a woman is "impure" during her menstrual period and cannot be touched by any man. Indeed, all objects on which she has been lying or sitting become *treyf,* impure. For that reason, the married couple had to have separate beds. It was not until seven days after the end of her menstruation that a woman became *kosher* again, following immersion in the *mikva,* the ritual bath built by the community. This prohibition meant that for two weeks of every month a man could not sleep with his wife. "Half of the time she belongs to him, half of the time to God" (*ibid.,* 1952, 287). This also explains why Orthodox Jews are afraid of touching any woman—they have no means of telling whether she happens to be pure or impure. Only pregnant women are certain to be pure. After giving birth, women are once again considered to be impure for several weeks, the interval being shorter following the birth of a boy than it is after the birth of a girl (Leviticus 12:2–5).

Sex was not a fit subject for conversation between the married couple, although the husband was expected to discuss the sexual commandments with other men as part of his Torah studies. Neither partner was informed in theory about sexual intercourse, which had to take place in the dark, unobserved by any living creature. Since so few homes had separate bedrooms, this meant a long, quiet wait for the married couple until all the children were fast asleep. Any sexual indulgence except for procreating—in particular masturbation or extramarital sexuality—was considered a grave sin (Zborowski/Herzog, 1952, 287).[11] Another strict rule stated that the body must be kept at least partially covered at all times. Nakedness was considered shameful. Normally, only the face and hands could be shown uncovered, for all other parts of the body, even the arms and feet, were subject to the prohibition against baring oneself (Somogyi, 1979, 50).

The birth of a boy was deemed a far greater blessing than that of a girl, since only male Jews could enter into the covenant God had signed with Abraham. This was done by circumcision on the eighth day after birth. In some communities the ceremony was performed in the synagogue, in others in the parental house (M. Friedlaender, 1890). During the ceremony a respected friend of the family acts as *sandak,* sitting with the baby in his lap on a special chair while the *mohel,* or professional circumciser, cuts off the child's foreskin and all those present recite the solemn prayer of dedication (Zborowski and Herzog, 1952, 318ff.).

Every Jewish father longed for a son who would dutifully say *Kaddish* three times a day after his parents' death, thus helping to assure their heavenly well-being. A son who did not say this prayer committed a grave sin (Zborowski/Herzog, 1952, 309). Sons were also wanted because they might become scholars and so add to their parents' *yikhus*. A girl could only do that by contracting a good marriage. This meant that the parents had to find her a dowry, which in view of the general poverty posed a grave problem. A particularly great blessing was a "child of old age," that is, a child born late in the parents' life *(ibid.)*.

The typical Jewish family had a large number of children, for a "good marriage" was expected to yield one child every year. Childlessness was considered a disgrace, and a man was entitled to sue his wife for divorce if she remained barren for ten years. Other causes for divorce were grave misdemeanor by the wife, and estrangement, especially due to desertion by the husband. In either case, however, only the husband could sue for divorce (Zborowski and Herzog, 1952, 288; M. Friedlaender, 1890).

During the early years of a boy's life, his mother alone took care of him. But as soon as the boy started attending the elementary Hebrew school, or *kheyder,* his father would take him in hand, testing his knowledge every Sabbath. The father thus became the embodiment of respect for the Law, and a lofty figure in his son's eyes. By contrast, the father would take no interest in a daughter's intellectual education although he would be emotionally very close to her. "Actually, short of incest, there are no norms prescribed in the Codes or elsewhere in tradition to guide a father in relations with his daughter, and he appears to follow a need to cultivate in this rather overlooked relationship a haven fairly free of tension" (Landes and Zborowski, 1950, 456). The father was also expected to find his daughter a husband, generally a man after his own heart, with whom he would then have a closer and better relationship than with his own sons.

The relationship between mother and son was closer still. A mother could share her bed with her son—which she could not do with her own husband because of the purity taboo—until he became a *bar mitzvah* boy (literally: "son of the commandment") at the age of thirteen, thus attaining the adult state. Landes and Zborowski comment that

There is no avoidance between mother and son, except that intercourse is forbidden. Mother is the embodiment of warmth, intimacy, food, unconditional love, security, practical reality. This inclusive libidinal character . . . is in complete contrast with the spiritualized, remote character of the father. Father's life is as dedicated to the study of the Law as mother's is to material comforts for the family; he is remote from his son physically and emotionally, being mentor and guide rather than comforter and nurse, and occupied outside of the home. . . . Yet the father and son bear a similar relationship to the wife and mother, except that the woman owes respect to the husband because such is her defined obligation, and the son owes respect to the mother because that is his obligation. Indeed, rivalry between father and son is a familiar theme, expressed in large and small ways, privately and publicly (*ibid.,* 1950, 454).

The Jewish child was obliged by the Fifth (or Fourth, depending on the respective partitioning of the Decalogue which is not consistent) Commandment to honor and obey his parents without question. That commandment was applied regardless of how the parents behaved toward their child or toward the Torah: "Even if the parents were criminals and had acquired no claim to their children's love and gratitude, or had never cared for them, the children were nevertheless expected to fulfill their duties toward their parents reverently, because respect and reverence toward parents was not meant to be repayment for services rendered" (Barta, 1975, 81; translated from the German). East European Jewish immigrants in the United States interviewed by Zborowski remembered the "enormous" awe which filled them whenever their father entered the house. Indeed, their *tateh,* remained a respected person even when they themselves had become fathers or mothers in their turn (Zborowski and Herzog, 1952, 295ff.).

The children also owed *derekh erets* (respect) to their *mammeh.* However, their feelings toward her were different because her position vis-à-vis her husband was similar to theirs. The ultimate authority was the father, and the children's education consisted first and foremost in their being taught to subordinate their own will to his.

This attitude of respect and obedience toward one's parents was based on the relationship of the people of Israel to God: "You shall be unto them as matter, educable matter, you shall have no will to set up against theirs. You shall respect them and honor them next to God, for only through them can you reach God. Whensoever you honor your father and mother as priests in God's temple of mankind . . . look upon them as God's, mankind's and Israel's messengers . . . then your God-given existence will blossom forth into true life" (S. R. Hirsch: *Versuche über Jissroels Pflichten in der Zerstreuung.* Frankfurt, 1909. Quoted after Barta, 1975, 82; translated from the German).

Magical and mystical ideas were widespread among East European Jews. These poor and persecuted people were helped by superstition to make sense of their tenuous existence as a persecuted minority. Their magical ideas were based above all on kabbalistic traditions and on number mysticism. We saw that, because the letters of the Hebrew alphabet also stand for numerals, it is possible to "translate" words into numbers (Trachtenberg, 1939, 262). Their addition, multiplication, and so on, followed by translation back into words, can lead to an almost infinite number of interpretations of a particular text, for purposes of prophecy. Moreover, belief in the miraculous powers of amulets, in the possibility of telling the future from dreams, in the power of spirits, of evil thoughts, curses, and so forth, was often a mere extension or exaggeration of the normal religious practices of pious Jews.

We might also dwell on other aspects of Jewish life in the Galician *shtetl,* for instance, the Jewish festivals which helped to integrate individuals even further into *shtetl* life. However, they seem less relevant in the present context, for we are more concerned with the general social and religious environment in which Jacob Freud grew up, the better to discover what radical changes the move from Tysmenitz to Freiberg and later to Vienna wrought in his life.

2.3 Tysmenitz

Tysmenitz (Polish: Tyśmienica), the birthplace of Jacob Freud, lies some ninety miles south of Lemberg (Lvov), at the edge of the Carpathians, on a tributary of the Dniester (see Fig. 1). Today it is part of the Ivano-Frankovsk Administrative District (formerly Stanislav) of the Ukrainian SSR. There is no Jewish community left in Tysmenitz. Apart from the handful who were able to flee, the entire Jewish population of Tysmenitz was murdered during the German occupation, either in death camps or by mass execution.[12]

The precise number of inhabitants at the beginning of the nineteenth century, when Jacob Freud lived there, is not known. In 1765, 856 Jews were registered as taxpayers (Balaban, after Blond, 1974, 155).[13] Sajner states that in about the middle of the nineteenth century, Tysmenitz had 6,000 inhabitants, of whom 50 percent were Jews (1968, 170). According to official census figures the town had approximately 7,000 inhabitants in 1880, of whom about 2,500, or 36 percent, were Jews (*Encyclopaedia Judaica,* Vol. 16, 1492). The rest of the population was made up of Russian Orthodox Ruthenians (Ukrainians, Russians) and Catholic Poles (*ibid.,* 1326).

Jews had been living in Tysmenitz since the sixteenth century (Blond, 1974, 153), a Jewish community first settling there under the benevolent rule of Count Potocki and his descendants. Tysmenitz eventually became a religious and administrative center for the smaller Jewish communities nearby which could not afford to run all the institutions needed for the strict observance of the Law, for instance, a *mikva,* or ritual bath. The town probably boasted a synagogue from the end of the seventeenth century (Blond, 1974, 152). After a fire in 1764, this was rebuilt in stone (*ibid.,* 157, see Fig. 5).

Tysmenitz was an important commercial center whose influence at times exceeded that of Brody. Commerce was predominantly in the hands of the Jews, who regularly attended the great markets of Breslau, Leipzig, and other German cities (*ibid.,* 157).

In addition, Tysmenitz was a hub of Jewish learning. M. Balaban has called Tysmenitz the second most important cultural center in Galicia, following closely behind Cracow and taking precedence over Stanislav and Lemberg. Thus the Tysmenitz *yeshiva* produced a number of important rabbis and Talmudic scholars. Tysmenitz Jews were represented in all important Jewish institutions in Galicia (Blond, 1974, 155; cf. Aron, 1971, 169f.).

The fact that Tysmenitz was a center of rabbinical learning and as such enjoyed renown far afield probably explains why the mystical movement of Hasidism failed to take root there at the beginning of the nineteenth century.[14] The *Encyclopaedia Judaica* (Vol. 16, 1492) tells us that Hasidim were being persecuted in Tysmenitz at that time, which suggests that although Hasidism had reached the town, its spread was fiercely resisted by the dominant Mitnaggedim, staunch opponents of the mystical movement. Only in the late nineteenth century did Tysmenitz produce its own Hasidic leaders (Blond, 1974, 175; Aron, 1971, 169).

Thus while Hasidism failed to receive general recognition in Tysmenitz during Jacob Freud's childhood—although some Tysmenitz Jews must have made secret pilgrimages to a *tsaddik (zaddïc),* or Hasidic miracle-working rabbi, in the immediate or more distant neighborhood—the Haskalah, or Jewish Enlightenment movement, was able to recruit disciples in Tysmenitz as early as the turn of the eighteenth century.

It would even seem as if the spirit of the Enlightenment began to stir extremely early in the town; at the beginning of the eighteenth century, even before Moses Mendelssohn advanced his new ideas, many Jews in Tysmenitz and in other Galician towns had already begun to strive for worldly learning. From the memoirs of Beer of Bolekhov (Beer, 1922), who was born in 1723 and lived in Tysmenitz for several years, it appears that a group of Jews there were reading books in Latin and Polish, and "versing themselves in worldly matters," that is, breaking the strict rules of orthodoxy which premitted no studies other than Torah exegesis on the basis of the Talmud and other traditional writings. M. Wischnitzer, who published Beer's memoirs, writes:

In Bolekhov and Tysmenitz, in Brody and in other towns and villages of eastern Galicia, a new movement sprang up in the eighteenth century which established a bridge between secular culture and loyalty to the Hebrew language. It was the eve of a new epoch. Here we see the pioneers of the Haskalah at work long before Mendelssohn propounded his ideas. These pre-Haskalitic pioneers of Beer's generation were still unable to pass across the threshold of the old tradition and observed the ancient Jewish customs in much the same way as did the broad masses of Orthodox Jews. Later, in the middle of the nineteenth century, eastern Galicia once again became a main centre of the Haskalah. I am convinced that there is a connection between the later blossoming of the Haskalah and those first beginnings almost a hundred years earlier. Brody, Lemberg, Tysmenitz, Bolekhov and other towns in the eighteenth no less than in the nineteenth century were constantly engaged in trade with the outside world, mainly at the great German markets. These contacts naturally awakened an interest in general education and secular culture (Wischnitzer in Beer, 1922, 17; translated from Yiddish into German and from German into English).

It was possibly thanks to these Haskalitic precursors that the reforming ideas of the new Austrian rulers did not receive the same cold reception from Tysmenitz Jews as they did elsewhere. When a new school for Jewish children was opened in 1788, for example, it was one of the German-language Jewish schools created by Naphtali Herz Homberg under the reign of Joseph II (personal communication by S. Blond). And while elsewhere such schools

FIGURE 4 Part of Market
Square in Tysmenitz
*(D. Chirowski: Dzieje Miasta
Tysmienicy, Lvov, 1938)*

FIGURE 5 The interior of the
Great Synagogue in Tysmenitz
*(D. Chirowski: Dzieje Miasta
Tysmienicy, Lvov, 1938)*

were quickly closed again because pious Jews refused to expose their children to non-Jewish ideas, we know that the one in Tysmenitz still stood in 1817.[15]

Several influences—the early influx of enlightened ideas, the opening of the German-language school, and certainly the trading contacts with the world outside—were thus responsible for turning Tysmenitz into a center of the Haskalah movement. Some of the most active *maskilim,* champions of the Haskalah, came from Tysmenitz.[16]

It is therefore highly probable that Jacob Freud's introduction to the ideas of the Enlightenment, which were to stamp his life and those of his children, did not take place only when he himself traveled to Moravia, but that he had already been exposed to that intellectual current in his birthplace. He may even have been a friend of some of the active *maskilim* in Tysmenitz, quite a few of whom were his own generation.

In 1848, Tysmenitz saw the opening of a "Reading and Cultural Circle," whose object it was to spread secular knowledge and the ideas of the Enlightenment (Blond, 1974, 155). In a letter to the Polish leader Franciszek Smolka, this circle called for the establishment of Polish schools and agricultural settlements for Jews so that they could commit themselves even more actively to the cause of Polish liberation.[17]

This reference to a pro-Polish current among Tysmenitz Jews is relevant here inasmuch as there are indications that one of Jacob Freud's brothers sympathized actively with the Polish liberation movement (see 3.3.4 below).

2.4 Jacob Freud's Childhood and His First Marriage to Sally Kanner in Tysmenitz

Following this general survey of Jewish life in Galicia, and particularly in Tysmenitz, we can now assemble what facts we have about Jacob Freud's life there (cf. Table 3).

In contrast to Freiberg/Moravia, the birthplace of Sigmund Freud, in which some records of the Jewish inhabitants have been preserved, no such records have been discovered in Tysmenitz. The reason is simple: in Galicia, the Jewish inhabitants kept their births and marriages secret, the better to escape the oppressive regulations imposed on them by the Austrian authorities. But even if registers of births, marriages, and deaths had been kept in Galicia, they would certainly have been destroyed in the course of the Nazi atrocities. Thus there is no hope of ever reconstructing the life of Jacob Freud from local archives.

Jacob was born on 18 December 1815.[18] In his autobiographical study,

Sigmund Freud has this to say about his ancestors: "I have reason to believe that my father's family were settled for a long time on the Rhine (at Cologne), that, as a result of the persecution of the Jews during the fourteenth and fifteenth centuries, they fled eastwards, and that, in the course of the nineteenth century, they migrated back from Lithuania through Galicia into German Austria" (1925d, 7f.). According to the family tree of the Freud family compiled by Hellreich from inscriptions in the Jewish cemetery at Buczacz and from other documents (see Table 2, based on Kohn, 1955), the family had been resident in Buczacz, some thirty-five miles east of Tysmenitz, for at least four generations. The name "Freud" was probably derived from Freide, the great-grandmother of Schlomo and wife of Jesucher, who also lived in Buczacz.[19] It was adopted in 1787, when all Jewish inhabitants of Galicia, a province recently annexed by Austria, were forced to assume a family name (Haas, 1908, 167).

It would seem that Schlomo Freud, Jacob's father, was the first of the Freud family to settle in Tysmenitz. S. Blond (written communication) thinks that he came to Tysmenitz from Buczacz as a *yeshiva* student. It is possible that he married Peppi (or Pepi, Yiddish: Pessel) Hofmann in Tysmenitz and that he lived *in kest* with his father-in-law Siskind (Yiddish: Zisie) Hofmann as a *yeshiva-bokher.*

The date of Schlomo Freud's birth is not known, but that of Siskind Hofmann, Jacob's grandfather, can be computed from documents discovered by J. Sajner and R. Gicklhorn in Czechoslovak archives. It appears that Siskind was born either in 1775 or else in 1768 (see p. 89 below), so that Peppi, Jacob Freud's mother, could not have been born before 1790 or 1783—at which time her father would have been fifteen—or after 1800, which would have made her fifteen at the birth of her son Jacob. She was probably no older than thirty when Jacob was born.

In that case, Siskind Hofmann, Jacob's maternal grandfather, must have been only forty (or perhaps forty-seven) years older than Jacob. Siskind Hofmann was a merchant who began traveling between Galicia and Moravia in 1804. Schlomo Freud was a merchant. Schlomo Freud was a merchant as well, occasionally accompanying his father-in-law to Moravia from 1838 onward. Quite possibly Siskind Hofmann and Schlomo Freud had that characteristic Jewish relationship between father-in-law and son-in-law which was often so much easier than that between father and son.

For Jacob Freud this may have meant growing up under the influence of his mother's family, which would explain why he eventually joined his grandfather Siskind Hofmann on his travels. We know nothing about Jacob's relationship to his other grandparents, the parents of Schlomo Freud.

As the latest researches of P. Swales have shown (see Table 3), Schlomo and Peppi Freud had three sons and one daughter, of whom Jacob was probably the eldest. Freud described his uncle Abae, who later moved to Breslau, as follows: "He is a younger brother of my father, a rather ordinary man, a merchant, and the story of his family is very sad. Of the four children, only one daughter is normal, and married in Poland. One son is hydrocephalic and feeble-minded; another, who as a young man showed some promise, went insane at the age of 19, and a daughter went the same way when she was 20-odd" (1960a, 222f., 10 February 1886).

Freud also mentioned that "one of the sons of the other (very unhappy) uncle in Vienna died an epileptic" *(ibid.)*. This "other uncle" was Josef Freud, about whom, following R. Gicklhorn's recent searches in Viennese archives, we now know a little more (Gicklhorn, 1976, 22, 43; see 3.3.4 below). Josef was ten years younger than Jacob.

Because we do not know to which of the three intellectual currents in Jewry Schlomo adhered, we cannot tell what kind of education he gave his sons. As we saw, Tysmenitz boasted not only a traditional *kheyder* but also a German-speaking Jewish school which, although it was opposed by Orthodox Jews of both the rabbinical and the Hasidic persuasion, nevertheless did have pupils, or else it would not have had to be financed from a special fund as late as 1817.

Jacob signed all the documents that have come down to us in a German hand, while his grandfather Siskind Hofmann signed in Hebrew (personal communication by Sajner). Had Jacob perhaps attended a German-language school? Had he learned the German language and script even as a child; and above all had he gained the kind of knowledge no Jewish child ever acquired in a *kheyder*? In that case, his father Schlomo must have been an early adherent of the Haskalah, which, from what we know of the long tradition of enlightened ideas in Tysmenitz, is not impossible though unlikely. Schlomo did not come from Tysmenitz but from Buczacz, of which we do not know whether, like Tysmenitz, it had a Haskalitic tradition. In any case we know that Jacob could read Hebrew even in later years (Heller, 1956, 419), which suggests that his father, Schlomo, sent him to a *kheyder,* and that, like all little Jewish boys there, he read the Bible from morning to night. Perhaps he also continued his education at the *yeshiva.*

Freud once stated that his father "did indeed come from a Chassidic [Hasidic] background. He was 41 when I was born and had been estranged from his native environment for almost twenty years" (1960a, 394). Did he mean that Schlomo, too, had been a Hasid? He could well have been, for Hasidism had spread to Tysmenitz by the beginning of the nineteenth century. A "Chassidic background" might, however, have simply meant that Schlomo's relatives or those of his wife rather than Schlomo himself were Hasidim. In that case, Jacob could have been introduced to mystical ideas by relatives.

Freud's remark that Jacob had lived in his "native environment" only during his first twenty years is important. This could mean that Jacob shook off his Orthodox background in about 1835, that is, shortly after his marriage and the birth of his two sons, and adopted the new ideas of the Haskalah. Perhaps until then he had lived the life of the pious Jew, the strict observer of the Law of his fathers; perhaps the *shtetl* had been his entire world, and remained so until he met other worlds on his travels.

There is evidence to support this view, not least his early marriage to Sally Kanner, which took place in the middle of 1832 at the latest, when he was about sixteen and a half—if we may take it that his son Emanuel was, in fact, born in April 1833.[20] This marriage had in all probability been arranged between the Freud and Kanner families. Because the bridegroom was so young, it seems likely that he lived *in kest* with his parents-in-law. Of Sally Kanner's parents nothing is known, and all we know of Sally herself is her name.

Emanuel was probably born very soon after the wedding; and Jacob's second son, Philipp, probably one and a half years later, some time between August and October 1834.[21] Jacob had two other children with Sally, as Swales has recently discovered (cf. Table 3). Both died in childhood.

2.5 The Break with Tradition

2.5.1 JACOB FREUD, THE WANDERING JEW

Whatever may have persuaded Jacob Freud to join his grandfather on his travels to Moravia, the experience must have been a tremendous one for him. It is true that on their 350-mile journey, which they had to cover by horse and cart,[22] most of their contacts were probably fellow Jews. They spent the nights in *kosher* hostelries, and perhaps also traveled as part of a group of Galician merchants. Even so, life outside the Galician *shtetl* must have astounded Jacob, for in Moravian Jewish communities the new forms of life had most probably been further disseminated than in his own backward Galicia.

Besides, these trips may have offered Jacob his first opportunity to escape from the strict control of his family and community. True, he traveled with his own people, but it was quite impossible for traveling Jews to keep all the commandments that pious *shtetl* Jews observed as a matter of course. Hence it may well have dawned on Jacob, perhaps for the first time, that it was possible to brush some of the old traditions aside. I am thinking in particular of the absolute ban on extramarital intercourse and on masturbation. One may take it that the temptation to break the rules must have been all the greater for Jacob as the young man was separated from his wife for many months at a time.

The position of Moravian Jews differed markedly from that of their Galician co-religionists. In Moravia, the Austrian authorities were, on the one hand, much more determined to ensure Jewish assimilation; all Jewish children were expected to attend German-language public schools, often in the face of strong parental opposition (Haas, 1908, 18ff.).

On the other hand, it was much easier to implement the anti-Semitic measures promulgated during the first half of the nineteenth century in Moravia than in distant Galicia. Jews were not allowed to settle outside of fifty-two designated Jewish communities, and non-resident Jews were only allowed to stay in a given community when they had been declared "tolerated Jews." This explains why the number of Jews in Moravia remained constant over several decades (*ibid.*, 15ff.).

Jacob Freud and his grandfather experienced these restrictions in person, as the documents discovered by J. Sajner and R. Gicklhorn in the District Archives of Neu Titschein (Nový Jičín) make only too clear. Because they were merely "tolerated" Jews in Moravia, they had to wage a constant battle to have their residence permits extended. Their passports, too, were valid for short periods only. The earliest document in which Jacob Freud is mentioned by name, the "Register of Foreign Jews Resident in the City of Freiberg, together with an account of the reasons for their stay" of 30 April 1844, lists thirteen Jews, including, in ninth place, Siskind Hofmann.[23] That entry reads as follows:

9 Süsskind Hoffmann
Place of origin: Tysmenitz
In possession of passport dated: None, as the passport held was sent home for renewal last March when it expired, and no new passport has yet been issued.
Duration of stay to this date: I have been staying here on and off for the purposes of trade for the past forty years. At the beginning my visits alternated with those of my associate, Salomo Britwitz, but for the past six years I have been accompanied by my son-in-law, Salamon Freit, whose place is often taken by his son Kallamon Jakob Freit. Our stay usually lasts for five to six months a year, during which time, however, we pay several visits to various places in the neighborhood. This time, Freit having departed some seven weeks ago, I arrived here a little later than usual and have been present here for about five weeks.
Period of required extension: Until after the Easter holidays, at which time Freit will return to continue the business for the necessary, but at this time not precisely determinable, period, and I shall return home.
Occupation: The selling of various products such as wool, hemp, tallow, honey, furs, and the buying of untreated cloth and seeing to its complete finishing.
Possession of trading tax certificate: Although I hold an 8 Fr. [florins = Austrian guilders] trading tax certificate, Freit having his own, that certificate is not kept here but with my family at home.
Use of rented premises: I rent a room in the house belonging to the widow Theresia Bohaž, No. 27, for carrying on business during the day, as well as two cellars at the same address for storing goods. Apart from that, for overnight stays I have my quarters in the town hostelry. [Signature in Hebrew script] Süsskind Hoffmann
(District Archives, N. Jičín, copied by J. Sajner; translated from the German).

In the same year, on June 24, Siskind Hofmann and Jacob Freud applied for "toleration" in Freiberg:

Esteemed Magistrate
Whereas I am known to trade in linen, wool, honey, tallow, etc., and have been resident partly in Freiberg and partly in its environs for several years for purposes of

business, it is now my intention to establish my domicile in Freiberg, because that town is most advantageous to my trade for more than one reason, firstly because it is on the main road, secondly because the whole populace is engaged chiefly in the manufacture of cloth, and thirdly because Freiberg lies in the midst of numerous villages devoted to the clothmaking trade and is therefore an extremely propitious trading center.

Because I buy woolen cloth in Freiberg and its environs and have it dyed and finished in the locality and despatch it as merchandise to Galicia: and in return convey Galician products such as wool, honey, hemp, and tallow for sale in Freiberg; and because Freiberg is visited by foreign merchants who buy this merchandise from me and also because I rent cellars in which this merchandise is deposited, the need arises for my permanent stay in Freiberg.

Because I, as an old man, now counting sixty-nine years, can no longer negotiate the difficulties of trade without assistance, I have engaged as a trading partner my grandson Kalman Freud, who will direct the outside trade, while I myself will be solely concerned with buying and selling in Freiberg itself. For the purpose of trade, I have also obtained from the respected Lemberg Regional Authorities the adjoined traveling passport issued for the duration of one year both to myself and also to my grandson Kalman Freud. I accordingly pray the Esteemed Magistrate to be gracious enough to intervene in our behalf in the appropriate high places that we may be granted certificates of toleration in Freiberg for the duration of the passport, namely, until 18 May [1]845.

Freiberg, 24 June [1]844. Siskind Hoffman Koloman Jacob Freud.
(Sajner, 1968, 169, additions from the original as copied by Sajner; translated from the German).

To this application the town magistrate appended an affidavit by the Clothmakers' Guild declaring that the stay of these two merchants was as necessary as it was useful:

Siskind Hoffmann and his grandson Kallmann Freud are known to us as honorable and trustworthy merchants, who purchase the products of local cloth masters, have them finished locally and forward them to Galicia, and import Galician products in return. The presence of these merchants in Freiberg is of great benefit both to the local inhabitants and also to the surrounding villages because the products of the clothmakers can invariably be sold through them. By virtue of the presence of these merchants in our midst, local commerce benefits considerably so that we feel in duty bound to endorse the application for a certificate of toleration by Siskind Hoffman and Kallmann Freud.
(Sajner, 1968, 169, changes following the original; translated from the German).

The district administration of Prerau granted the request on 10 September 1844, but imposed a toleration tax of 10 guilders "common coin" per person for the one year's stay. Both men protested, not only to the magistrate of Freiberg but also to the "Royal and Imperial Moravian-Silesian Provincial Government." In this letter of protest, they stressed that the toleration tax was disproportionate to their income:

Firstly the writer of the previous petition committed an error inasmuch as he also applied for a certificate of toleration for me, Siskind Hoffmann, who has never had the intention of spending a whole year in Freiberg. I, Siskind Hoffmann, am an old man of seventy-six, bent by age, and one whose infirmity and illness make him incapable of carrying on independent trade. I have come to Freiberg solely for the purpose of settling a number of outstanding matters and intend immediately afterwards to return to my home in Tysmenitz, in Galicia, which I intend to do immediately after the Festival of the Tabernacles. Hence I humbly beg that I, because my name has only been entered in the petition by an error, and because I neither now nor then had the intention of spending a whole year in Freiberg, be, by highest mercy, exempted from the payment of the toleration tax assessed at 10 FCM for the year.

As for me, your most obedient Kallman Freud, I humbly submit that the toleration tax imposed upon me, and assessed at 10 FCM, is much too high for the size of my business and income, inasmuch as I am only a beginner in business, carry on an insignificant trade with Galician country products and merely concern myself with the purchase of cloth on commission on behalf of others for sale in Moldavia and Wallachia.

Both of us are moreover expected to pay all the prescribed taxes and community dues in our domicile, and if we are now to pay a special toleration tax of 10 FCM as well then we shall be burdened beyond our means and shall have to give up our business altogether, which would be of the greatest disadvantage to Freiberg, since that town, which has declined considerably, owes to us and our trade with Galician products and the purchase of cloth and other Moravian manufactured goods, a large part of its surviving trade.

With full confidence in the understanding and courtesy of the gracious Royal and Imperial Provincial Government we therefore respectfully present the following humble petition: that the gracious Government be indulgent enough to exempt me, Sisskind Hoffmann, who intends in the near future to return to his home and does not intend to make use of the residence permit in Freiberg, from the toleration tax assessed at 10 FCM, and to reduce the toleration tax imposed on me, Kallmann Freud, assessed equally at 10 FCM, to 5 FCM (District Archives, N. Jičín, copied by J. Sajner; translated from the German).

This application was turned down, and on October 29 both men paid "20 guilders common coin in cash to the local taxation office" *(ibid.)*.

Quite apart from the light these documents cast on the life of Jacob Freud in Freiberg, they also bear witness to the extreme handicaps under which "tolerated" Jews had to labor. True, Jacob Freud and his grandfather may have exaggerated their plight, but 20 guilders was in fact a large sum, if one considers that their joint enterprise had a turnover (not a profit) of about 1,000 guilders a year (see Table 6).

Each year they had to apply for renewal of their residence permits until, on 19 October 1847, Jacob made an application for "toleration" for himself alone. On that occasion he wanted to stay in Freiberg for six months only. Once again the Clothmakers' Guild endorsed his application as well as the applications of seven other Jews.[24] Apparently his was turned down, because he made a new application on February 22, again with the support of the Clothmakers' Guild. His letter read as follows:

I am in partnership with my grandfather, Siskind Hoffmann, and we deal in wool, cloth and tallow, though in actual fact I am merely the appointee of Abraham Halpen in Stanislaus, who sends me these articles, and further of Nathan Tenner and M. N. Herdan of Tysmenitz. As my grandfather's partner I pay income tax in Tysmenitz at 3 Fl. annually, while my grandfather pays 8 Fl. My income tax certificate is kept in the above-mentioned place and, every year, when applying for a new passport, I am obliged to produce it, the certificate being in the hands of my Fany Freud in Tysmenitz (Sajner, 1968, 170, corrections following the original; translated from the German).[25]

On this occasion Jacob was issued with a toleration certificate for three months only, the Prerau District Administration informing him that his own and his grandfather's passports were running out and that they had no proof that they actually did pay income tax in their home towns. The Freiberg magistrate was instructed by the district administration to expel these Jews after the lapse of three months, or immediately "if they cannot satisfy the passport and police regulations" (District Archives, N. Jičín, copied by J. Sajner).

This decision was dated 10 July 1848—almost three months after the March Revolution which shook the whole of Western Europe and was eventually to bring Austrian Jews full political and civic rights, leading to the abolition of all restrictions, particularly in respect of free movement and the contraction of marriages. As Haas has stressed, it all heralded a new epoch for the Jews (1908, 22).[26] Even so, we need not be surprised that, three months after the Revolution, Jacob should still have been treated as harshly as he was; in all probability the new laws were not implemented until later in 1848.

We may take it that when the new laws did come into force, Jacob immediately applied for permanent domicile in Freiberg. In any case, the 1852 Register of Jews shows him as holder of a certificate of domicile issued by the Klogsdorf municipality, which bordered on Freiberg (see Table 4). It is likely, however, that Jacob Freud never actually lived in Klogsdorf, merely acquiring domiciliary rights there because such rights were easier to obtain in a village than in a town.[27]

The year 1848 must have been the turning point for Jacob Freud and for many Austrian Jews. It was probably then that he took the great step from the narrow life of the Orthodox Jew to that of the emancipated bourgeois and that he began to cut what ties still bound him to his old world.

Jacob Freud had in his possession a copy of an illustrated Bible published in the Hebrew and German languages by Ludwig Philippson. On a commemorative page in that Bible, the date 1 November 1848 appears under Jacob Freud's signature (Roback, 1957, 89; E. Freud, 1977, 46). The first edition was published between the years 1838 and 1854, and it became the Bible used by enlightened and assimilated Jews.[28]

Since Jacob Freud acquired a copy of it either on or within only a few years of publication, we may conclude that he was a close adherent of Jewish assimilation. And the appearance of the date 1 November 1848 on a page where he later recorded the death of his father, Schlomo, and the birth of his son Schlomo (Sigmund) may indeed signify that the year 1848 was a turning point in the life of Jacob Freud.

2.5.2 JACOB'S MARRIAGE TO
REBEKKA

We do not know what happened to Jacob between 1848 and 1852. But the period must have been a crucial one for him, for by the year 1852 he and his two sons Philipp and Emanuel, himself married by that time, were registered in Freiberg, together with a certain thirty-two-year-old Rebekka, given out as Jacob's wife (see Table 4). If the ages entered were correct, then Rebekka could not have been Emanuel's mother, for she was a mere thirteen years older than he. She was also, as the name suggests, not the same person as Sally, Jacob's first wife. Sajner and Gicklhorn, followed by other biographers, have accordingly assumed that she was, in fact, Jacob's second wife (see Sajner, 1968, 170; Gicklhorn, 1961, 41; Schur, 1972, 20; Ellenberger, 1970, 425; and Eissler, 1978).

If we agree with them, we must also accept the authenticity of this particular registration document. That authenticity, however, is not very great, for other verifiable age entries are plainly wrong. We know that Jacob was not thirty-eight in 1852, but at most thirty-seven; Emanuel was not twenty-one but nineteen; and Philipp not sixteen but eighteen. Furthermore, when he eventually married Amalie, Jacob declared that he had been "a widower since 1852" (see note 2 to Table 3). If he was indeed still married to Rebekka on 31 October 1852 (see the date in Table 4), she must have died before December 1852.

Recently, J. Sajner and P. Swales have discovered Rebekka's name in a passport register in Freiberg, where she is recorded under the date of 31 October 1852 as Jacob Freud's thirty-one-year-old wife. But this entry has been crossed out (see Table 5). We might therefore conclude that no Rebekka ever existed, that her name was struck from the passport register, and that the authorities simply forgot to do the same in the Register of Jews. P. Swales, however, believes that the two original entries are clear proof of Rebekka's existence. He assumes that she must have died between October and December 1852, possibly on a journey to Galicia in the company of Jacob, Emanuel, and Philipp, all of whom had been issued with passports. Swales believes that the reason for this journey was Emanuel's marriage to Maria.

We might also suppose that Rebekka's name was struck out in the passport register because her application for a passport had been turned down. In any case, I feel it is more appropriate to speak of Jacob's second marriage to Rebekka as "alleged," for it is possible that she was Sally after all, and that only her name and age were altered. Alternatively, Jacob might well have entered another woman as wife simply to procure her a residence permit in Moravia.[29]

But if we assume that he was indeed married to Rebekka, then we must ask what happened to Sally, the mother of his two sons, whose presence in Freiberg in 1852 is also recorded. Did she die later that very year? Had Jacob divorced her?

It is idle to speculate about the attitude of Jacob's parents—his father, Schlomo, was still alive, and his mother, Peppi, may have been—and of his grown-up sons to this alleged marriage. What seems worth mentioning, though, is that some relatives of Jacob's first wife may have lived in Freiberg in 1852, for several persons with the name of Kanner from Tysmenitz were registered there.[30]

The marriage of Jacob to Rebekka—if indeed there was one—must have been of short duration, because Rebekka is no longer listed as Jacob's wife in the 1854 Register of Freiberg inhabitants (Sajner, 1968, 171) and one year later he was married to Amalie, Sigmund Freud's mother. R. Gicklhorn believes that Jacob may have repudiated Rebekka because she failed to give him a child which, according to Orthodox practice, was a cause for divorce (1969, 41). However, at that time Jacob was most probably no longer an Orthodox Jew; furthermore, the infertility clause applied only if a woman had not borne her husband a child after ten years (Zborowski/Herzog, 1952, 288), so that Gicklhorn's assumption seems unfounded. Besides, Jacob already had two sons from his first marriage.

2.5.3 JACOB'S MARRIAGE TO AMALIE NATHANSOHN

In December 1853, Jacob Freud transferred his business to his son Emanuel while he himself was away in Vienna. Emanuel did not take full charge until January 1854, when he also paid the taxes (District Archives, N. Jičín, according to J. Sajner). It is not known whether this was a temporary transfer or whether the thirty-eight-year-old Jacob retired permanently in favor of his son, as Gicklhorn believes he did (1969, 42). It seems more likely that Emanuel merely managed the business while Jacob was away in Vienna to arrange his wedding to Amalie on 29 July 1855 (see Table 7).[31]

Amalie (Amalia or Malka) Nathansohn (or Nathanson) was born in Brody in eastern Galicia (see Fig. 3). As a young girl she spent several years in Odessa, where two of her brothers, who must have been thirteen and ten years older respectively, had settled (see Table 3). Her parents moved with her to Vienna when she was still a child (Jones, 1953, I, 3).

How did it come about that Jacob, aged forty, married the "virgin" Amalie Nathansohn, who was not yet twenty (see Table 7)? The couple could not have known each other very well, for though Jacob visited Vienna four times in 1854 (Sajner, 1968, 171), it seems most unlikely that they could have developed a close emotional relationship on those few occasions. And even if they had known each other longer, the idea of marriage could not have existed for long, because in 1852 Jacob was still married to Sally or to that mysterious Rebekka.

Was theirs then an arranged marriage, as used to be the rule among Jews? But why should Jacob Nathansohn choose for his daughter a man old enough to have been her father? Was Jacob Nathansohn too poor to give her an adequate dowry, so that she was forced to accept an older man with a seemingly respectable income? Or did the two men, whose difference in age was a mere ten years and who probably did business with each other, agree to this marriage for some business reason? Did they perhaps plan to enter into a partnership?

R. Gicklhorn believes that Amalie was "bartered" by her parents, who were deceived about Jacob Freud's real circumstances in Freiberg. She contends that Amalie was very disappointed when she first saw their one-room apartment in Freiberg, since she and her parents had shared an apartment of one and a half rooms in Vienna (Gicklhorn, 1976, 17–18, 23). However, the difference in size does not appear great; moreover, we do not know how many people were included in Jacob Nathansohn's household.[32] And since most Jews lived in cramped quarters at that time, it could be argued that Jacob was fortunate in having a whole room for himself and his wife.

Jacob's financial situation in 1852–55 is set out in a table listing the turnover of Freiberg importers (Table 6).[33] It is not possible to compute Jacob's actual income from the table, which would have been made up of the difference between the selling and buying prices of the products, less expenses, plus what profits he made in Galicia from the sale of woolen cloth bought in Moravia. Nevertheless a comparison with the other eighteen merchants shows that Jacob was among the top six importers.

Even so, Jacob may well have misled his parents-in-law about his financial situation, for such a great age difference between partners was most unusual among Jews, indeed, not in keeping with the rules of marriage-broking. Amalie, far from being visibly flawed, had marked good looks (M. Freud, 1957, 11), as we can also tell from photographs taken later (see Fig. 17). Did she perhaps have an invisible flaw? We are unlikely ever to discover the answer to such questions.

But we may take it that this marriage marked a new beginning for Jacob, a final break with his old life in Tysmenitz. The wedding was solemnized by Rabbi Mannheimer of the Reform movement (Aron, 1971, 166), a clear sign that the Nathansohns too were *maskilim,* followers of the Enlightenment. Did Jacob seal his complete break with Orthodox Judaism by his last marriage? From an incidental remark made by Freud in *The Interpretation of Dreams,* we know that during his first years in Freiberg Jacob still wore a *shtreymel,* the fur-trimmed hat of Galician Jews, and undoubtedly a kaftan as well (1900a, 197; cf. Simon, 1957, 271). Was it after his marriage that he first discarded these in favor of Western dress, as his later photographs show (see Fig. 16)?[34]

It is also possible that Jacob tried to prove to himself by this marriage that he was not yet an old man, still sexually potent and virile, perhaps because he had no wish to allow his grown-up sons to usurp his position. Emanuel became a father one month after Jacob's wedding (see Table 3). I shall return to the question of what the unmarried Philipp, twenty-one years old, must have thought when his father took a twenty-year-old wife (see 3.1.6 below). Jacob may also have intended partially to free himself from the burden of piety toward his own parents. For in Tysmenitz and on his travels with his father and grandfather, he had surely obeyed the Law and submitted himself to paternal authority. Was it that with his new marriage he began to feel like a patriarch himself, who had to be the sole authority for his sons?

2.5.4 THE DEATH OF SCHLOMO FREUD

Six months after Jacob's wedding, his father died in Tysmenitz. On the memorial page in his Bible he made the following entry in Hebrew:

My father Rabbi [probably "Reb" — Mr., M.K.] Schlomo of blessed memory, son of Rabbi [Reb, M.K.] Ephraim Freud, entered into his heavenly home on the 6th day of the week, Friday at 4 o'clock in the afternoon on the 16th Adar Rischon [5]616, and on the 18th of the same month was buried in the town of Tysmenitz, where I was born. May he rest in his resting place . . . [illegible] until the time of the end, until the day when it shall be said to those who sleep in the dust: "Awake in peace, Amen." According to Christian reckoning he died on 21 February, and was buried on 23 February [1]856 (E. Freud, 1977, 46 and 324).

It is possible but unlikely that Jacob Freud attended his father's burial in Tysmenitz. Thus he was probably unable to fulfill his filial duty of saying *Kaddish* at his father's grave.

I suspect that this event was a crucial experience in Jacob's life; that—not unlike what happened to Sigmund Freud forty years later—his father's death at a time when he himself was turning his back on all the old traditions must have produced deep feelings of guilt. Jacob had become a *maskil,* had cut his links with Orthodox Judaism—to which his father had probably subscribed to the end of his life—and so had betrayed his religion. It is possible that he felt guilty in other ways as well, perhaps in connection with his two marriages away from home.

If Jacob was indeed guilt-ridden, then the birth of the son whom Amalie brought into the world ten weeks later, and whom he called Schlomo in Hebrew and Sigismund in German after his own father, must have been charged with deep emotional significance for him. One can imagine that Jacob hoped through the newborn boy to assuage the guilt he felt toward his own father, to be provided with an instrument of atonement and expiation. I believe that from the moment of his son's birth, Jacob gave him the ambivalent mandate to expunge Jacob's guilt, rooted as it was in the past, but to refrain from uncovering its precise nature.

In Part 3 we shall see how young Freud shouldered this mandate, and how traumatic Jacob's unexpressed feelings and expectations proved to be in his life.

2.6 Conclusions: The "Old Man's" Secret

Let us now attempt, from what sparse biographical material there is, to discover those secrets Jacob tried to keep from his son. Not much can be said with certainty; at best we can advance a number of "if-then" speculations.

What does seem to be established is that there was a break in Jacob's life, and that it occurred when, in his early twenties, he left the traditional Jewish *shtetl* of Tysmenitz and started to travel to Moravia. Because he had been brought up as an Orthodox Jew, and probably because his first marriage had helped to cement his bonds with the Orthodox Jewish community, we may take it that his encounter with the other, non-Jewish, world and also with followers of the Haskalah was a turning point in his life. He eventually embraced the new doctrine and with it the idea of Jewish assimilation.

Since we do not know how his parents, grandparents, and parents-in-law reacted to this change, we can only assume that Jacob had bitter struggles with them, or even that he broke with them. In that case, he would also have broken the sacred commandment to honor one's father and do his bidding. Moreover, he would have committed the grave sin of betraying his Jewish heritage, which according to the Orthodox view can only be preserved by the strictest observance of all divine commandments and by the unquestioned acceptance of the Bible as the revealed Word of God.

Thus, even if he did not fall out with his parents, the break with tradition —which Jacob's was probably the first generation to make—must have filled him with deep guilt, especially at times of crisis or misfortune. Assimilated Jews of the first generation, as Simon (1957, 294) has stressed, freed themselves from the yoke of the Torah but not from the yoke of its morals. It could even be that Jacob engineered such crises to satisfy an unconscious need for punishment.

It is likely that the death of his own father, whose will he most probably did not fulfill, represented just such a crisis; in other words, that the first years of the life of Sigmund Freud were stamped by massive guilt feelings on Jacob's part. Perhaps his stay in Freiberg was so traumatic for little Sigmund precisely because it coincided with the peak of Jacob's own crisis. Perhaps in 1896, when *his* father died, Sigmund Freud not only relived his own childhood trauma but also directly repeated his father's crisis, which had caused that childhood trauma in the first place. He too was then forty years old, just as Jacob had been at the time of his son's birth. There are some indications that Jacob felt guilty not only in a general way for abandoning the old traditions but also for highly personal reasons, namely, his sexual behavior. As a merchant, and still a young man, Jacob was on the road for many months at a time. At such times he was much further removed from the control of his family and of the community than he was at home. Hence it is quite possible that he was guilty of breaking the Seventh Commandment. His concealment of his second marriage to the mysterious Rebekka—if such a marriage ever took place—might well have reflected such guilt feelings.

But even if he withstood this temptation, it must have been very difficult for him on his journeys to observe the biblical injunction against masturbation. It is conceivable that Jacob's "perversion," to which Freud, when he still upheld the seduction theory, tried to trace his own neurotic problems (see 1.2.2 above), was nothing other than masturbation. Because Judaism considers masturbation a grave sin, and because Jacob probably felt the same way despite his new attitude, it is quite conceivable that masturbation accounted for a large part of his guilt.

Perhaps he also reproached himself for having linked his life with so young a woman. That might have struck him as yet another breach of the injunction to be temperate in all things, not least in the sexual sphere, every form of excess being abhorred as "un-Jewish" behavior.

It is almost inconceivable that Jacob should ever have spoken to his son about his sexual lapses—if they were the reason for his feelings of guilt. Jewish fathers did not discuss their own sexuality with their children; sex was the great taboo, and not even liberal Jews were likely to have broken it.[35] To Sigmund Freud, therefore, this part of his father's life would have been a closed book, all the more important to him if his father felt burdened and guilty about it.

And so I am bold enough to suggest that the two central threads running through Freud's entire theoretical and therapeutic work—the subject of sexuality, which was to become the pivot of his theory of human behavior, and the subject of the guilt of the sons toward the father, which can be followed through many of his writings and which became the centerpiece of his last work, *Moses and Monotheism*—were the very areas in which Jacob Freud himself felt beset with guilt.

The better to appreciate that link, we shall now look at Sigmund Freud's relationship with his father and with the other people who cared for him in his childhood.

3. The Trauma:
Sigmund Freud's Childhood
and Youth

A traumatic event in early childhood marked Freud for life and apparently had a direct bearing on the crisis of 1897. That event was the departure of the Freud family from Freiberg in 1859, which Sigmund —he was just three years old at the time—later described as a catastrophe (1899a, 314). To understand why this move to Vienna proved such a blow to him, we must first look at the individuals who were his primary caretakers at the time, at their relationship to him and to one another, and at how they structured his experiences.

The main problem of any such reconstruction is that most of the data have to be taken from the dreams and dream associations which Freud recorded at the age of forty, and passed on to us in severely fragmentary form. Although much of these data can be corroborated by other information, a good deal must remain speculative.[1]

3.1 The Web of Relationships in Freiberg

Freiberg (Příbor), the birthplace of Sigmund Freud, is in northeastern Moravia, now part of Czechoslovakia. The town is less than 150 miles northeast of Vienna (see Fig. 3), with the Silesian and Polish borders only some 25 miles away. Until World War I, Moravia was part of Austria-Hungary. The official language at the time was German, although the population was Czech.[2]

Sigmund Freud was born on 6 May 1856 (see Table 8). At that time Freiberg had 4,500 inhabitants, of whom about 3 percent, or 130 persons, were Jews (Sajner, 1968, 167). Many of these were traders from Galicia, like Jacob. The nearest rabbinate was in Neu Titschein (Nový Jičín), some six or seven miles away; Freiberg itself probably had a simple prayer house only. The nearest Jewish cemetery was in Weisskirchen (Hranice), about twenty miles away (Sajner, 1968, 173).

TABLE 11 The Network of Sigmund Freud's Relationships in the Summer of 1859.[30]

Freiberg

117, Schlossergasse

Father **Jacob**, 43½

Mother **Amalie**, 24

Sigmund, 3

Brother **Julius**, died ½ year old, one year ago

Sister **Anna**, ½

Family **Zajic**, with children

42, Marktplatz

Half-brother **Emanuel**, 26

Aunt **Maria**, 25 or 23

Nephew **Johannes (John)**, 4

Niece **Pauline**, 2½

Niece **Bertha**, ½

House No. 416, opposite No. 117

Half-brother **Philipp**, 24½

Nursemaid **Resi Wittek**
(in jail)

(**Rebekka**, father's second wife,
presumably dead)

Other Jewish families in Freiberg, e.g., the
Fluss family, with children; the **Berisch
Kanner** family. Other people in Freiberg

Tysmenitz

(ca. 350 miles east of Freiberg, in Galicia)

Grandfather **Schlomo**, died 3½ years ago)

Grandmother **Pepi**, date of death unknown)

Sally, father's first wife, presumably dead)

(Great-grandfather **Siskind Hofmann**, presumably dead)

Breslau

(ca. 120 miles north of Freiberg)

Uncle **Abae Freud** and family

Vienna

(ca. 150 miles south of Freiberg)

Grandfather **Jacob Nathansohn**, 54

Grandmother **Sarah Nathansohn**, age unknown

(Uncle **Julius Nathansohn**, died aged 20, one year ago)

Jassy

(ca. 420 miles southeast of Freiberg, in Moldavia)

Uncle **Josef Freud**, 34, with Aunt **Rebekka** and children

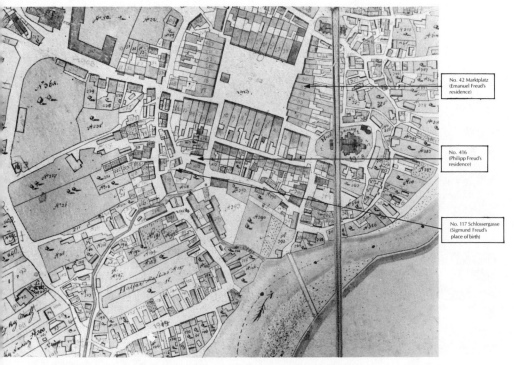

No. 42 Marktplatz
(Emanuel Freud's
residence)

No. 416
(Philipp Freud's
residence)

No. 117 Schlossergasse
(Sigmund Freud's
place of birth)

FIGURE 6 Detail from plan No. 2078 of Freiberg Municipality (1833)
(State Archives, Brno; photograph, Sajner)

FIGURE 7 Panorama of Freiberg (in Czech: Příbor)

PŘÍBOR

FIGURE 8 The vicinity of Freiberg with the Carpatian Mountains in the background

FIGURE 9 The Market Square of Freiberg at about 1890. The house in which Emanuel Freud lived with his family is the first from the left *(photograph, Sajner, Swales)*

FIGURE 10 The house in which Sigmund Freud was born in Freiberg (about 1931) *(Sigmund Freud Copyrights Ltd., Colchester, England)*

FIGURE 11 The staircase in the house in which Sigmund Freud was born (1977) *(photograph, M. Krüll)*

Due to the sensational discoveries of Sajner (1968) and Gicklhorn (1969), there is quite a lot we do know about the way the Freud family lived. The 1883 cadastral map of Freiberg (see Fig. 6) shows the houses in which members of the family resided. Jacob and his wife and children rented a room on the first floor of the house of a blacksmith by the name of Zajíc, who lived in the other room with his family and used the ground floor as a smithy. This house, No. 117 (in Schlossergasse), has changed very little to this day (see Fig. 10).[3] Philipp rented a room in No. 416, directly opposite Jacob's. Emanuel and his family lived in No. 42, on Marktplatz.

For greater clarity, I have tried to show in Table 11 the spatial and age-related network of the relevant individuals in the Freiberg world of little Sigmund. To that end I have included, apart from those still alive at the time, those who had died but had apparently played a role of some importance in Sigmund's life. The relationships are shown as they were in the summer of 1859, shortly before the Freuds left Freiberg. For the exact dates, see the Freud family tree (Table 3).

3.1.1 JACOB, THE FATHER

Having tried in Part 2 to reconstruct the life of Jacob Freud up to the birth of his son Sigmund, I shall now turn to the relationship between father and son in Freiberg.

Jacob named his "second first-born" son after his father Salomon (Schlomo), who had just died. It was the custom of Jews to name their children, not after living parents or relatives, but after a dead person whose memory they wanted to honor. The name Sigismund, which was recorded in the Register of Births (see Table 8), was a Germanization of Schlomo and probably also an evocation of the German word *Sieg* (victory).[4] Freud's parents and close acquaintances probably called him "Sigi," and his mother still referred to him as "Sigi, my gold" when he was himself a grandfather (T. Reik, after E. Freeman, 1971, 80; Jones, 1960, I, 3).

In the family Bible, Jacob made the following entry in Hebrew:

My son Schlomo Sigismund [may he live long] was born on Tuesday [the third day] the 1st day of the month of Iar [5] 616 at 6.30 in the afternoon—6 May [1] 856. He entered the Jewish Covenant [was circumcised] on Tuesday [the third day] the 8th day of the month of Iar—13 May [1] 856. The moel [the man who performs the circumcision, M.K.] was Mr. Samson Frankl [Reb Schimschon Frankel] from Ostrau, the godparents were Mr. Lippa Horowitz [Reb Lippe Hurwitz] and his sister Mirl [Mirel], children of the rabbi from Czernowitz. The sandak [the man who holds the child during the circumcision, M.K.] was Mr. Samuel Samueli [Reb Schmuel Samueli] in Freiberg in Moravia . . . [illegible] 4 . . . ber [1] 856[5] (E. Freud, 1977, 46 and 324, with amplifications by Aron, 1956–57, and Roback, 1957).

No mention is made of any of the other nine (or if we include the deceased Julius, ten) of Jacob's children in that Bible. This fact alone may be taken as evidence that Jacob held Sigmund in particular esteem.

There are other indications as well. In connection with his dream of Count Thun, the so-called revolutionary dream (1900a, 208ff.), Freud recalled an episode from his life that had taken place in Freiberg: "It appears that when I was two years old I still occasionally wetted the bed, and when I was reproached I consoled my father by promising to buy him a nice new red bed in N. (the nearest town of any size]. . . .* This promise of mine exhibited all the megalomania of a child" (1900a, 216f.; partially retranslated from the German).

Little Sigmund, aged two, had clearly faced his father with confidence when proposing restitution for this mishap. He obviously had an anxiety-free relationship with his father since he even tried to console him, which suggests that he may already have realized how important he was to Jacob. Freud, in his own interpretation, only stressed the child's megalomania; but must not the father too have had megalomaniacal expectations of his son for the child to react in the way he did?

The father was certainly proud of his son when he heard of another of Sigmund's "heroic acts." He had been given a hiding by his older and stronger nephew John, but had had the courage to hit back, whereupon the children were summoned before father/grandfather Jacob. Freud reports the scene as follows: ". . . in my later years I have often been told of the short speech made by me in my own defence when my father, who was at the same time John's grandfather, had said to me accusingly: 'Why are you hitting John?' My reply —I was not yet two years old at the time—was, 'I hit him 'cos he hit me' " (*ibid.*, 424f., 484).

One would like to know how Jacob reacted to this reply. But the very fact that both these incidents became part of the stock of family stories shows plainly enough how much delight Jacob took in his son. However, there was still more to the story than meets the eye (see pp. 121f. below).

How may little Sigmund have felt about his father? Jacob was clearly an impressive figure (see Fig. 16). In a passport issued in 1847, his appearance is described as follows: "Figure slim, face oval, hair blond, eyes brown, nose turned up" (Gicklhorn, 1976, Table I, from a copy taken by J. Sajner). Documents from the years 1852–57 recently discovered by J. Sajner and P. Swales in Freiberg confirm this description. Jacob is invariably described as "fair," "of medium build," and with "brown eyes." Martin, Sigmund Freud's son, has described his grandfather as tall and broad-shouldered (1957, 10).

As to his character, Freud himself said that his father was a man of "deep wisdom and imaginative lightheartedness" (1950a, 170), "an interesting human being, intrinsically very happy," that he was a man of "dignity and demeanor" (Schur, 1972, 105); that he had "a sense of humour, a shrewd scepticism about the uncertain vicissitudes of life"; that he was in the habit of "pointing a moral by quoting a Jewish anecdote"; that he was "kindly, affectionate and tolerant, a talented man of above-average intelligence"; and that

* This would be Neu Titschein, according to Jones, 1960, I, 7—M.K.

he was "always hopefully expecting something to turn up" (Jones, 1960, I, 3f., 7, 2). He was often "grouchy" but otherwise "the greatest optimist" (1960a, 40). Freud liked to identify himself with his father and even remarked that "he was the duplicate of his father physically, and to some extent mentally" (Jones, 1960, I, 2; see also Freud's letters to Fliess after his father's death, quoted on pp. 38ff. above).

Freud's son Martin wrote that Jacob "used to tell us stories, mostly with a little twinkle in his great, brown eyes, as if he wanted to say: 'Isn't everything we are doing and saying here a great joke?' " (1957, 10). Freud's sister Anna said of him that her father's motto was to think morally and to act morally. She called him a "happy optimist" and a nature-lover (Bernays, 1930, 5, 8). His granddaughter, Judith Bernays Heller, has also stressed Jacob's humor and his friendly, gentle manner (1956, 419).

It may well be that in Freiberg, when he was forty, Jacob did not yet have the twinkling humor he displayed at eighty; in any case little Sigmund undoubtedly saw him as larger-than-life, the more so as two grown-up men, Sigmund's half-brothers Emanuel and Philipp, looked up to Jacob as well. He was the patriarch of the family and his was invariably the last word. Yet young Sigmund must have known that his own position in the household was a special one, for while his two playmates, John and Pauline, called his father "Grandfather," he was allowed to call him "Father" like the two big men, one of whom was actually the father of his two friends. What is more, the great patriarch was much more attentive and affectionate to him than he was to John, although the latter was much better than he was at sports.

The fact that Jacob was often away on business may also have affected his relationship with his son. We do not know whether Jacob still made regular trips to Galicia at that time or whether he confined his visits to the vicinity of Freiberg, in other words, whether he was away from home for months, weeks, or just a few days at a time.

Another open question is whether Jacob was also a threatening figure in his son's eyes; there are a number of indications that he enjoined little Sigmund not to play with his genitals, and even threatened him with castration if he did. This is borne out first of all by the fact that, in his discussion of child masturbation, Freud seems to take such parental threats for granted (1908c, 270). Moreover, several of Freud's dreams contain associations that point to fear of being castrated by father figures.

In this connection, it must be remembered that the threat of castration is particularly realistic to a Jewish boy, since it is easy to establish a connection between ritual circumcision and castration (see 2.2 above). Freud himself said that "Fear of castration plays an extremely large part, in the case of youthful neurotics whom we come across, as an interference in their relations with their father. . . . When our [Jewish] children come to hear of ritual circumcision they equate it with castration" (1912–13, 153). It is even possible that little Sigmund was present at a circumcision ceremony, and thus had a clear idea of what happens on such occasions, so that he was unlikely to dismiss the threat of castration as just another idle exhortation. There was another reason, too, why he should have taken that threat very seriously: he and his nephew John had recently made the discovery that little Pauline lacked a penis (see 3.1.8 below).

In one of Freud's dreams, the relationship between masturbation and castration is particularly clear:

Old Brücke must have set me some task; strangely enough it related to a dissection of the lower part of my own body, my pelvis and legs, which I saw before me as though in the dissecting-room, but without noticing their absence in myself, and also without a trace of any gruesome feeling. Louise N. was standing beside me and doing the work with me. The pelvis had been eviscerated, and it was visible now in its superior, now in its inferior, aspect, the two being mixed together. Thick, flesh-coloured protuberances (which, in the dream itself, made me think of haemorrhoids) could be seen. Something which lay over it and was like crumpled silver-paper had also to be carefully fished out. . . . Finally I was making a journey through a changing landscape with an Alpine guide who was carrying my belongings. Part of the way he carried me too, out of consideration for my tired legs. The ground was boggy; we went round the edge; people were sitting on the ground like Red Indians or gipsies—among them a girl. Before this I had been making my own way forward over the slippery ground with a constant feeling of surprise that I was able to do it so well after the dissection. At last we reached a small wooden house, at the end of which was an open window. There the guide set me down and laid two wooden boards, which were standing ready, upon the window-sill, so as to bridge the chasm which had to be crossed over from the window. At that point I really became frightened about my legs, but instead of the expected crossing, I saw two grown-up men lying on wooden benches that were along the walls of the hut, and what seemed to be two children sleeping beside them. It was as though what was going to make the crossing possible was not the boards but the children. I awoke in a mental fright (1900a, 452f.).

If we seek the reality content of these dream images, we shall find that some of them probably refer back to Freiberg. First, they have a rural setting; second, Freud is being carried by an adult, which suggests that he was at most three years old; and finally, the two "grown-up men" and the two children could be Emanuel and Philipp and John and Pauline, respectively, in whose joint company he lived in Freiberg and in Freiberg only.

Freud himself tells us that the dissection stood for his self-analysis, in which he had to "give away so much of my own private character."[6] However, as other authors have pointed out (see for example Grinstein, 1968, 436ff.), the dream also introduces clear sexual images. The task of "dissection of the pelvis," which was set him by a father figure, the revered Professor Brücke, is thus a very vivid description of an admittedly rather comprehensive castration.[7]

Perhaps the most significant part of the dream is that Freud could not walk because of that dissection/castration and had to be carried by an "Alpine guide"—another father figure. If one assumes that this dream image corresponds to a real event in Freud's childhood, then it is probable that the father carried his small son, tired of so much running, on his back or on his shoulders.

It is not impossible that the child became genitally excited in the process and frightened because he had been threatened with severe punishment for just that sensation. The fear he felt when his father put him down would then be understandable; in a sense his father must have seemed a "seducer," someone tempting him to enjoy forbidden pleasures.[8]

All in all we may take it that this dream expressed, among other things, Freud's childish fears of being castrated as a punishment for masturbation, a fear he later embodied in his theory of actual neuroses, which after all also asserts that masturbation weakens the sexual potency of men, and hence in a metaphorical sense castrates them (see 1.1.2.2 above).

This theme is also reflected in the dream image of the "wooden house" which, Freud points out, was really a coffin and suggested to him that "children may perhaps achieve what their father has failed to" (1900a, 455). That passage has generally been taken to mean that Freud was thinking here of his own failure. However, the dream image is also reminiscent of that other dream in which Jacob gave him the ambivalent order to close his eye(s). I believe that the forty-two-year-old Freud woke up in a "mental fright" precisely because the dream reminded him again of his father's expectation that he would turn into a scholar and of his own fear that he would be "castrated" as a punishment for masturbation, that is, in a wider sense, become mentally impotent and hence unable to live up to Jacob's expectation.

It is quite likely that Jacob himself already had these fears, for it is most probable that he shared the common belief of his times that masturbation would lead to mental decay. In that case, the discovery that his son, in whom he had placed such great hopes, was guilty of "self-abuse" must have filled him with doubts about all his ambitious plans for Sigmund's future.

If we start from this assumption, then the various urination scenes in Freud's dreams (1900a, 216ff., 468ff., 210, 402), which he himself associated with ambition, must either have been screen memories for masturbation or else conscious attempts to censor the dream content. From the Fliess correspondence, we know that Freud replaced all references to his own sexuality with *"drekkologikal"* (fecal or urinary) statements (see 1.3.2 above), so that conscious censorship is probably the more likely explanation. Now, if these urination scenes were in fact masturbation scenes, then Jacob's reaction becomes much more understandable. He was afraid that "the boy will come to nothing" (*ibid.,* 216). The association of masturbation with ambition is in any case much more convincing than that of urination with ambition.

Freud may have applied his substitution of "urination" for "masturbation" to his father's case as well, for there is a revealing scene in the "Count Thun" or "revolutionary" dream:

Once more I was in front of the station, but this time in the company of an elderly gentleman. I thought of a plan for remaining unrecognized; and then saw that this plan had already been put into effect. It was as though thinking and experiencing were one and the same thing. He appeared to be blind, at all events with one eye, and I handed him a male glass urinal (which we had to buy or had bought in town). So I was a sick-nurse and had to give him the urinal because he was blind. If the ticket-collector were to see us like that, he would be certain to let us get away without noticing us. Here the man's attitude and his micturating penis appeared in plastic form (*ibid.,* 210f.).

By the blind or purblind "elderly gentleman," Freud was really referring to his father. In the dream, he said, he had changed roles out of revenge: he himself had once obeyed the call of nature in his parents' bedroom and been punished for it by his father; now the dream had placed his father in a compromising situation. "The older man (clearly my father, since his blindness in one eye referred to his unilateral glaucoma⁹) was now micturating in front of me, just as I had in front of him in my childhood. In the reference to his glaucoma I was reminding him of the cocaine, which had helped him in the operation,* as though I had in that way kept my promise. Moreover, I was making fun of him; I had to hand him the urinal because he was blind, and I revelled in allusions to my discoveries in connection with the theory of hysteria, of which I felt so proud" (*ibid.,* 216f.).

If I am right in thinking that by urination or micturition Freud was really referring to masturbation, then it becomes obvious why the dream should have filled him with a sense of triumph. Despite his own masturbation, he had achieved success, had developed a theory of hysteria, and had discovered the medical importance of cocaine. However, we must remember these discoveries were no real successes. For when he wrote *The Interpretation of Dreams,* that theory had received no recognition; moreover, he had just discarded his earlier theory of hysteria, the seduction theory, in favor of a new fantasy theory whose validity he still had to establish. His reference to cocaine, too, was not all it seemed to be. True, he had discovered the anesthetic effects of cocaine in 1884; but it was a colleague who was credited with the use of this anesthetic in eye surgery, and Freud later reproached himself severely for having missed that step (see Jones, 1953, I, 88f.; 1900a, 169ff.). One could therefore interpret Freud's associations to this dream fragment equally well as self-reproaches, as the regretful conclusion that his masturbation had stopped him from becoming a famous scientist and thus from keeping the promise he had given his father.

The reversal of the original situation—that his father, not he, was found urinating (masturbating)—might have indicated that Freud was trying to blame his own failure on his father's: because the father, too, had been weak enough to succumb to masturbation, the son had to suffer from the same debility and could not meet the father's expectations.

It is remarkable that, in his associations, Freud should have ignored an important element of the dream, the double attempt at concealment: "I thought of a plan for remaining unrecognized" and "the ticket-collector . . . would be certain to let us get away without noticing us." Might Freud as a child have surprised his father in the act of masturbation? Or had he perhaps merely come upon him during urination but had so startled him as to gain the

* Freud discovered the anesthetic properties of cocaine—M.K.

impression that he had caught him in some forbidden act? The reader must remember that although Orthodox Jews may not show themselves naked to their children, the crowded conditions in the Freuds' Freiberg apartment would have rendered such incidents almost inevitable. Or else the incident might have happened in the course of the traumatic departure from Freiberg, since a station also figured in the dream. In that case, little Sigmund must have had one more terrifying experience to add to all the traumatic events on the day or days of their departure (see 3.2).[10]

Freud's further associations with the above dream fragment all contain reproaches against various father figures:

Handing him the glass [urinal] reminded me of the . . . way in which the father in Zola's *La terre* was treated among the peasants after he had grown feeble-minded.—The tragic requital that lay in my father's soiling his bed like a child during the last days of his life; hence my appearance in the dream as a sick-nurse.—"Here it was as though thinking and experiencing were one and the same thing." This recalled a strongly revolutionary literary play by Oskar Panizza in which God the Father is ignominiously treated as a paralytic old man. . . . My making plans was a reproach against my father dating from a later period. And indeed the whole rebellious content of the dream, with its *lèse majesté* and its derision of the higher authorities, went back to rebellion against my father. A Prince is knows as the father of his country; the father is the oldest, first, and for children the only authority. . . . (1900a, 217, footnote).

Grinstein (1968, 141ff.) has examined these associations at some length, and has shown that the literary references are all to fathers who ruin their sons through their own debility, for example, senility, syphilis, impotence—all weaknesses that can ultimately be traced back to sexual lapses. The sons in these works either suffer passively out of devotion for their fathers, sometimes even sacrificing their lives in the process, or else reject the claims of what, in their eyes, are unworthy fathers, in extreme cases even committing patricide.

In connection with the dream image of the "male glass," Freud mentions that one merry evening in Vienna "a male urinal of the type used in hospitals" was jokingly compared to a "poisoned chalice belonging to Lucrezia Borgia." This association is in line with the rest, for Lucrezia Borgia, daughter of a Pope, was the issue of her father's illicit sexual adventures.[11]

All these reproaches against fathers are clear reflections of Freud's concern with his own father's "perversion," which he had begun to search out during 1896–7. There is no doubt that he assumed his father to have had sexual problems. However, as a three-year-old, he surely would not have been able to hold such ideas. Only much later does he seem to have had some suspicion in that direction, the traumatic departure from Freiberg having probably been a key experience for his toppling of the father ideal. Certain events in Freiberg or during the departure from that town assumed a symbolic significance for him, so that they reappeared in his dreams when he was forty years old. There are several other dreams reflecting Freud's ambivalent feelings toward his father, but this is not the place to analyze them in detail.[12]

3.1.2 AMALIE, THE MOTHER

Freud once called himself the "first-born son of a youthful mother" (1960a, 406). Amalie was barely twenty-one years old when she brought Sigmund, her first child, into the world. Now, while Jacob, or a father figure representing him, appears in very many of his dreams, few if any include Amalie or a mother figure like her. In particular, Freud has reported no dreams in which the mother is the central figure, whereas there are several such dreams about his nursemaid. Whenever his mother does appear in a dream, she is one of two or three mother figures. In "Screen Memories" (1899a, 311; cf. p. 123 below), these are a peasant woman and a "children's nurse," and it is not even clear whether the peasant woman is in fact Amalie and not Maria, Emanuel's wife, because her two children also play a part in the dream. In *The Interpretation of Dreams,* Freud mentions three women: "I went into a kitchen in search of some pudding. Three women were standing in it; one of them was the hostess of the inn and was twisting something about in her hand, as though she was making *Knödel* [dumplings]. She answered that I must wait till she was ready. . . . I felt impatient and went off with a sense of injury" (1900a, 204).

In his interpretation of this dream fragment, Freud explains that the women were the three Fates "who spin the destiny of man." One of them, the "inn-hostess," was "the mother who gives life and furthermore (as in my own case) gives the living creature its first nourishment. Love and hunger, I reflected, meet at a woman's breast." And, as if he wished to emphasize this link between the nourishing and the erotically exciting breast, Freud added an anecdote about a young man who was "a great admirer of feminine beauty," and who, talking of the good-looking wet-nurse who had suckled him as a baby, remarked, "I'm sorry that I didn't make a better use of my opportunity" *(ibid.).* [13] Was Freud implying that he too had looked upon his mother as an erotically exciting person first and foremost, and less as the traditional mother figure who affords her child protection and warmth?

Another reference to the three Fates strengthens this impression. In "The Theme of the Three Caskets," Freud describes the three Fates as follows:

We might argue that what is represented here are the three inevitable relations that a man has with a woman—the woman who bears him, the woman who is his mate and the woman who destroys him; or that they are the three forms taken by the figure of the mother in the course of a man's life—the mother herself, the beloved one who is chosen after her pattern, and lastly the Mother Earth who receives him once more. But it is in vain that an old man yearns for the love of woman as he had it first from his mother; the third of the Fates alone, the silent Goddess of Death, will take him into her arms (1913f, 301).

Once again the protective mother figure is absent. The actual mother is the model for the beloved, for whose love the old man (in 1913 Freud was fifty-seven years old) yearns in vain.

It seems to follow—and other authors have expressed the same opinion (see for example Grinstein, 1968, 191)—that Freud's tripartition of the mother figure is based on the three women who tended him in Freiberg: Amalie, Maria, and Resi Wittek.[14] Of these three women, Amalie was undoubtedly the least experienced. The nursemaid had more experience because of her age, and Maria was already a mother when Sigmund was born and could thus feel superior to her young stepmother-in-law.

If I am right in thinking that Amalie was physically attractive not only to her very much older husband but also to her stepson Philipp, then she was bound to appear a picture of beauty and charm to little Sigmund. These qualities would thus have seemed more pronounced in his eyes than those more normally associated with a mother—maternal love and care—for these he received from another woman, his nursemaid. I think it is reasonable to see the roots of Freud's theory of the Oedipus complex in this rather untypical constellation. Did he not, in fact, raise his own mother relationship to the level of a general principle (see 1.3.1.6 below)?

His nursemaid, as we know from Freud's dreams, exerted a much more incisive influence on his cognitive and emotional development than did his mother. This may well be because when he was only sixteen months old Amalie gave birth to a second son, who died six months later. Although infant mortality was still very high at the time, so that every mother had to take into account the possibility of losing a child, this tragic event could not have passed her by without trace.

Recent searches by P. Swales in the archives of the Israelitic Congregation in Vienna have shown that, exactly one month before the death of her son Julius, Amalie's brother, also called Julius, died at the age of twenty from pulmonary tuberculosis (see Table 3). It is therefore probable that the young mother, having just suffered the loss of her youngest brother, to whom she was presumably close since she named her second son after him, reacted with panic when her baby came down with enteritis. His subsequent death, following so closely upon that of the other Julius, must have been a heavy blow and would certainly have had repercussions on her relationship with two-year-old Sigmund. And if we knew how long Julius Nathansohn had been suffering from tuberculosis, we should be able to tell whether Amalie named her child after a brother whose life was already in the balance.

However, it also seems possible that Amalie was not a particularly warm-hearted woman. Neither Judith Bernays Heller nor Martin Freud, her grand-children, has drawn a very flattering portrait of her. Martin, Sigmund Freud's son, describes his grandmother as a "tornado," and says that she was not a real lady because in his opinion she had few manners. It would seem that even in Vienna she did not speak German but retained her Galician Yiddish speech (Reik, after Freeman, 1971, 80). Her tremendous vitality and her impatience were as impressive as her hunger for life, her indomitable spirit, her intelli-gence, and her astuteness (M. Freud, 1957, 11; 1967, 202). Both grandchildren stress that Amalie was highly emotional and given to frequent outbursts. According to Judith Heller, she was very impulsive, often moody, strident, and domineering. True, she could radiate charm in the presence of strangers, but she was a self-centered tyrant to her family, and vain to boot, as both grandchildren have stressed. Martin Freud states that at the age of ninety she refused to buy a hat that she felt made her look too old (1957, 11; cf. Jones, 1960, I, 3).

Judith Heller calls her grandmother cold-hearted because at the time of the tragic death of her twenty-three-year-old granddaughter Cecilia, the daughter of Rosa Graf, she made no attempt to console the grief-stricken mother, indeed never asked for details of the death (1956, 421). Moreover, both grandchildren were convinced that Amalie exploited and enslaved her unmarried daughter, Adolfine (Dolfi). Roazen, who interviewed many of Freud's relatives and acquaintances who had known her personally, gained the impression that Amalie was "a classic Jewish matriarch" and "a tyrant to her daughters" (1975, 45). According to Judith Heller, she greatly preferred her sons to her daughters, Sigmund serving her as a moral support, and Alexander, who was ten years younger, as an aide in more practical matters.

Both grandchildren agree that she was an impressive figure. Her looks stood her in good stead even in old age, and she had obviously been a great beauty in her youth. Judith Heller was particularly struck by her strength of will and her ability to accept blows of fate. Roazen thinks she was "a tough old bird," as witness her successful fight against tuberculosis, for which she regularly took the cure at Roznau in the Carpathian Mountains, (1976, 45; 1933a, 141; 1969a, 780). Martin Freud calls her one of "the race who fought the German army on the ruins of Warsaw," who showed violence or belligerence instead of the meekness sometimes associated with the Jewish people (1957, 11).[15]

It is not of course reasonable to draw too many conclusions about the twenty-one-year-old Amalie in Freiberg and her relationship with little Sigmund from these accounts by grandchildren of their very old grandmother; all we can say is that their descriptions do not conflict with Freud's dream images of her. Thus he was quite possibly thinking of his own mother when he wrote: "A mother is only brought unlimited satisfaction by her relation to a son; this is altogether the most perfect, the most free from ambivalence of all human relationships. A mother can transfer to her son the ambition which she had been obliged to suppress in herself, and she can expect from him the satisfaction of all that has been left over in her of her masculinity complex" (1933a, 133).

I believe that, to her son, Amalie must have appeared a "masculine" woman in that sense, i.e., one who wanted to have her unfulfilled ambitions achieved by her sons. I also believe that her "golden Sigi" tried to oblige her by outshining his father, in whom she may at first have placed high hopes but who had patently disappointed her. Perhaps Freud's ambition was partly rooted in the wish to be a better partner for her than his father was.

When he called the mother–son relationship "free from ambivalence," Freud clearly meant that it was so for the mother rather than for the son. Amalie no doubt reveled in her son's growing fame. She loved being the center of attention at Freud's birthday parties or other family celebrations, as her two grandchildren have described so graphically. Freud's own relationship with his mother, however, was anything but tension-free, and he would have "attacks of indigestion" before his regular visits to her on Sunday mornings (Jones, 1962, II, 391; Roazen, 1976, 46). We might agree with Roazen that in this he allowed himself to regress to childhood and so to elicit her tenderness. Conversely, we might also interpret this psychosomatic symptom as repressed aggression in response to his mother's excessive demands.

At the same time, Freud had great power over his mother—according to his sister Anna, he had his way with her even as a child. Thus a piano was removed from the Freud home because Sigmund found it annoying, although his mother was fond of playing and the sisters wanted to take lessons (Bernays, 1940, 337).[16]

There could, it is true, have been few signs of all this in Freiberg, where Sigmund's nursemaid was probably still his chief caretaker. However, when she eventually disappeared and he was left with his mother in a new city, he was bound to have ambivalent feelings toward the latter, not least when he compared her to his lost mother substitute. Like his father image, Freud's mother image, too, was probably shattered in the wake of the family's departure from Freiberg.

In contrast to most of Freud's biographers, therefore, I hold that Amalie was not a giving mother figure but one who loved her son demandingly and selfishly. Accordingly, I see the following two of Freud's oft-quoted remarks on the mother–son relationship, not as happy reflections on maternal love but rather as wry comments on maternal exactions. The first can be found in an essay on one of Goethe's childhood memories, and goes as follows: "If a man has been his mother's undisputed darling he retains throughout life the triumphant feeling, the confidence in success, which not seldom brings actual success along with it" (1917b, 156). The second comes in a footnote Freud added in 1911 to *The Interpretation of Dreams:* "I have found that people who know that they are preferred or favoured by their mother give evidence in their lives of a peculiar self-reliance and an unshakeable optimism which often seem like heroic attributes and bring actual success to their possessors" (1900a, 398, footnote).

Freud thus believed that one must be preferred or favored by one's mother or be her darling if one is to attain success in life—but did not say that one has to be *loved* by one's mother to reach that desirable goal. For being a favorite does not mean being loved unconditionally. Did Freud ever imagine that one could also be loved by one's mother without having to satisfy all her demands and expectations, that is, loved "maternally" in the full sense of the word?

Admittedly, we cannot be at all certain that, in both cases, Freud was thinking of his own rather than of Goethe's relationship to his mother, for he is unlikely to have described himself as an "unshakeable optimist"; from his *Autobiographical Study* one would be inclined to agree with Jones that he considered himself "a cheerful pessimist" (Jones, 1962, II, 413).[17] Hence it is conceivable that Freud's identification with Goethe did not include their relationship to their mothers. It is quite likely, therefore, that Freud's biographers went too far in their zeal to present Amalie as a loving mother.[18]

3.1.3 FREUD'S NURSEMAID, RESI WITTEK

Freud's nursemaid, as we have said, played a role of extraordinary importance during his early life in Freiberg. Since R. Gicklhorn's and J. Sajner's researches on her identity, most biographers, including myself, had assumed that she was Monika Zajíc, a member of the family in whose house the Freuds lived. However, J. Sajner and P. Swales have recently discovered an entry in the list of visitors taking the cure at Roznau (see Table 13) which makes it most likely that she was in fact Resi Wittek, by which name I shall refer to her in what follows.

She was "ugly, elderly but clever," a Czech and a Catholic,[19/20] and it is possible that she was solely responsible for little Sigmund at the time of Julius's death and Amalie's new pregnancy followed by the birth of Anna, from April to December 1858. It is not known if Resi Wittek was married and had children of her own, but she had obviously taken little Sigmund to her heart, and he supposed later that he must have loved her in turn (1900a, 248). Perhaps she wanted to make a Catholic of him, for she was always talking to him about church, Heaven, and Hell. So impressed was Sigmund, the little Jewish boy, that he would play the preacher at home in front of his parents, telling them in the course of his sermon "all about how God conducted His affairs."

This, incidentally, is some indication of how liberal Freud's parents really were. In an Orthdox Jewish home, a Gentile nursemaid would never have been allowed to exert so strong an influence on a child (Barta, 1975, 114, and *passim*).

But it is unlikely that Freud's parents exposed their son to such Christian influences deliberately, in order, say, to encourage his assimilation; rather, they most probably did not realize the full extent of Resi Wittek's sway over the young boy's mind. Apparently she spoke to him in Czech, for when Freud later heard a Czech nursery rhyme he remembered it very easily, though he had no notion what it meant (1900a, 196).

I believe that these early contacts with a world to which his parents did not belong, although it was the world of most Freiberg adults and children, all of whom spoke Czech, went to church, and were "different," struck young Sigmund as perfectly natural and at the same time colored his emotional attitudes. The very fact that he knew so little about this "other world" and could only take it in sensuously, in the form of striking images—dark church interiors, burning candles, the solemn atmosphere—must have rendered it all the more fascinating for him.

Above all, his nursemaid—as Freud and his mother remembered—was a clever and wise woman, who loved him and probably conveyed her own world to him with great intuitive power. What he saw and heard became fused with her person into one emotional whole that he would never be able to resolve because Resi Wittek was suddenly to disappear, to be followed soon afterward by the whole of his Freiberg world vanishing into "prehistory." That world and the person of the nursemaid became part and parcel of his unconscious, and as such were only accessible to him in his dreams; consciously he had forgotten everything.

I agree with Grinstein (1968, 76 and 91) that Freud's longing for Rome was the symbolic expression of his wish to regain his Freiberg world. Freud did not visit Rome until 1901, having returned home from places close to Rome on his previous travels through Italy. His was a strange inhibition, and one that also expressed itself in a number of dreams, several of which Freud has examined in his *Interpretation of Dreams* (1900a, 193ff.): all refer to the inaccessibility of Rome. In his dream associations he brought up Hannibal, the Semitic general from Carthage, who also failed to reach Rome and had to turn back at Lake Trasimene—just like Freud himself on one of his trips. "Hannibal and Rome symbolized the conflict between the tenacity of Jewry and the organization of the Catholic Church" (*ibid.*, 196).

Freud realized that his longing for Rome was symbolic of his search for fame, for recognition by the non-Jewish world—that is, of an ambition both parents had probably tried to inculcate in him. In my view, he failed to appreciate that Rome was also a symbol of his wish to return to Freiberg. It seems to me that this was also the unconscious leitmotif of his book on Moses, which he did not finish until shortly before his death (see 4.2 below): the fantasy that Moses was the child of a non-Jewess, of an Egyptian princess, was a mirror of his own fantasy that he was Resi's child. She too was an "Egyptian," a non-Jewess who revered many gods in the shape of saints. His later passion for collecting gods in the form of relics of antiquity might equally have sprung from his identification with his "idol-worshipping" nursemaid.

Religious experiences were not the only explanation of little Sigmund's strong attachment to her. Freud called her his "primary originator," his "instructress in sexual matters," said that she "chided" him for being "clumsy and not being able to do anything," that she washed him in reddish water in which she had previously washed herself, that she followed him up the stairs in their Freiberg house and that he became erotically excited as a result.

Now why did she think Freud clumsy and incompetent? Perhaps it was because of his toilet training, his inability to urinate without wetting the floor? Freud himself put it as follows: ". . . her treatment of me was not always excessive in its amiability and her words could be harsh if I failed to reach the required standard of cleanliness. . . . It is reasonable to suppose that the child loved the old woman who taught him these lessons, in spite of her rough treatment of him" (1900a, 248).

However, because Freud dwelled on the sexual element in these dream associations, we may take it that something else was also involved. Did Resi perhaps manipulate his penis, not simply when teaching him to urinate but on other occasions, too? In his essay on infantile sexuality, Freud wrote: "It is well known that unscrupulous nurses put crying children to sleep by stroking their genitals" (1905d, 180, footnote; cf. 1931b, 232). Did his nursemaid also send little Sigmund to sleep in this way?

If we may take it that the staircase dream was a memory of a real incident, then his nursemaid might have excited him in other ways as well. Further, it is conceivable that Freud was thinking of his experiences with his nursemaid when he wrote: "The 'affection' shown by the child's parents and those who look after him, which seldom fails to betray its erotic nature ('the child is an erotic plaything'), does a very great deal to raise the contributions made by eroticism to the cathexes of his ego-instincts. . . ." (1912d, 181). "A child's intercourse with anyone responsible for his care affords him an unending source of sexual excitation and satisfaction from his erotogenic zones. This is especially so since the person in charge of him, who, after all, is as a rule his mother, herself regards him with feelings that are derived from her own sexual life: she strokes him, kisses him, rocks him and quite clearly treats him as a substitute for a complete sexual object" (1905d, 223). That Freud was thinking of his own experiences may be deduced from the fact that he spoke of "the person in charge of him . . . as a rule his mother," a qualification he might not otherwise have added.

But no matter what Resi Wittek actually did with or to him, Freud himself had the feeling that he had been sexually seduced by her, as we know from his dream of 3 October 1897 (see p. 56 above). There is little doubt but that his nursemaid's relationship with Sigmund had sexual overtones to which the small boy reacted with sexual feelings, for only in this way do Freud's associations to his dreams about the nursemaid become comprehensible. It is quite conceivable that she herself tried to repress these feelings in the child with threats of punishment, because she felt guilty about them. It is equally possible that she thought nothing of playing sexual games with him, but that at one point she was caught by Freud's parents, and that it was not until then that the child gathered that something was wrong. Nor, finally, is it impossible that he was punished either by his parents or by Resi Wittek when he tried to recapture the pleasant sensation his nursemaid had first awakened in him by resorting to masturbation. If that was the case, he must have suffered violent conflicts, for the combination of active stimulation by adults with threats of castration for self-stimulation must have utterly confused him.

The woman who played so crucial a role in little Sigmund's life was later caught in the act of stealing by his brother Philipp, indicted, and sent to prison. Whether all she took was the "shiny Kreuzers and Zehners and toys" his parents had given him and which he in turn had handed over to her (1950a, 221f.; cf. p. 56 above), or whether "considerable thefts in the house" (1901b, 51) were involved, is not clear. What is certain is that this episode occurred early in January 1859, just as Amalie was confined with Anna, who had been born on 31 December 1858. Sigmund, aged two and a half, probably did not understand why Resi disappeared so suddenly, let alone that he himself had contributed to her departure, as witness his dream of 3 October 1897. She was simply gone, and he missed her very much. The picture of a screaming child who asked Philipp to open the box because he was afraid that his mother had been "boxed up" like the nursemaid who had just disappeared (cf. pp. 57f. above, and 1901b, 51), clearly reflects this feeling. That the episode was traumatic is also borne out by the fact that he kept recalling it year after year without really understanding what had happened. The lesson he drew might perhaps be formulated as follows: You must expect mother figures to disappear, and you have good cause to fear that the love you receive and offer in return will suddenly cease to be.

I would not hesitate to trace Freud's cardiac neurosis back to this incident —Freud's own reference to his heart condition in his report of the staircase dream clearly corroborates this view, as Grinstein, too, has emphasized (1968, 196). Separation in early childhood from emotionally important caretakers is, according to Richter and Beckmann (1969), a crucial element in the etiology of all cardiac neuroses.

The central dichotomy in Freud's thinking and feeling, which runs like a red thread through his work—from the earliest psychoanalytical papers to *Moses and Monotheism*—namely, the dichotomy between death and sexuality, or between Thanatos and Eros in his later formulation, may also have its origins in his early separation from his nursemaid. Sexuality as he experienced it at her hands was threatening, dangerous, and caused people to vanish. Freud's "prehistoric old nurse" (1900a, 248) might thus have colored his picture of one of the three Fates, the Goddess of Death. Just as no man can grasp his own death, so the sudden disappearance of the nursemaid who had given him love, warmth, and erotic satisfaction must have seemed incomprehensible to young Sigmund. I believe that, to him, she became a symbol of the great universal mother, meting out love and destruction. That she was not a Jewess but someone from "the other side" contributed significantly to his inner conflicts and lent a particular color to his attitude to the Jewish religion (cf. 4.2 below).

3.1.4 FREUD'S HALF-BROTHER EMANUEL

While in high school, Freud had fantasies of "how different things would have been if I had been born the son not of my father but of my brother" (1901b, 219f.; cf. 1900a, 444, footnote). It is impossible to say whether he first entertained such thoughts at the age of two or three. After all, at that time Jacob was still in the prime of life and in all probability the undisputed head of his family.

We know very little about Emanuel's personal life or appearance, although the researches of J. Sajner and P. Swales in Freiberg have recently shown that in 1855–57 he was of "medium stature," and had "brown hair and brown eyes." He was probably born in April 1833 (see Table 3), grew up in Tysmenitz, and was presumably brought up almost exclusively by his mother, Sally, née Kanner, since his father, Jacob, was away on business most of the time. If Jacob lived *in kest,* which was very likely because he was only seventeen when Emanuel was born, then Emanuel would have grown up in the Kanner household. This would explain his marked independence from his father.

Emanuel seems to have been very fond of his little half-brother. When Freud visited him in England in 1875, Emanuel wrote enthusiastic letters about him back to Vienna (Bernays, 1940, 340). Freud too liked his big half-brother very much (1950a, 321), and in later years felt much more drawn to Emanuel than he did to Philipp. In a letter written to Martha Bernays in 1883 in which he reported what was in fact a meeting both his half-brothers, he almost completely ignored the presence of Philipp (1960a, 92ff.). Freud's first visit to England seems to have intensified their relationship even further (cf. 3.5 below). His "strict eldest brother" enjoined him to show "filial piety" to his father, because "you really belong not to the second but the third generation in relation to your father" (1901d, 227 and 220), a remark that made a great impression on young Freud. In general, Emanuel remained a person Sigmund respected and whose advice he did not dare to ignore.[21] It might also be that Emanuel made him privy to family secrets, perhaps involving his father's past.

In the Freiberg days, Emanuel might well have struck little Sigmund as the ideal husband. "Real" couples were about the same age, without the difference in years of his own parents. Jones believes that from young Sigmund's viewpoint it was not unnatural to "pair off Jacob and Nanny, the two forbidding authorities. Then came Emanuel with his wife, and there remained Philipp and Amalie, who were just of an age" (1960, I, 10). It is not clear whether this passage is a free association on Jones's part, or whether he based it on remarks by Freud in unpublished letters. In any case, Freud was to marry a woman roughly his own age, one who like Emanuel's wife, Maria, came of "good" Jewish stock: a long line of rabbis and Talmudic scholars.

3.1.5 Maria, Emanuel's Wife

Emanuel's wife, Maria (see Table 3), then twenty-three or twenty-five, was the daughter of Rabbi Ferdinand Rokach (or Kokach) and his wife, Babeth Kanner. Ferdinand Rokach lived in Ragewilla (or Ragewitza). Maria was born in Milov (see Table 8).[22]

To Freud, Emanuel's wife might have been the third mother figure, the "companion" in the dream of the three Fates. That would accord with my belief that Emanuel's marriage to Maria served in some way as a model for Freud. However, even without that assumption, it is easy to imagine that Maria, whom John and Pauline called "Mother," acted as a mother to little Sigmund.

3.1.6 FREUD'S HALF-BROTHER PHILIPP

Freud's other big brother, Philipp, was twenty-four in the winter of 1858, and single—he married rather late, at the age of thirty-nine, in England (see 3.5 below and Table 3). Philipp played a special role in the life of little Sigmund because it was he who caught the nursemaid in the act of stealing and had her "boxed up." Why Jacob delegated that task to him is not clear. Possibly he was away from home at the time.

Sigmund probably addressed his half-brother as Philipp, while John and Pauline, Sigmund's playmates, called him "Uncle Philipp." To little Sigmund, too, the connection between "Uncle" and "Philipp" must have been close, as we shall have occasion to observe in connection with several of his dream associations in which the term "Uncle" occurs.[23]

Freud called him his "naughty brother" and mentioned that Philipp was in the habit of answering people in an elusive and punning fashion (1901d, 51), and that at the age of sixty-three he was still fond of "humorous expressions" (1950a, 223). Did Freud then think of Philipp as a joker, as someone who was not to be taken very seriously, and who made fun of other people?[24] All we can be certain of is that Philipp was not someone to whom Freud looked up as he did to Emanuel.

More important to him was Philipp's relationship to Amalie. Several dreams and dream associations suggest that Freud's mother was not indifferent to Philipp and that she had feelings for him, or he for her, or both for each other, which went beyond the normal feelings between stepmother and stepson. In connection with the childhood scene of the "boxed-up" nurse (1950a, 223; 1901b, 51), Freud explained:

> Anyone who is interested in the mental life of these years of childhood will find it easy to guess the deeper determinant of the demand made on the big brother. The child of not yet three had understood that the little sister who had recently arrived had grown inside his mother. He was very far from approving of this addition to the family, and was full of mistrust and anxiety that his mother's inside might conceal still more children. The box or chest was a symbol for him of his mother's womb. So he insisted on looking into this chest, and turned for this to his big brother, who (as is clear from other material) had taken *his father's place as the child's rival.* Besides the well-founded suspicion that this brother had the lost nurse "boxed up," there was a further suspicion against him—namely, that he had in some way *introduced the recently born baby into his mother's womb.* (1901b, 51, footnote, italics added; partially retranslated from the German).

Little Sigmund suspected his big stepbrother of having made a little sister with his mother. To him, Philipp was a rival with whom he had to share his mother's love. It was not his father who had deprived him of his mother, but his big brother. Jones has put it as follows: "Well, there was his half-brother Philipp, so given to joking as Freud himself remarked, whom he suspected of being his mother's mate, and whom he tearfully begged not to make his mother again pregnant" (1962, II, 434; cf. Jones, 1953, I, 10f.).

Elsewhere, Freud produces an association to a dream which points just as unequivocally to a sexual relationship between Philipp and his mother.[25] That dream, he said, was

a very vivid one, and in it I saw *my beloved mother, with a peculiarly peaceful, sleeping expression on her features, being carried into the room by two (or three) people with birds' beaks and laid upon the bed.* I awoke in tears and screaming, and interrupted my parents' sleep. The strangely draped and unnaturally tall figures with birds' beaks were derived from the illustrations to Philippson's Bible. I fancy they must have been gods with falcons' heads from an ancient Egyptian funerary relief. Besides this, the analysis brought to mind an ill-mannered boy, a son of a janitor, who used to play with us on the grass in front of the house when we were children, and who I am inclined to think was called Philipp. It seems to me that it was from this boy that I first heard the vulgar term for sexual intercourse, instead of which educated people always use a Latin word, "to copulate," and which was clearly enough indicated by the choice of the falcons' heads. I must have guessed the sexual significance of the word from the face of my young instructor, who was well acquainted with the facts of life. The expression on my mother's features in the dream was copied from the view I had had of my grandfather a few days before his death as he lay snoring in a coma. The interpretation carried out in the dream by the "secondary revision" must therefore have been that my mother was dying; the funerary relief fitted in with this. I awoke in anxiety, which did not cease till I had woken my parents up. I remember that I suddenly grew calm when I saw my mother's face, as though I had needed to be reassured that she was not dead (1900a, 583f., italics in the original)

Even Jones found it incomprehensible that Freud should, on that occasion, have failed to associate the name of Philipp with his half-brother (1953, I, 9). I assume that he omitted to do so—consciously or unconsciously—because Philipp and Amalie were the chief actors in this scene. In support of the—admittedly tenuous—assumption that Amalie committed adultery with her stepson, it should first of all be remarked that this dream scene involves the observation of sexual intercourse by a child. This emerges from Freud's further associations: "It is, I may say, a matter of daily experience that sexual intercourse between adults strikes any children who may observe it as something uncanny and that it arouses anxiety in them. I have explained this anxiety by arguing that what we are dealing with is a sexual excitation with which their understanding is unable to cope and which they also, no doubt, repudiate because their parents are involved in it, and which is therefore transformed into anxiety" (1900a, 585).

We can therefore suppose with Grinstein (1968, 458ff.) that shortly after the son of the janitor had taught him the meaning of the verb *vögeln,* * nine-and-a-half-year-old Sigmund surprised his parents during intercourse and then had his dream about the figures with birds' beaks. This also suggests that the dream

* To copulate; derived from *Vögel,* meaning "birds"—Trans.

associations of a patient Freud mentions in the same context were either his
own, or very similar to his own. This patient suddenly remembered something
that had happened when he was nine:

> His parents had come home late and had gone to bed while he pretended to be asleep;
> soon he had heard sounds of panting and other noises which had seemed to him
> uncanny, and he had also been able to make out their position in the bed. Further
> thoughts showed that he had drawn an analogy between this relation between his
> parents and his own relation to his younger brother. He had subsumed what happened
> between his parents under the concept of violence and struggling; and he had found
> evidence in favour of this view in the fact that he had often noticed blood in his mother's
> bed (1900a, 584f.).

In particular, the reference to struggling with a younger brother—which
might have been a hidden allusion to a slightly older nephew or a niece with
whom Freud had fought on his own admission (see 3.1.7 and 3.1.8 below)—
makes it reasonable to assume that Freud was in fact writing about himself.
In that case, though, the dream must refer to Freud's childhood in Freiberg.
Did his sex games with John and Pauline then have some bearing on his
observation of his parents during sexual intercourse? In view of the cramped
quarters in which the Freuds lived in Freiberg, this supposition has a high
degree of probability.

But why then did Freud come up with the name of Philipp in this connection? If once again we recall Freud's childhood memories of the box or chest,
we cannot help noticing that he had been anxious about his mother both in
the childhood memory and also in his dream. He screamed, and only calmed
down when he saw that his mother was back. In the chest scene, he suspected
Philipp of making Amalie pregnant. I believe that the "sex education" he
received when he was ten helped him to understand what he had witnessed
at the age of about two or three in Freiberg. We cannot tell, of course, what
really happened, though it is quite possible that little Sigmund actually surprised his mother with Philipp. He may merely have realized that there was
a secret between the two, of which no one must know anything, because it was
something forbidden.[26]

This association of Freud's seems to have been facilitated by the illustrations
in Philippson's Bible (see p. 125 above, 3.3.3 below, and Figs. 19 and 22).
Grinstein (1968) has analyzed the text and the commentaries accompanying
these illustrations. The one mentioned by Freud—an Egyptian funerary relief
—accompanies 2 Samuel 3–4 (Philippson, 1858, II, 394; cf. Fig. 40). It admittedly does not depict gods with falcons' heads, but oddly draped, exceptionally
tall female figures with bare breasts. The relevant Bible passage tells of King
David's grief over the murdered General Abner. According to Grinstein, it is
a tale of "death and castration . . . murder and the possession of a forbidden
woman" (1968, 452).

The text of another illustration, 2 Samuel 19, which contains human figures
with birds' heads (Philippson, 1858, II, 459), deals with a conflict between a

father and his son. In it, Absalom plots against his father, King David, appoints himself king, and sleeps with his father's concubines (2 Samuel 16), whereupon he is killed by King David's retainers. According to Grinstein (1968, 454), the tragic element in this story is the bitter grief King David feels about the execution of his son, although that son wanted to kill him.

These passages thus deal with seduction and punishment, and in a framework not dissimilar to that of the Freud household in Freiberg: King David undoubtedly corresponds to Jacob Freud, who must have seemed a kind of super-father to his little son. Sigmund, for his part, might easily have identified himself with Solomon, the son of David and Bathsheba (2 Samuel 12). This is suggested not only by the fact that both bore the same name but also because it was Solomon who succeeded to the throne of David. Absalom, Solomon's half-brother, was a "naughty" boy: he slept with his father's wives and wanted to usurp the crown. For this sin he was killed. If Freud did in fact feel that Philipp and Amalie had sinned, then he may well have identified Philipp with Absalom.

Freud also makes other allusions to a possible sexual relationship between Philipp and Amalie. Thus, in connection with the forgetting of names, he made the following comment:

> I have a whole quantity of examples to illustrate further the positively predatory activities of the *"family complex."* There came to my consulting-room one day a young man who was the younger brother of a woman patient. I had seen him countless times and used to refer to him by his first name. When I wanted to speak about his visit I found I had forgotten his first name *(which was,* I knew, *not at all an unusual one),* and nothing could help me to recover it. I thereupon went out into the street to read the names over the shops, and recognized his name the first time I ran across it. The analysis of the episode showed me that I had drawn a parallel between the visitor and *my own brother,* a parallel which was trying to come to a head in the repressed question: *"Would my brother in the same circumstances have behaved in a similar way, or would he have done the opposite?"* The external link between the thoughts concerned with my own and with the other family was made possible by the chance fact that in both cases the mothers had the same first name of *Amalia.* Later in retrospect I also understood the substitute names, Daniel and Franz, which had forced themselves upon me without making me any wiser. These, like Amalia, too, are names from Schiller's [play] *Die Räuber,* which were the subject of a jest made by Daniel Spitzer. . . . (1901, 23f., italics added).

Freud unfortunately did not make it clear to which of his brothers he was referring in this passage, but it seems more than likely that he meant Philipp.[27] If my assumption is correct, then Freud once again coupled Amalie and Philipp in one of his associations. Moreover, Schiller's *Die Räuber* is a family drama with great similarities to the assumed entanglements in the Freud family.[28]

All these similarities, to which we must add the Hamlet theme and last but not least the Oedipus legend (cf. 1.3.1 above), are treated by all Freud's biographers, and also by himself, as expressions of Oedipal fantasies. But are they, in fact, pure fantasies without any basis in reality? I do not believe it would have occurred to young Sigmund to try to possess his mother without further ado had he not had the "model" of Philipp before him. I believe that it was only after Philipp disappeared that he directed incest-wishes at his mother, putting himself, so to speak, in the place of his mother's lost lover. Little Sigmund, in fact, looked upon his mother as a desirable object only after their departure from Freiberg. Thus he informed Fliess that his "libido towards matrem" was aroused during a journey with her from Leipzig to Vienna, when "we spent a night together, and I must have had the opportunity of seeing her nudam" (1950a, 219; cf. p. 55 above, and 3.2). During that journey, incidentally, which took place in the winter of 1859, his mother would have been visibly pregnant, for Freud's sister Rosa was born on 21 March 1860 in Vienna. Was it on this occasion that little Sigmund developed the fantasy of occupying the place Philipp had vacated in her affections, not least because Amalie was turning increasingly to him?

We might perhaps go further still and claim that, for little Sigmund, Philipp became the embodiment of the power and danger of sexuality. For if my assumption is correct and Jacob sent his sons to England in order to separate Philipp and Amalie (see 3.2 below), among other reasons, then Philipp was indeed punished with banishment for his unbridled instinctuality. From his brother's enforced exile Freud might have drawn the lesson that, to avoid being castrated or destroyed by one's father, it is best to repress one's instincts and desires. Freud's image of the primal horde, of the sons' rebellion against the imposition of abstinence by their primitive father, would then stem from his own family life (cf. 4.1.2.2 below).[29]

3.1.7 FREUD'S NEPHEW JOHANNES (JOHN)

Freud invariably refers to Johannes (Hebrew: probably Jochanan), the son of Emmanuel and Maria, as John, probably because that was the name by which the boy was later known in England. John was born on 13 August 1855 (Opava State Archives, according to Sajner), and was thus nine months older than Sigmund. The two children seem to have been like brothers, playing happily with each other but also often quarreling and fighting. The younger of the two remembered that their relations were "sometimes friendly, but sometimes warlike" (1900a, 198), that they had "loved each other and fought with each other" (412, cf. 231), that they were "inseparable friends" but also "fought and denounced each other" (483), and that the elder was his earliest "friend and opponent" (486). He wrote to Fliess that John was his "companion in crime" (1950a, 219; cf. p. 55 above).

John certainly set the tone, and the younger boy looked up to his more "experienced" nephew. But at some point Sigmund must have discovered that "big" John was far from indomitable:

The two children had a dispute about some object. (What the object was may be left an open question, though the memory or pseudo-memory [sic] had a quite specific one in view.) Each of them claimed to have *got there before the other* and therefore to have a better right to it. They came to blows, and might prevailed over right. On the evidence of the dream, I may myself have been aware that I was in the wrong. . . . However, this time I was the stronger and remained in possession of the field. The vanquished party hurried to his grandfather—my father—and complained about me, and I defended myself in the words which I know from my father's account: "I hit him 'cos he hit me" (1900a, 483f., brackets added).

It is a pity that Freud gives us no indication what the object of the fight might have been. All we are told is that he felt in the wrong but nevertheless received the approval of his father, who apparently took his son's word rather than his grandson's. We do not know how John reacted to this rebuff, and whether Emanuel backed his son, or whether he too sided with Sigmund.

In any case, when John was older, he was either sent away from home or himself left his parents, with no further contact between them. The Freud family tree (S. Freud Archives, New York) bears a note to the effect that John disappeared when eighteen years old, but gives no further details. Other references, however, including one by Freud himself in a letter he wrote in 1897 (see p. 55 above) and in a letter to Silberstein written in 1875 (see p. 158 below), suggest that John did not disappear at the age of eighteen but somewhat later. In any case, John's disappearance remains unexplained.

The two boys received special attention from the rest of the family, no doubt because they, so to speak, embodied the complicated family relationships. We may take it that the boys realized this, and that they adapted their behavior to suit the conflicting wishes, emotions, and quarrels of the grown-ups around them. Not only the two fathers and "Uncle" Philipp, but also the two mothers and the nursemaid could very easily have projected their mutual likes and dislikes onto these two children, which the latter were then forced willy-nilly to act out. This was probably the main reason for Sigmund's highly ambivalent attitude toward John.

When associating to dreams, Freud also remembered games with John that went further than the occasional harmless scrap. In particular, the two of them played forbidden games—and in the full knowledge that they were doing wrong. As the reader will see below (3.1.8), these games were probably sexual and involved their two-year-old-niece/sister Pauline. But it is equally possible that the two boys played homosexual games, competing, for instance, as boys are wont to do, to see who could urinate further, or touching each other's genitals in play. They seem to have been caught in the act, possibly after Sigmund betrayed them, since, in connection with the *"Non-vixit"* dream he reproached himself for being unable to keep anything to himself and traced these feelings of treachery back to the memory of a childhood situation:

. . . my warm friendships as well as my enmities with contemporaries went back to my relations in childhood with a nephew who was a year my senior; how he was my superior, how I learned to defend myself against him, how we were inseparable friends, and how, according to the testimony of elders, we sometimes fought with each other and—made complaints . . . about each other. All my friends have in a certain sense been re-incarnations of this first figure who *"früh sich einst dem trüben Blick gezeigt"* [Goethe, *Faust* Dedication]: they have been *revenants* [people returned from the grave, ghosts, M.K.]. My nephew himself re-appeared in my boyhood, and at that time we acted the parts of Caesar and Brutus together. My emotional life has always insisted that I should have an intimate friend and a hated enemy. I have always been able to provide myself afresh with both, and it has not infrequently happened that the ideal situation of childhood has been so completely reproduced that friend and enemy have come together in a single individual—though not, of course, both at once or with constant oscillations, as may have been the case in my early childhood (1900a, 483).

It is impossible to determine whether, in this account of his relationship to John, Freud deliberately used words that normally refer to homosexual relationships,*[30] but we do know from Jones that Freud admitted to having had "unruly homosexual feelings," for instance, for Jung and Fliess. We may take it that both were "revenants" of John (Jones, 1953, I, 317).

Freud was to repeat this pattern—friendship with almost slavish dependence on an apparently superior man, followed by hostility and guilt feelings, together with a compulsion to justify himself—several times in his life, particularly in his relationship with Wilhelm Fliess. From Schur, we know of an event that had many parallels to an incident in Freiberg. I am referring to the Anna–Emma–Irma episode, in which Fliess performed an operation on a friend of the Freud family and failed to remove a length of iodine gauze from the wound (see 1.1.2.3 above). To Freud, this event must have been reminiscent of the scene with John and Pauline in Freiberg (see 3.1.8 below), and hence evoked the same reaction: the end of a friendship and reproaches mixed with guilt feelings.[31]

In childhood, however, Sigmund must also have had a feeling of triumph, for shortly after the event John left the field to him and disappeared from Freiberg. Freud admitted that he was glad to have survived him, that John, not he, had been eliminated: "Thus it seemed to me quite natural that the *revenants* should only exist for just so long as one likes and should be removable at a wish" (1900a, 485).

3.1.8   FREUD'S NIECE PAULINE

Pauline, the daughter of Emanuel and Maria, was born on 20 November 1856 in Freiberg (see Table 8) and was therefore seven and a half months younger than Sigmund, which made her just two years old in the winter of 1858. In a letter to Fliess, Freud admitted that he and John treated her "brutally" on occasion (1950a, 219 "brutally" retranslated from the German).

* For example, "warm friendship," which in German has clear homosexual connotations— Trans.

What exactly the two boys did with the girl is something we can only guess at, largely by using Freud's remarks in his *Screen Memories:*

> I see a rectangular, rather steeply sloping piece of meadow-land, green and thickly grown; in the green there are a great number of yellow flowers—evidently common dandelions. At the top end of the meadow there is a cottage [in German: farmhouse, M.K.] and in front of the cottage door two women are standing chatting busily, a peasant-woman with a handkerchief on her head and a children's nurse. Three children are playing in the grass. One of them is myself (between the age of two and three); the two others are my boy cousin, who is a year older than me, and his sister, who is almost exactly the same age as I am. We are picking the yellow flowers and each of us is holding a bunch of flowers we have already picked. The little girl has the best bunch; and, as though by mutual agreement, we—the two boys—fall on her and snatch away her flowers. She runs up the meadow in tears and as a consolation the peasant-woman gives her a big piece of black bread. Hardly have we seen this than we throw the flowers away, hurry to the cottage and ask to be given some bread too. And we are in fact given some; the peasant-woman cuts the loaf with a long knife. In my memory the bread tastes quite delicious—and at that point the scene breaks off (1899a, 311).

S. Bernfeld (1946) has shown that this scene represents a genuine childhood memory, in other words, that the two "cousins" were John and Pauline. Whether the peasant-woman was Freud's mother or Maria, the mother of the other two children, is impossible to say. If that scene—a sloping meadow and a house with a door giving onto it—represented a real place in Freiberg, then it could not have been 117, Schlossergasse, the house in which Freud was born, or Emanuel's house at 42, Marktplatz, for neither had a large sloping garden at the back (cf. Figs. 6 and 10). Probably, then, the event took place in a peasant's house, and the peasant-woman was someone to whom Freud's nurse-maid had taken the children. We cannot say whether or not that nursemaid was Resi Wittek.

From Freud's remarks about the flowers, we can tell during which season this episode occurred: dandelions flower in April or May depending on weather conditions. In other words, this screen memory refers to an event that took place in April or May 1859—a year earlier, Pauline would have been only one and a half years old and much too small to pick a real bunch of dandelions. Sigmund was therefore three or just coming up to three, John was three and three quarters, and Pauline was two and a half. In that case, the nursemaid could not have been Resi Wittek, who had been sent to prison for ten months in January 1859.

Freud produced the following association to this dream: "Taking flowers away from a girl means to deflower her" (1899a, 316); "the most seductive part of the whole subject . . . is the picture of the marriage night" *(ibid.);* "being helped in deflowering someone" (p. 319). Can we take it then that John and Sigmund tried to deflower little Pauline? In that case they must have had fairly accurate knowledge of the female genitals and of the nature of sexual intercourse, which seems most unlikely in children of their age. A more probable explanation is that both of them were simply curious to find out what a girl looked like "underneath"; or that John was keen to demonstrate to an incredulous Sigmund something he had seen earlier. It is also possible that both boys were persuaded to make this investigation following the recent birth of their sisters: Sigmund's sister Anna had been born in December, and Bertha, John's sister, in February. Both boys must therefore have been puzzling about where the two new babies had sprung from.

In any case, they had some difficulty in carrying out their "investigation" of Pauline, who seems to have resisted, otherwise she would not have run away screaming in the end. Sigmund and John had to "fall upon her" in order to have a closer look.

In his *Interpretation of Dreams,* Freud describes the dream of "a man" which might have been a continuation or a part of the same screen memory:

He saw two boys struggling—barrel-maker's boys, to judge by the implements lying around. One of the boys threw the other down; the boy on the ground had ear-rings with blue stones. He hurried towards the offender with his stick raised, to chastise him. The latter fled for protection to a woman, who was standing by a wooden fence, as though she was his mother. She was a woman of the working classes and her back was turned to the dreamer. At last she turned round and gave him a terrible look, so that he ran off in terror. The red flesh of the lower lids of her eyes could be seen standing out (1900a, 201).

In his interpretation, Freud explained that the boy on the ground, the one with the earrings, represented a prostitute. "The other boy was called Marie (i.e., was a girl)." The woman who gave the dreamer a terrible look was stooping to micturate. Her gaping genitals, reminiscent of something "seen in his childhood," appeared in subsequent memories as "proud flesh"—as "a wound." Freud went on to explain that his dream combined two opportunities the man had had as a little boy of seeing the genitals of girls: when they were thrown down and when they were micturating. Moreover, it emerged that he had a recollection of being chastised or threatened by his father for the sexual curiosity he had evinced on such occasions *(ibid.).* If Freud himself was indeed the dreamer of this dream, then the opportunity when the little girl was thrown down so that he could look at her genitals may have occurred in the dandelion meadow.[32]

Because they had been told that masturbation would be punished with castration, the two boys, and particularly little Sigmund, must have felt horrified when they saw the rosy, woundlike genitals of little Pauline in the place of a penis. Characteristically, Freud's association in "Screen Memories" led him from defloration to masturbation. Freud asked his fictitious subject, who was none other than himself, to produce associations to another screen memory, that of a child pulling off a branch from a tree while he was on a walk, and of his being helped to do it by someone. The answer he gave himself was: "in German 'to pull one out' is a very common vulgar term for masturbation" (1899a, 319).

If we can take it that this association—which Freud placed in the mouth of his *alter ego*—was in fact his own, then he himself must have linked castration with masturbation, the phrase "pulling one out" applying to both acts. The child Sigmund had suddenly been brought to the realization that castration was no idle threat by adults but had, as it seemed to him, actually been performed on Pauline. The peasant woman standing in front of the house and holding a knife could then have become his symbol of the castration threat. If she was the mother of John and Pauline, it was she who had circumcised Pauline; if she was his own mother, then she was waiting to perform the same operation on him! Even if she was a stranger, the mere fact that she held a knife in her hand probably sufficed to turn her into the symbol of the terrible threat. Freud himself has described a child's thought processes in this type of situation as follows:

Infantile sexual researches begin very early, sometimes before the third year of life. They do not relate to the distinction between the sexes, for this means nothing to children, since they (or at any rate, boys) attribute the same male genital to both sexes. If, afterwards, a boy makes the discovery of the vagina from seeing his little sister or a girl playmate, he tries, to begin with, to disavow the evidence of his senses, for he cannot imagine a human creature like himself who is without such a precious portion. Later on, he takes fright at the possibility thus presented to him; and any threats that may have been made to him earlier, because he took too intense an interest in his little organ, now produce a deferred effect. He comes under the sway of the castration complex (1916–17, 317; Cf. 1908c, 1909b, 1924d, 1925).

The fact that Freud must have been thinking of his own case becomes clear from the phrase "before the third year of life" and the remark that a boy makes the discovery of the vagina "from seeing his little sister or a girl playmate." It is striking how often Freud in his theoretical writings keeps generalizing his own, quite specific experiences, implying that they are valid for all human beings. Apparently his childhood memories had so strong a hold on him that he focused his theoretical searchlight exclusively on them and ignored the experiences of all others. The result was a highly unrealistic conception of female sexuality, which he completely ignored in the above account of infantile sexuality. Much as he did with his Oedipus theory, Freud now declared the castration complex, too, a universal phenomenon shared by all children, for had he not done so he would undoubtedly have been forced to delve more deeply into his own relationship with his parents, something he had to avoid at all costs.

Regrettably, Freud omitted to tell us in "Screen Memories" what sensations he had during the meadow incident. It would, however, seem that the exaggerated delight he took in the taste of the bread was a screen memory for his anxiety; perhaps in this sense that he was relieved at the discovery that he still had his penis. Sigmund may then have resolved never to masturbate again so as to escape castration. Since nothing had happened, as yet, he did not have to remember the anxiety he certainly felt at the time, but only the lesson he drew from it:—you must not masturbate. The lesson could be stored in the memory as a positive feeling: all will be well so long as you never masturbate.

Pauline thus became the living proof of the dangers of masturbation: they might "pull his own off" as well. I shall try to demonstrate that the Freuds' departure from Freiberg, which followed soon afterwards, assumed a symbolic significance thanks to his experience with Pauline, and that this experience rendered the event truly traumatic for little Sigmund. In "Screen Memories," he merely hints at the link: his *alter ego* mentions "two small occurrences during the railway-journey" from his birthplace. These incidents, he said, came up in the analysis of "my phobia." That this remark might be a reference to Freud's own travel anxiety is something Bernfeld has already stressed (1946, 16).

Like John, Pauline was a figure Freud kept re-encountering; in other words, she was another *revenant*. Thus there is little doubt but that Emma Eckstein (the Anna–Irma–Emma mentioned in 1.1.2.3), was a reincarnation of Pauline. Freud and Fliess secretly "doctored her up," much as John and Sigmund had "doctored up" Pauline. Freud's panic when he realized how careless his friend had been during that operation was certainly a direct repetition of the emotions he had felt when playing with John and Pauline.[33]

3.1.9   FREUD'S SISTER ANNA

The birth of his sister on 31 December 1858 was something of which Freud retained no memory (1899a, 310), although the birth and lying-in undoubtedly took place in the family's single-room apartment. We may therefore take it that two-and-a-half-year-old Sigmund observed certain things that struck him as being uncanny and frightening although he did not consciously remember them.[34]

As I mentioned earlier (3.1.6), he had the vague feeling that his brother Philipp was Anna's father. Did he reach that conclusion all by himself, or did he overhear some remark? Did he perhaps have some tangible evidence for his suspicions?[35]

In any case, Freud does not seem to have been particularly fond of Anna. Rosa and Adolfine were his favorite sisters (Jones, 1953, I, 10). In later years, Anna was jealous of her brother, as we know from her memoirs. She begrudged him privileges at home which she felt he enjoyed at the expense of his five sisters. In particular, he usually had his way even if it ran contrary to the interest of his mother and his sisters. On the other hand, it would seem that Anna was able to stand up to him much more forcefully than her other sisters (Bernays, 1940).

In Freiberg, Anna was, of course, a mere infant, and their later dislike can at best have been fostered there. Was it jealousy, rage at the fact that the baby should have taken up so much of his mother's time and attention? Did he feel that, having just lost his nursemaid, he was in danger of being rejected by his mother as well? It is even possible that little Sigmund blamed the baby for all the changes in his life that had followed her arrival.

Grinstein (1974; 1968) believes that later on, in Vienna, he played the same game with Anna as he had played in Freiberg with Pauline. To some extent, therefore, Anna may be called the first reincarnation of Pauline.[36]

3.1.10 FREUD'S BROTHER JULIUS

Julius was born in October 1857,[37] as we know from the official record of his death (see Table 10), which states that he died on 15 April 1858 at the age of six months from "bowel infections," and that he was buried in the Jewish cemetery at Weisskirchen (Hranice), some twenty miles from Prague.

Sigmund was seventeen months old when Julius was born. Since children of this age do not yet have much command of language, Sigmund could not have put his feelings about his new brother into words. And at the time of his brother's death he was just two years old and still incapable of communicating his feelings verbally.

Freud nevertheless claimed later that his brother's birth and death had been of great importance to him. "I can only say . . . that I welcomed my one-year-old brother (who died within a few months) with ill wishes and real infantile jealousy, and that his death left the germ of guilt in me" (1950a, 219). In his analysis of one of Goethe's childhood memories (1917b, 151ff.), Freud explained that at the age of fifteen months Goethe could not possibly have made his newly born sister an "object of jealousy," but that he must have reserved his hatred for siblings born later. I believe that this explanation also applied to Freud himself—that he was jealous not of Julius, but of Anna, born a year later (see 1916–17, 204f.; 1908c, 212f.).[38]

Hence it is impossible to tell how Sigmund felt about his brother's death. Since he was probably being looked after by his nursemaid at the time, his life could not have been changed very drastically by that event—the nursemaid must have shielded him from what would have been a traumatic experience had he been in his mother's exclusive charge. This "shield" was all the more necessary if we can take it that Amalie was already in mourning for her brother Julius, who had died one month earlier.

3.1.11 REBEKKA, JACOB'S SECOND WIFE

I have said that it cannot be established whether or not Jacob took a second wife, Rebekka, before his marriage to Amalie. If Rebekka really did exist, it would be of interest to know whether little Sigmund had heard anything about her. According to Schur, Freud had no conscious knowledge of her. "The fact of this secret is important enough, however, to warrant our searching carefully through Freud's reports about his self-analysis, his letters, reconstructions and dreams" (1972, 21). Jacob's sons Philipp and Emanuel, as well as Emanuel's wife Maria, would have known of her existence, and almost certainly Amalie too, since a secret of that sort could not have been hidden from her. I would also suggest that it would be natural for all those in Freiberg who had had any dealings with Jacob from 1852 to 1854 to have been aware of this marriage, so that had Jacob really wanted to conceal his alliance with Rebekka he would certainly not have moved with Amalie to Freiberg.

Schur has searched Freud's writings for references to this mysterious person. In this connection he cites an "absurd dream" Freud mentions in *The Interpretation of Dreams* (1900a, 435ff., 441ff.; Schur, 1972, 184ff.). That dream goes as follows:

I received a communication from the town council of my birthplace concerning the fees due for someone's maintenance in the hospital in the year 1851, which had been necessitated by an attack he had had in my house. I was amused by this since, in the first place, I was not yet alive in 1851 and, in the second place, my father, to whom it might have related, was already dead. I went to him in the next room, where he was lying on his bed, and told him about it. To my surprise, he recollected that in 1851 he had once got drunk and had had to be locked up or detained. It was at a time at which he had been working for the firm of T——. "So you used to drink as well?" I asked; "did you get married soon after that?" I calculated that, of course, I was born in 1856, which seemed to be the year which immediately followed the year in question (1900a, 435f.).

Freud has given detailed interpretations of this dream. From a critical analysis of these,[39] Schur concludes, and I would agree with him, that the dream points clearly to Rebekka. "Could it be that Freud was really asking his father who[m] he had married 'soon after' 1851? Could the 'conclusions' he was drawing in the repetitive search for the wish-fulfillment that 'four to five years don't matter' be an expression of the same theme? Could his association about his patients who used to parody his claim of the importance of early memories by saying that they were ready to look for recollections 'dating from a time at which they were not yet alive' also refer to this unknown wife of his father, about whom he perhaps had learned during his 'prehistoric' time in Freiberg? Finally, could this mysterious date, 1851, also have contributed to Freud's preoccupation with the critical age of 51?" (Schur, 1972, 190).

I have already pointed out (p. 54 above) that the crucial letter to Fliess in which Freud explained his "renunciation" of the seduction theory contains a strange sentence to which Schur also draws our attention: "Rebekka, you can take off your wedding-gown, you are not a *Kalle* [bride—M.K.] any longer..." (1950a, 218, retranslated from the German; Schur, 1972, 191). Was this sentence cut short by the editors of the Fliess letters, or did Freud himself end it with three dots? In any case, Schur seems to have been familiar with the Jewish joke in which the phrase occurs, and explains its point as follows: "You were once a proud bride, but you got into trouble, the wedding is off— take off your bridal gown" *(ibid.).*

Schur, too, was puzzled: "Why just this joke at this time? Why a joke in which Freud identifies himself with a disgraced woman? And a joke, the punch line of which contains the name of this mysterious second wife of his father?" (1972, 191). Was Rebekka perhaps Jacob's great secret, to which his son had to close his eyes? Had Jacob tried to conceal from his son his lapse with Rebekka or his rejection of one wife in favor of another? And did Freud perhaps remember her name in his renunciation letter because it was indeed on her account that he had to stop his search into his father's past, a search his seduction theory would have forced him to continue?

FIGURE 12 Josef Pur, Municipal Medical Doctor in 1857 (Announcement Leaflet of the Town of Freiberg) *(photograph, J. Sajner)*

3.1.12 OTHER CONTACTS IN FREIBERG

The Freud family undoubtedly had close links with other Jewish merchants and their families in Freiberg. Sigmund's friends included the sons of the Fluss family from Tysmenitz (see 3.4 below). Emil Fluss and he were the same age (see Table 8), and it is possible that the Fluss children were his playmates. Moreover, it is probable that other Jewish families in Freiberg were related to the Freuds, for instance, the family of Berisch Kanner (see p. 93 above and Table 6). Freud must thus have been familiar with the sounds of Yiddish, the language all Galician Jews spoke among themselves, and which, we may take it, Jacob and Amalie spoke to each other. We know that Amalie spoke Yiddish even in her old age (T. Reik, after E. Freeman, 1971, 80).

Important Gentile figures in young Sigmund's life certainly included the Zajíc family, in whose house the Freuds lived. Johann Zajíc, the son of locksmith Zajíc, was Sigmund's senior by a few years, and remembered young Freud many years later as a "plucky well-developed, lively and deft boy," who liked to visit the locksmith's shop, and who had exceptional "manual dexterity and imagination when it came to fashioning toys out of tin off-cuts" (communication by Mrs. Balcárková, daughter of Johann Zajíc; in J. Sajner, 1968, 173). The one-eyed Freiberg physician—whose name, according to J. Sajner, was Dr. Josef Pur, and who was also the mayor of the town—was probably present during the death of Freud's brother Julius, and treated two-year-old Sigmund when he fell and cut his chin, thus becoming an important person to him (1900a, 17, 560; 1916–17, 201; 1950a, 222; and Sajner, 1968, 175, see Fig. 12).

3.1.13 RELATIVES OF FREUD'S FATHER IN TYSMENITZ, JASSY, BRESLAU, VIENNA, AND ELSEWHERE

As far as we can tell, Freud himself never visited Tysmenitz. But as a child he must have heard about his relatives there, for it is likely that Jacob, Emanuel, and Philipp were still traveling in Moravia and Galicia on business.

There is no doubt that little Sigmund was told things about his grandfather Schlomo after whom he was named, and also about his grandmother Pessel (Peppi), who might still have been alive in the winter of 1858. However, he probably never met his grandparents and so would not have had the important experience of seeing his own father treated as a child. In Freiberg, Jacob was the oldest member of the family, and there was no one to diminish his towering importance in the child's eyes. Hence Sigmund must have been all the more shocked in Vienna when he heard his other grandfather, Amalie's father, rebuke Jacob in his presence (see 3.3.1 below).

Possibly Sigmund also learned about Sally, Jacob's first wife. It seems unlikely that she was still alive in the summer of 1859, in other words, that she had been divorced by Jacob (see 2.4 above). But little Sigmund might just as well have known nothing at all about her existence. Did he know anything about his great-grandfather Siskind Hofmann? After all, Siskind had been in Feiberg quite often with Jacob, and before that with Schlomo (cf. 2.4 and 2.5 above), and Sigmund could easily have learned something about his great-grandfather from family friends in Freiberg. We do not know where and when Siskind Hofmann died, but he may still have been alive in 1859. However, at that time he certainly did not live in Freiberg, because he is not listed in the local Register of Jews.

We know the precise number of Freud's uncles and aunts on his father's side from P. Swales's researches (see Table 3). Jacob, who was probably the oldest son of Schlomo and Pessel Freud, had two brothers and one sister. Abae Freud was a wool merchant in Breslau. Freud had only "seen him three times in my life, on each occasion for a quarter of an hour" (1960a, 222). In 1859, the other brother, Uncle Josef, probably lived with his wife and children at Jassy on the River Moldau (Vltava), and it is quite possible that Sigmund met both uncles during visits they may have paid Jacob in Freiberg—both were merchants and spent much time on the road. We may also take it that Jacob visited his brothers in their respective homes, for we know that he went to Breslau several times in 1847. It is even possible that Uncle Josef, who was later involved in the counterfeiting affair (see 3.3.4 below), had something to do with Jacob's sudden departure from Freiberg, thereby helping to change the life of little Sigmund. Nothing is known about Jacob's sister, except that by a second marriage she was the wife of one Lüstmann, in Hungary.[40]

3.1.14 RELATIVES OF FREUD'S MOTHER

In Freiberg, Sigmund must certainly have heard about his relatives on his mother's side, particularly Jacob and Sarah Nathansohn. Jacob Nathansohn, who called himself a commercial agent, may have visited Freiberg on business, and it is certain that the families corresponded. If it is true that Amalie had no relatives of her own in Freiberg but lived far from her old home, then such contacts must have been doubly important to her, and little Sigmund may well have been aware of that. However, Grandfather and Grandmother Nathansohn did not impinge on Sigmund's life directly until he moved to Vienna, where they became close neighbors.

From P. Swales's searches, it appears that Amalie had four brothers (see Table 3): Hermann, Nathan, and Adolf, who were much older than she was; and Julius, who was two or three years younger. By 1859, Hermann and Nathan had moved to Odessa, and Julius had just died of pulmonary tuberculosis at the age of twenty. An unpublished letter from Freud's son Oliver to S. Bernfeld makes it clear—according to P. Swales—that the uncle whom Freud "loved and honoured" (1900a, 138, footnote) was in fact Hermann Nathansohn. We may perhaps take it, then, that Amalie too was on good terms with this, her oldest, brother. However, elsewhere Freud deplores the man's lack of generosity (1960a, 56f.; cf. p. 141, note 55, below). It is of course open to question whether little Sigmund met these relatives of his mother in Freiberg.[41]

3.2   The Departure from Freiberg

If we bear in mind the complicated network of family relationships during the first three years of Freud's life, then it becomes clear that his special position must have stamped him for life. However, the family's departure from Freiberg altered his circumstances radically: the network of interacting partners was cut by more than half; the familiar environment was replaced by a completely different world; and, not least, even those people who remained in Sigmund's life were not the same as they had been.

The precise date of the Freuds' departure from Freiberg and the length of their intermediate stay in Leipzig before the family settled in Vienna are not known. The earliest possible date of Amalie's departure is 11 August 1859, when she was issued with a passport in Brünn (Brno) "for a further stay in Leipzig" (Sigmund Freud Gesellschaft, 1975, 13); the latest possible date of her arrival in Vienna is 21 March 1860, when Rosa Freud was born.[42]

It is not known if all the family left Freiberg at the same time, nor can we tell if they all stayed in Leipzig together and whether Emanuel, with his family and Philipp, traveled straight on to Manchester.[43] Since Freiberg was not then served by the railway, the Freuds would have had to repair to the nearest railway station, probably Ostrau, some eighteen miles from Freiberg, in a horse-drawn carriage, there to board the train to Leipzig via Breslau.

Freud refers briefly to their departure in a number of his writings, for instance, in a letter to Fliess of 3 December 1897: "Breslau plays a part in my childhood memories. At the age of three I passed through the station when we moved from Freiberg to Leipzig, and the gas jets [gas lamps], which were the first I had seen, reminded me of souls burning in Hell. I know something of the context here. The anxiety about travel which I have had to overcome is also bound up with it" (1950a, 237). And in his autobiographical "Screen Memories," we read: "For at the age of three I left the small place where I was born and moved to a large town. . . ." (1899a, 309); ". . . my departure, my first sight of the railway and the long carriage-drive before it—none of these has left a trace in my memory. On the other hand, I can remember two small occurrences during the railway-journey; these, as you will recollect,*

---

* Freud was addressing his *alter ego*—see p. 62f above.

came up in the analysis of my phobia" (*ibid.*, 310); ". . . my father had meant well in planning . . . to make good the loss in which the original catastrophe had involved my whole existence" (*ibid.*, 314).

What could there have been to frighten little Sigmund so much that he still suffered from it as an adult? Why was this, presumably his first, railway journey not the happy event one might have expected it to be for a lively young boy of three, but one that filled him with panic? The explanation can be found in another letter to Fliess, this time about a patient:

Buried deep beneath all his phantasies we found a scene from his primal period (before twenty-two months) which meets all requirements and into which all the surviving puzzles flow. It is everything at the same time—sexual, innocent, natural, etc. I can hardly bring myself to believe it yet. It is as if Schliemann had dug up another Troy which had hitherto been believed to be mythical. Also the fellow is feeling shamelessly well. He has demonstrated the truth of my theories in my own person, for with a surprising turn [in his analysis] he provided me with a solution of my own railway phobia (which I had overlooked). . . . My phobia, if you please, was a poverty, or rather a hunger phobia, arising out of my infantile gluttony and called up by the circumstance that my wife had no dowry (of which I am proud) (1950a, 305f., 21 December 1899, omission by the editors).[44]

I have quoted this passage at length because it shows that whereas, at the time, Freud based his approach on the reality of his patients' childhood traumas, he denied their reality when it came to himself—as witness his "Screen Memories," which was published in the same year, 1899.

The *Three Essays on the Theory of Sexuality* of 1905[45] contains a passage which treats railway travel by children as a source of infantile sexual excitation. It is quite possible that the insight his patient afforded him in 1899 received its theoretical formulation in that very passage:

. . . the existence, then, of these pleasurable sensations, caused by forms of mechanical agitation of the body, is confirmed by the fact that children are so fond of games of passive movement, such as swinging and being thrown up into the air, and insist on such games being incessantly repeated. (Some people can remember that in swinging they felt the impact of moving air upon the genitals as an immediate sexual pleasure.) It is well known that rocking is habitually used to induce sleep in restless children. The *shaking* produced by riding in *carriages* and later by *railway-travel* exercises such a fascinating effect on older children that every body, at any rate, has at one time or other in his life wanted to be an engine driver or a coachman. It is a puzzling fact that boys take such an extraordinarily intense interest in things connected with railways, and, at the age at which the production of phantasies is most active (shortly before puberty), use those things as the nucleus of a symbolism that is peculiarly sexual. A compulsive link of this kind between *railway-travel and sexuality* is clearly derived from the *pleasurable character* of the sensations of movement. In the event of repression, which turns so many childish preferences into their opposite, these same individuals, when they are adolescents or adults, will react to rocking or swinging with a feeling of nausea, will be terribly exhausted by a railway journey, or will be subject to attacks of *anxiety on the journey* and will protect themselves against a repetition of the painful experience by a *dread of railway-travel* (1905d, 201f., italics added, except for the last phrase; cf. 1900a, 393 and 271f.).

If we can take it once again that Freud was describing a personal experience, then the above passage may be considered an accurate account of his feelings during the journey by carriage and train from Ostrau to Leipzig. The child had felt sexually excited but recalled that the punishment for this forbidden pleasure was castration. Moreover, he had recently discovered that this punishment had actually been carried out on little Pauline, so that he must have gone in acute fear of losing his own penis in retaliation for what had been an involuntary and uncontrollable sensation. It is also quite possible, of course, that he masturbated in fact and was caught in the act. Now he was done for; now the terrible punishment would be meted out to him, too! And when he spotted the gas lamps on Breslau station, he lost what little composure he had left, for now the threat of Resi, his nursemaid, that he would be sent to Hell if he misbehaved again seemed to have come true as well. (I suppose that it was his nursemaid's threat because Jews do not believe that Hell is peopled with burning spirits.) The masturbation hypothesis is borne out by another of Freud's dreams, which also involved a train:

> Thus, I dreamt on one occasion that I was sitting on a bench with one of my first University teachers, and that the bench, which was surrounded by other benches, was moving forward at a rapid pace. . . . Another time I was sitting in a railway carriage and holding on my left an object in the shape of a top-hat ["Zylinderhut," literally "cylinder-hat"], which however was made of transparent glass. The situation made me think at once of the proverb *"Mit dem Hute in her Hand kommt man durch das ganze Land"* ["If you go hat in hand, you can cross the whole land"]. . . . I soon saw that I should like to make a discovery that would make me . . . rich and independent. . . . In the dream I was travelling with my discovery, the hat in the shape of a glass cylinder (1901a, 651f.).

That he considered hats to be phallic symbols has been stated by Freud himself (1900a, 355, 360ff.), so that the dream of holding a hat in one's hand must have been a clear reference to masturbation.[46]

If my assumption is correct, then it is obvious not only that little Sigmund had an extraordinarily vivid imagination, but also that the fearful conclusions he drew were not at all irrational, but in the context of his experiences, fully justified. He had been threatened with castration for the crime of masturbation, that is, for feeling sexual excitation in his genitals; had seen that Pauline had been "castrated"; had again experienced sexual excitation on the train and was terrified that his penis was about to be cut off.[47]

I do not, however, think that this was the sole reason why he was so shaken by the train journey; in my view, the adults, and his parents in particular, must also have displayed agitated, perhaps even panicky, behavior. For a three-year-old boy would not have suffered such pangs of remorse about what was after all a purely involuntary lapse had his companions on the journey been carefree and cheerful. His own panic about his sexual feelings may thus have been a symptom to which he clung as his only explanation of his family's incomprehensible gloom and despondency.

This leads us to the question of why Jacob Freud and his family left Freiberg in the first instance; why little Sigmund had to suffer this "catastrophe" (1899a, 340; cf. p. 132 above).

Jones (1950, I, 12) and most other Freud biographers mention the economic crisis that swept the Moravian textile industry in the 1850s and hence threatened the existence of all Jews engaged in this branch of commerce. Jones claims that the weaving industry had been in decline for twenty years because the introduction of machines was rendering handwork redundant, and that Freiberg suffered particularly because the Northern Railway from Vienna, built in the 1840s, bypassed that town.

However, this whole theory is completely unfounded, and Jones in fact fails to adduce solid evidence for it.[48] In reality, Moravia experienced an economic boom during those very years, industrialization having led to enormous increases in productivity. As a result, Brünn, which was some ninety miles west of Freiberg and the center of the Moravian textile industry, became the "Moravian Manchester," not only supplying the home market but also receiving large orders from abroad (Jordan, 1959; J. Sajner's translation).

Similarly, Jones's argument that Freiberg suffered special economic damage because the Northern Railway did not call there is not valid—at least as far as Jacob Freud's business was concerned. For Jacob's trade was not confined to Freiberg but also took him regularly to nearby railway centers. In particular, the Prerau–Ostrau line, built between 1841 and 1847 (according to Sajner), was less than twenty miles from Freiberg. In any event, there is documentary evidence that Jacob was economically successful well into the 1850s (see 2.5 above).

But even in the worst case he could have adapted himself, for instance by becoming a manufacturer like his friend Ignaz Fluss, who also came from Tysmenitz. In 1854 Fluss, too, had been a wool merchant with a far smaller turnover than Jacob Freud (see Table 6), but soon afterwards he managed to establish himself in Freiberg as the owner of a successful textile mill,[49] with a branch in Vienna.[50] All in all, therefore, there are no grounds to claim that Jacob's move from Freiberg was caused by a general economic depression.

Nor was Jones right to claim that Jacob Freud left Freiberg to escape the rising tide of anti-Semitism. For if Ignaz Fluss could become a factory owner in Freiberg, what militant anti-Semites there were would not have stopped Jacob Freud either. Sajner has produced further evidence against Jones's theory of anti-Semitism, an affidavit signed by the mayor of the district of Klogsdorf and issued at Jacob's request in 1859, a few months before his departure. It reads as follows:

The undersigned Mayor of the District of Klogsdorf hereby certifies that Herr Jacob Freud, born in Tysmenitz on 18 December 1815, his wife Amalie Freud, née Nathansohn, and the two children of this marriage, Sigmund Freud, born in Freiberg on 6 May 1857* and Anna Freud, born in Freiberg on 31 December 1858, as well as all future children born from this marriage fall under the jurisdiction of this district, are entitled to be domiciled in it and will be admitted here at any time provided they have not acquired citizens' rights elsewhere. Further, the undersigned Mayor of the District certifies that Herr Jacob Freud and his wife are of good repute in every way and that nothing untoward in their conduct has ever become known (Sajner, 1968, 176; additions from a copy procured by J. Sajner; translated from the German).

Jacob asked for a similar affidavit from the Freiberg Municipal Council and was issued with one on 23 March 1879. A copy was discovered by J. Sajner and R. Gicklhorn in the District Archives of Nový Jičín:

Jacob Freud from Tysmenitz in Galicia, formerly a local dealer in produce, requests a certificate of good conduct covering his fifteen years' residence here, i.e., from 1844 to the present.

Certificate of good conduct

The G.R.d.St.F.N.T. [the Municipal Council of the Town of Freiberg Neu-Titschein] in M.M. [the Margravate of Moravia] hereby certifies that Herr Jacob Freud from Tysmeniz born in Galicia and currently registered in the District of Klogsdorf has been a tax-paying produce dealer in this town from the year 1844 to the present, i.e., that he has been a resident for the past fifteen years, during which time he has been above reproach both in moral respects and also in respect of his civic duties (District Archives, N. Jičín; copy by J. Sajner; translated from the German).

Even if these testimonials were issued as a matter of routine, they nevertheless make it seem highly unlikely that anti-Semitic persecution was the real reason for Jacob's departure from Freiberg. All in all, therefore, I feel entitled to assert that Jacob Freud must have had different reasons for his departure. True, he may have left Freiberg for economic reasons, may, as Freud wrote, have "lost all his means" and been "forced" to move to a large town (1899, 312; cf. p. 132 above). But if he did so, it was not because of a general economic decline, nor because of repressive measures against the Jews, but solely because of his personal failings.

This conclusion is of great importance to any assessment of Sigmund Freud's relationship with his father. For if Jacob Freud was indeed forced to leave Freiberg because of his own incompetence, then it follows that his son, when looking back at this "catastrophe" in later years, must have felt highly critical of his father.

On the other hand, Jacob may have gone to Leipzig for the express purpose of keeping his older sons out of the Austrian Army. We know that on 21 May 1857 the Royal District Office requested the Municipal Council of Freiberg for information "within three days as to whether the Israelites Moises Kanner and Pinkas Freud, domiciled in Tysmenitz, are resident there and with what legitimization." The Municipal Council replied on May 28:

Following your instructions of 21–23 inst., No. 1891, we hereby declare as requested that Moises Kanner, son of the produce dealer Berisch Kanner from Tysmenitz and

* This is obviously a mistake. It should read 1856—M.K.

domiciled here, is, according to information supplied by the latter, presently in Galatz, in Moldavia; that he is daily expected to return by his father who has specially asked him to do so for the purpose of reporting for military service; Pinkas Freud, son of the local resident Jacob Freud, is resident here and holds a Certificate of Citizenship issued by the Glogsdorf [sic] Municipality and dated 15 May 1853 in the home of his father whose commercial agent he is (District Archives, N. Jičín, copy by J. Sajner; translated from the German).

We may take it that "Pinkas Freud" was Philipp Freud, the then twenty-three-year-old son of Jacob, for as far as we know, Jacob had no grown-up sons other than Philipp and Emanuel. In the present context it is important that another young Jew from Tysmenitz, Moises Kanner, son of Berisch (see Table 6), was called up for military service. Hence it is likely that Philipp too, and perhaps even the married Emanuel, were due to be called up, and that the family had to leave Austria in a hurry. By 1859 Austria was at war with Sardinia, and according to Leslie Adams (quoted in Roazen, 1975, 27), Philipp would have had to serve in that conflict.

Emanuel and Philipp probably emigrated to England because there, and particularly in Manchester, the center of the textile industry, they had high hopes of making their way. But in that case why did not Jacob, who after all was only forty-four years old and had so much experience in the wool trade, accompany them? Why did he go on to Vienna, where he was to fare so badly, and why did he go to Leipzig first, which was not on the route from Freiberg to Vienna?

R. Gicklhorn's searches in Viennese archives suggest yet another possibility: Jacob and his sons may have become involved in a venture that was to lead to the arrest in 1865 of Josef, Jacob's brother, for possession of counterfeit money (see Gicklhorn, 1976, and 3.3.4 below). From the available documents, it appears that forged fifty-rouble notes began to circulate in Europe in 1863 and that their source was the same as that of the notes with which Josef was caught red-handed. All these notes had originated in England, and the Austrian authorities suspected that Josef Freud's nephews in Manchester were implicated.[51]

If Emanuel and Philipp did indeed go to England for the express purpose of joining the counterfeiters in some capacity, then it is most unlikely that Jacob Freud knew nothing about it. He might even have sold his business in Freiberg so as to enable his sons to go to England on the proceeds and to start a new life there, in the expectation that his generosity would pay dividends. In that case, he might have been left without funds and forced to go to Vienna, where he could count on support from his relatives.

And there could have been yet another reason for Jacob's departure from Freiberg and his sons' emigration to England, namely, the presumed love relationship between Amalie and Philipp to which I referred earlier (see 3.1.6 above). If my assumption is correct, then Jacob would have done all he could to ensure that his wife and son were separated. Emanuel, his older and more reliable son, with a family of his own, could be expected to keep an eye on Philipp in England and become a father substitute for him. In other words,

Jacob banished his son. That would also explain why Sigmund Freud, during his separation from his rival John but also in adult life, felt so relieved whenever he cut his ties with rivals. Identification with his father may have taught him that the best way of ridding oneself of rivals is to break with them completely. To corroborate this hypothesis we would, of course, have to know if Jacob did indeed break off all contact with Philipp.

Which of these various reasons was resonsible for the Freuds' departure from Freiberg can no longer be ascertained. However, there is enough evidence to support my belief that the adults in whose company little Sigmund left Freiberg were in a state of anxiety or even panic, and that no explanation for this was given to Sigmund. He would then have been forced to seek an explanation of his own for all the tense and anxious behavior about him. That explanation, though rather fantastical, was nevertheless quite adequate and realistic in view of the experience he had had as a three-year-old: he had done something his father had expressly forbidden him to do; he felt guilty for it; and now he was being punished, which was just.

In *The Interpretation of Dreams* Freud describes a "farewell" dream, and I agreee with Grinstein (1968, 323f.) that its subject was in fact the Freuds' departure from Freiberg:

> Professor M. said: "My son, the Myops. . . . On account of certain events which had occurred in the City of Rome, it had become necessary to remove the children to safety, and this was done. The scene was then in front of a gateway, double doors in the ancient style (the "Porta Romana" at Siena, as I was aware in the dream itself). I was sitting on the edge of a fountain and was greatly depressed and almost in tears. A female figure —an attendant or nun—brought two boys out and handed them over to their father, who was not myself. The elder of the two was clearly my eldest son; I did not see the other one's face. The woman who brought out the boy asked him to kiss her good-bye. She was noticeable for having a red nose. The boy refused to kiss her, but, holding out his hand in farewell, said *Auf Geseres* to her, and then *Auf Ungeseres* to the two of us (or to one of us). I had a notion that this last phrase denoted a preference (1900a, 441f., first omission by the editors in the original).

Freud himself explains: " . . . the situation in the dream of my removing my children to safety from the City of Rome was distorted by being related back to an analogous event that occurred in my own childhood: I was envying some relatives who, many years earlier, had had an opportunity of removing their children to another country" (*ibid.*, 444, footnote). Freud had once again equated Rome with Freiberg. He has to remove children from the city, but he himself is one of these children. It is very likely that the obviously Catholic "attendant or nun" was his old nursemaid Resi Wittek, who had come back specially to say goodbye; if the Freuds did not leave before October 1859, she might well have finished her ten months' prison sentence by then. Grinstein also believes that this dream figure was Freud's old nursemaid.

The boy—supposedly Freud's son, but who certainly reports Freud's own feelings—says *Auf Geseres* to her and *Auf Ungeseres* to Freud. Now, *Geseres,* according to Freud, may be translated by "weeping and wailing" but also by "leavened bread." Freud's private neologism, *Ungeseres,* is the unleavened bread Jews eat on the Passover feast in memory of the exodus from Egypt. When he claimed that this word expressed a preference, Freud therefore indicated that being a Jew is preferable to being a Catholic. Moreover, Bergmann (1976, 13) has pointed out that the Hebrew word *geserot* also means "anti-Jewish laws," and he believes that Freud knew this meaning—at least unconsciously. *Auf Ungeseres* would then have positive significance even in this sense, for Freud was welcoming the fact that he was turning his back on anti-Jewish laws. Incidentally, when he went on to mention *The New Ghetto,* a Zionist play (cf. Grinstein, 1968, 318ff.), but failed to name its author, Theodor Herzl, the spiritual founder of the state of Israel, he might well have been expressing his negative attitude to Zionism (Falk, 1977; Loewenberg, 1970).

From Freud's remark that he envied Emanuel and his family (1900a, 444, footnote; cf. 1901b, 219), it appears that he would have preferred to go to England rather than to Vienna. But I believe that most of all he would have wanted to stay in Freiberg.

It seems reasonable to me to suppose that Freud must have felt desolate about leaving Freiberg, as the dream indicates. At the same time he must have been filled with a diffuse sense of outrage, which later, when he grasped the full story, became directed against the person of Jacob. Since that rage could never be expressed—Sigmund, unlike Philipp, was determined to be his father's devoted son—it turned into a mainspring of hostile emotions. Even his Oedipal hatred of his father was, considered in this light, quite rational and explicable: his father had robbed him of an entire world, and the new world to which he had taken him had brought nothing but misery and distress—at least in the beginning. Jacob had turned out to be a failure and eventually made his son shoulder responsibility for the whole family. As a result, Sigmund became the family breadwinner, his brothers' and sisters' "father," and his mother's real partner.

3.3. The Early Years in Vienna

3.3.1 THE FREUDS' MATERIAL CIRCUMSTANCES

Jacob Freud took his family to Leopoldstadt, Vienna's Jewish district. According to the census of 1857, 17 percent of the quarter's 50,000 inhabitants were Jews, and this number accounted for half of Vienna's entire Jewish population (Statistical Survey of the City of Vienna, 1857, IX, copied by R.

Sieder). In the years that followed, the proportion of Jews grew rapidly; by 1890, 31 percent of the population of Leopoldstadt, which had grown to 160,000, was Jewish.

Leopoldstadt did not become part of the city of Vienna until 1861 (Artner, 1937, 146f.). Before then it had been a separate suburb, separated from the city by the Danube Canal. It had contained a Jewish ghetto ever since the Middle Ages. Though it boasted several stately buildings and gardens (Augarten Castle, Prater), the center of Leopoldstadt was a slum. A burst of building activity in the 1860s admittedly improved matters, but the improvement was offset the continuous influx of immigrants from the eastern regions.

Arthur describes the appalling conditions they encountered:

The new buildings contained many offices and large apartments, but these were not accessible to the greater part of the population because the rentals were too high. To alleviate the rent burden, tenants usually sublet parts of their single rooms. Conditions were horrifying: often, only a line drawn with chalk separated the area reserved for the "roomlord" or the "bedholder" from the rest. The grave psychological and physical dangers conjured up by these conditions need no special emphasis. Hand in hand with miserable housing went a rising rate of inflation, which was only just tolerable because work was still available, but which nevertheless had serious repercussions on the health of the poorer sections. For the first time even the official reports referred to the horrible specter of "the Viennese disease": "of every 10,000 inhabitants 77 persons died of tuberculosis" (1897) (1937, 157; translated from the German).

The Freuds too had to be numbered among the poor, as we know from many remarks made by Freud himself (Jones, 1953, I, 15, 157ff.; 1950a, 298; 1960a, 101, 188). Amalie came down with tuberculosis and had to be sent to the Carpathians while Freud was still at school (1969a, 117, footnote; Roazen, 1976, 45).[52]

Apparently Jacob and his family changed home several times during the first few years in Vienna. From the Register of Births (Israelitic Congregation, Vienna), we can tell that in March 1860 the Freuds lived at "Weissgärber 3" (3, Obere Weissgärberstrasse) in the Third District, near the Danube Canal. At this address the Vienna directory of 1863–64 lists one Selig Freud, distiller. In other words, Jacob, his wife, and three children were subtenants of one of his relatives, and must have lived in the overcrowded conditions we have just been describing. In March 1861 and July 1862, the family lived at 114, Weissgärberstrasse; in May 1864, at 5, Pillersdorfgasse, on the other side of the Danube Canal in the Second District; and in April 1866, at 1, Pfeffergasse, also in the Second District. Later still they moved to 5, Pfeffergasse, as we know from Freud's high school reports (Gicklhorn, 1965, 23). It was not until 1875, by which time Freud was a university student, that the family moved to 3, Kaiser-Joseph-Strasse (now Heinestrasse). The house must have been fairly new, since the 1863 map of Leopoldstadt (see Fig. 13) does not show any building on the site (then in Augartenstrasse).[53]

Changing homes was not unusual among poor Jews at that time. These

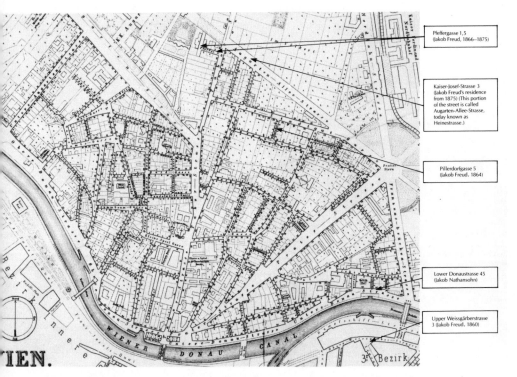

Pfeffergasse 1,5
(Jakob Freud, 1866–1875)

Kaiser-Josef-Strasse 3
(Jakob Freud's residence
from 1875) (This portion
of the street is called
Augarten-Allee-Strasse,
today known as
Heinestrasse.)

Pillerdorfgasse 5
(Jakob Freud, 1864)

Lower Donaustrasse 45
(Jakob Nathansohn)

Upper Weissgärberstrasse
3 (Jakob Freud, 1860)

FIGURE 13 Detail from a map of Leopoldstadt, the Second District of Vienna (1863) *(Vienna Town and Country Archives)*

changes were not really "moves" in the modern sense, because people owned few pieces of furniture and other moveable assets. It is all the more noteworthy, therefore, that Jacob and Sarah Nathansohn, Amalie's parents, always lived in the same apartment.[54]

Anna Bernays, Freud's sister, has described one of the Freuds' apartments. It was probably the one in Kaiser-Joseph-Strasse, to which the family did not move until 1875. They had a parlor, a dining room, three bedrooms "which the rest of us shared," while Sigmund had a small room all to himself, long and narrow, with a window giving onto the street (Bernays, 1940, 336). We know nothing about the Freuds' other apartments, but Anna Bernays states that Sigmund always had a room to himself, "no matter how crowded our quarters" *(ibid.).*

It is unclear how Jacob made a living in Vienna, although until he was a very old man he continued to describe himself as a wool merchant (see Lehmann's Directory; Gicklhorn, 1965, 23). In all probability he did not follow a regular trade, for as Gicklhorn has discovered, his name appears neither in the Vienna trade directory nor on the roll of commercial ratepayers, which means that he had no taxable income. However, it is most unlikely that he would have been able to maintain a family of nine purely on the alms of his

FIGURE 14 Leopoldstadt,
Vienna: Untere Donau-Strasse
with Jacob Nathansohn's
house (second from the right),
1851 *(Vienna City Museum)*

FIGURE 15
"Coppersmith-House", Obere
Augartenstrasse, at the corner
of Grosse Sperlgasse in
Vienna at about 1860
(probably part of Freud's way
to school) *(in Artner 1937)*

relatives; more likely his income was such that he had no need to declare it officially. Grünwald (1941) assumes that Jacob acted as broker for various Jewish merchants from outside the city, and that he provided them with introductions. Gicklhorn (1976), for her part, claims that Jacob Freud kept his family on the circulation of forged banknotes (cf. 3.3.4 below).

Neither of these claims has been corroborated. We only know that Freud himself reproached his father for making so many plans that came to nothing and that kept bringing the family into financial difficulties. Thus in 1884 he wrote to his fiancée: "Yesterday I met Father in the street, still full of projects, still hoping. I took it upon myself to write to Emanuel and Philipp urging them to help Father out of his present predicament. He doesn't want to do it himself since he considers himself badly treated. So I sat down last night and wrote Emanuel a very sharp letter" (1960a, 101; 1900a, 217). In 1884 Jacob was seventy-nine years old, so that his lack of business acumen could not really have been held against him. However, he seems to have been something of a failure even in earlier years, for Jones describes him as one "who was never a very enterprising or successful man," who in old age relapsed "into a state of fatalistic helplessness and even childishness" (1953, I, 157). Martin Freud, too, writes that Jacob was always in dire financial straits, and that as he grew older he became gradually "helpless and ineffective in his efforts to bring up his family really well" (1957, 20, 24).

We do not know who helped him, apart from his sons in England, but Jones suggests that he must have received financial assistance from Amalie's family (1953, I, 17).[55]

3.3.2 SIGMUND FREUD'S EARLY YEARS IN VIENNA

For little Sigmund, aged three and a half, the sudden change of environment must have posed tremendous problems. A familiar world that despite its pitfalls and anxieties had been full of life and cheer had to be forgotten, to make way for a new, much less pleasant, world. The move took him from a small Moravian village, with its Czech and Catholic population in which the few Jewish families constituted a minority, to overcrowded Leopoldstadt, in the midst of the hectic hustle and bustle of a mass of poor, predominantly Jewish inhabitants (see M. Freud, 1957, 19). More important probably for the child, however, was the loss of so many people who had meant so much to him. In Freiberg, he had had three "mothers": Amalie, Resi, and Maria; in Vienna, he had just one. He had also had three "fathers": Jacob, Emanuel, and Philipp; in Vienna, there was again only one. In addition he had lost his playmates, and soon after he arrived in Vienna had to contend with the birth of a little sister, Rosa, followed during the next four years by the birth of another three sisters, and, in 1866, by that of his brother Alexander.

Worse still, the remaining characters had changed roles. His mother was far from being the same person in the circle of her parents and relatives that she

FIGURE 16 Jacob Freud (about forty-eight years old) and Sigmund Freud (about eight years old) *(Sigmund Freud Copyrights Ltd., Colchester, England)*

FIGURE 17 Amalie Freud with Sigmund, Rosa (or Anna?) and Dolfi in 1864
(Copyright Omir David Male, London.)

had been in the alien surroundings of Freiberg. In particular, she must have seemed more self-assured to her son. And perhaps it was during these first few years of poverty and hardship that she developed those qualities which later made such an impression on her grandchildren: her impatience, selfishness, and impulsiveness. His father, by contrast, had been reduced from a more than lifesize patriarch to a humble petitioner. In Vienna, the real patriarch was Grandfather Nathansohn. If one considers that in Freiberg Sigmund had only known one "grandfather," namely Jacob, this particular experience must have made a deep impression on him.

Perhaps seeing his father as a weakling and feeling sorry for him helped Freud to develop that enormous ambition which was to mark his creative energies in later life. It would seem that it was here, in Vienna, that he first realized the true meaning of his father's mandate—that he must do better than Jacob had done. This mandate was admittedly ambivalent, because it also involved the duty of not acknowledging Jacob's weaknesses and of honoring him despite his faults. Jacob, it would seem, could let himself go more and more, become increasingly helpless, because Sigmund could grow, or rather *so that* Sigmund could grow to ever-increasing brilliance. Sigmund, we may take it, suppressed his justified anger at his incapable father because Jacob loved him more than himself, turning him into his ideal ego, into a delegate of his own unfulfilled wishes.

There are countless references in Freud's work, and particularly in *The Interpretation of Dreams,* to his inordinate ambition and its causes.[56] The following is probably the most revealing passage of all:

I may have been ten or twelve years old, when my father began to take me with him on his walks and reveal to me in his talk his views upon things in the world we live in. Thus it was, on one such occasion, that he told me a story to show me how much better things were now than they had been in his days. "When I was a young man," he said, "I went for a walk one Saturday in the streets of your birthplace; I was well dressed, and had a new fur cap on my head. A Christian came up to me and with a single blow knocked off my cap into the mud and shouted: 'Jew! get off the pavement!' "And what did you do?" I asked. "I went into the roadway and picked up my cap," was his calm reply. This struck me as unheroic conduct on the part of the big, strong man who was holding the little boy by the hand. I contrasted this situation with another which fitted my feelings better: the scene in which Hannibal's father, Hamilcar Barcas, made his boy swear before the household altar to take vengeance on the Romans. Ever since that time Hannibal had had a place in my phantasies (1900a, 197; partially retranslated from the German).

In this much quoted passage, Freud was undoubtedly critical of his father. But was he not making a false comparison? Was the behavior of Hamilcar Barcas really so much more heroic than that of his father Jacob? In fact, there is a great similarity between the two father–son relationships: both fathers were failures, both were humiliated by "Rome," both wanted their sons to avenge them. Hence Freud was not so much criticizing his father as expressing his willingness to obey Jacob's mandate.

Yet this decision was not free of ambivalence. Here too he was like Hannibal, who ultimately also refused, consciously or unconsciously, to fulfill his father's mission. He did not enter Rome. Did Freud also rebel unconsciously against Jacob's order? It would seem to me that he did, as witness a significant slip when he wrote this section of *The Interpretation of Dreams:* instead of giving the name of Hannibal's father, he put down the name of the latter's brother, Hasdrubal. Freud himself considered this slip (1901b, 219f.) the expression of his wish to have been born the son of Emmanuel rather than the son of Jacob. For, we can imagine him going on to think, Emanuel would undoubtedly not have given him so tough an assignment. Emanuel had become "great" in his own right and had attained an honored place in bourgeois society (see 3.5 below).

Jacob, on the other hand, expected Sigmund to excel him, but not too overtly, and to close his eyes to his weakness. Freud has described the ambivalent nature of this mandate in a letter to Romain Rolland written late in his life:

It must be that a sense of guilt was attached to the satisfaction in having gone such a long way: there was something about it that was wrong, that from earliest times had been forbidden. It was something to do with a child's criticism of his father, with the undervaluation which took the place of the overvaluation of earlier childhood. *It seems as though the essence of success was to have got further than one's father, and as though to excel one's father was still something forbidden* (1936a, 247, italics added).

It was this ambiguous and, because of its inherent contradiction, quite impossible mission which, in my opinion, caused Freud during his crisis of 1896–97 to abandon his seduction theory (see Part 1). In connection with a dream in which a father is once again shown in a despicable light even while being set on a pedestal, Freud himself admitted as much: "The authority wielded by the father provokes criticism from his child at an early age, and the severity of the demands he makes upon the child leads him, for his own relief, to watch keenly for any weakness of his father's; but the filial piety called up in our minds by the figure of a father, particularly after his death, tightens the censorship which keeps any such criticism from becoming conscious" (1900a, 435; partially retranslated from the German).

His father's death, which, as I have tried to show, was the principal cause of Freud's crisis, mobilized the same repressive mechanisms he had learned to deploy as a child in Vienna, when he had also been forced to repress rage against his father and had learned to cover up Jacob's weaknesses with his own brilliance.

Freud became a model son. His father is said to have told an acquaintance who had had an argument with his own father: "What, you contradict your father? My Sigmund has more intelligence in his little toe than I have in my whole head, but it would never ever occur to him to contradict me" (Wittels, 1924, 242).

However, Freud's attempts to repress his anger and doubts do not seem to have been completely successful, for there are indications that even in Vienna little Sigmund could not repress all the problems that had worried him so much in Freiberg. Thus the memory of an episode that occurred when he was five may be called a repetition of the scene on the dandelion meadow. In connection with his interpretation of the dream of the "botanical monograph," Freud has related it as follows:

It had once amused my father to hand over a book with coloured plates (an account of a journey through Persia) for me and my eldest sister to destroy. Not easy to justify from the educational point of view! I had been five years old at the time and my sister not yet three; and the picture of the two of us blissfully pulling the book to pieces (leaf by leaf, like an artichoke, I found myself saying) was almost the only plastic memory that I retained from that period of my life. Then, when I became a student I had developed a passion for collecting and owning books. . . . I had become a book-worm. I had always, from the time I first began to think about myself, referred this first passion of mine back to the childhood memory I have mentioned. Or rather, I had recognized that the childhood scene was a "screen memory" for my later bibliophile propensities (cf. my paper on screen memories). And I had early discovered, of course, that passions often lead to sorrow (1900a, 172f.).

The fact that Freud, when talking about the "pulling to pieces" of a book —in the metaphorical sense of a flower—makes direct reference to his "Screen Memories" (cf. 3.1.7 and 3.1.8 above) leads me to suppose that what we have here is yet another reversal. The memory was not meant to be a "screen" for Freud's later bibliophilia (which would have clashed with Freud's own theoretical ideas (just as it did in his "Screen Memories")), but was intended to cover an earlier, less harmless scene. Had he perhaps been playing the same games with his sister Anna as he played two years earlier with Pauline? Grinstein believes that he had, and contends that the same chain of associations (pulling the petals off a flower—defloration—looking at the genitals of a little girl) which Freud put into the mouth of his *alter ego* in "Screen Memories" was at work here as well. The latent content of the dream, accordingly, was the genital organ of Anna and/or Pauline, reflecting the incestuous wishes of five-year-old Sigmund to possess his sister Anna (Grinstein, 1968, 66f.). Grinstein has analyzed the links between the many associations Freud brings up in connection with this dream and his "Screen Memories," and has argued convincingly that there is little doubt but that the "defloration scene" in Freiberg, when Sigmund and John "inspected" Pauline, was repeated in Vienna, this time with Sigmund and Anna as the dramatis personae.

3.3.3　LEARNING WITH HIS FATHER

During his latency period Freud seems to have been occupied almost exclusively with learning. It seems that his formal education did not begin until he entered the Gymnasium (high school). His sister, Anna Bernays, tells us that

מ ק ר א

תורה נביאים וכתובים.

Die

Israelitische Bibel.

Enthaltend:

Den heiligen Urtext,

die deutsche Uebertragung,

die

allgemeine, ausführliche Erläuterung mit mehr als 500 englischen Holzschnitten.

Herausgegeben von

Dr. Ludwig Philippson.

Erster Theil: Die fünf Bücher Mosche.
Mit einem Stahlstiche.

Zweite Ausgabe.

Leipzig, 1858.
Baumgärtner's Buchhandlung.

FIGURE 18 Title page of Philippson's Bible

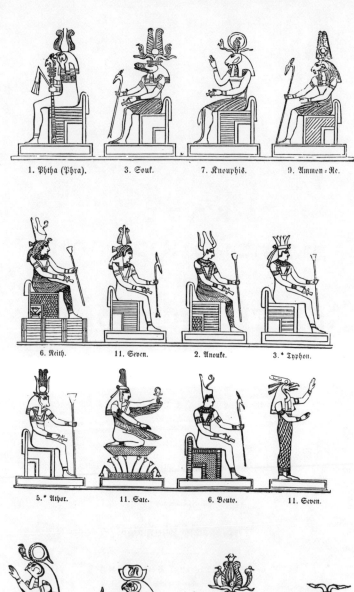

1. Phtha (Phra).   3. Souf.   7. Knouphis.   9. Ammen-Re.

6. Neith.   11. Seven.   2. Anouke.   3. * Typhon.

5. * Athor.   11. Sate.   6. Bouto.   11. Seven.

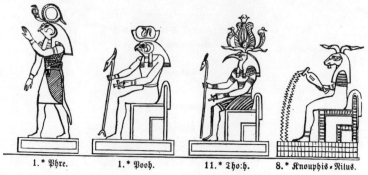

1. * Phre.   1. * Pooh.   11. * Tho:h.   8. * Knouphis-Nilus.

FIGURE 19 Egyptian gods, woodcuts from Philippson's Bible,
1:869–871 (illustrating Deuteronomy 4: 15–31)

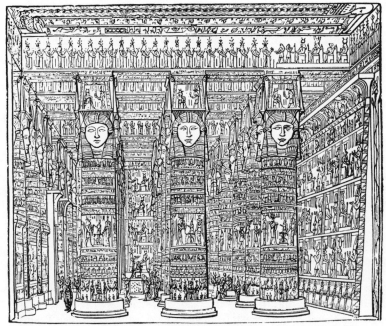

Bilderkammer. Das Innere des Portikus des großen Tempels von Denderah.

FIGURE 20 Egyptian temple, woodcut from Philippson's Bible, p. 1164 (illustrating Hezekiah 8: 7–13)

Aegyptische Fähre. Von einer Skulptur, die das Todtengericht darstellt.

מ״ב 58*

FIGURE 21 Egyptian funeral ferry, woodcut from Philippson's Bible, 2:459 (illustrating 2 Samuel 19: 17–20)

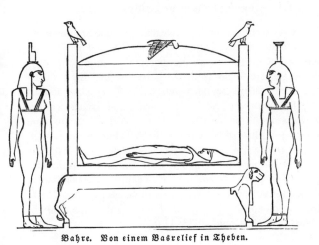

Bahre. Von einem Basrelief in Theben.

FIGURE 22 Egyptian funeral bier, woodcut from Philippson's Bible, 2:394 (illustrating 2 Samuel 3: 31–35)

he did not attend a primary school (1940, 336) because his father, who was an autodidact, taught him privately. Freud himself wrote that he had received his first lesson in his father's house and that he then attended a private elementary school (1960b, 125).[57]

It seems unlikely that Jacob tried, in these lessons, to educate his son in the old tradition. Jacob and Amalie were assimilated Jews, whose ideas on child education Barta has characterized as follows:

> The few festive occasions apart, the Jewish tradition, so basic a part of Jewish education, barely made itself felt in the homes of Central European assimilated Jews. Instead, they forged ambitious plans . . . to ensure their children's future by helping them to attain a good social position. In so doing they lost more and more of their traditional Jewish foundations and hence the very foothold of Jewish thought, namely true piety. The assimilated Jew did not want to be a member of a "people without a future" and preferred to live without his so fateful past. In their eyes, tradition was a hindrance to their efforts to be fully accepted by their surroundings (1975, 116).

Jones writes that after moving to Vienna, the Freuds discarded the Jewish dietary observances and most of the customary rituals (1957, III 350). They nevertheless kept certain Jewish festivals. At the age of seventeen Freud wrote to his friend Emil Fluss that his brother and sisters had celebrated Purim (the Jewish festival during which people disguise themselves) (1969a, 114). J. Heller remembers a *seder* on the eve of the Passover in 1892 or 1893 in the house of her grandfather Jacob Freud, and tells us that although Jacob's was not an Orthodox home, he conducted the ceremony in a most impressive way and knew all the prayers and recitations by heart (1956, 419).

But though he was assimilated—the Freuds even celebrated Christmas (M. Freud, 1957, 11)—Jacob was obviously anxious to hand down to his son those parts of the Jewish religion that seemed particularly important to him. This is also borne out by the fact that he read the Bible with Sigmund. On the occasion of Freud's thirty-fifth birthday he made him a present of his Bible, to which he had added the following dedication in Hebrew:[58]

> My dear son Schlomo (Salomo), in the seventh . . . [illegible] of your life the Spirit of the Lord began to move you [cf. Judges 13:25] and said to you: Go, read in My Book that I have written, and there will be opened to you the sources of wisdom, of knowledge and understanding. See, the Book of Books, from which the wise men dug out their wisdom and the lawmakers learnt law and justice [cf. Numbers 21:18]. You have looked upon the face of the Almighty [cf. Numbers 24:4;16], have heard and striven to climb upwards and you flew upon the wings of the Spirit [cf. Psalms 18:10]. For a long time the Book has been hidden [kept safe] like the fragments of the Tables of the Law in the shrine of his servant, [yet] for the day on which you have completed your 35th year I have had it covered with a new leather binding and given it the name "Spring Up, O Well! Sing ye unto it!" [cf. Numbers 21:17], and offer it to you for a remembrance and a memorial of love—From your father, who loves you with unending love—Jacob, son of Rabbi [probably "Reb," meaning Mr., M.K.] Sch. Freud. In the capital city of Vienna, 29 Nisan 5651, 6 May 1891 (E. Freud, 1977, 134).[59]

Should we take it from this dedication, doubtless written with deep religious feeling, that Jacob handed down the Bible to his son as a set of religious precepts, as God's revealed Word? In his *Autobiographical Study,* Freud, writing about his choice of profession, mentions his curiosity, which, as he explained, was "directed more towards human concerns than towards natural objects": "My deep engrossment in the Bible story (almost as soon as I had learnt the art of reading) had, as I recognized much later, an enduring effect upon the direction of my interests" (1925d, 8; this sentence was added in 1935).

I suppose therefore that Jacob was less concerned to fill his son's mind with traditional Jewish learning than to share with his son—as Freud himself put it—the biblical story, or rather, the stor*ies* of the Jews. Since Freud claimed that he could not read Hebrew (1960a, 394), it is probable that he and Jacob did not read the Bible in the Hebrew original but in the German translation.

Furthermore, if Jacob taught his son in the spirit of the Haskalah, or viewing the Bible as a history or storybook with the help of which one could learn to read and write German, then it would be interesting to know what stories struck him as particularly worthy of being handed on to his son. From Freud's frequent references to the story of Jacob and his sons, we may take it that this exerted a great fascination on Jacob as well. It is a "family romance" with a striking resemblance to Jacob's own story.

Like Jacob Freud, the Jacob of the Bible had children from several marriages. Of his twelve sons he loved Joseph best because—like Sigmund Freud—he was the fruit of his father's old age. Joseph's stepbrothers hated him as a result and sold him to Egypt, where he attained power and riches and then sent for his old father and brothers (Genesis 28–46).

Sigmund Freud's identification with the biblical Joseph has been stressed by himself: "It will be noticed that the name Josef plays a great part in my dreams (*cf.* the dream about my uncle). My own ego finds it very easy to hide itself behind people of that name, since Joseph was the name of a man famous in the Bible as an interpreter of dreams" (1900a, 484, footnote). In his letter to Fliess, he called *The Interpretation of Dreams* an "Egyptian dream book" (1950a, 294). And Egypt had yet another symbolic meaning for Freud: it was "the other side," as M. Robert (1975, Chap. 3 and *passim*) has put it, the country in which one could strive for recognition and success—or better, had to strive for them if one wanted to lead one's family out of misery.

I feel certain that it was through this story in particular that Jacob conveyed his mission to his son; he saw himself as the biblical Jacob, and cast his son in the role of Joseph. Sigmund, for his part, must have realized that his father wanted him to be a second Joseph: upright, clever, the support of his father in old age, and—I would add—a son who did not enquire into his father's past, let alone reproach him for it. For the biblical Jacob had committed several sins. He had bought his birthright from his brother Esau and obtained the father's blessing by deceit; he had outwitted his father-in-law Laban; and one can even say that he was not entirely innocent of Joseph's betrayal by his brothers, for he had preferred Joseph to the others and then abandoned him to their hatred. And finally, Joseph might well have asked himself why Reuben, his oldest half-brother, "went and lay with Bilhah, his father's concubine" (Genesis 35:22), and whether Jacob might not have condoned it. Joseph ignored all these lapses, did not criticize his father but loved him unconditionally—and that was precisely how Jacob Freud wanted to be loved by his son.

The joint Bible readings seem to have pleased father and son alike, and to have strengthened their mutual bond. It may well have been on these occasions that Jacob first noticed that he could incite his son's intellectual curiosity and realized that Sigmund promised to become a scholar and hence to fulfill a great Jewish ideal. Sigmund, in his turn, must have discovered how important he and his intellectual progress were to his father. Perhaps he also felt how good it was to be a Jew, one of a people who had always excelled in intellectual acumen over the *goyim* (cf. 4.2 below). It is not surprising that these joint Bible readings should have turned Sigmund into a bookworm, an intellectually curious young man, open to new ideas and full of enthusiasm for them, and at the same time treasuring his Judaism.

From Freud's associations to the dream of "people with birds' beaks" (1900a, 583ff.; cf. 3.1.6 above), we also know that the illustrations in Philippson's Bible affected him deeply. These woodcuts, 685 in all, depicted a variety of subjects: landscapes, town views, genre scenes from the contemporary Orient, animals and plants from the Mediterranean, representations of customs in classical antiquity and particularly in ancient Egypt, and many others. Looking at these rather striking illustrations, one can imagine how much they must have captured the imagination of a precocious young boy, particularly when the accompanying text was read out and explained to him by his father with deep emotion, and when it seemed to relate personally to him or to his father. Perhaps these illustrations even contributed to Sigmund's strong visual memory (1901b, 47), not least because the Egyptian gods were often depicted as female figures with bare breasts (see Figs. 19 and 22). It might be that these pictures made a deep impression on him because they offered "graphic" answers to secret questions he had—for example, regarding his mother's body.

On the other hand, since Jacob Freud had most probably been given an Orthodox Jewish education based on studying the Bible and biblical commentaries in the original, he must have felt rather guilty about presenting his son with an illustrated modern Bible. In particular, when reading out passages stating that the making of idolatrous images or of "any likeness of any thing that is in heaven above, or that is in earth beneath, or that is in the water under the earth" is forbidden under threat of dire punishment (Exodus 20:3; Deuteronomy 4:23; Deuteronomy 5:8), Jacob must have realized time and again that what he was doing offended deeply against the Orthodox Jewish code: he read the Bible in translation to his son—a Bible, furthermore, that contained idolatrous illustrations—instead of presenting it to him in its true form as a revelation of God to His people.

Did Sigmund sense his father's ambiguous attitude? Did he feel that Jacob was half-hearted when initiating his children into the old tradition because he wanted them to be assimilated but also felt guilty about betraying his fathers? Did Freud, when he later collected "idols" himself, filling his consulting room and his study with antique statuettes (see Engleman, 1977; cf. Fig. 25), have the same ambiguous feelings? The passages in Deuteronomy in which the Ten Commandments are once more enjoined upon the people of Israel shortly before Moses' death are illustrated in the Philippson's Bible with a particularly large number of wood carvings of Egyptian gods, in order, as the commentary explains, "to drive home to the reader the difference between these abominations of the human spirit and the pure doctrine of Divine Revelation" (Philippson 1858, I 872; translated from the German; cf. Fig. 19). The accompanying text contains the most terrible threats of punishment by Moses for breaking the Law, and at the same time God's promise that He will keep faith with His people, even if they should sin against Him.

The resemblance of these illustrations to the small statues Freud collected and placed on his desk (see Figs. 25 and 26) is striking. True, we do not actually know what Freud thought when he looked at the little figures, but he may have felt that by venerating these alien gods he flew in the face of the God of his fathers, and in so doing proved that he had indeed become an emancipated Jew, thus obeying Jacob's mandate. On the other hand, in secret he may well have implored the protection of the new gods to save him from the wrath of Jehovah.[60]

We know that Freud, much like his father, had such fears, and that they were connected with his passion for collecting statuettes and also with his "worship of alien gods" in the modern form of bourgeois culture and science. It was only with the utmost exertion that he managed to brave the curse of the God of his ancestors and at long last pay a visit to Rome (see p. 60 above). Moreover, his sense of depersonalization upon beholding the Acropolis (1936a), a "heathen temple" not only of the Greeks but also of the educated bourgeoisie in Freud's own day, may be considered a sign of his fear that the ancient Jewish God would punish him. His last book, *Moses and Monotheism*, is at heart an account of his struggle with the God of Moses whose retribution he feared, but to whom he nevertheless would not submit because his father's ambivalent mission had required him not to do so (see 4.2 below).

In my view, Freud's behavior during the crisis of 1896–97 was molded by his Bible readings with his father in these early years. For it was at that time —and against the background of the awe-inspiring tradition of Judaism—that Jacob's mandate acquired its tremendously binding force over his son, which was later reflected in the dream of the "closed eyes," and drove Sigmund to confront himself again with Jacob's mandate even in the last of his writings (1939a).

3.3.4 THE COUNTERFEIT MONEY AFFAIR

We know little about the years preceding Freud's enrollment in the Gymnasium in 1865, a year in which an event occurred of which the details have become clearer from R. Gicklhorn's investigations (1976). I am referring to the arrest of Josef Freud, Jacob's brother, on 20 June 1865, for possession of counterfeit money. In this connection, Freud had the following dream: "I.) . . . My friend R. was my uncle.—I had a great feeling of affection for him. II.) I saw before me his face, somewhat changed. It was as though it had been drawn out lengthways. A yellow beard that surrounded it stood out especially clearly" (1900a, 137; omission in the original).

Freud's associations to this dream, particularly relevant to our discussion, were:

"R. was my uncle." What could that mean? I never had more than one uncle—Uncle Josef. (Footnote: It is astonishing to observe the way in which my memory—my waking memory—was narrowed at this point, for the purposes of the analysis. Actually I have known five of my uncles, and loved and honoured one of them. But at the moment at which I overcame my resistance to interpreting the dream I said to myself that I never had more than one uncle—the one that was intended in the dream.) There was an unhappy story attached to him. Once—more than thirty years ago,—in his eagerness to make money, he allowed himself to be involved in a transaction of a kind that is severely punished by the law, and he was in fact punished for it. My father, whose hair turned grey from grief in a few days, used always to say that Uncle Josef was not a bad man but only a simpleton; those were his words. . . . But there was the face which I saw in the dream, with its elongated features and yellow beard. My uncle did in fact have a face like that, elongated and framed in a handsome fair beard. . . . my uncle was a criminal . . . I had naturally never had any feeling of affection for my Uncle Josef (1900a, 138ff.).

In that dream, Freud went on to say, "the antithetical, affectionate affect probably arose from an infantile source (as was suggested by the later part of the dream), for the uncle–nephew relationship, owing to the peculiar nature of the earliest experiences of my childhood . . . had become the source of all my friendships and all my hatreds" (1900a, 472).

The Viennese press carried detailed reports of Josef's arrest and trial (see Table 12). In addition, the affair was mentioned in an official exchange of letters between the Austrian minister of police, Belcredi, the foreign minister, Mensdorff, and various Austrian embassies abroad. Particularly revealing is a memorandum sent by the minister of police to the foreign minister on 16 October 1865. The relevant passages in it read as follows:

A third case of an attempt to issue forged rouble notes occurred in Vienna. On June 20 of this year the Israelite Josef Freud was apprehended in the act of attempting to pass on a relatively large sum of counterfeit money, namely, 100 forged fifty-rouble notes. Altogether he was found in possession of 359 such notes with a nominal value of 17,950 roubles. From his own statement it appears that Josef Freud is an Israelite, married and the father of two children; he was born in Tysmenitz in the Stanislav district of Galicia, but has for a long time resided in Moldavia; married in 1849 at Jassy, he later traded in English ironware in Galatz. Since 1861, he has been resident in Vienna, whence he has paid three visits to London, Manchester and Birmingham, has been to Leipzig, Breslau, etc., and maintained a large correspondence with foreign countries. His son-in-law, Adolf Kornhauser of Trencsin in Hungary, is suspected of complicity in Freud's offense, for which reason Kornhauser, too, has been apprehended. Regarding the source of the notes which he knew to be forgeries, Josef Freud stated during his first interrogation that he obtained them from one Osias Weich from Czernowitz—whom he claims to have met in Galatz—during the latter's stay in Vienna last year. . . . In this case, too, there are indications that the forgeries originated in England, as may be surmised from letters of a very suspicious nature, written by two sons of the brother of Josef Freud, now in England. One of these letters states that they, the brother's two sons, have money like sand on the seashore, that, since they were wise, clever and very circumspect, fortune could not but smile on them. In another letter they enquire whether the lucky star of the House of Freud had risen for him as well, and ask the recipient to find a banking house for the goods, one with larger, quicker and more profitable outlets" (Gicklhorn, 1976, 39f.; checked against the original and translated from the German).[62]

Unfortunately, the two letters from the "brother's two sons" which Belcredi quotes have not been preserved. It is however very probable that their authors were Emanuel and Philipp, because as far as we can tell Josef Freud had no other nephews in England. One important comment is found in the conclusion Belcredi draws from reports about the rouble forgeries:

"The forgers of the fifty-rouble notes are based in England; the notes were first issued at the end of 1862 or the beginning of 1863; those responsible were Polish emigrants who printed and supervised the circulation of the notes for the benefit of rebellious, national causes. The actual circulation of the notes was placed almost exclusively in the hands of Israelites of Polish origin" (from the original; translated from the German).

When dealing with the possible reasons for the departure of the Freud family from Freiberg, I have already mentioned that Jacob Freud's older sons may have had contacts with the forgers even then, and that they may have gone to Manchester to join them. If the minister of police was right, their decision may even had had a political motive. Perhaps Emanuel and Philipp, both of whom had come from Tysmenitz, had links with Polish nationalists, who, particularly in the Russian part of the former Polish Empire, were fighting for their independence. There is clear evidence that such a pro-Polish movement flourished in Austrian Galicia, indeed in Tysmenitz itself (Friedmann, 1929, 199; Blond, 1974, 155).

The trial of Josef Freud and Osias Weich was held on 21 February 1866. Both were sentenced to ten years' imprisonment. Josef Freud's wife Rebekka drafted annual petitions for clemency from 1866 to 1870. We may take it that her husband obtained an early release in 1870, since otherwise she would presumably have continued to enter petitions for remission in succeeding years (Gicklhorn, 1976, 6; additional information supplied by the Vienna State Archives).

Sigmund Freud was nine years old when his uncle was arrested and sentenced, and Professor Gicklhorn is convinced that Jacob Freud's house underwent a police search at the time as well (*ibid.,* 17). But since the name of Jacob Freud did not appear in any press report, this assumption is highly speculative. It is quite possible that the police failed to trace the father of the "brother's two sons"—provided of course they were Emanuel and Philipp—back to Vienna, Josef having managed to keep his brother out of the investigation.

Gicklhorn's sweeping conclusions about the effects of this affair on little Sigmund Freud are, in my view, ill-founded (*ibid.,* 17f.). It is even possible that Sigmund had no idea at the time of how close to disaster his uncle's "misfortune" had brought the whole family, and that he knew nothing about the involvement of his half-brothers (if indeed they were involved). Nor is it at all certain that his schoolmates teased him about his uncle's arrest and sentence, as Gicklhorn describes so graphically. She is, however, certainly right when she claims that Sigmund must have realized something was amiss, or else he would not have recalled in a dream association thirty years later that his father's hair turned "grey from grief in a few days."

3.3.5 FREUD'S BROTHER ALEXANDER

On October 3 of that same year, 1865, Jacob Nathansohn, Amalie's father, died. From the Vienna Register of Deaths we know that he died at 9, Seegasse, presumably in the Israelitic Hospital located there. He was sixty years old. The cause of death was given as "senile mortification," or gangrene. When Sigmund, aged nine and a half, visited his grandfather for the last time, he found him "snoring in a coma" (1900a, 583; cf. p. 117 above). This scene clearly made an impression on him, which is not at all surprising. We may take it that his mother accompanied him on that occasion, and perhaps he could sense Amalie's emotional turmoil as she watched her father struggling with death.[62]

At the time of Jacob Nathansohn's death, Amalie was two months pregnant with Alexander, her last child. Alexander was born on 19 April 1866. From Freud's associations to the dream of the "persons with birds' beaks" we know that, shortly after the death of his grandfather, he was taken aside by the "ill-mannered son of a janitor," Philipp by name, and informed about the sexual behavior of adults. So it is quite possible that this, his mother's last pregnancy, had a meaning for him different from the many that had gone before. This time he probably realized that even his mother, in order to become pregnant, must have had sexual intercourse in the way his playmate had described to him.

If we may also take it that this knowledge awakened vague memories of certain glimpses he had had in Freiberg of his mother and Philipp, and of which he could suddenly make sense, then the violent emotion he experienced in the dream becomes comprehensible: the unexplained, unmentionable anxiety he had experienced in Freiberg at the age of two or two and a half because he had felt his mother's excitement was repeated in the dream in association with the strong emotion Amalie had shown by the bedside of her dying father.[63]

Anna Freud Bernays reports that Freud himself chose the name of Alexander for his new brother, his father having asked him for a suggestion (1940, 337). Was Sigmund able, as a result, to continue his fantasy of having displaced his brother Philipp in his mother's affections? Suzanne Bernfeld believes that this is what happened, adding that Alexander was the son of Philip of Macedonia (1951, 126). In that case, the paternal role Freud later assumed toward his brother may well have been founded on such fantasies. In 1895 he referred to Alexander, then twenty-nine, as "my little brother" (1950a, 122). He went on journeys with him, and supported him financially and intellectually. It is also possible that in his relations with Alexander Freud repeated Emanuel's relationship to himself: Emanuel had probably been a father substitute as well (see 3.1.4 above and 3.5 below).

Alexander is said to have resembled his mother in temperament. He was highly musical and an excellent storyteller, who could imitate the various accents of the characters in his tale—quite unlike his brother Sigmund (M. Freud, 1957, 17). Although we know very little about Philipp, it is quite possible that Emanuel and Philip were as different from each other as were Sigmund and Alexander.[64] Both Alexander and Philipp married late in life, Philipp in 1873 at the age of thirty-nine and Alexander in 1909 when he was forty-three.

The twelve months between the summer of 1865 and the summer of 1866 were thus filled with important experiences and events for little Sigmund: the arrest of his uncle Josef with its threatening implications for Sigmund's father and hence for the whole family; his own enrollment in the Gymnasium; the death of his grandfather; his sex education by the son of a janitor; possibly his observation of sexual intercourse between his parents; the birth of Alexander. Perhaps it was also during this period that Sigmund had that deeply upsetting conversation with his father during which he learned that his father once allowed a Christian to knock his hat from his head (Freud said he was ten or twelve years old at the time; 1900a, 197; cf. p. 142 above).

Freud's "militaristic phase" (Jones, 1953, I, 23) seems also to have started during this period. He began to worship heroes and warriors, to revere Hannibal, Napoleon, Alexander the Great, and many others (Grubrich-Simitis, 1971, 29). It was as if he had set out to capture the bourgeois world, "the other side." The times seemed favorable. Austrian Jews were being increasingly freed from political restrictions—the official proclamation of their emancipation coming in 1866–67 (Kinder/Hilgemann, 1966). Freud's fantasies were realistic, his hopes justified.

3.3.6 AT THE GYMNASIUM

In the autumn of 1865, Sigmund Freud enrolled in the newly established "Leopoldstädter Communales Real- und Obergymnasium" (1960b, 125).[65] In other words, he was accepted when he was one year younger than the normal enrollment age, an indication that his father or mother must have provided him with solid educational foundations. He was top of his class almost throughout his eight years at high school (Gicklhorn, 1965, 20). This too demonstrates that Jacob must have inculcated a love of learning and intellectual achievement in his son which made life at school seem easy for him.

Nevertheless, his spirit of opposition had not been entirely stifled, as we may gather from a remark in a letter he sent to Martha in 1886: "One would hardly guess it from looking at me, and yet even at school I was always the bold oppositionist, always on hand when an extreme had to be defended, and usually ready to atone for it. As I moved up into the favoured position of head boy, where I remained for years and was generally trusted, people no longer had any reason to complain about me" (1960a, 215).

In 1914, he wrote:

> From his nursery, the boy begins to cast his eyes upon the world outside. And he cannot fail now to make discoveries which undermine his original high opinion of his father and which expedite his detachment from his first ideal. He finds that his father is no longer the mightiest, wisest and richest of beings; he grows dissatisfied with him, he learns to criticize him and to estimate his place in society; and then, as a rule, he makes him pay heavily for the disappointment that has been caused by him. . . . It is in this phase of a youth's development that he comes into contact with his teachers. So that we can now understand our relation to our schoolmasters. These men, not all of whom were in fact fathers themselves, became our substitute fathers. . . . We transferred on to them the respect and expectations attaching to the omniscient father of our childhood, and we then began to treat them as we treated our fathers at home. We confronted them with the ambivalence that we had acquired in our own families, and with its help we struggled with them as we had been in the habit of struggling with our fathers in the flesh. Unless we take into account our nurseries and our family homes, our behaviour to our schoolmasters would be not only incomprehensible but inexcusable (1914f., 244).

This attitude of opposition expressed itself, as Freud reported, in a "conspiracy" against an "unpopular and ignorant master" in which he, at the age of fifteen, was the ringleader (1900a, 211). Gicklhorn believes that Freud also protested when several of his classmates were reprimanded and punished for misbehavior (1965).[66]

But this spirit of opposition vanished, as Freud himself admitted, as soon as he became head of his class. He was declared a "preferential pupil," that is, one whose average marks were better than 1.5 (*ibid.,* 20).*

Nevertheless, Freud also had time for extracurricular activities. For example, he and his friend Eduard Silberstein taught themselves Spanish:

---

* The marks ranged from 1 (top) to 5 (bottom)—Trans.

We became friends at a time when one doesn't look upon friendship as a sport or an asset, but when one needs a friend with whom to share things. We used to be together literally every hour of the day that was not spent on the school bench. We learned Spanish together, had our own mythology and secret names which we took from some dialogue of the great Cervantes. Once in our Spanish primer we found a humorous-philosophical conversation between two dogs which lie peacefully at the door of a hospital, and appropriated their names; in writing as well as in conversation he was known as Berganza, I as Cipion. . . . Together we founded a strange scholarly society, the *Academia Castellana* (AC), compiled a great mass of humorous work . . . we shared our frugal suppers and were never bored in each other's company" (1960a, 112, Letter to Martha Bernays, 7 February 1884).

It is regrettable that the seventy letters Freud wrote to Silberstein have not yet been released, though they are currently being prepared for publication. Stanescu (1965) tells us that they contain "a wealth of facts and ideas," and these are bound to throw fresh light on our understanding of the development of Freud's personality.

3.4 Visits to Freiberg

Freud and his friend Eduard Silberstein—who may also have been related to him (Stanescu, 1965, 127)—paid a visit to Freiberg in the winter of 1870. Sigmund was fourteen and a half years old at the time, though most Freud biographers say he was sixteen or seventeen, presumably because he has his *alter ego* in "Screen Memories" say that he did not return to Freiberg before that date. However, from his letters to his friend Emil Fluss, who had grown up in Freiberg (see p. 63 above), it appears that this information is incorrect. Thus, on 7 February 1873 he wrote to Emil Fluss about a "now two-year-old" story which happened during his "first" visit to Freiberg (1969a, 113). I. Grubrich-Simitis, the editor of the Fluss letters, claims that Freud must have been mistaken about the date because she too assumes that Freud did not return to Freiberg before 1872 (1971, 104). Yet it seems highly improbable that a young man of almost seventeen should have forgotten whether an event took place one or two years before. Hence it is much more reasonable to trust Freud himself and to set his first return to the place of his birth in the winter of 1870.

It is possible that he went to Freiberg on other occasions as well, for his mother was in the habit of taking the cure at Roznau, where he often visited her during the school holidays (1933a, 141). Freiberg was just fifteen miles from Roznau.

In the winter of 1870, he visited Freiberg with Silberstein alone; in the summer of 1872, he took two friends with him (1969a, 107). This stay lasted for six weeks, from the beginning of August to the middle of September.

During this visit Freud fell in love with Gisela Fluss, whom he called "Ich-thyosaura" (an extinct marine reptile) in his letters to her brother, Emil Fluss. Why he chose this humorous but unflattering name for her is not clear.[67] In "Screen Memories," he describes this event as follows:

I was seventeen, and in the family where I was staying there was a daughter of fifteen, with whom I immediately fell in love. It was my first calf-love and sufficiently intense, but I kept it completely secret. After a few days the girl went off to her school (from which she too was home for the holidays) and it was this separation after such a short acquaintance that brought my longings to a really high pitch. I passed many hours in solitary walks through the lovely woods that I had found once more and spent my time building castles in the air. These, strangely enough, were not concerned with the future but *sought to improve the past.* If only the smash had not occurred! If only I had stopped at home and grown up in the country and grown as strong as the young men in the house, the brothers of my love! And then *if only I had followed my father's profession* and if I had finally married her—for I should have known her intimately all those years! I had not the slightest doubt, of course, that in the circumstances created by my imagination I should have loved her just as passionately as I really seemed to then. A strange thing. For when I see her now from time to time—she happens to have married someone here—she is quite exceptionally indifferent to me. Yet I can remember quite well for what a long time afterwards I was affected by the yellow colour of the dress she was wearing when we first met, whenever I saw the same colour anywhere else (1899a, 313, italics added).

As in other passages of his "Screen Memories," Freud was not altogether honest here (cf. pp. 63, 123f above): in 1872, he was sixteen, not seventeen; nor did he keep his calf-love secret. Emil Fluss seems to have had some idea of what was going on. "If you insist on being kept informed about Ichthyosaura," Freud wrote to him, "let me tell you that the flirtation had more irony, indeed mockery, than seriousness about it. True, you have never attended a meeting of the 'Spanish Academy' (as our society of two is called). If you had, you would have heard how we ran this poor girl down, and would have had quite different ideas about 'our' relationship to her" (1969a, 110, 28 September 1872; translated from the German).

If he and his friend Silberstein, the only other member of the "Academia Castellana," did indeed scoff at Gisela Fluss, then his feelings for her may not have been very deep. Quite possibly this flirtation was just one of many adolescent flings, for we know that even during the train journey back from Freiberg to Vienna Freud tried to flirt with a girl through the carriage window (1969a, 108f.)[68]

He may of course have had deeper feelings for Gisela Fluss than he admitted to his friends. He once wrote to his fiancée: "Did I ever tell you that Gisela was my first love when I counted sixteen springs? No, well then, have a good laugh at me, firstly because of my taste, and then because I have never spoken a neutral, let alone kindly, word with that child. When I think about it now I think that I must have grown soft at the time, upon seeing my birthplace again" (*ibid.,* 109, footnote, 28 October 1883; translated from the German).

What had moved Freud so much during his visit to Freiberg for his meeting with Gisela to have had an importance that he would not admit to his friends and perhaps not even to himself? To answer that question, we must put ourselves in the shoes of an adolescent in the second half of the nineteenth century who, being largely ignorant of sexual matters, tries to come to terms with his burgeoning sexuality. We must also remember that his descent from a Jewish family which, though it aimed at assimilation, nevertheless had its roots in the Orthodox tradition of Eastern Europe, probably made him more ill at ease about sex than non-Jewish boys might have been. If, furthermore, we may take it that because of Jacob Freud's own guilt feelings, he made his son consider sex a taboo subject (see 2.6 above), then we can easily imagine how deeply sixteen-year-old Freud must have suffered from his sexual urges. Masturbation was generally believed to cause mental and physical damage, so that its practice caused anxiety and guilt, and other forms of sexual satisfaction were unattainable for moral and other reasons. In these circumstances, the company of a young girl, who during his earlier visit would still have looked like a child and now suddenly stood before him as a young woman, must have thrown him into a turmoil of emotion.

We know that at the time he was given to fantasies, all involving forbidden sexuality. "Screen Memories" contains the following telling passage:

Taking flowers away from a girl means to deflower her. What a contrast between the boldness of this phantasy and my bashfulness on the first occasion and my indifference on the second [his meeting with Gisela Fluss, M.K.]. . . . The most seductive part of the whole subject for a young scapegrace is the picture of the marriage night. (What does he care about what comes afterwards?) But that picture cannot venture out into the light of day: the dominating mood of diffidence and of respect towards the girl keeps it suppressed. So it remains unconscious—(1899a, 316).

Elsewhere Freud had this to say on the subject of sexual fantasies:

If these impulses do not quickly pass, there is no outlet for them other than to run their course in phantasies which have as their subject his mother's sexual activities under the most diverse circumstances; and the consequent tension leads particularly readily to his finding relief in masturbation. . . . The precondition of the loved one's being like a prostitute . . . is simple to understand as a fixation on the phantasies formed by the boy in puberty. . . . There is no difficulty in assuming that the masturbation assiduously practised in the years of puberty has played its part in the fixation of the phantasies (1910h, 171f.).

Freud's particular fantasies may have had another explanation as well. He himself thought it strange that on his lonely walks after his meeting with Gisela he should have built castles in the air, by which he tried to "improve the past." Why did he not imagine that he might possess the girl one day in real life instead of imagining what would have happened had he remained in Freiberg and possessed her there?

His claim that he would then have "followed my father's profession" might be a reference to what I believe was Jacob's contradictory mandate (see 3.3.3

above). It could well be that having "grown soft" upon seeing his birthplace again, Freud wished that he too had become a merchant, because then he would have been free of all the onerous duties Jacob's mandate entailed—to become a great scholar, to attain fame in the non-Jewish world to which end he had to defer his financial independence, to forego a comfortable life, and last but not least to delay marriage, i.e., what to him was the only "natural" way of obtaining sexual satisfaction.

Perhaps it was no accident that on this visit to Freiberg Freud should have been the same age his father was when he married Sally, his first wife, in Tysmenitz. Jacob had become a merchant like his father and grandfather, and perhaps he had given his son to understand that he must not copy their example if he wanted to better himself. Sigmund could have gained the impression that his father regretted having become a merchant instead of an intellectual.

If these assumptions are correct, then Freud's idea of "improving the past" referred not only to his own childhood but also to his father's past, which he was not to repeat. It seems to me that Freud's return to Freiberg, where childhood memories flooded back and impressed themselves upon him with particular poignancy, gave him his first chance to grasp these associations and hence to accept his fate.[69]

His letters to Emil Fluss also show that it was during this period that Freud began to sign letters as "Sigmund" instead of "Sigismund" (1969a, 109f., footnote). As I pointed out earlier (see p. 100, note 4), many biographers have concluded from this change of name that Freud had an identity crisis at the time. Although this view admittedly agrees with my own assumptions about the links between Freud's return to Freiberg and the discovery of his own destiny and identity, to me there is not enough evidence to say that Freud himself felt there was a significant difference between "Sigmund" and "Sigismund." He may simply have chosen to drop the longer name for the sake of convenience.

From a letter to Emil Fluss, we also know that Freud took his *Matura* (school-leaving examination) at the beginning of 1873, that he passed it with distinction (1969a, 21f., 16 June 1873), and that he decided to become a "natural scientist," giving up his plan to study law (*ibid.,* 116, 1 May 1873).

3.5 Freud's Half-Brothers in England

After his school-leaving examination, Freud intended to visit his half-brothers in Manchester. This visit, however, had to be postponed until 1875, by which time Freud had already been studying medicine in Vienna for two years.

In 1875, Emanuel lived at 12, Green Street, Ardwick, one of the "better suburbs" of Manchester. His occupation is given as "fent" dealer, a dealer in remnants of cloth. His business address was 69, Thomas Street, Shudehill, in the center of the city (Manchester Directories, from information supplied by F. Shepherd).

He had five children: John, Pauline, and Bertha, born in Freiberg; Solomon (Samuel, Sam), born on 28 June 1860 in Lower Broughton; and Matilda, born on 12 May 1862 in Central Manchester (London, General Register Office). Since Matilda, Emanuel's youngest daughter, does not figure on the Freud family tree (Sigmund Freud Archives, New York), and since the 1871 Census does not list her among the children of Emanuel and Maria (according to information supplied by B. Williams), she may have died in early childhood. However, no entry to that effect could be found in the General Register Office (research by E. Kuhne).

Philipp Freud married Bloome (Bloomah) Frankel from Birmingham on 15 January 1873 (London, General Register Office; see Table 3). They had two children, Pauline (Poppy), born on 23 October 1873, and Morris Herbert Walter, born on 2 April 1876 *(loc. cit.)*. Both the marriage certificate and the birth certificate give Philipp's address as 96, Shudehill, which means that he had not yet moved to a "better" district; he was first listed as a resident of Ardwick in 1879 (Manchester Directories; information supplied by F. Shepherd).

Philipp called himself an "importer of foreign fancy goods," but also stated on his marriage certificate that he was a jeweler.

A letter from Sigmund Freud to Eduard Silberstein contains a very graphic description of the visit he paid his two half-brothers in Manchester:

Vienna, 9 Sept. 1875   ¡Querido Berganza!
Two mornings ago I returned to good old Vienna after my seven and a half weeks' long travels, have made use of the first two days to wean myself from English habits, and now that my little room looks comfortable once again, all my treasures have been put in place and my mind is settled, I am sitting down by the light of a miserable, sight-destroying oil lamp (in England, every beggar uses gas) in order to reply to your letter, which reached me while I was busy packing my bags in Manchester. . . .[70]
You will, no doubt, wish to know who my relatives in England are and how I feel about them. I cannot have told you much about them in the past. They are two brothers on my father's side, that is, from my father's first marriage, twenty and twenty-two years older than I, the older, Emanuel, having married when very young, the younger, Philipp, two and a half years ago. They used to live with us in Freiberg, where the oldest three children of my elder brother were born. The unfavorable turn their business took there caused them to move to England, where they have been since 1859. It is true to say that they now hold a generally respected position, not because of their wealth, for they are not rich, but because of their personal attributes. They are shopkeepers, the elder selling cloth and the younger jewelry, in the sense that word seems to have in England. My two sisters-in-law are good and cheerful women, one of them being English, which made my conversations with her extremely agreeable. Of those members

of our family of whom I am privileged to call myself uncle, you are already acquainted with John; he is an Englishman in every sense and has a knowledge of languages and technical skills well beyond the normal commercial education. Unknown to you, and, until recently, to me, are two charming nieces, Pauline, who is nineteen, and Bertha, who is seventeen, and a fifteen-year-old boy by the name of Sam'l, which, I believe, has been fashionable in England ever since Pickwick, and who is generally considered to be a "sharp and deep" young fellow. I would have less to criticize than to praise, and in many respects to praise warmly, in my relatives, if my biased position of brother and uncle and the cordial reception I was accorded did not disqualify me from occupying the judge's and critic's bench. As for England itself, I need not observe such restrictions and can say straight out that I would sooner live there than here, rain, fog, drunkenness and conservatism notwithstanding. Many peculiarities of the English character and country that other continentals might find intolerable agree very well with my own nature. Who knows, dear friend, but that after I have completed my studies a friendly wind might not blow me across to England and allow me to practice my hand there. Let me confess to you: I now have more than just one ideal, a practical one having been added to the theoretical of earlier years. Had I been asked last year what was my dearest wish, I would have replied: a laboratory and free time, or an ocean liner with all the instruments a scientist needs; now I am unsure whether I would not rather reply: a large hospital and ample funds to mitigate or eradicate some of the ills that ravage man's body. If then I wished to reach a large number of people instead of seeing a small host of people or fellow scientists, then England would be just the place for that purpose. A respected man, supported by the press and rich patrons, could do wonders in curing physical ills, if only he is enough of an explorer to enter new curative paths. All these are still vague ideas, and I must stop here.

I saw nothing of London, Sheffield, Birmingham, Oxford and so on, all of which the tourist is expected to visit; they flattered me with the hope that I might see England again next year or the year after. To touch the poet in you as well, just think: I have seen the sea, sacred thalatta, following the waves of the flood as with fury they fled from the shore and catching crab and starfish on the beach!

I have brought over only a few books, but what English scientific writings I have read over there will ensure that all my own studies follow in the steps of those Englishmen toward whom I happen to be most favorably inclined: Tyndall, Huxley, Lyell, Darwin, Thomson, Lockyer, et al.

I am more suspicious than ever of philosophy, but you will probably prefer to learn that I have a fine penknife and a good razor for you, for about 9 sh = 3 thaler. And you will believe me when I say that I am waiting impatiently for the day when I shall see you again. Tell me the date and time of your arrival; I am a devotee of waiting-at-the-station.

Warm regards from your

Cipion.

P.S. My mother asks you to remember her to your mother and to let her know whether her health is as good as all of us wish it to be.*

* Letter kindly supplied by Freud Copyrights Ltd., Colchester, from an unpublished copy of the Freud–Silberstein correspondence, transcribed and translated by A. J. Pomerans.

This letter strikes me as being very important not only for what it tells us about Freud's half-brothers but also for the light it throws on Freud's professional aspirations.

With respect to his English relatives, it appears that as late as 1875 John was still living with his parents; in other words, he had not disappeared "at the age of eighteen" (see 3.1.7 above). The letter also confirms my assumption that both the half-brothers had risen in England within about ten years from the status of poverty-stricken immigrants to respected citizens. Thus, while they first lived in Lower Broughton, one of the poorest quarters in the north of the city, they had managed by 1871 to settle in Ardwick (1861 Census, 1871 Census, information supplied by B. Williams).[71] B. Williams, the author of *The Making of Manchester Jewry* (1976), also informed me that most middle-class Jews lived in North Manchester and that only a minority succeeded in settling in the southern suburbs. The migration of the Freuds from the north of the city to the south was the typical reaction of better-off Jews to the influx of poorer co-religionists from Eastern Europe into the north of the city. Ardwick, and Chorlton-on-Medlock where Emanuel moved later, were admittedly not the most elegant districts; but Jews lived here amid English and German inhabitants in surroundings that were undoubtedly more respectable than their earlier quarters (Williams, 1976, 310f.).

According to B. Williams, Emanuel and Philipp were even founder members of the South Manchester Synagogue, established in 1872 in Chorlton-on-Medlock by Jews dissatisfied with the composition of the old congregation. The new group wanted to distance itself both from the poor new immigrants and also from the established Jewish residents who dominated the Great Synagogue, and by whom they felt snubbed (*ibid.,* 310ff.). The fact that Emanuel and Philipp were founder members of the South Manchester Synagogue is a reflection of their social advancement, which did not involve their turning their backs on Judaism. Probably they were simply interested in not having their still shaky social status put to the test by constant contact with both the poorer and the more fashionable Jewish circles.

When he was much older, Emanuel apparently rented a second house in Southport, a seaside resort not far from Manchester.[72] It was here that Freud visited him in 1908 (Jones, 1965, II, 52). Martin, Sigmund Freud's son, had this to say about a visit to his uncle's home in Southport:

Uncle Emanuel, as the son of Jacob Freud, the small and not successful textile merchant of Freiberg in Moravia, had no importance, social or otherwise, when he reached Manchester. But when, in 1913, I went from Vienna to stay with him for a short holiday, I found him living in a large and comfortable house in Southport. This might be natural enough in a man who by hard work and ability had won wealth, but what has struck me since . . . is the fact that Uncle Emanuel had become in every possible detail a dignified English gentleman. Indeed, while I have been received in many English homes, I have never enjoyed one that seemed so typically English as that of my Uncle Emanuel at Southport; and this applies to his dress, his manners and his hospitality. . . . My impression of Uncle Emanuel's metamorphosis was gained when he, then about eighty, had retired from business and left his control to his son Sam. I have earlier memories, also, of Uncle Emanuel. During my youth in Vienna, being very fond of his half-brother (my father), Uncle Emanuel came to see us occasionally, events I recall because of the presents he bought us children. He liked to spend money, but he hated to waste it. In consequence, the selection of the presents was always a great and highly methodical occasion in which the cost of the gift was of much less importance than its uses or entertainment value (1957, 12–13).

Did Freud, during his 1875 visit, have the same impression of Emanuel, then forty-three, as, nearly forty years on, his own son would have of the old man at almost eighty years old? Did Emanuel strike Freud, too, as a model of successful assimilation? Did the two "oldest sons" of Jacob, Emanuel and Sigmund, realize that, by turning their backs on orthodoxy, they were obeying their father's mandate? They seem to have spoken about their relationship to Jacob, for Emanuel admonished his younger brother to show filial piety toward him (see p. 115 above).

It is odd how little information there is about Philipp. Jones thinks he ended up as a peddler (1955, II, 434), and the official death entry simply states that he was a former traveler in fancy goods. Freud's son Martin never visited him, since Philipp died in 1911 and Martin did not go to Manchester until 1913. But Freud himself said nothing about meeting Philipp, and confined most of his comments to his half-brother Emanuel.[73] For this lack of concern, too, there may be an explanation in the unpublished family correspondence.

With this visit to England, it would seem, Freud's childhood and youth drew to a close, in the sense that all his later experiences were, so to speak, built on those foundations. His student years until he graduated in 1881, his postgraduate research during the engagement to Martha Bernays between 1882 and 1886, his early years as a medical practitioner and husband before the crisis of 1896–97, may be considered—just like the crisis itself—as consequences of the earlier events we have examined, and hence contribute nothing further to our understanding of his great crisis. For the rest, it is precisely the later years that have been described in great detail by all of Freud's biographers.

3.6 Conclusions: Jacob Freud's Mandate and the Crisis of 1896–97

The data on Freud's family of origin assembled here are numerous and yet fragmentary. At best they yield an incomplete picture, like a broken mosaic of which many small pieces have been preserved but of which a great deal is still missing. Any reconstruction can only be one of many equally plausible options. The discovery of further pieces would bring us much closer to the original picture, but would then call for a revision of all previous reconstructions. This is of course true of my own attempt as well.

Can we say that Freud's crisis of 1896–97, which led to the creation of psychoanalysis, may be traced back to his childhood? Can that crisis be considered a repetition of a childhood trauma which was caused by events in Freiberg and the abrupt move to Vienna and which, in turn, may be traced back to the experiences of Jacob Freud? I believe that there is a series of parallels to support this claim.

A comparison of the course and nature of the crisis of 1896–97 with Freud's experiences during his departure from Freiberg in 1859–60 readily reveals that both have a similar structure:

In Freiberg, Freud, I believe, stumbled upon the subject of sexuality in the course of childish exploration by which he had tried to answer the question of where little children come from; he had discovered the physical differences between the sexes by examining the body of little Pauline. This discovery became associated with a terrible threat—the threat of castration—which his father had uttered as a warning against masturbation. True, that threat had not been implemented, and he had retained his penis; but he had lost Freiberg, and, it would seem, felt personally responsible for that loss. The events related to that loss of his world were repressed. They sank into his unconscious, combined with his feeling of guilt for having caused them. And out of his unconscious they had a motivating force upon his ambition, his quest for recognition through achievement.

Similarly, during his crisis of 1896–97 Freud also stumbled upon the subject of sexuality, and more precisely of infantile sexuality, while trying to discover the etiology of the neuroses of defense. This time his research was cut short by his father's death, which must have rekindled the repressed childhood fear that forbidden investigations invite terrible punishment. The memories which had just been released from repression were consigned back into the unconscious, with the result that once again there was a prodigious increase in Freud's creative efforts, culminating in the development of psychoanalysis as a theory.

It would seem that this scheme—search for the secret of sexuality; sanctions against this search by threat of punishment; panic from the experience of punishment; repression of guilt feelings; and compensation for these feelings by increased intellectual activity—was repeated in Freud's life not only during these two crises but on many other occasions as well. His experience with Gisela Fluss also fits into this scheme, as does the later Emma–Irma–Anne episode (see 1.1.2.3 above).

I believe, however, that the substantive similarities are even more important than these purely external structural parallels:

Both crises hinged on Freud's ambivalent attitude toward sexuality. In Freiberg, his "seduction" by his nursemaid Resi Wittek had felt exciting and pleasant, and yet highly dangerous because of the allied threat of castration.

As a forty-year-old man he thought he had discovered that sexuality was the cause of neurosis—precisely because of this bipolarity. It was liberating on the one hand but dangerous on the other; if diverted into "the wrong channels," it was bound to lead to a kind of castration, that of neurotic debility.

During both periods in Freud's life, guilt was a central concern. As a child he had been guilty of sexual curiosity and masturbation, for which in his fantasy he was punished with a "journey to Hell," the departure from Freiberg. True, he probably suspected that his parents also were not entirely blameless for that journey, but the fantastic explanation seems to have struck him as the more plausible one. As an adult he felt guilty because he had broken the commandment of filial piety. At the same time, his father's death rekindled the memory of this repressed childhood experience, which he was once again unable to assimilate except by a fantasy—that of the universal Oedipus conflict, according to which the child's own sexual desires are responsible for his guilt so that the parents can be exonerated.

I believe that this very myth prevented Freud from grasping the causes of his crisis, that is, from realizing that his childhood fantasies, although in keeping with his childish powers of reasoning, prevented him from seeing the truth. Thus he did not understand that Jacob probably had very sound reasons of his own for folding his tents in Freiberg, that these reasons involved Jacob's own guilt feelings which were probably also rooted in a conflict between sexuality and filial piety. I believe that Freud was, so to speak, forced in both crises to invent a fantasy theory to make sense of the problems that were worrying him, and this because Jacob had placed a taboo on the discovery of the real answers.

In the crisis of 1896–97, Freud did not realize that the answer to the problem that was torturing him, the cause of his own neurotic symptoms, was that his conflict was a repetition of the conflict Jacob had faced when, at the same age, he too had just lost his father. Freud did not realize that Jacob had turned him into a "bound delegate" (Stierlin), who was expected to fulfill conflicting missions. He was meant to be a better or more loyal son than Jacob believed himself to have been; at the same time he was to abandon the narrow Orthodox tradition and seek success in bourgeois society. Now, in my view, the ambivalence of the mandate was precisely that the son was expected to turn his back on tradition but not on one of its most central tenets, that of filial piety on which, ultimately, the entire Jewish tradition is based.

I believe that with this mandate to his son Schlomo or Sigmund, Jacob tried to rid himself of the guilt feelings he had toward his own father, Schlomo. For the clearer it became that little Sigmund had a brain, a *"kop,"* and hence was capable of fulfilling Jacob's mandate, the more relieved of his own burden of guilt Jacob could feel. I believe that here we may also have an explanation of Jacob's growing failure in business. It was as if he did not have to strive for success any longer, indeed, that he had to fail if he was to assuage his guilt toward his father. His son could be—in fact had to be—successful in his stead. Perhaps, unconsciously, Jacob even invited those personal defeats I have assumed he suffered—the relationship between Amalie and Philipp, the business failure in Vienna, and possibly an earlier one in Freiberg.

Freud did not see these connections, but I am certain that he felt them. This can be inferred from his feelings of rage and hatred against his father, secretly stored up for years, until they emerged in his dreams before and after the crisis of 1896–97. He hated his father for tying him down with his mandate, and his hatred might also explain why he chose a field of activity in which he was bound to come into conflict with that mandate. For there is reason to ask why Freud felt so drawn to the study of the human psyche, to the "archaeology of the soul," a subject in which he had perforce to delve into his own history, why he did not continue with neurophysiology or choose another, less "hazardous" profession. Here Freud's unconquered rage against his father seems to have acted as a spur: he had been "seduced" or "misled," first by Resi's eroticizing activities and then by his father's mandate. For every delegation is necessarily seducing or misleading, especially when it involves contradictory instructions and so frustrates the need for unequivocal ego definition.

Throughout his life Freud struggled with his father's mandate, and it was this struggle, I believe, which caused his neurotic symptoms. Just when it reached its climax, when Freud was on the track of his father's "perversions," Jacob died. And although I do not think Freud would ever have spoken to his father about the latter's past—and this precisely because he had internalized Jacob's taboo—his father's death placed an even more insurmountable obstacle in the path of any further investigation. Nearly a year passed before Freud wrote his letter of recantation (see 1.2 above), and throughout the interval he struggled to save his seduction theory. But then his father prevailed, and Freud shouldered his mandate with all its contradictions: he stopped looking into his father's guilty past, renounced the seduction theory, and instead, dutiful son that he was, took the guilt upon his own shoulders with the help of his Oedipus theory. We shall see how this feeling of self-surrender was given an even further, symbolic expression in his confrontation with "Moses" (see 4.2 below).

The ultimate victory, however, went to Schlomo, Freud's grandfather, for son and grandson alike remained loyal to him and hence to the Jewish tradition. Jacob expunged his guilt toward him by charging his own son, Schlomo, to observe the traditional Jewish ideal of the perfect father-son relationship: a Jewish son must excel his father in learning, must bring him, his family, and the people of Israel closer to redemption by his scholarship. At the same time, and above all, he must also obey the Fifth Commandment, to honor his parents. True, Sigmund Freud's learning was not that of the Orthodox Jewish scholar, whose study is confined to Torah and Talmud, thereby promoting the ultimate end of the exile and the arrival of the Messiah. Freud studied modern science; but he too did as much as he could to further the redemption of his people, at least in the eyes of the assimilated Jew, Jacob Freud.

By becoming the kind of son his father wanted him to be, Freud helped Jacob to assuage his guilt toward his own father. To that end, he abandoned his seduction theory, which compromised not only his own but every other father as well. Jacob conquered his guilt feelings with the help of his actual child; Sigmund conquered his with the help of a "theoretical child"—psychoanalysis based upon Oedipus theory. But the psychic structure presiding over the mastery of their respective father conflicts was identical. Neither of them rebelled against his father, and both shouldered the contradictory mandate of making their own way, even while remaining dutiful sons.

For us, however, it is very sobering that Freud should have invented psychoanalysis because his father most probably had problems with his own sexuality and fought with his own father about matters of religion; that Freud, dutiful son that he was, did no more than obey his father's mandate, so that the motive of his epoch-making contribution was a childish wish to please his father. As Stierlin has pointed out in his book on Hitler (1975b), the real motives of great works—for good or evil—are invariably based on childish and, judged by the criteria of the adult world, extremely banal wishes. It is disappointing to detect the small child in the great man—the small child that he has remained even in the act of creating work admired all over the world. But we can bear this knowledge not least because Freud himself has taught us to look at our own thoughts and actions in the mirror of childhood experience and to realize that in our deepest feelings we have all remained the little children we once were.

4. The Fulfillment of
the Mandate

It is tempting to set out in detail how Jacob's mandate affected Freud's scientific work and his personal relationships, how Freud—much as he had done during the crisis of 1897—continued to avoid all questions that might have infringed his father's taboo. Anyone examining Freud's views on family life and the development of psychoanalytical theory must be struck, time and again, by the limitations this taboo imposed on his theoretical work and practical life.

Thus, though his relationship with his wife and children is largely a matter of speculation because there are few references to it in his writings, all the available evidence[1] suggests that Freud expected his children, and probably his wife as well, not to delve too deeply into his personal life and to respect the taboo that he, like his father before him, had set up as a barrier before his own past. His children do not seem to have known much more about his childhood and antecedents than the outside can glean from his biographers.

Martin Freud's book about his father contains several indications that Freud, even in his dealings with his children, and above all with his sons, repeated certain attitudes and views of his own father. For example, Freud's extraordinarily close relationship with his daughter Anna, who in his old age was obviously closer to him than his wife,[2] must probably be considered yet another consequence of Jacob's taboo. It would seem that Freud passed on to her much the same mandate as he had received from his father, without however, offering her the chance to excel him. It is not known whether she too tried to lay down her mandate as Freud had tried to do before Jacob's death. She is reported to have fallen in love several times, her close ties with her father always holding her back (Roazen, 1975, 438).[3]

It is also remarkable that Freud's wife should have known next to nothing about psychoanalysis, and that she seems to have been ignorant of many of Freud's views, for instance on sexuality, which must after all have concerned her intimately (Reik, after Freeman, 1971, 80f.). Simon has compared Freud in this respect to the Orthodox Jew who feels free to discuss the Talmudic commentaries on the sexual commandments and prohibitions with absolute frankness in *shul* (synagogue), but cannot exchange a single word on the subject with his wife. Undoubtedly, quite a few non-Jews in Franz-Joseph's Vienna[4] suffered from similar inhibitions, but precisely in this sphere we can detect a narrowing of Freud's normally wide horizon, linked indubitably to the ideas Jacob had handed down to him.

Freud's relations with his followers, too, were colored by Jacob's taboo. It appears that he had two kinds of disciples: those who subscribed to his views fully, or at least without overt reservations (Abraham, Jones, Ferenczi, Rank, Sachs, Reik, Federn, Nunberg, and others);[5] and those who challenged him openly and went their own way (see 4.1.2.1 below), or else succumbed to the conflict, like Tausk and Silberer, both of whom took their lives.[6] In each case it can be shown that Freud's feelings toward these men, whom he treated like sons, were a repetition of his relationship with his father, albeit with a reversal of roles: he put himself in Jacob's shoes and made the same demands on his "sons" as his father had made on him.

A detailed analysis of Freud's relationships with his patients would reveal to what large extent his own father conflict was reflected in his case histories. It would seem that his patient Dora (1905e), for example, broke off her analysis not least because Freud's own unresolved conflict caused him to misinterpret the dynamics of that young girl's family life (Stierlin, 1975c, 137; Slipp, 1978, 138). In his most detailed case history, that of the "Wolf Man" (1918b), Freud again failed to trace the patient's neurotic symptoms back to seduction in early childhood and other highly traumatic infantile experiences, and instead treated them as so many expressions of the Wolf Man's Oedipal fantasies (Stierlin, 1975c, 183; Gardiner, 1972). And finally, in the Schreber case (1911c), Freud chose to ignore the patient's family history, although it was known to him (Schatzman, 1973, 1976; Krüll, 1977b; cf. p. 35, note 33, above).

Above all, it would be interesting to examine all Freud's writings for the purpose of determining whether his theory, with its subsequent developments and changes, continued to provide him with such explanations of his own behavior as allowed him to keep Jacob's taboo. I, for one, am certain that such an examination would explain—as I shall try to show in connection with Freud's studies on Moses—not only the many gaps, incongruities, and contradictions in his work but also his extreme emotional involvement with particular subjects.

In my view, it is no accident that Freud should never have succeeded in writing a "metapsychology" of the kind he had first tried vainly to produce with his *Project* as early as the 1890s (1950a; cf. 1.1.2.4 above). In 1915 he made another attempt, in the twelve "Papers on Metapsychology," to provide a systematic overview of his theoretical ideas, but failed again. Only five of these papers were published (1915c, 1915d, 1915e, 1917d, and 1917e); he seems to have destroyed the other seven (see editorial introduction to 1915c, 105ff.). Freud's theoretical opus is made up of many individual books and papers, each of which is brilliant in itself; but taken together, they do not constitute a coherent whole. I believe that this failure must be blamed on a motive of which Freud himself was unconscious. His theory had to have a provisional character, had to remain adaptable so that it could serve him during all future external or internal changes as protection against the intrusion of repressed childhood memories.

Thus the Oedipus theory was transformed into a theory of patricide, just as soon as Freud himself became a "patriarch" (see 4.1.2 below); the libido theory had to make way for the dual instinct theory (sexual and death instincts) when he himself had lost people he loved (1920g). And even the introduction of his structural theory (1923b), involving Ego, Id, and Superego, came during a phase of personal reorientation that coincided with the onset of cancer. I believe that these and other changes in his theory can all be understood as reactions to personal experiences. I am not of course suggesting that there was a direct causal link, for instance, between his death instinct theory and the death of a close friend,[7] but merely that these personal experiences seem linked with his childhood traumas so that the transformation of his theoretical views can once again be said to have been dictated by Jacob's taboo.

Probably even Freud's peculiar inability to explain female sexuality can be traced back to that taboo. It was in the Fliess letters that he first expressed regret at being unable to include female sexuality in his theory (1950a, 302, 5 November 1899), and as late as 1926 he was still writing: "We know less about the sexual life of little girls than of boys. But we need not feel ashamed of this distinction; after all, the sexual life of adult women is a 'dark continent' for psychology" (1926e, 212).

Not until he was seventy-five did Freud present a theory of female sexuality, the precise nature of which need not detain us here but which obviously struck him as a surprising discovery, for he commented: "Our insight into this early, pre-Oedipus, phase in girls comes to us as a surprise, *like the discovery, in another field, of the Minoan-Mycenean civilization behind the civilization of Greece.* Everything in the sphere of this first attachment to the mother seems to me *so difficult to grasp in analysis*—so grey with age and shadowy and almost impossible to revivify—that it was as if it had succumbed to an especially inexorable repression" (1931b, 226, italics added).

That repression, I believe, was present not only in Freud's female patients but also in Freud himself, as the archeological comparison may indicate. His belated interest in the subject may also have been connected with the death of his mother in 1930—one year before the publication of "Female Sexuality" —at the age of ninety-five. It is as if he had been unable to deal with this question while his mother was still alive, once again thanks to Jacob's taboo.

All these matters deserve a deeper analysis, which would take us far too far afield. I am, however, convinced that a study of Freud's work against the background of Jacob's mandate would bring us a great deal closer to an answer to many difficult questions thrown up by recent studies of psychoanalysis.[8]

In what follows, I shall confine myself to looking at Freud's writings on Moses against this background. These writings—"The Moses of Michelangelo" (1914b) and *Moses and Monotheism* (1939a)—are central to our theme because they reflect Freud's relationship to his father in a multiplicity of ways.

4.1 Sigmund Freud and the *Moses* of Michelangelo

In September 1901, when Freud finally overcame his inhibitions and traveled to Rome, the *Moses* of Michelangelo in the Church of St. Peter in Vincoli moved him very deeply: "For no piece of statuary has ever made stronger impression on me than this. How often have I . . . essayed to support the angry scorn of the hero's glance! Sometimes I have crept cautiously out of the half-gloom of the interior as though I myself belonged to the mob upon whom his eye is turned—the mob which can hold fast no conviction, which has neither faith nor patience, and which rejoices when it has regained its illusory idols" (1914b, 213; see Fig. 24).

During his later visits to Rome, Freud never failed to return to this statue. In 1914, he published "The Moses of Michelangelo," in which he tried to reconstruct the artistic intentions he attributed to Michelangelo, but which in fact reflected his own confrontation with Moses. This can be deduced, above all, from the fact that Freud published this paper anonymously, although his friends and followers had protested that the style would identify the author (Jones, 1955, II, 366). Just as he had tried to hide the autobiographical character of "Screen Memories," albeit he did not publish it anonymously, he also tried to hide the Moses paper, and only as late as 1924 admitted publicly that he was the author.

Freud once told E. Weiss that his relationship to this paper was "something like that to a love-child," adding that he had not legitimized this "non-analytical child" until much later (1960a, 412, 12 April 1933). By this remark, he probably meant that his paper sounded so strong a personal note that he did not want to include it among the "legitimate" body of his scientific writings, which apparently had to be devoid of any biographical "taint."

In this paper, Freud flies in the face of a whole series of art experts by maintaining that Michelangelo did not depict Moses in an outburst of rage shortly *before* he smashed the tablets, but during a moment of reflection *after* the tablets had almost slipped out of his hands. Freud believed that Michelangelo, using his artistic licence, had changed the Bible story to create a Moses who did not destroy the tablets but saved them at the last moment from his own passion:

> In his first transport of fury, Moses desired to act, to spring up and take vengeance and forget the Tables; but he has overcome the temptation, and he will now remain seated and still, in his frozen wrath and in his pain mingled with contempt. Nor will he throw away the Tables so that they will break on the stones, for it is on their especial account that he has controlled his anger; it was to preserve them that he kept his passion in check. In giving way to his rage and indignation, he had to neglect the Tables, and

FIGURE 23 Moses, steel engraving
from Philippson's Bible

FIGURE 24 Michelangelo's *Moses*
in S. Pietro in Vincoli, Rome

the hand which upheld them was withdrawn. They began to slide down and were in danger of being broken. This brought him to himself. *He remembered his mission and for its sake renounced an indulgence of his feelings.* His hand returned and saved the unsupported Tables before they had actually fallen to the ground. In this attitude he remained immobilized, and in this attitude Michelangelo has portrayed him as the guardian of the tomb [of Pope Julius II, M.K.]. . . . Michelangelo has placed a different Moses on the tomb . . . one superior to the historical or traditional Moses. He has modified the theme of the broken Tables; he does not let Moses break them in his wrath, but makes him be influenced by the danger that they will be broken and makes him calm that wrath, or at any rate prevent it from becoming an act. In this way he has added something new and more than human to the figure of Moses; so that the giant frame with its tremendous physical power becomes only a concrete expression of *the highest mental achievement that is possible in a man, that of struggling successfully against an inward passion for the sake of a cause to which he has devoted himself* (1914b, 229f., 233, italics added).

Like all other interpretations of Michelangelo's artistic intentions, Freud's is speculative, the artist himself not having made us privy to his intentions.

Freud's detailed analysis of the *Moses* statue, its posture, its facial expression, its flowing beard, and so on, is very convincing and indeed makes it seem plausible that Michelangelo did wish to represent Moses as a man in control of his passions. However, Freud felt he was on uncertain ground here (Jones, 1955, II, 365ff.; Freud/Abraham, 1965, 171), which was one of the reasons he himself mentioned for keeping the authorship of the essay a secret. In any case, he did not proceed to publish it until after his visit to Rome in 1913, when he sat daily before the statue and felt strengthened in his original opinion.

It is strange, however, that in support of this opinion Freud should have quoted a biblical passage that does not bear out very well Moses' alleged mental state. That passage[9] deals with Moses' descent from Mount Sinai after he had received the tablets. Finding the Israelites dancing round the golden calf, he smashed the tablets and punished the renegades, three thousand of whom were killed by their own brothers, the Levites (Exodus 32:27–28); this punishment ordered by Moses, incidentally, is not mentioned in Freud's paper. Then Moses returned to Mount Sinai, where he received the Ten Commandments from God once again.

On his second descent, he did not find cause to be angry with the Israelites, who greeted him with due deference. This is how the Bible puts it:

And it came to pass, when Moses came down from mount Sinai with the two tables of testimony in Moses' hand, when he came down from the mount that Moses wist not that the skin of his face shone while he talked with him. And when Aaron and all the children of Israel saw Moses, behold, the skin of his face shone; and they were afraid to come nigh him. And Moses called unto them; and Aaron and all the rulers of the congregation returned unto him: and Moses talked with them (Exodus 34:29–31).

Now, Freud did not realize that Michelangelo had probably intended to depict Moses after his *second* descent, as the horns on Moses' head indicate. That peculiar ornament seems to rest on an erroneous translation (Bergmann, 1976, 16): the Hebrew word *karan,* rendered in this passage as "his face shone," means both "to radiate" and "to have horns." This explains why Moses was said to be "cornute" in an early Latin translation of the passage, and why there are so many medieval representations of Moses adorned with horns. Michelangelo seems to have been under the same misapprehension. In any case, the Bible does not use *karan* in connection with Moses' *first* stay on Mount Sinai.

In other words, Michelangelo did in fact depict a composed Moses, one who had reined in his passion, who, having destroyed the first tablets in anger, now wished to save the second gift by which God had sealed His covenant with the people of Israel. Why then did Freud not quote the relevant biblical passage instead of the one in which Moses rages at the renegade Israelites? Had he chosen the correct text he would not have had to assume that Michelangelo engaged in a "re-elaboration of the *motif* of the broken Tables of the Law" (1914b, 216). Did Freud simply fail to read another two chapters of Exodus and hence miss the point?

That assumption is implausible, because Freud knew his Bible well and because he quoted the passage in question in a later work (1921c, 125). In my view, Freud overlooked the most obvious interpretation—consciously or unconsciously—simply because the image of a composed Moses, sure of himself and of his adherents, did not lend itself to a projection of his own feelings. This he could only accomplish with a Moses who struggled "successfully against an inward passion for the sake of a cause," who fulfilled his "mission," and to that end "renounced an indulgence of his feelings."

4.1.1 SIGMUND FREUD, THE SON OF MOSES

To my mind, Freud's fascination with Michelangelo's statue reflected his own emotional ambivalence. On the one hand, he identified himself with Moses, the self-controlled lawgiver; on the other hand, Moses was a father image of whom he was afraid, whose "disdainful and wrathful expression" consigned him, Freud, to the "mob" that danced around the false idol. In what follows I shall start out by examining Freud's filial feelings toward Moses, leaving his identification with the founder of the Jewish religion until later (see 4.1.2 below).

Freud's description of the feelings of shame and guilt which he experienced in the dark of the Roman church in the face of the awe-inspiring *Moses* reminds me of his dream the night after his father's funeral (see 1.2.1 above). In that dream, a "tablet" had appeared to him, warning him not to trespass the Fifth Commandment. Now he feared to look into Moses', the tablet-bringer's eyes because he felt like one of the Israelites who had trespassed against his commandments by worshipping idols.

Bakan points out that Freud found himself in a wholly paradoxical situation as he stood before the statue of Moses. As a Jew, he felt that the great Jewish lawgiver admonished him to keep the commandments; yet by his extremely emotional response to the "graven image" of the statue he had broken the Law of God—and a special irony lay in the fact that it was a statue erected for a papal tomb in a Catholic church (Bakan, 1958, 134; cf. Robert, 1975).

Bakan believes that it was not by chance that Freud omitted the biblical passage in which Moses orders the Levites to kill the rebellious Israelites; he did so because of an unconscious feeling that he deserved the same kind of punishment (1958, 156). Above all, Bakan is convinced that Freud's central concern to present Moses not as a violent hothead but as one who has gained control of his passion reflected his own attempts to surmount his unconscious fears of punishment by the God of his Fathers (*ibid.*, 128).

In my view, these very fears were linked with Freud's childhood trauma in Freiberg. Once again he felt himself caught in a forbidden act.

The Interpretation of Dreams contains a passage that was originally written by Hanns Sachs (1900a, 378ff.). Since it is well known that Freud only accepted contributions from colleagues or pupils with whom he was in full agreement, we are entitled to take Sachs's views for Freud's own (see Simon, 1957). The passage deals with an episode in one of Bismarck's dreams ("then, with my whip in my left hand, I struck the smooth rock and called on God. The whip grew to an endless length . . ."), which Sachs interprets as a masturbation fantasy based on "childish desires in the remote past." Moreover, Sachs argues that Bismarck may have identified himself with Moses in this dream:

It would not be unlikely that in this time of conflict Bismarck should compare himself with Moses, the leader, whom the people he sought to free rewarded with rebellion, hatred and ingratitude. Here, then, we should have the connection with the dreamer's contemporary wishes. But on the other hand the Bible passage contains some details which apply well to a masturbation phantasy. Moses seized the rod in the face of God's command, and the Lord punished him for his transgression by telling him that he must die without entering the Promised Land. The prohibited seizing of the rod (in the dream an unmistakably phallic one), the production of fluid from its blow, the threat of death —in these we find all the factors of infantile masturbation united (1900a, 380).

I believe that there is a very similar explanation for Freud's attitude to Moses, indeed, that Freud may even have suggested the interpretation of the Bismarck dream to Sachs. In that case, the sentences following the above passage can be considered an account of Freud's own attempts at concealment: "We may observe with interest the process of revision which has welded together these two heterogeneous pictures (originating, the one from the mind of the statesman of genius, and the other from the impulses of the primitive mind of a child) and which has by that means succeeded in eliminating all the embarrassing elements" (*ibid.,* 380f.; partially retranslated from the German).

Does it not seem reasonable to suppose that Michelangelo's statue of Moses helped Freud too to build a bridge between his actual problems and his childhood trauma? Did Freud's enthusiasm perhaps stem from the rekindling of early infantile emotions? His experience in San Pietro had, in any case, the same structure as the original trauma and its many repetitions. He had broken a commandment, had worshipped before a graven image, and probably had also broken what in his eyes was a sexual taboo, namely, the prohibition against masturbation, since we must take it that he had been practicing marital abstinence ever since the birth of his daughter Anna in 1895 (see 1.1.2.2 above). Hence he felt guilty, and so developed a theory about Michelangelo's intentions—a theory that blunted the subjective danger of the situation and once again prevented his real childhood experiences from reaching his consciousness.

4.1.2 SIGMUND FREUD, PATRIARCH IN THE PRIMAL HORDE

To Freud, however, Michelangelo's *Moses* was a father figure toward whom he not only felt like a son but with whom he identified himself as well. Jones has stressed that Freud's various feelings toward Moses were connected with changes in his personal circumstances (1955, II, 366f.). In 1901, when he visited Rome for the first time, he was an unknown Viennese neurologist, who admittedly hoped to become famous one day but whose real situation at the time lent little substance to such hopes. In 1912 and 1913, on the other hand, when he spent many hours before the statue to gather material for his paper, his position had completely changed. He had been made a professor in 1902,[10] and in the years that followed he had seen his new theoretical and therapeutic ideas being accepted by an ever-growing number of people. His publications were being read by interested circles all over the world, psychoanalytical associations had sprung up in many cities, there were international congresses, and in 1909 he had been invited to give a course of lectures at an American university. Psychoanalysis had grown into a movement and, like Moses, Freud had become a lawgiver and the head of a large body of disciples.

4.1.2.1. The "sons": Adler, Stekel, and Jung

But like Moses, Freud too discovered that some of his disciples refused to accept his doctrine in its entirety. Alfred Adler, one of his earliest disciples, broke with him in October 1911 because Adler's approach, later known as "individual psychology," differed from Freud's in several essential points: in respect of the Oedipus complex, of repression, of infantile sexuality, of dreams, and of various other elements (1914d, 15ff.; cf. Freud/Jung, 1974, 447; Nunberg/Federn, 1976/1977, *passim;* Jones, 1955, II, 129ff.; and Stekel, 1950, 139ff.). Adler was president of the Vienna Psychoanalytical Society and with Wilhelm Stekel had been editor of the *Zentralblatt für Psychoanalyse,* the official journal of the International Psychoanalytical Association, of which Freud was listed as publisher. Adler had largely provoked the break, but Freud was obviously glad to be rid of him.

Stekel was the next to go—in the autumn of 1912. Even before he had heard of Freud's psychoanalysis, Stekel had been using psychotherapeutic methods in his general practice, and in so doing had discovered links between childhood experience and later neurotic illness. As early as 1895 he had published a paper on "Coitus in Childhood" which Freud mentions in his "Aetiology of Hysteria" (1896c, 207). Stekel was very impressed with Freud's writings (which at the time meant *The Interpretation of Dreams* and early papers from the seduction theory period) and became one of the leading champions of the new doctrine. In particular, he wrote numerous articles on psychoanalysis that did a great deal to bring Freud's theory before a wider public, first of all in Vienna (Stekel, 1950; Jones, 1955, II, 134ff.).

Stekel left the Psychoanalytical Society ostensibly because he had clashed with Freud over the *Zentralblatt.* The deeper reason, however, was that he had gradually come to reject some of Freud's views. In 1908, he published his *Nervous Anxiety States and Their Treatment,* in which he developed a theory of anxiety that differed considerably from Freud's theory of the actual neuroses. In particular, Stekel refused to accept that anxiety neurosis and neuras-thenia were due to actual "abnormal" sexual practices and tried to convince Freud that *all* neuroses stemmed from psychic conflicts (Stekel, 1921a, V, 35ff.). But Freud refused to budge; the only concession he was prepared to make was to allow Stekel to refer to these psychogenic anxiety states as "anxiety hysteria," thus distinguishing them clearly from the anxiety neuroses, which Freud continued to attribute to "abnormal" sexual practices, i.e., to forms of sexual intercourse deviating from the heterosexual norm or to use of contraceptives (cf. Freud/Jung, 1974, 168f.; Nunberg/Federn, 1976, I, 165ff., and *passim;* 1977, II, 320, and *passim*).

Stekel, on the other hand, argued that all neuroses spring from irreconcilable emotions which have their roots in infantile experiences. Thus he did not consider masturbation itself a cause of psychic disorders but only the guilt feelings about it provoked by parental or other reproaches (Stekel, 1950, 16ff.; Nunberg/Federn, 1976 I, 513ff.).

If one agrees that Freud's theory of the actual neuroses, as I have tried to show (see 1.1.2.2), had a self-protective function, then he was bound to find Stekel's theory highly dangerous. His deep dislike of Stekel must thus be attributed to his former disciple's insistence that Freud's neuroses too must have had psychic causes.

Stekel, I believe, was the only one of Freud's disciples to take over the seduction theory which Freud himself had upheld until 1897, and to develop it consistently. He abandoned Freud's fixation on exclusively sexual seduction experiences in childhood, maintaining instead that every conflict between desires that are first aroused and then forbidden can produce a neurosis. I believe that Freud's highly emotive rejection of Stekel's theoretical and thera-peutic views (Jones, 1955, II, 135ff.; Stekel, 1950, 142ff.) was due not least to Freud's defensive attitude toward a theory he himself had renounced in 1897. If Stekel did in fact come close to the mainsprings of Freud's own neurosis, as I believe he did, then Freud's defense mechanism had to be all the stronger.[11]

Much more painful than Stekel's defection was that of Jung at about the same time. Freud's ideas had influenced Jung as soon as they were published. Jung had read *The Interpretation of Dreams* immediately after its appearance in 1900 and had tried soon afterward to apply psychoanalysis in the Zurich psychiatric clinic where he was a senior physician.[12]

After their first meeting in the spring of 1907, Freud became convinced that he had found a successor in Jung (Freud and Jung, 1974, 27, 7 April 1907), and he accordingly tried to ignore Jung's attempts—which started almost from the outset of their association—to disassociate himself from some of his theo-retical views. He loved Jung, his young, dynamic, and above all non-Jewish "crown prince," to whom he was anxious to bequeath his life's work, psychoa-nalysis. As he wrote to Jung: "If I am Moses, then you are Joshua and will take possession of the Promised Land of psychiatry, which I shall only be able to glimpse from afar" (*ibid.,* 196f., 17 January 1909; cf. 219f., 16 April 1909).

Jung's reaction was ambivalent. On the one hand, he was anxious to execute the mandate of his revered teacher; on the other, he had a resistance that expressed itself chiefly in his rejection of certain aspects of Freud's sexual theory. Very early on, even before the two men first met, Jung had had reservations about Freud's view that sexuality was the cause of all neuroses (*ibid.*, 6f., 23 October 1906). And when Jung later revised the libido theory (Jung, 1912), Freud was so deeply hurt that he broke with him for good.

However, Freud too had all along been ambivalent in his feelings toward his "successor to the throne." Thus, after Jung had been working on symbolism in myth and fable for some time (since about October 1909, Freud/Jung, 1974, 251f.), Freud began to turn his own attention to the subject. But characteristically he did not mention his plan to publish something in this field to Jung until shortly after he had been deeply upset by Jung's *Symbols of Transformation* (1952, Part I), in which Jung openly declared his rejection of Freud's libido concept. Freud's own four papers on the origins of religion were published soon afterward under the title of *Totem and Taboo* (1912–13), and in the last of them, written after Jung's defection, Freud tried to get even with his former disciple.

The point of contention, I believe, was the father fixation of both men, a fixation they tried to project onto each other. It was his own ambivalent father relationship that caused Jung to admire his paternal friend and at the same time made him want to oust Freud from his almighty position, doubtless so as to appear less puny by comparison (Jung, 1962).

It seems to me that Freud, for his part, brought to the relationship everything that had gone into his relationship with his own father, except that this time he adopted the position of Jacob, thus experiencing Jung as a kind of reincarnation of himself.[13] He expected Jung to submit to him in the same way that he, however reluctantly, had bowed to his father, Jacob. But Jung rebelled, asking Freud to be more open and to admit his own weaknesses.

Jung had provoked Freud as early as 1909, during their voyage to America: "Freud had had a dream, the contents of which I am not entitled to divulge. I interpreted it as best I could but added that much more could be said if he cared to impart to me some more details from his private life. Upon these words Freud looked at me strangely—his look was full of suspicion—and he said: 'How can I possibly risk my authority?' " (Jung, 1962 162; retranslated from the German). Jung reminded Freud of this exchange in his letter of 3 December 1912, which introduced the final phase of their friendship. Shortly before that, in November, Freud had fainted during a meeting with Jung and other members of the International Psychoanalytical Association in the dining room of a Munich hotel. His explanation of this incident to Jung read as follows:

My attack in Munich was not more serious than the similar one at the Essighaus in Bremen;* my condition improved in the evening and I had an excellent night's sleep. According to my private diagnosis, it was migraine (of the M. ophthalm. type), not

* Where Jung and he had set out for America in 1909—M.K.

without a psychic factor which unfortunately I haven't time to track down now. The dining-room of the Park Hotel seems to hold a fatality for me. Six years ago I had a first attack of the same kind there, and four years ago a second. *A bit of neurosis that I ought really to look into* (Freud/Jung, 1974, 524, 29 November 1912, italics added).[14]

It is difficult to know what to make of this episode because we know nothing about Freud's emotional state on this or on the previous occasions. What is certain is that shortly before his attack in 1912 he had scored a personal victory over Jung, and that the theme of death and dying was being discussed when Freud fell unconscious.[15]

In my view, these attacks may be linked directly to Freud's relationship to his father. Jacob too had gained a victory over his son—with his taboo—and had then died, or rather, was already dead. Now, if Freud did indeed see himself in the role of a father to Jung, then a victory over him must have filled Freud with forebodings: in Freud's own experience the father had to die in order to subdue the son.

Referring to Freud's confession that his fainting spell had had a neurotic cause, Jung told him that he himself was suffering from this neurosis of Freud's and implored him to take it "very seriously indeed" (*ibid.*, 525, 3 December 1912). Freud would have none of it and retorted bluntly: "In one point, however, I venture to disagree most emphatically; you have not, as you suppose, been injured by my neurosis" (*ibid.*, 530, 5 December 1912). Jung reacted with a slip of the pen which clearly betrayed his intention to break with Freud.[16] When Freud pointed this out to him, Jung replied in a furious letter and hastened the final break:

I would, however, point out that your technique of treating your pupils like patients is a *blunder*. In that way you produce either slavish sons or impudent puppies (Adler-Stekel and the whole insolent gang now throwing their weight about in Vienna). I am objective enough to see through your little trick. You go around sniffing out all the symptomatic actions in your vicinity, thus reducing everyone to the level of sons and daughters who blushingly admit the existence of their faults. Meanwhile you remain on top as the father, sitting pretty. For sheer obsequiousness nobody dares to pluck the prophet by the beard and inquire for once what you would say to a patient with a tendency to analyse the analyst instead of himself. You would certainly ask him: "*Who's* got the neurosis?" . . . You know, of course, how far a patient gets with self-analysis: *not* out of his neurosis—just like you. If ever you should rid yourself entirely of your complexes and stop playing the father to your sons and instead of aiming continually at their weak spots took a good look at your own for a change, then I will mend my ways and at one stroke uproot the vice of being in two minds about you (*ibid.*, 534f., 18 December 1912).

Freud replied with a proposal that they terminate their personal relationship. Jung concurred.

4.1.2.2 *Totem and Taboo*

Freud and Jung were both distressed as a result, Jung nearly suffering a mental breakdown and Freud once again encapsulating himself in the narrow circle of his Viennese disciples and a few other faithful followers—most of them Jews. Freud apparently did his mourning in the fourth section of his *Totem and Taboo,* which he concluded in May 1913, that is, after the break with Jung. That work contains Freud's famous thesis that patricide in the primeval horde has been handed down to us, and that it is the phylogenetic cause of the Oedipus complex. Freud described the primeval horde as follows:

a violent and jealous father who keeps all the females for himself and drives away his sons as they grow up. . . . One day the brothers who had been driven out came together, killed and devoured their father, and so made an end of the patriarchal horde. . . . The violent primal father had doubtless been the feared and envied model of each one of the company of brothers: and in the act of devouring him they accomplished their identification with him, and each one of them acquired a portion of his strength (1912–13, 141f.).

In Freud's view, this mythological murder of the primal father was the cause of the introduction of father gods to whom the sons could atone for their guilt. The family, for its part, was a "restoration of the former primal horde" (*ibid.,* 149). Above all, Freud believed that the murder of the primitive father affected every male child ever born, and this precisely because "psychical dispositions" are handed on from one generation to the next, and because, in the unconscious, the memory of the primal horde is preserved for millennia (*ibid.,* 158).

Here I am not concerned with the question of whether this theory is sensible or absurd, but merely wish to demonstrate that it once again provided Freud with an explanation of his own situation, an explanation that, like its predecessors, simply obscured the real facts.

At that time, with so many of his followers in open rebellion, Freud felt that he himself was a primal father whom the horde of envious sons wished to overthrow. In a letter to Jung, he wrote: "Old age is not an empty delusion. A morose senex deserves to be shot without remorse" (Freud/Jung, 1974, 453, 2 November 1911). But such insight did not in any way mean that he was prepared to let himself be "slain by his sons"; on the contrary, he cast them out in the same way as I believe Jacob had cast out Philipp, a son who had tried to subdue him.

Freud could not bear Jung's destructive ambitions, but was also unable to look for the explanation of the anxiety Jung's desperate attacks caused him, as that would have meant taking a closer look at himself and at his own father. Instead, he once again invented a theory that shifted the cause of his anxiety back into a legendary past: Jung was bound to hate him, because some primeval horde had turned against some father once upon a time. This "solution" obviated any need to ask himself to what extent his own behavior had provoked Jung's reaction—or, more generally, how the behavior of the fathers elicits the hatred of the sons.

Small wonder then that Freud's feelings in 1912 and 1913, when he sat daily before Michelangelo's *Moses,* should have been different from his feelings during the 1901 visit. He had become a Moses himself, one who watched his followers' "dance round the golden calf" and did so with seething rage. And even his interpretation of the emotional attitude in which Moses was shown corresponded to his own. Like Moses he was concerned to save the "Tables of the Law," in his case of psychoanalysis. In pursuit of that mission, he too had to struggle against an "inward passion" (1914b, 230, 233). It was a twofold emotional ambivalence which Freud felt in front of the *Moses* statue: he was both a son and a father, and in each of the two roles the feeling of passion had to be subdued in favor of an attitude of temperance. As a "son," he would gladly have given in to his wild—probably sexual—passion, but was prevented from doing so under threat of dire punishment by the "father" Moses and his Law. As a "father," he had to control his anger at his rebellious "sons," who ignored his commandments—lest he himself break these commandments by venting his primitive rage on them.

4.2 Sigmund Freud, the Man Moses

Freud came to grips with Moses in yet another work, one that, together with *The Interpretation of Dreams,* is his most personal contribution of all: his *Moses and Monotheism.* It is his only book on a specifically Jewish subject (Simon, 1957, 285), one in which he deals with his own "Jewishness," and which may therefore be called a résumé of his own life and work. It is also his final confrontation with his father.

Freud had been suffering from cancer of the buccal cavity since 1923, and by 1933, when it apparently occurred to him to offer a new interpretation of the Moses theme, he had had numerous operations.[17] Writing the Moses book seems to have been a form of therapy for him, supporting him in his fight against the disease and helping him to bear his last six years with heroic fortitude. And even his expulsion from Nazi-occupied Vienna fifteen months prior to his death seems to have been easier for him to cope with than most people would have expected, since he could hope for publication of *Moses and Monotheism* in England. During the terrible period of waiting for his exit permit, he continued working at revising the third part of the book (Jones, 1957, III, 216).

The work, to which he devoted all his intellectual acumen during the last five or six years of his life (*ibid.,* 367), has a chaotic structure. Bakan has called it "incredibly bad" (1958, 137), adding that no one would have paid it the least attention had it not come from Freud's pen.[18] Other critics have blamed its poor quality on Freud's advanced years and fading intellectual powers, but this view is refuted by the fact that, at the same time, Freud also wrote the (incomplete) *Outline of Psychoanalysis* (1940a), which is both systematic and perfectly logical. If, therefore, his *Moses and Monotheism* seems to be a patchwork of whose poor quality Freud himself was in no doubt—the text is full of apologies—then there must have been a very special reason.

Several leads can be found in the unusual history of the work. In 1934, Freud told Arnold Zweig that he had finished the book but felt he could not publish it because it was too explosive; moreover, he was not altogether certain of his conclusions (Freud/Zweig, 1968, 91f., 30 September 1934; Jones, 1957, III, 216f.). After rewriting the work in 1936 and 1937, he released the first of the three essays of which it is composed in the spring of 1937, planning to hold the other two back. Contrary to this plan, he published the second essay at the end of 1937, and started to revise the third once again. Only after he had turned his back on Nazi Vienna and moved to London in June 1938 did he finish that revision, and in the spring of 1939 he published all three essays under the title *Moses and Monotheism.*

Strangely enough, he added the original version of the third essay to the book (as *Moses and Monotheism III,* Part II), explaining that he had been unable to include the whole of this material in his second version (1939a, 103f.). Freud also mentioned another reason for this unusual decision: "I found myself unable to *wipe out the traces [die Spuren . . . zu verwischen]* of the history of the work's origin, which was in any case unusual" (1939a, 103, italics and German added).

It is striking that Freud should have used almost the same words here as those he chose in the preface to the second edition of *The Interpretation of Dreams.* There, after explaining that his inability to replace his own dreams with less dated specimens was due to his realization that the book was his reaction to his father's death (see pp. 3f. above), he also went on to say that he "felt unable to *obliterate the traces [die Spuren . . . zu verwischen]* of the experience" (1900a, xxvi; italics and German added). I think this parallel is no accident but indirect proof that both works were written for the same reason, to help Freud to grapple with his father's mandate. When he wrote *The Interpretation of Dreams* shortly after Jacob's death, the emotional repercussions had just become clear to him. Forty years later, anticipating his own death, he submitted, so to speak, a statement of accounts—his third essay on Moses—in which he explained how he had fulfilled Jacob's mission.[19]

It is as if *Moses and Monotheism* as well as *The Interpretation of Dreams* had been dictated by Freud's unconscious. In either case, all personal references impinging on Jacob's taboo have been "censored" or "coded." In *Moses and Monotheism,* the coding is far more comprehensive and thorough than it is in *The Interpretation of Dreams,* which was still allowed to contain numerous personal reminiscences of Freud's own childhood. In *Moses and Monotheism,* by contrast, all biographical material lies veiled behind the symbolic language of Freud's theory. The theoretical constructs he had developed during the forty years since his *Interpretation of Dreams* provided him with a stock of symbols that helped him to explain his deepest feelings without having to hold them up before his readers, and to a large extent even to himself, as his own.

That this assumption is justified is borne out by several statements in the first essay. The myths of the birth of great men, Freud wrote, have their origins in the "family romance" of their authors:

> . . . the source of the whole poetic fiction is what is known as a child's "family romance,"[20] in which the son reacts to a change in his emotional relation to his parents and particularly to his father. A child's earliest years are dominated by an enormous overvaluation of his father; in accordance with this a king and queen in dreams and fairy tales invariably stand for parents. Later, under the influence of rivalry and of disappointment in real life, the child begins to detach himself from his parents and to adopt a critical attitude towards his father. *Thus the two families in the myth—the aristocratic one and the humble one—are both of them reflections of the child's own family as they appeared to him in successive periods of his life* (1939a, 12, italics added; cf. 71f.)

We cannot, of course, be sure that Freud was thinking of himself and of his own childhood, but the parallel is clear, not least because he confined his argument again only to male children. Above all, the reference to the father points clearly to Jacob. In other words, Freud had let it slip out that *his* fiction, *his* Moses myth, was a cover for his own family romance, in which he was taking a fresh interest in the face of his imminent death. M. Robert is convinced that his "historical novel" about Moses, as Freud originally intended the book to be styled, absorbed him so much because it was the novel of his own life, a novel he had to finish before he could die (Robert, 1975, 145).

If we read *Moses and Monotheism* with the knowledge that it contains coded autobiographical confessions then we are no longer surprised at the confused style, the many repetitions, incongruencies, and open contradictions—which Freud partly acknowledged himself. These inconsistencies now appear as forms of the code he used to hide the actual meaning.[21]

These forms can be distinguished in respect of time, content, and level of consciousness. I believe that there are at least five "encoding planes" in *Moses and Monotheism:*

—The reconstruction of the historical events surrounding the life of Moses and the description of the peculiarities of the Jewish religion from which Christianity later emerged. This plane is the most obvious and, on a first reading of the book, seems to be the only one used by the author. I shall call it the "plane of historical reconstruction."

—In addition, the book contains an account of the ontological development of the normal and the neurotic personality. Here Freud once again presents the essential ideas of his theory, and to that end not only uses the terminology of his later, structural theory (Ego, Id, Superego; cf. 1923e) but oddly enough keeps reverting to his earlier seduction theory. I shall call this the "plane of personality theory."

—There are some passages in *Moses and Monotheism* that reflect Freud's own feelings at the time of writing. These involve attempts to come to terms with his approaching death, mixed with feelings of pride about the success he has achieved in life. This may be called the "plane of Freud's confrontation with his own aging."

—Behind these three planes, which could be assigned to the dimension of consciousness, there appears—as it were, in the preconscious sphere—an account of Freud's own history and above all of his relationship with Jacob. This is partly presented as a general description of psychic development (i.e., on the plane of "personality theory") and partly in the light of his identification with the people of Israel or with the person of Moses (i.e., on the plane of "historical reconstruction"). I call this the "plane of Freud's confrontation with his own childhood."

—And finally, Freud presents, within the sphere of the "unconscious," as it were, fantasies about what might have happened in Freiberg and Tysmenitz before his birth, and about events that had puzzled him in Freiberg (the disappearance of his nursemaid Resi; the relationship between Philipp and Amalie; the behavior of his father; the loss of his Freiberg world; etc.), and subsumes them all under the heading of the murder of the primal father. That version served him as an explanation not only for the Moses story but also for the ontological development of every single (male!) child, including his own development and that of his father. The patricide of yore, he fantasized, is the inheritance of man. I call this the "plane of fantasized prehistory."

Let us now examine the various parts of *Moses* to see how these planes interlock and where the preconscious or unconscious dimensions predominate, which might help to reveal the hidden meaning of Freud's last work to us. To facilitate this examination, I shall condense Freud's central arguments into eight theses.

1. The first thesis, developed in Part I ("Moses an Egyptian," 1939a, 7–16), falls mainly into the plane of historical reconstruction. In it, Freud claimed that Moses was not a Jew but the son of an Egyptian princess who had him put out on the banks of the Nile. His two "proofs" of this claim did not seem very convincing even to himself: the name "Moses" was probably Egyptian, and the biblical myth of Moses' birth and exposure conflicts with the majority of myths concerning the births of heroes. According to such myths, the hero is invariably of noble descent and is saved and brought up by a commoner until, one day, his true origins are discovered.

Freud's decision to declare Moses a child of noble Egyptian birth—despite his own reservations, in the absence of any historical evidence, and purely on the basis of "phantasy" and of "fabrications and assumptions" (1939, 14–15) —was not his only attempt to ennoble great men he admired. He similarly made Shakespeare a nobleman although he could not adduce a single serious argument in support of that claim (see Jones, 1957, III, 428ff.).

It therefore seems highly probable that this thesis reflected Freud's own wish for other origins (see *ibid.,* 430; Robert, 1975, 149), which means that his view of Moses' origins also involved the plane of confrontation with his own childhood.

We know that the idea of Egypt had exerted a strong emotional attraction

on Freud ever since childhood, when he and Jacob had read Philippson's Bible
and admired the many Egyptian figures illustrated in it. Egypt was the symbol
of the "other side," of the non-Jewish world (Robert, 1975, 42ff.), into which
Freud had been initiated by his nurse maid. It was she who probably made him
feel so much at home in that world that he came to identify himself with a
Moses of non-Jewish descent.

However, as we shall show below, "Egypt" had yet another symbolic significance for Freud.

2. Still on the plane of historical reconstruction, Freud advanced in the
second essay ("If Moses Was an Egyptian . . ." 1939a, 17–53) the further thesis
that Moses had originally been a follower of the Aten religion, a monotheistic
sun cult introduced into Egypt by the pharaoh Akhenaten, and replaced by
the old polytheistic religion after that pharaoh's death. Moses, Freud argued,
chose the Israelites living in Egypt as the group to continue the Aten cult,
which in Freud's eyes was greatly superior to all other religions. "Egypt"
accordingly had two contradictory meanings for Freud: on the one hand, it
was the quintessence of non-Jewishness; on the other hand, it was a symbol
for all that distinguished Judaism from other religious groups.

But let us first look at Freud's own dramatic description of the choice of
Israel by Moses:

> There is no doubt that it was a mighty prototype of a father which, in the person
> of Moses, stooped to the poor Jewish bondsmen to assure them that they were his dear
> children. And no less overwhelming must have been the effect upon them of the idea
> of an only, eternal, almighty God, to whom they were not too mean for him to make
> a covenant with them and who promised to care for them if they remained loyal to his
> worship. It was probably not easy for them to distinguish the image of the man Moses
> from that of his God; and their feeling was right in this, for Moses may have introduced
> traits of his own personality into the character of his God—such as his wrathful temper
> and his relentlessness (*op.cit.*, 110).

In other words, the Egyptian Moses was like a father to the people of Israel,
who loved the new God because they loved the father. Clearly, on the plane
of his confrontation with his own childhood, Freud did not identify himself
with Moses but with the people of Israel. That also emerges from the passage
preceding the one I have just quoted:

> It is a longing for the father felt by everyone from his childhood onwards, for the
> same father whom the hero of legend boasts he has overcome. And now it may begin
> to dawn on us that all the characteristics with which we equipped the great man are
> paternal characteristics. . . . The decisiveness of thought, the strength of will, the energy
> of action are part of the picture of a father—but above all the autonomy and indepen-
> dence of the great man, his divine unconcern which may grow into ruthlessness. One
> must admire him, one may trust him, but one cannot avoid being afraid of him too
> (*ibid.*, 109f.).

Here Freud, in my opinion, erected a memorial to his own father as he had
known him in Freiberg, where Jacob had seemed to be so Godlike, had shown

so much strength of will, so much decisiveness and independence in his deal-ings with his grown-up sons, and had condescended to him, the little boy who had looked up to him with admiration and trust but also with fear. Moreover, Jacob had forced "his people" to join in the exodus from the "Egyptian" Freiberg to Vienna, which though it did not become Jacob's Promised Land was where his son attained great renown.

In particular, Jacob-Moses had brought a new and splendid "religion" to little Sigmund-Israel: that of the Haskalah, which gave the Jews the new, enlightened spirit of science and led them from the ghetto into bourgeois society.

This also fits in with Freud's claiming that Moses had not invented the new religion but had merely taken it over from King Akhenaten, a father figure: "If on the one hand we thus see the figure of the great man grown to divine proportions, yet on the other hand we must recall that the father too was once a child. The great religious idea for which the man Moses stood was, on our view, not his own property: he had taken it over from King Akhenaten" (*ibid.*, 110).

As I have tried to show earlier (see 2.5 above), Jacob was probably intro-duced to the Haskalah by his grandfather Siskind Hofmann, or by other *maskilim* from Tysmenitz—the parallel with Moses and Akhenaten can thus be drawn even here. Furthermore, Freud may also have felt that the new movement had helped his father to turn his back on Orthodox (rabbinical or Hasidic) practices, which shared certain features with "Egyptian" polytheism, so that in Freud's eyes the Haskalah seems to have fused with Akhenaten's Aten religion, and mystical-Orthodox Judaism with the polytheistic Amun religion of ancient Egypt.

The picture of the elect character of the people of Israel that Freud drew on the plane of historical reconstruction thus had an analogy on the plane of his childhood memories: Freud too felt "chosen" by his father, chosen to transform the idea of the Haskalah into reality. Like the people of Israel, he too was the "declared favourite of the dreaded father" (*ibid.*, 106); he too was meant to conquer a Promised Land, that of intellectual enlightenment and of science—a land Jacob was not allowed to enter and could only see from afar.

3. It was for the express purpose of underlining the special character of the new religion and hence driving home to the Israelites that they were the chosen people that Moses, according to Freud, commanded them not to make graven images of their God and introduced the custom of circumcision among them. The first of these two commands involved an instinctual renunciation and was "a triumph of intellectuality over sensuality" (*ibid.*, 113):

The religion which began with the prohibition against making an image of God, develops more and more in the course of centuries into a religion of instinctual renun-ciations. It is not that it would demand sexual *abstinence;* it is content with a marked restriction of sexual freedom. God, however, becomes entirely removed from sexuality and elevated into the ideal of ethical perfection. But ethics is a limitation of instinct.

. . . God requires nothing other from his people than a just and virtuous conduct of life—that is, abstention from every instinctual satisfaction which is still condemned as vicious by our morality to-day as well (*ibid.*, 118f.).

Freud himself seems to have realized that this interpretation involved the plane of confrontation with his own childhood, because he went on to add: "
. . . it is the authority of the child's parents—essentially, that of his autocratic father, threatening him with his power to punish—which calls on him for a renunciation of instinct and which decides for him what is to be allowed and what forbidden" (*ibid.*, 119).

It was Jacob who had demanded instinctual renunciation from him and who at the same time had guided Sigmund's steps toward "intellectuality," much as Moses had done by the Second Commandment.

And finally, Freud's claim that Moses introduced circumcision among the Israelites—which was even more far-fetched than his other speculations since it is fairly certain that the practice of circumcision was widespread among Semitic people before the Egyptian exile—must clearly be assigned to the plane of childhood experience. The castration threat with which Jacob had so forcefully brought about his son's "instinctual renunciation" and devotion to "intellectuality" is given due emphasis in Freud's "Moses romance":

When we hear that Moses made his people holy by introducing the custom of circumcision we now understand the deep meaning of that assertion. *Circumcision is the symbolic substitute for the castration* which the primal father once inflicted upon his sons in the plenitude of his absolute power, and *whoever accepted that symbol was showing by it that he was prepared to submit to the father's will,* even if it imposed the most painful sacrifice on him (*ibid.*, 122, italics added).

4. With his fourth thesis, Freud alleged that the Egyptian Moses was murdered by the Israelites because the new religion proved too heavy a burden. That view is admittedly shared by several historians of religion, but seems to be as little proven as the thesis of Moses' Egyptian origin (Robert, 1975, 152ff.; Jones, 1957, III, 373ff.).

This thesis also can be transferred from the plane of historical reconstruction to that of Freud's confrontation with his own childhood. The guilt feelings rekindled in him by his father's death (see 1.2.1 and 4.1.2 above) tied in with the idea of Moses' murder; Freud, like the ancient Israelites, found the Mosaic religion an oppressive burden and had tried to escape from it with the help of his seduction theory. True, he had not murdered his father; but Jacob's death, I believe, incited feelings in him that were not dissimilar to those he attributed to the Israelites after their alleged murder of Moses. He himself drew a comparison between that murder and the natural death of Akhenaten, in which he presented both men as fathers who had made too heavy demands on the people they "patronized" and who had to pay for it with their lives:

Moses, deriving from the school of Akhenaten, employed no methods other than did the king; he commanded, he forced his faith upon the people. The doctrine of Moses may have been even harsher than that of his master. . . . *Moses, like Akhenaten, met with the same fate that awaits all enlightened despots.* The Jewish people under Moses were just as little able to tolerate such a highly spiritualized religion and find satisfaction of their needs in what it had to offer as had been the Egyptians of the Eighteenth Dynasty. The same thing happened in both cases: those who had been dominated and kept in want rose and threw off the burden of the religion that had been imposed upon them. But while *the tame Egyptians waited till fate had removed the sacred figure of their Pharaoh,* the savage Semites took fate into their own hands and rid themselves of their tyrant (1939a, 47, italics added).

His own father too, Freud seems to have fantasized, died because he was an "enlightened despot," one who had asked too much of his son. He, the son, had not slain him like the "savage Semites" but had waited for "fate" to "remove" him.

Finally, the idea of the murder of Moses might also have involved the plane of Freud's confrontation with his own aging. Freud's despair and sorrow at his approaching end were easily linked with Moses' fate: anyone who gives birth to a new idea and is able to make it prevail in the face of rather stiff resistance must expect to atone for it with his death.

5. In his fifth thesis, Freud argued that two or more generations after the murder of Moses there arose a new leader of the Israelites. That leader, who also called himself Moses, was a Midianite shepherd who worshipped the volcano god Yahweh. Under his leadership, the Israelites conquered Canaan. This second Moses, according to Freud, was altogether different from the "aristocratic Egyptian" who had "presented the people with a religion in which all magic and spells were proscribed in the strictest terms" (*ibid.,* 36). Their respective views of God were distinct as well. The "universal god Aten" was hardly comparable with the "demon Yahweh in his home on the Mount of God." The solitary Aten was much mightier and more radiant than the primitive volcano god, of whose kind there were many. In the tradition, Freud claimed, both Moses figures became fused, as did the two conceptions of God.

On the plane of historical reconstruction, Freud used the fusion of the two Moses figures and their respective conceptions of God to explain the contradictions in the character of the biblical Moses: "He is often pictured as domineering, hot-tempered and even violent, yet he is also described as the mildest and most patient of men. These last qualities would evidently have fitted in badly with the Egyptian Moses, who had to deal with his people in such great and difficult matters; they may have belonged to the character of the other Moses, the Midianite" (*ibid.,* 41).

This argument is easily transposed onto the plane of Freud's childhood experiences. Freud himself even supplied the "translation key" when he said that the two contrasting images of humble and noble origins are often "reflections" of one and the same person at various periods of his life (*ibid.,* 13; cf. p. 182f above). This suggests that both Moses figures represented Jacob, first as he had appeared in the eyes of little Sigmund in Freiberg, when he had still seemed the quintessence of strength and power, and next as seen through the eyes of the growing Freud, who looked on his father as a comparatively weak man. Freud accordingly likened the god Aten to the strong Jacob-Moses while turning Yahweh into the god of the weak Jacob-Moses.

It is remarkable that in another passage of the same book, Freud should have given a diametrically opposite description of the two Moses figures and of their gods: "Aten had been a pacifist like his representative on earth—or more properly, his prototype—the Pharoah Akhenaten, who looked on passively while the world-empire conquered by his ancestors fell to pieces. No doubt Yahweh was better suited to a people who were starting out to occupy new homelands by force" (ibid., 63).

There is nothing to suggest that Freud was aware of this contradiction. But what caused him to describe Aten on one occasion as the strong god and Yahweh as weak, and on another to reverse their roles? In my view, the answer is that he simply confused his planes of reference. In the first passage, he was arguing on the plane of confrontation with his childhood and identified himself with the people of Israel; in the second, he was arguing on the plane of confrontation with his own aging and thought himself the equal of Moses by virtue of his own struggles with his followers. By his reference to the incompetent father, Akhenaten-Jacob, he perhaps tried to justify his choice of "substitute fathers" and his consequent betrayal of Jacob. Although the pacifist Akenaten-Jacob might have been powerful once upon a time, he could not assist in the conquest of the Promised Land, so that the son had to turn to other, mightier gods.[22]

6. Freud believed, however, that the descendants of those Israelites who had lived in Egypt had not forgotten "their" Moses and his Aten religion, and that, in the long run, the Mosaic god prevailed over the volcano god. After a "latency period" lasting several generations, the Mosaic god eventually became the God of the Jews:

The Egyptian Moses had given to one portion of the people a more highly spiritualized notion of god, the idea of a single deity embracing the whole world, who was not less all-loving than all-powerful, who was averse to all ceremonial and magic and set before men as their highest aim a life in truth and justice. . . . The tradition of it remained, and its influence achieved (only gradually, it is true, in the course of centuries) what was denied to Moses himself. . . . No one can doubt that it was only the idea of this other god that enabled the people of Israel to survive all the blows of fate and that kept them alive to our own days (ibid., 50f.; cf. 69f.).

This thesis too can be shown to have a connection with Freud's personal life. On several occasions he had been forced, after periods of turning toward "the other side," to remember his origins, often at the cost of painful renunciations. Thus his arguments with Jung taught him to rely largely on Jewish followers. The "Aten religion" had remained the stronger, had proved itself in his own "tradition," and had given him the strength to withstand the terrible blow of expulsion from his home in the face of his imminent death.

7. Freud published the above theses as early as 1937. There was yet another,

however, which he kept back until after his arrival in England because he thought it particularly "open to objection" and "dangerous" (*ibid.*, 103). It concerned the link between the Moses story and the murder of the primal father as he had first developed it in *Totem and Taboo* (1912–13). Freud believed that he had not yet said all there was to say about the reemergence of the Egyptian Moses and of monotheism. It was not enough to assert that the Israelite tradition had preserved the memory of an ancestor and of his firm monotheistic faith; over and above that, the return of Moses was the "reestablishment of the primal father in his historic rights" (1939a, 86). Because the Jews had murdered Moses, Freud claimed, they were shouldered with "the archaic inheritance" of murder in the primal horde, the memory of which had been repressed in the "latency period" of the Yahweh cult, only to reemerge all the more vigorously and to cement the Jewish faith for all time. This is how he emphatically described the return of the "primal father":

> . . . finally the decision was taken of giving all power to a single god and tolerating no other gods beside him. Only thus was it that the supremacy of the father of the primal horde was re-established and that the emotions relating to him could be repeated. The first effect of meeting the being who had so long been missed and longed for was overwhelming and was like the traditional description of the law-giving from Mount Sinai. Admiration, awe and thankfulness for having found grace in his eyes—the religion of Moses knew none but these positive feelings towards the father-god. *The conviction of his irresistibility, the submission to his will, could not have been more unquestioning in the helpless and intimidated son of the father of the horde*—indeed those feelings only become fully intelligible when they are transposed into the primitive and infantile setting. A child's emotional impulses are intensely and inexhaustibly deep to a degree quite other than those of an adult; only religious ecstasy can bring them back. *A rapture of devotion to God was thus the first reaction to the return of the great father (ibid., 133f., italics added).*

The highly emotional tone of this account suggests that Freud was once again expressing his own feelings, in other words, that he was once again back on the plane of his confrontation with his childhood. We do not know if he himself ever had the feeling of reencountering "the being who had so long been missed and longed for," i.e., his father in Freiberg. If he did, he probably remembered him as he was at the time when they began to read the Bible together, which would also explain the association with religious ecstasy.

To lend plausibility to his thesis of the return of the first Moses, Freud drew on his theory of infantile development, according to which incestuous wishes experienced in childhood remain repressed during the latency period and do not reemerge until puberty.[23] He tried to illustrate this theoretical point with a case history that looks singularly unsuitable in the frame of historical reconstruction (*ibid.*, 78f.) but has a surprising number of parallels with Freud's own life: the patient in question observed parental coitus as a child, had been threatened with castration because of masturbation, had become a model boy, and so on. In other respects the two biographies, admittedly, do not agree, but one nevertheless gains the impression that Freud was relating his own child-

hood experiences, albeit in coded form. While he had still described his childhood with relative candor in *The Interpretation of Dreams,* he became less
frank as time went on. Yet the images that oppressed him seem to have
remained the same.

On the plane of historical reconstruction, this turning back to the theory of
the primal horde helped him to offer an interpretation of the bond between the
people of Israel and their God. Because the Israelites were not only guilty of
the murder of the primal father, like all human beings on earth, but had also
murdered the first Moses, they were doubly culpable, and hence experienced
the "supremacy of the father of the primal horde," when he reappeared to
them in the form of the second Moses, as an act of grace. Yet, Freud continued,
their feeling of exaltation was not free of ambivalence: the hatred "which had
once driven the sons into killing their admired and dreaded father" (*ibid.,* 134)
was rekindled as well. But whereas the primal horde had expressed that hatred
in action, the Moses religion now bade the Israelites to rein in their hatred of
the primal father: "There was no place in the framework of the religion of
Moses for a direct expression of the murderous hatred of the father. All that
could come to light was a mighty reaction against it—a sense of guilt on
account of that hostility, a bad conscience for having sinned against God and
for not ceasing to sin" (*ibid.*).

Moreover, "things were going badly for the people," so that they found it
difficult "to maintain the illusion, loved above all else, of being God's chosen
people" (*ibid.*). Fortunately, there was one way out of this impasse:

> If they wished to avoid renouncing that happiness, *a sense of guilt on account of their
> own sinfulness offered a welcome means of exculpating God:* they deserved no better
> than to be punished by him since they had not obeyed his commandments. And, driven
> by the need to satisfy this sense of guilt, which was insatiable and came from sources
> so much deeper, they must make those commandments grow ever stricter, more metic-
> ulous and even more trivial. *In a fresh rapture of moral asceticism they imposed more
> and more new instinctual renunciations on themselves and in that way reached—in
> doctrine and precept, at least—ethical heights* which had remained inaccessible to the
> other peoples of antiquity (ibid., italics added).

One cannot help wondering why, in a penetrating analysis of Jewish morality and its psychological basis, Freud should have felt the least need to introduce the idea of the murder of the primal father. This was not only superfluous
but also extremely awkward, because it entailed the further assumption of
phylogenetic inheritance, that is, of the inheritance of acquired characters in
the sense of Lamarck's theory. In contrast to *Totem and Taboo,* where Freud
had left the question of the genetic transmission of cultural traditions open
(1912–13, 158f.), he seemed quite clear about the answer in *Moses and Monotheism:* "We must finally make up our minds to adopt the hypothesis that the
psychical precipitates of the primaeval period became inherited property
which, in each fresh generation, called not for acquisition but only for awakening" (1939a, 132). Freud asserted that this assumption was as essential in
"mass psychology" as it was in individual psychology, where certain individual

questions can only be explained phylogenetically; so "the behaviour of neurotic children towards their parents in the Oedipus and castration complex" could only be explained by "their connection with the experience of earlier generations" (*ibid.*, 99).

I believe that Freud had once again—and for the same reasons as in 1897–99, when he presented his Oedipus theory in *The Interpretation of Dreams*—invented a theory that enabled him to write his "family romance" without having to probe too deeply into its background. Like the Oedipus theory, the theory of hereditary guilt helped him to project his hatred of his own father into a mythical past and hence to spare the person of Jacob. Freud's illustrations of the primal horde were clearly drawn from the situation of his family in Freiberg. In Freiberg, too, there had been "sons"—Freud's half-brothers—who in all probability envied their father's power (cf. Part 3). He, the "second first-born," had not grown up with the "primal horde," and yet he bore the guilt of his "primal brothers." And when he found favor in the eyes of the returned "Father God"—probably because the father realized that the son was clever enough to justify his hopes in his future—it became utterly impossible to show feelings of hatred toward him. Because these hostile thoughts nevertheless existed, the son felt culpable; and although he "exculpated" his father, he could do so only through "instinctual renunciation." Yet precisely by doing so, he too reached "ethical heights in doctrine and precept" that allowed him to become so admirable a human being.

The theory of the murder of the primeval father and the associated hypothesis of the inheritance of acquired character traits were principles Freud could "not do without" (*ibid.*, 100; cf. 89), although even his most loyal disciples advised him to discard them (Jones, 1957, III, 312ff.). They spared him from having to work out his own "prehistory" and that of his father. Murder in the primal horde and the murder of Moses did not greatly matter to him on the plane of historical reconstruction—which probably explains his reluctance to come out with this part of his book—but he did indeed have need of them on the plane of confrontation with his own childhood and also to substitute fantasy for prehistory, into which Jacob had forbidden him to delve.

8. *Moses and Monotheism* ends with another thesis which Freud had already presented twenty-five years earlier in *Totem and Taboo* (1912–13, 153ff.), but now—not least because of its position at the end of the book—it became a central statement. Christians, unlike Jews, need feel no guilt for the murder of the father by the primal horde. As Paul, the Roman Jew, had phrased it: "We are freed from all guilt since one of us has sacrificed his life to absolve us" (1939a, 135). Although Paul was in no way referring to the murder of the primeval father, Freud was convinced that the sacrifice of Christ, the son, must have been in expiation of the murder of the father committed by the primal horde.

Thanks to this idea of expiation, the new religion became a religion of the son, while Judaism remained the religion of the father (*ibid.*, 136). In this connection, Freud remarked:

It is worth noticing how the new religion dealt with the ancient ambivalence in relation to the father. Its main content was, it is true, reconciliation with God the Father, atonement for the crime committed against him; but the other side of the emotional relationship showed itself in the fact that *the son, who had taken the atonement on himself, became a god himself* beside the father and, actually, *in place of the father.* Christianity, having risen out of a father-religion, became a son-religion. *It has not escaped the fate of having to get rid of the father* (*ibid.,* italics added).

According to Freud, Paul also "abandoned the chosen character of his people," the Jews, by dispensing with circumcision, the visible mark of their covenant with God. And finally, according to Freud, Paul abandoned pure monotheism. The Christian religion "was no longer strictly monotheist, it took over numerous symbolic rituals from surrounding peoples, it re-established the great mother-goddess and found room to introduce many of the divine figures of polytheism only lightly veiled" (*ibid.,* 88).

These innovations, claimed Freud, brought in their wake a liberating sense of redemption. By obviating the need to repress the murder of the father, by renouncing the idea that the Jews were the chosen people, and by abandoning undiluted monotheism, the new religion assumed a progressive aspect that the old had discarded long since. "With the strength which it derived from the source of historical truth, this new faith overthrew every obstacle. The blissful sense of being chosen was replaced by the liberating sense of redemption" (*ibid.,* 135). From that time on, "the Jewish religion was to some extent a fossil" (*ibid.,* 88).

However, Freud also believed that Christianity was unable to maintain the high level of spirituality which Judaism had achieved. Christianity, unlike the Aten religion and the Mosaic one that followed it, did not exclude "the entry of superstitious, magical and mystical elements, which were to prove a severe inhibition on the intellectual development of the next two thousand years" (*ibid.).* And Freud continued: "The triumph of Christianity was a fresh victory for the priests of Amun over Akhenaten's god after an interval of fifteen hundred years and on a wider stage" (*ibid.).* "It was as though Egypt was taking vengeance once more on the heirs of Akhenaten" (*ibid.,* 136).

In Freud's view, the advantages of Christianity were thus converted into their very opposites: although Christians had been released from the guilt of primal patricide, they had grown less enlightened and intellectual and more susceptible to magic and mysticism. If we transpose these ideas from the plane of historical reconstruction to that of Freud's confrontation with himself and his doctrine in the face of his imminent death, we cannot but conclude that with these ideas he was expressing his pride in his Jewishness. His work, his own great intellectual achievement, the new "religion of psychoanalysis," could only have issued forth because he was a Jew, because he had not allowed himself to be exonerated but preferred to bear the onus of guilt himself.

And so he, like all Jews who refused to adopt Christianity and who "with their habitual stubbornness continued to disavow the father's murder" (*ibid.,* 90), opened himself up to persecution by Christians. Christians accused the

Jews of the murder of God and, according to Freud, not without justification inasmuch as their accusation really amounted to saying that the Jews "will not accept it as true that they murdered God whereas we admit it and have been cleansed of that guilt" (*ibid.*, 136). For, since the murder of the primal father is a sin that weighs upon all mankind, it is incumbent on every man to confess it. *Moses and Monotheism* ends with the following remarks: "A special enquiry would be called for to discover why it has been impossible for the Jews to join in this forward step which was implied, in spite of all its distortions, by the admission of having murdered God. In a certain sense they have in that way taken a tragic load of guilt on themselves; they have been made to pay heavy penance for it"[24] (*ibid.*).

If we transpose this enquiry onto the plane of Freud's self-confrontation, then it becomes the problem of why he himself could not have chosen the easier path but had to carry instead the yoke of his religion. He did not oblige his readers with an answer, did not say why he could not admit to having "murdered God," to having hated his father. In my view, he failed to do so because he did not know the answer. He did not know that his father had forbidden him to carry feelings of hatred against him, that he had furthermore forbidden him to be aware of that prohibition, thereby establishing the taboo in all its binding force. And in that sense Freud's unanswered question in *Moses and Monotheism* is really an answer. Because he could not name the taboo, i.e., could not give reasons for having remained loyal to Judaism, the most he could do without breaking the taboo was to pose the question.

In this last of his eight theses, as the reader will have gathered, the various planes of interpretation and Freud's various identifications intersect in a host of different ways. It would appear that Freud identified himself with the loyalty of the Orthodox Jew to God the Father no less than with the liberating, redeeming belief of the Christian in the Redeemer; with the rigid obstinacy of Judaism no less than with the openness of Christianity; with the sensuality of Christianity no less than with the spirituality of Judaism; with the suffering of the Jewish people no less than with the triumph of Christianity. For had not Freud as the son of Jacob on the one hand taken "the atonement upon himself," thus stepping "in the place of the father"; and had he not on the other hand with "habitual stubbornness" continued to adhere to the "religion of the father" when he bowed to his father's taboo? Had he not on the one hand worshipped the "false gods of polytheistic Egypt," and on the other hand rendered homage to the "Mosaic Aten religion"? Had he not, on the one hand, rejected the rigid orthodoxy of rabbinical Judaism and adopted the progressive ideas of the Haskalah, somewhat akin to those of messianic Christianity, while on the other hand refusing to condone the least deviation from the principles he himself had laid down, and visiting the severest sanctions upon the heterodox amongst his disciples? And in this connection, had not Freud given birth with psychoanalysis to an idea of redemption similar to Paul's? If Freud believed that Paul was the first to interpret Christ's Crucifixion as an expiation on behalf of all Christians, then he could indeed draw a parallel with his own discovery, that of the Oedipus complex. He too had brought men a message that offered them redemption from guilt: he had made it possible for them to look upon the murderous hatred they felt for their father as a universal feeling shared by every male child, and thus to exonerate themselves as well as their fathers. Alas, the Christian who had been exonerated by Paul could escape "the fate of having to eliminate the father" no more than the patient exonerated by Freud. That fate reappears with every generation and no liberating idea can hope to do more than to render it less intolerable.

4.3 Conclusions: Reckoning Up

Freud's arguments in *Moses and Monotheism,* and especially in his last thesis on the relationship between Christianity and Judaism, are laden with meaning. They not only involve the historical development of Judaism but also provide a terse summary of the most essential theories of psychoanalysis (see Robert, 1975, 191) as well as a coded biography of Freud.[25]

And *Moses and Monotheism* is even more. It may be considered Freud's last will and testament, in which he both accounts to his father and also settles accounts with him. M. Robert has given us a very perceptive analysis of the second aspect (*ibid.,* Chap. 5). She believes that in his last book, and also in his great psychoanalytic study *The Interpretation of Dreams,* Freud was trying to free himself of his "socially and intellectually mediocre Jewish father" (*ibid.,* 156). By identifying himself with Moses and turning him into an Egyptian, Freud was, so Robert maintains, trying to deny his own origins. He was neither "Salomon, the son of Jacob . . . nor Sigmund, the son turned apostate, whose very name held the promise of a great future. He was no more a Jew than Moses or Moshe had been a Jew . . . wanted to be nothing but the son of No-one from Nowhere, the son of his work and of nothing but his work. . . ." (*ibid.,* 158; translated from the German).

It is odd that Robert should have arrived at that conclusion, because elsewhere in her book she calls Freud's Jewish origins his great inner strength, and claims that he himself recognized them as such.[26]

With this somewhat one-sided interpretation, she shows that she failed to appreciate the full complexity of Jacob's mandate to his son, and hence the fact that Freud's last book was an attempt to come to grips with that mandate. I agree with her that—in his fantasy that Moses was a noble Egyptian—Freud indicated that he would have preferred not to have been born a Jew, but to have been reared as the child of Christian parents and hence to have been spared the heavy burden of "atonement" imposed on the Jewish people. Yet that wish, and hence his resentment of his father for being a Jew, was only one

FIGURE 25 Sigmund Freud's study at 19, Berggasse, Vienna (1938), photographed by Edmund Engelman. *(Copyright Edmund Engelman, New York.)* Note the similarities with the illustrations from Philippson's Bible (Figs. 19–22)

FIGURE 26 Sigmund Freud's desk at 19, Berggasse, Vienna (1938), photographed by Edmund Engelman. *(Copyright Edmund Engelman, New York.)* Note the similarities with the illustrations from Philippson's Bible (Fig. 19)

FIGURE 27 Sigmund Freud at his desk in 19, Berggasse, Vienna, shortly before his enforced emigration to England in 1938, photographed by Edmund Engelman. *(Copyright Edmund Engelman, New York.)*

part of his "balance sheet." In the other part he exonerated his father. Jacob had given him a mandate that had opened up great prospects: it had set him on the path of scientific enlightenment. To his son, Jacob was not only the petty and self-seeking "primal father" whom he either had to murder or to ignore if he was to achieve anything; he was also a "Moses" who provided his "people of Israel" with a wonderful vision, one that Freud, at the end of his life, could pride himself on having fulfilled. It had been a hard road. Things would have been much easier for Freud had he been a Christian; but because it had been so hard, he could look back on his life's work—the work he had produced in pursuit of his mission—with all the more pride. He had truly become a great man, just what his father had expected of him.

I believe, however, that Freud's satisfaction with his life's work, expressed in *Moses and Monotheism,* was not solely based on this worldly success, on the international renown for his ideas and person, but also even more on the fact that he had obeyed yet another part of Jacob's mission: he had not smashed the tablets (Simon, 1957, 305), had remained a loyal son not only to his father but also to the people of Israel.

I feel certain that it was not least from his compliance with the second part of his mandate that Freud drew the strength to face his own death with equanimity. This is how Max Schur, Freud's personal physician, has described Freud's last hours:

On the following day, September 21, while I was sitting at his bedside, Freud took my hand and said to me: "Lieber Schur, Sie erinnern sich wohl an unser erstes Gespräch. Sie haben mir damals versprochen mich nicht im Stiche zu lassen wenn es so weit ist. Das ist jetzt nur noch Quälerei und hat keinen Sinn mehr." ("My dear Schur, you certainly remember our first talk. You promised me then not to forsake me when my time comes. Now it's nothing but torture and makes no sense any more.") I indicated that I had not forgotten my promise. He sighed with relief, held my hand for a moment longer, and said: "Ich danke Ihnen" ("I thank you"), and after a moment of hesitation he added: "Sagen Sie es der Anna" ("Tell Anna about this"). All this was said without a trace of emotionality or self-pity, and with full consciousness of reality. I informed Anna of our conversation, as Freud had asked. When he was again in agony, I gave him a hypodermic of two centigrams of morphine. He soon felt relief and fell into a peaceful sleep. The expression of pain and suffering was gone. I repeated this dose after about twelve hours. Freud was obviously so close to the end of his reserves that he lapsed into a coma and did not wake up again. He died at 3:00 A.M. on September 23, 1939 (Schur, 1972, 529).

In concluding, I wish to raise the question of the relevance of Freud's theories of man to us today. Does not the recognition of the obvious subjectivity of his ideas force us to reject his theoretical work as a mere generalization of highly personal experiences?

If we were to answer this question in the affirmative, then we would also have to reject all sociological and psychological theories, because every contribution, to the social sciences reflects the person of its author, is part of his confrontation with the economic and social problems of his day. If for anything, Freud could be criticized for failing to appreciate his own subjectivity and for believing that he had discovered absolute truths. But that too cannot be held against him, for in his day, when positivism prevailed, it was unthinkable that scientific truths might be relative.

I am of the opinion, however, that Freud's theories should not be accepted unreservedly; they must be tested carefully with a view to determining which of them merely served Freud to disguise important problems that impinged on Jacob's taboo. Such theories certainly include the myth of primal patricide based on the belief in phylogenetic inheritance, and hence, ultimately, the entire Oedipus theory and all concepts and constructs based upon it. These are mystifications that obscure the interhuman dimension, ignoring the role of the social environment in the socialization of man, and hence its role in the emergence of "normal" or of socially deviant behavior. They have led psychoanalysis, in theory and therapeutic practice, into a blind alley, as so many of its critics have already pointed out.

But those parts of Freud's theory by which Freud, despite—or perhaps precisely because of—his own involvement, tried to trace neurotic or "normal" behavior back to childhood experiences, to the overall "family romance" of human beings, have remained an exceedingly sharp instrument for the analysis of human existence. Only the systematic inclusion of Freud's own history in the evaluation and application of his theory makes it possible to separate the mystical from the (in the above sense) heuristically useful elements of his intellectual edifice.

It is my hope that the present work will contribute in its small way to that essential separation. If it does so, it will have facilitated the execution of an important task, one that Helm Stierlin has defined as follows: "It remains a —perhaps the—task of psychoanalytical theorists to do justice to the interhuman and family spheres neglected by Freud, without sacrificing the pioneering insights he has bequeathed to us" (1975c, 138; translated from the German).

Chronology

In this Chronology, special prominence has been given to events in Sigmund Freud's personal life and to the development of his ideas during the period 1893–1900. The years before and after his crisis, by contrast, have been set out in broad outline only. What few data we have on Freud's childhood and Jacob Freud's "prehistory" have also been included. For sources, see Notes.

1768 or 1775
Birth of Zisie (Siskind) Hofmann (father-in-law of Schlomo Freud, great-grandfather of Sigmund Freud).[3]

1783 or 1790
Earliest possible year of birth (because of conflicting statements about the birth of her father Zisie Hofmann) of Peppi (Pepi, Pessel) Hofmann (mother of Jacob Freud, grandmother of Sigmund Freud).[3]

1800
Latest possible year of birth (because of the birth of Jacob Freud) of Peppi (Pessel) Hofmann.[3]

1805
Jacob Nathansohn (father of Amalie Freud, grandfather of Sigmund Freud) born in Brody.[6]

1815
December 18: Birth of Jacob (Kallamon Jacob) Freud (Sigmund Freud's father) in Tysmenitz.[4]

1825
Josef Freud (Sigmund Freud's uncle) born in Tysmenitz.[15]

1832
Summer or earlier: Marriage of Jacob Freud to Sally Kanner in Tysmenitz.

1833
About April: Emanuel Freud (Sigmund Freud's half-brother, first child of Jacob and Sally Freud) born in Tysmenitz.[21]

1834 or 1836
Maria Rokach (Kokach) (Emanuel's wife) born in Milov, Russia.

1834
Between the end of August and the middle of September: Philipp Freud (Sigmund Freud's half-brother, second child of Jacob and Sally Freud) born in Tysmenitz.[22]

1835
August 18: Amalie (Amalie, Malka) Nathansohn born in Brody (Sigmund Freud's mother, daughter of Jacob and Sarah Nathansohn, née Wilenz).[4]

1838
(Probably) and following years: Jacob Freud travels with his father Schlomo and his grandfather Siskind Hofmann to Freiberg in Moravia.[3]

1844–45

Jacob Freud and Siskind Hofmann stay in Freiberg as tolerated Jews for several months.[3]

1847–48

Jacob Freud spends several months in Freiberg as a tolerated Jew.[3]

1847

June, July, August: Jacob Freud travels several times from Freiberg to Breslau.[3]

1848

March Revolution.

(Probably) Jacob Freud is granted domicile in Freiberg, or in Klogsdorf, near Freiberg.

1852

Or earlier: Emanuel Freud marries Maria Rokach.

Jacob Freud, Rebekka (wife), Emanuel Freud, Maria (his wife), and Philipp register as residents in Klogsdorf.[14]

Jacob's wife (either Rebekka or Sally) dies.[2]

1854

January: Jacob Freud hands over his produce business to Emanuel. Makes several visits to Vienna.[3]

1855

July 29: Jacob Freud marries Amalie Nathansohn in Vienna.[2]

August 13: Johann (John) Freud (Sigmund Freud's nephew, first child of Emanuel and Maria) born in Freiberg.[17]

1856

February 21: Schlomo Freud dies in Tysmenitz.[7]

May 6: Sigismund (Salomo, Schlomo) Freud born in Freiberg (first child of Jacob and Amalie). Circumcision on May 13.[17] [7]

November 20: Pauline Freud (Sigmund Freud's niece, second child of Emanuel and Maria) born in Freiberg.[17]

1857

June 5: "Amalie Freud, wool merchant's wife, with child Sigmund and maid Resi

Wittek from Freiberg" take the cure at Roznau.[28]

October: Julius Freud (Sigmund Freud's brother, second child of Jacob and Amalie) born in Freiberg.[16]

1858

March 15: Julius, Freud (Amalie's brother) dies of T.B. in Vienna[37]

April 15: Julius Freud dies in Freiberg.[16]

December 31: Anna Freud (Sigmund Freud's sister, third child of Jacob and Amalie) born in Freiberg.[17]

1859

January: Resi Wittek, Sigmund's nursemaid, is caught stealing by Philipp and "boxed up" (i.e., locked up).[11]

February 22: Bertha Freud (Sigmund Freud's niece, third child of Emanuel and Maria) born in Freiberg.[17]

Spring: "Screen memory": Sigmund's games with John and Pauline in the dandelion meadow in Freiberg (cf. 1.3.2 above).

August 11: Traveling papers issued to Amalie Freud "for a further stay in Leipzig."[27]

August 1859–March 1860: Jacob Freud and family leave Freiberg, stay in Leipzig, and then move to Vienna. Emanuel Freud, his family, and his brother Philipp move to Manchester, England.[11]

1860

March 21: Regine Debora (Rosa) Freud (Sigmund Freud's sister, fourth child of Jacob and Amalie) born in Vienna, at 3, Weissgärber[strasse].[18]

June 28: Sam Freud (Sigmund Freud's nephew, fourth child of Emanuel and Maria) born in Manchester.[20]

1861

March 22: Maria (Mitzi) Freud (Sigmund Freud's sister, fifth child of Jacob and Amalie) born in Vienna, at 114, Weissgärber[strasse].[18]

July 26: Martha Bernays (Sigmund Freud's wife, daughter of Berman Bernays and Emmeline, née Philipps) born in Wandsbek, near Hamburg.[26]

1862

May 12: Matilda Freud (Sigmund Freud's niece, fifth child of Emanuel and Maria) born in Manchester.[20]

July 23: Esther Adolfine (Dolfi) Freud (Sigmund Freud's sister, sixth child of Jacob and Amalie) born in Vienna, at 114, Weissgärber[strasse].[18]

1864

May 3: Pauline Regine (Paula) Freud (Sigmund Freud's sister, seventh child of Jacob and Amalie) born in Vienna, at 5, Pillersdorfgasse.[18]

1865

July 20: Arrest of Josef Freud (uncle of Sigmund Freud) for circulating forged rouble notes in Vienna.[15]

Autumn: Sigmund Freud enrols in the Leopoldstädter Real- und Obergymnasium (1960b, 125).

October 3: Jacob Nathansohn (Sigmund Freud's maternal grandfather) dies in Vienna.[6]

1866

February 22: Josef Freud sentenced to ten years' imprisonment.[15]

April 19: Alexander Gotthold Efraim Freud (Sigmund Freud's brother, eighth child of Jacob and Amalie) born in Vienna, at 1, Pfeffergasse.[18]

1868

Summer: Amalie Freud and family visit the health resort of Roznau.[28]

1869

Summer: Amalie Freud and family visit Roznau.[28]

1870

John (Sigmund Freud's nephew) visits Vienna from Manchester.[11]

Summer: Amalie Freud and two children visit Roznau.[28]

1870–71

Winter: Sigmund Freud and a school friend (Silberstein) visit the Fluss family in Freiberg (1969a, 113).

1871

Summer: Amalie Freud, six children, and maid visit Roznau.[28]

1872

Early August to September 15: Freud visits the Fluss family in Freiberg with two school friends (Silberstein and Rosanes). Freud falls in love with Gisela Fluss (see 3.4 above).

Summer: Amalie Freud and two children visit Roznau.[28]

1873

July: Freud passes the *Matura* examination (school-leaving certificate) (1960b, 125).

Autumn: Freud's immatriculation in the medical faculty, Vienna University *(ibid.).*

1875

(Probably) Freud family moves to 3, Kaiser-Josef-Strasse.[25]

Freud visits his half-brothers Emanuel and Philipp in Manchester (Jones, 1953, I, 24).

Summer: Amalie Freud visits Roznau with three children.[28]

1876

Freud receives a research grant to work at the Zoological Experimental Station of the University of Vienna in Trieste (Jones, 1953, I, 37).

1877

Freud enters Brücke's Physiological Institute *(ibid.,* 39ff.).

1880

Josef Breuer, medical practitioner in Vienna, friend and patron of Freud, begins to treat Anna O. (Bertha Pappenheim) *(ibid.,* 223ff.).

1881

Sigmund Freud obtains his medical qualification *(ibid.,* 57).

1882

April: Freud falls in love with Martha Bernays *(ibid.,* 103ff.).

June 17: Freud becomes engaged to Martha Bernays (*ibid.*).

October: Freud starts work in the Vienna General Hospital, serving in various departments, including Professor Meynert's psychiatric clinic (*ibid.*, 64).

1883

Freud moves into the hospital (*ibid.*).

June 14: Martha Bernays moves with her mother and sister to Wandsbek, near Hamburg (*ibid.*, 120).

October: Anna Freud (Sigmund Freud's sister) marries Eli Bernays (Martha Bernays's brother) (*ibid.*, 119).

December: Freud travels to Leipzig and Dresden to meet his half-brothers (1960a, 91ff.).

1884

April–June: Research on cocaine; paper "On Coca" (1884d) (Jones, 1953, I, Chap. 6).

September: Holiday in Wandsbek. Freud stays with Martha Bernays's family (*ibid.*, 114f.).

1885

September 5: Freud appointed *Privatdozent* (*ibid.*, 70ff.)

Beginning of October: Freud visits Wandsbek on his way to Paris (*ibid.*, 135).

October 11: Study trip to Paris. Freud becomes a student of J.-M. Charcot at the Salpêtrière, the famous neurological clinic (*ibid.*, 207ff.).

December 20–27: One week's visit to Wandsbek from Paris (*ibid.*, 135).

1886

February 28: Return from Paris via Berlin (*ibid.*, 212).

March: Several weeks' stay in Berlin, "in order to learn . . . something of the general diseases of children" (*ibid.*)

Translation from the French of J.-M. Charcot's lectures (English title: "New Lectures on the Diseases of the Nervous System, Especially on Hysteria" (1886f) (Jones, 1953, I, 209).

April 15: Freud opens a private practice at 7, Rathausstrasse, Vienna (*ibid.*, 143).

September 13: Sigmund Freud's marriage to Martha Bernays in Wandsbek (*ibid.*, 150).

1887

October 16: Mathilde Freud (first child of Sigmund and Martha) born in Vienna at 8, Maria-Theresia-Strasse (*ibid.*, 152).

November: Beginning of the Freud–Fliess correspondence (1950a).

December: Freud starts to treat patients by hypnosis (1950a, 53).

1888

Translation from the French of H. Bernheim's *De la Suggestion et de ses applications à la thérapeutique (Hypnotism and Suggestion)* (1889) (Jones, 1953, I, 228).

Freud publishes several papers (probably "Aphasia," "Hysteria," "Hystero-epilepsy," "Brain," "Infantile Paralyses," and "Coca") in A. Villaret, ed.: *Handwörterbuch der gesamten Medizin* (1888b and 1891c).

Freud writes "Quelques considérations pour une étude comparative des paralyses motrices organiques et hystériques" (1893c) (Jones, 1953, I, 233).

1889

May 1: Freud begins the treatment of Frau Emmy von N. (*ibid.*, 240).

Freud, accompanied by a patient (Emmy von N.?), visits H. Bernheim in Nancy with the idea of perfecting his hypnotic technique (*ibid.*, 238).

December 6: Jean Martin Freud (second child of Sigmund and Martha) born in Vienna at 8, Maria-Theresia-Strasse (*ibid.*, 152).

1889 or 1890

Freud starts to apply the cathartic method (recall of childhood traumas under hypnosis) in the treatment of Frau Emmy von N. (*ibid.*, 240).

1890

August: Meeting with Fliess in Salzburg-Berchtesgaden.

Attack of travel anxiety, train phobia (1950a, 60f., 285; Jones, 1953, I, 305, 307).

Paper on "Psychical (or Mental) Treatment" (1890a).

1891
February 19: Oliver Freud (third child of Sigmund and Martha) born in Vienna at 8, Maria Theresia-Strasse (Jones, 1953, I, 152).
Late summer: Move to 19, Berggasse (*ibid.*, 328).
"On Aphasia" (1891b).

1892–94
Translation from the French of J.-M. Charcot's *Leçons du mardi à la Salpêtrière* (1892–94).

1892
Translation from the French of H. Bernheim's *Hypnotisme, suggestion et psychothérapie: études nouvelles* (1892a).
April 6: Ernst Freud (fourth child of Sigmund and Martha) born in Vienna at 19, Berggasse (Jones, 1953, I, 152).
Wilhelm Fliess's marriage to Ida Bondy (a friend of J. Breuer) in Vienna. Freud begins to use the familiar "Du" instead of the more formal "Sie" in his letters to Fliess (1950a, 62).
Beginning of disagreement with Josef Breuer. Freud nevertheless persuades Breuer to collaborate with him in writing a treatise on hysteria *(ibid.).*
Autumn: Elisabeth von R. becomes Freud's patient. She is the first patient with whom he dispenses with hypnosis (Jones, 1953, I, 243).
December: Draft A. Problems raised by, and theses on, neurasthenia and anxiety neurosis (1950a, 64ff.).
"A Case of Successful Treatment by Hypnotism" (1892–93). General theoretical deliberations on and case examples of the emergence of hysterical symptoms.

1893
January: With Josef Breuer: "On the Psychical Mechanism of Hysterical Phenomena: Preliminary Communication" (1893a) and lecture on the same subject (1893h).
February 8: Draft B: "The Aetiology of the Neuroses." Neurasthenia in men and women. Freud starts to collect cases of anxiety neurosis and neurasthenia (1950a, 66ff.).
April 7 (Easter): Meeting with Fliess in Berlin (Jones, 1953, I, 332).
April 12: Sophie Freud (fifth child of Sigmund and Martha) born in Vienna at 19, Berggasse (*ibid.*, 152).
May: Freud writes *Zur Kenntriss der cerebralen Diplegien des Kindesalters* (1893b). The work is extremely well received (1950a, 73 and 84).
Summer: Three weeks' holiday in Reichenau (Jones, 1953, I, 331f.).
September: Freud writes "Charcot" (1893f) in memory of his teacher, who died in August.
Autumn: Heart symptoms. Freud cuts down his tobacco consumption in October, but writes to Fliess in November: "I am not obeying your smoking prohibition; do you really consider it such a great boon to live a great many years in misery?" (Schur, 1972, 42).
Autumn: Success as medical practitioner: "The sexual business attracts people" (1950a, 77).
At about Christmas: Meeting with Fliess in Vienna (*ibid.*, 80, footnote).

1894
January: "The Neuro-Psychoses of Defence" (1894a). Freud disassociates himself from Breuer by assuming "incompatible sexual notions as the cause of hysteria."
February: Freud's work with Breuer on hysteria is half finished (1950a, 81).
End of March: Gives up smoking. Shortly afterwards experiences "cardiac depression," "violent arrhythmia," constant tension, pressure and burning in the region of the heart, some dyspnoea, and "visions of death" (*ibid.*, 82; Schur, 1972, 43).
April–July: Cardiac symptoms, depressive states, fantasies of death. Freud implores Fliess to be honest about the gravity of his condition; he accuses Breuer of not having told him the truth (Schur, 1972, 46ff.).
May: Draft D. Plan for a book on the etiology and theory of the major neuroses (1950a, 86f.).

June: Draft E, *How Anxiety Originates.* Sexual tension is transformed into anxiety. Anxiety neurosis as the consequence of sexual practices (*ibid.,* 88ff.).

June: Freud believes that anxiety neuroses must be separated from neurasthenia (*ibid.,* 94).

Summer: Differences of opinion with Breuer, which lead to a break (Jones, 1953, I, 252ff.).

July: Freud starts smoking again, but stops again on Fliess's advice (Schur, 1972, 54).

Summer: Holiday in Reichenau (Jones, 1953, I, 332).

Beginning of August: Freud and Martha visit Fliess in Munich (*ibid.*).

August: Draft F. Two cases of anxiety neurosis in males (1950a, 96ff.).

September: With Martha and the children to Lovrano on the Adriatic (Jones, 1953, I, 333).

Christmas: Meeting with Fliess (1950a, 101, footnote).

1895

Freud joins the Jewish fraternal organization B'nai B'rith (Jones, 1953, I, 330).

January: "On the Grounds for Detaching a Particular Syndrome from Neurasthenia under the Description 'Anxiety Neurosis' " (1895c). Fundamental work on the theory of "actual neurosis" (Jones, 1953, I, 256ff.).

January: Draft G, *Melancholia.* "Melancholia consists in mourning over loss of libido"; sexually potent people contract anxiety neurosis, impotent people contract melancholia (1950a, 101ff.).

Draft H, *Paranoia.* Ideas intolerable to the ego are warded off by projection. Comparison of paranoia with hysteria, obsessions, and hallucinatory confusion (*ibid.,* 109ff.).

End of February: Fliess operates on Emma, a patient of Freud's and a good friend of the family (Schur, 1974).

March: Draft I, *Migraine.* Migraine is "a toxic effect produced by the stimulus of the sexual substance when this cannot find adequate discharge" (1950a, 116ff.).

Löwenfeld attacks Freud's theory of anxiety neurosis (*ibid.,* 119).

March 6: A strip of gauze which Fliess forgot to remove is discovered in Emma's nasal cavity.

March 8: Letter to Fliess (Schur, 1966, 56f.).

March and April: Emma has relapses (*ibid.,* 61ff.).

April: Cardiac symptoms. Freud refuses Fliess's invitation to Berlin. Helps himself with cocaine. Asks Fliess to stop discussing the "topic heart" (Schur, 1972, 83).

Spring: "Obsessions et phobies, leur mécanisme psychique et leur étiologie" (1895c). Identical with 1895h.

April: "Zwangsvorstellungen und Phobien. Ihr psychischer Mechanismus und ihre Aetiologie" (1895h). Obsessions are defensive neuroses; phobias are "psychical expressions of anxiety neurosis."

"Über die Bernhardt'sche Sensibilitätsstörung am Oberschenkel" (1895e). Description of a neurasthenic condition (*meralgia paraesthetica*) from which Freud himself suffered.

May: Practices for ten to eleven hours a day. Psychology is his "tyrant"; his work on neuroses gives him great satisfaction and he feels certain that "the cause of the matter is within one's grasp" (1950a, 120).

Freud suffers from empyema (pus in the nasal cavity) (Schur, 1972, 83).

Mid-May: *Studies on Hysteria* (1895d). Case histories of Anna O., Emmy von N., Lucy R., Katharina, and Elisabeth von R.; the work includes "The Psychotherapy of Hysteria," and (with Breuer) "On the Psychical Mechanism of Hysterical Phenomena."

May 25: Freud informs Fliess that Martha is pregnant (1950a, 120).

"A Reply to Criticisms of My Paper on Anxiety Neurosis" (1895f); Freud's reply to Löwenfeld.

June: Freud starts to smoke again, allegedly after having stopped for fourteen months; but see July 1894 (1950a, 120).

Summer: Freud takes his family to Bellevue, near Grinzig, in the immediate vicinity of Vienna (Jones, 1953, I, 331).

July 24: Interpretation of the "Irma" dream of July 23 (1950a, 403).

August: Freud returns to the problem of defense, believes he has a solution, but then drops the matter. He wants to "hear no more of it" (*ibid.,* 123).

Freud's first visit to Italy (Venice and environs). He is accompanied by his brother Alexander (Jones, 1953, I, 333). September 4: Meeting with Fliess in Berlin (*ibid.,* 381). Fliess performs a nasal operation on Freud (*ibid.,* 333).

On his return from Berlin, Freud starts on his "Project for a Scientific Psychology" (1950a, 347ff.). A dream provides him with confirmation that the motivation of dreams is wish-fulfillment (*ibid.,* 125).

October 8: Freud sends Fliess Parts I and II of his "Project," and the unfinished Part III. "What does not hang together yet is . . . the explanation of repression" (*ibid.,* 126; cf. pp. 00ff. above).

October or September: New cardiac symptoms (Schur, 1972, 91).

October 14, 21, and 28: Freud delivers three lectures on hysteria to the Doktorenkollegium of Vienna (1895g) (Jones, 1953, I, 262).

October 15 and 16: Hysteria is a consequence of infantile sexual shock; obsessional neurosis is a consequence of infantile sexual pleasure. Freud is sure that both neuroses are generally curable (1950a, 127f.). He stops smoking once more.

October 20: Freud is sure that he also understands the neurophysiological causes of the neuroses (*ibid.,* 129f.).

October 31: Freud starts doubting his "pleasure–pain explanation of hysteria and obsessional neurosis." He turns his attention to "migraine," for the sake of which he has made "an excursion into the mechanism of the sexual act." However, he must put everything to one side for two months to write a commissioned article on children's paralyses for a textbook by Nothnagel (1897a) (1950a, 116f.).

November 2: Euphoria, because a patient gives Freud confirmation of the sexual shock theory of hysteria *(ibid.).*

November 8: Freud puts his psychological studies to one side because he feels "incapable of mastering the thing." He

works instead on children's paralyses, in which "I am not in the least interested."

Breuer delivers a "big speech" on Freud's sexual theory of the neuroses but does not really believe in it (1950a, 133f.). November 29: Freud calls his "psychology" (the "Project"?) a kind of "aberration"; he can no longer understand the state of mind in which he "concocted it" (1950a, 134).

December 3: Anna Freud (sixth child of Sigmund and Martha) born in Vienna at 19, Berggasse.

Minna Bernays (Martha Freud's sister) moves in with the Freuds.

December 8: Freud's practice is doing well. "The town is gradually beginning to realize that something is to be had from me" (*ibid.,* 136).

Obsessional ideas are based on self-reproaches, hysteria on conflict. Freud nevertheless believes that he has not come any closer to a theoretical explanation of the neuroses and that he may have to content himself with a "clinical explanation" *(ibid.).*

Date uncertain: Draft J, Case History of Frau P. Freud's insistent probing into the sexual background of his patient's anxiety symptoms drives her away (1950a, 137ff.).

Christmas: Draft K, *The Neurosis of Defence (A Christmas Fairy Tale).* First formulation of the seduction theory of hysteria, obsessional neurosis, and paranoia (*ibid.,* 146f.).

1896

January 1: The letter accompanying Draft K contains a renewed attempt to adduce a physiological explanation of psychic processes. The explanation is linked to Fliess's nasal-sexual theory (*ibid.,* 140ff.). End of January–beginning of February: "Further Remarks on the Neuro-Psychosis of Defence" (1896b) and "L'hérédité et l'étiologie des névroses" (1896a). Both papers are based on the ideas outlined in Manuscript K. The French paper, which also presents Freud's theory of actual neuroses, is a "blanket account" of the seduction theory and of the sexual theory. The other essay sets out the seduction theory of hysteria and obsessional neurosis and presents the case of Frau P. as an example of a paranoid defensive psychosis.

Fliess disagrees with Freud's seduction theory (1950a, 155f.).

February 13: Freud suffers "frequent" migraine attacks (Schur, 1972, 99).

He writes to Fliess that he no longer agrees with Breuer but that he regrets Breuer's disappearance from his life (Jones, 1953, I, 255).

March 1: Freud comments on Fliess's manuscript "On the Relations between the Nose and the Female Sex Organs from the Biological Aspect" (1950a, 158f.).

March 16: Freud defends his objections to Fliess's periodic theory and plans a book on the "major neuroses."

April 2: Freud is euphoric. His youthful longing for philosophical knowledge is about to be satisfied "now that I have changed over from medicine to psychology." Freud is convinced that he can "definitely cure" hysteria and obsessional neurosis (ibid., 161f.).

April 9: Three-day meeting with Fliess in Dresden (Jones, 1953, I, 301 and 336).

April 16: Migraine, nasal secretion, and an attack of dread of dying following the death of the Viennese sculptor Victor Tilgner (Schur, 1972, 103f). Freud claims that he had a "surprising," i.e., psychic, explanation of Emma's hemorrhages following her abortive operation (ibid., 97).

He takes Fliess's advice to isolate himself completely (ibid.).

April 26–28: Freud reports that his lecture to the Verein für Psychiatrie und Neurologie on "The Aetiology of Hysteria" had an "icy reception from the asses" (ibid., 539).

May 2: Lecture on the interpretation of dreams (1950a, 162).

May 4: Freud calls Emma's hemorrhages "hysterical" (Schur, 1974, 80).

Freud is "isolated"; "a void is forming round me" (1950a, 162).

May 6: Freud's fortieth birthday (date at which he expected to die).

May 17: Freud mentions that he has passed a critical date (Schur, 1972, 104).

ca. May 23–30: Emanuel Freud arrives in Vienna on a week's visit (1950a, 167).

End of May: Publication of "The Aetiology of Hysteria" (1896c), the clearest account of Freud's seduction theory, with many details about the concrete sexual experiences in early childhood.

May 30: Further advancement of the seduction theory through specification of the occurrence of seduction in childhood (1950a, 163f.).

June 4: Freud continues to work on children's paralyses (ibid., 167).

Beginning of June: Martha and children go to Aussee, in Styria. Freud stays behind in Vienna (ibid.).

ca. June 16: Jacob, Freud's father, falls ill (Schur, 1972, 105).

June 30: Freud calls off meeting with Fliess because of his father's illness (1950a, 168f.).

July 15: Freud again postpones his meeting with Fliess because he realizes that his father is dying. "He was an interesting human being" (Schur, 1972, 105).

End of July: Freud joins his family on holiday in Aussee and stays until the end of August (Jones, 1953, I, 301 and 331).

End of August to middle of September: Journey of two and a half weeks with brother Alexander through Italy (Venice, Bologna, Florence) (ibid., 333).

September 29: Influenza and heart symptoms. Wants to attain the "critical age" of fifty-one. Father is "steadily shrinking" (Schur, 1972, 106).

October 9: Freud tells Fliess that he believes in "historical periods" and in the "symbolic presentiment of unknown realities." "Bows" before Fliess as "honorable astrologer" (ibid., 107).

October 23: Death of Jacob Freud (1950a, 170).

October 25: Funeral of Jacob Freud (ibid.).

Night of October 25: Dream of closing the eyes (1950a, 171).

October 26: Freud tells Fliess that his father has died: "It all happened in my critical period, and I am really down over it" (ibid., 170).

November 2: Freud describes his feelings about his father's death and his relationship to him (see 1.2.1 above). He is again working on his paper on children's paralyses. He is glad at having seven cases but has few other patients *(ibid.)*.

November 22: Freud moves into his consulting rooms on the first floor of 19, Berggasse. He is preoccupied "with the state of affairs after my death." Depressive mood (Schur, 1972, 110).

December 4: "My bad time has run its course in typical fashion . . . and I am not at all interested in life after death" *(ibid.)*.

Freud mentions the introductory quotations to the different chapters of his proposed book on the theory of neuroses (1950a, 172).

December 6: Freud works ten to eleven hours daily, feels well, but has a hoarse voice and wonders whether that is due to strain on his vocal chords or to anxiety neurosis. He has adorned his room with plaster casts of Florentine statues *(ibid.,* 180f.). Develops the theory of memory stratification through "transcriptions" or "translations." Repression is "a failure of transmission." Freud tries to link this system to Fliess's theory of periodicity. On hysteria: "It seems to me more and more that the essential point of hysteria is that it is a result of perversion on the part of the seducer; and that heredity is seduction by the father" *(ibid.,* 173ff.).

December 17: Freud proffers an explanation of the fears of prostitutes. Certain symptoms are due to "perversion of the seducers" *(ibid.,* 181f.).

1897

January 3: Solemn New Year greetings to Fliess. Freud again suffers from anxiety.

Neuroses due to infantile seduction originate during the first three years of life *(ibid.,* 183).

January 11: In the case of psychoses and epilepsy, infantile seduction occurs at the age of about fifteen to eighteen months. Case history of a family with several psychotic members over three generations with repeated incidents of sexual seduction *(ibid.,* 184ff.).

January 17 and 24: Freud draws parallels between his theory of hysteria and medieval ideas of devils and possession *(ibid.,* 187f.). Reference to a childhood experience of Emma's ("female circumcision")

(Schur, 1966, 84). Perversions could be the "remnants of a primitive sexual cult which in the Semitic east may once have been a religion" (1950a, 189).

January 24: Freud is passed over in favor of a younger colleague, and fails to be appointed associate professor.

The work on children's paralyses is finished.

"I think I have now passed the age boundary; I am in a much more stable state" *(ibid.,* 191).

February 8: Freud works eleven to twelve hours a day. "Work is progressing excellently."

Professor Nothnagel proposes Freud for a professorship *(ibid.,* 191f.).

February 11: Freud infers from the existence of hysterical symptoms in his brother and several sisters that even his own father has to be incriminated (Jones, 1953, I, 322).

February 29: Freud writes bitterly about Breuer in an unpublished letter *(ibid.,* 254).

April 6: Freud explains that hysterical fantasies result from "things heard in early infancy and only subsequently understood" (1950a, 193).

Mid-April (Easter): Meeting with Fliess in Nüremberg (Jones, 1953, I, 301, 318, 333).

April 28: Dream reflecting Freud's annoyance with Fliess.

Freud is given confirmation of his seduction theory by a patient who was sexually abused by her father (1950a, 195f.).

May 2: Freud informs Fliess that their "congress" has given him "pleasure and refreshment," that he has since been in a "continuous state of euphoria," and that he is working like a "young man" (Schur, 1972, 112).

May 2: Freud repeats that hysterical fantasies "arise from things heard but only understood later, and all the material is of course genuine" (1950a, 196).

Draft L, *Notes (I)* on the "Architecture of Hysteria" (symptoms, too, are built up from what is heard about past events in the life of parents and ancestors) *(ibid.,* 197ff.).

May 16: "Inside me there is a seething

ferment." Freud starts to write on dreams and compile the *Abstracts of the Scientific Writings of Dr. Sigm. Freud (1877–1897)* (1897b). One patient, "my banker," who had gone "furthest in his analysis," made off "at a critical point." Freud realizes that he does not yet know "all the factors that are at work." He looks at the literature on the subject of dreams and is pleased that no one has had the slightest suspicion that "dreams are not nonsense but wish-fulfilment" (1950a, 200f.).

May 24: Minna Bernays and Freud's children go to Aussee, in Styria. Freud remains in Vienna with his wife (*ibid.*, 202).

May 25: Draft M, *Notes (II)* on the "Architecture of Hysteria" (differences in the accessibility of the memory of childhood scenes); on "Phantasies" (fantasies serve to render the memory of childhood scenes inaccessible; all anxiety symptoms/phobias are derived from fantasies); and on "Repression" (the essential repressed element is always femininity; what men essentially repress is their pederastic element). The contents of fantasies are connected with the "family romance" (*ibid.*, 202ff.).

May 31: "Another presentiment tells me . . . that I am about to discover the source of morality."

Freud dreams that he is feeling over-affectionately toward his daughter Mathilde. That dream fulfills his wish to "pin down a father as the originator of neurosis." Freud also dreams the "staircase" dream, in which a woman comes up behind him and he finds himself paralyzed. "The accompanying emotion was not anxiety but erotic excitement" (1950a, 206f.).

Draft N, *Notes (III)* on "Impulses" (hostile impulses against parents are repressed at periods during which pity for one's parents is active, for instance, at times of their illness or death; the death wish in sons is directed against the father, in daughters against the mother); on "Motives for the Formation of Symptoms" (a symptom, like a dream, is a wish-fulfillment); and on "Definition of Holiness" (holiness is the sacrifice of the freedom to indulge in sexual perversions

"for the sake of the larger community") (*ibid.*, 207ff.).

Early June (Whitsun): Freud joins his family in Aussee, then returns to Vienna (*ibid.*, 206).

June 18: Freud longs for "the end of the season" and for a meeting with Fliess (Schur, 1972, 113). He mentions a pathological "inhibition about writing" (Jones, 1953, I, 325).

June 22: Freud expects to be appointed professor this summer.

He reports a period of intellectual paralysis; has been through "some kind of a neurotic experience" with "cloudy thoughts and veiled doubts."

He confides to Fliess that he has recently "made a collection of deeply significant Jewish stories." Freud has a nineteen-year-old woman patient who, he suspects, was seduced by older brothers.

"I believe I am in a cocoon, and heaven knows what sort of creature will emerge from it" (1950a, 210f.; according to Schur [1972, 112, note 20], the correct date of this letter is not June 12 but 22 June 1897).

July 7: "Something from the deepest depths of my own neurosis has ranged itself against my taking a further step in understanding of the neuroses"; his inability to write is directed at Fliess: it "seems to be aimed at hindering our intercourse."

Dreams contain the psychology of neurosis "in a nutshell." Defense against memories can cause "distortions of memory and phantasies" and also "perverted impulses." The subsequent repression of these fantasies and impulses gives rise to new symptoms.

The explanation of dreams is "the firmest point." It is "surrounded by huge and obstinate riddles."

Freud attempts an interpretation of exhibitionist dreams.

He still intends to have a meeting with Fliess (1950a, 212f.).

Mid-July: Freud meets Minna Bernays in Salzburg; they go on a walking tour and visit Emmeline Bernays (Freud's mother-in-law) in Reichenhall. Freud goes on to Vienna to procure a gravestone for his father. Beginning of self-analysis (Jones, 1953, I, 334).

End of July: Freud joins his family in Aussee, and stays there until the beginning of September *(ibid.)*.

August 13: Freud cancels his meeting with Fliess (1950a, 213).

August 14: "Things are fermenting inside me." "The chief patient I am busy with is myself. My little hysteria, which was much intensified by work, has yielded one stage further." "This analysis is harder than any other" *(ibid., 213f.)*.

August 18: Freud's handwriting is "more human again." He plans a journey with Martha, but confesses that he is afraid of traveling by train *(ibid., 214)*.

August 25 (or beginning of September): Journey to Italy with Martha, his brother Alexander, and one of his pupils, Dr. Gattl (or with Alexander and Dr. Gattl only). Venice, Pisa, Leghorn, Siena, Orvieto (Signorelli frescoes), Spoleto, Assisi, Perugia, and Florence *(ibid.; Jones, 1953, I, 334)*.

September 20: Return from Italy to Vienna (1950a, 215).

September 21: Renunciation letter. Freud no longer believes in the seduction theory of the defensive neuroses *(ibid., 215ff.; see 1.2.4 above)*.

September 26–29: Freud visits Fliess in Berlin *(ibid., 217)*.

October 3: Freud's self-analysis has been making progress in dreams for four days. He dreams about his "primary originator," an "ugly, elderly but clever woman," who told him "a great deal about God and Hell" and gave him "a high opinion of my own capacities." He dreams of having seen his mother in the nude during a journey from Leipzig to Vienna. He dreams about Julius, John, and Pauline. He hopes that these memories will "succeed in resolving my own hysteria" but cannot yet interpret the scenes himself. "The old man," his father, played "no active role" in them *(ibid., 218f.)*.

October 4: Freud has another dream about his "instructress in sexual matters." She washed him in "reddish water" and encouraged him to steal " 'Zehners' (ten-Kreuzer pieces) to give to her." He wonders whether this is a "genuine rediscovery" *(ibid., 220)*.

October 15: "My self-analysis is the most important thing I have in hand." Freud's mother tells him about his nursemaid and confirms the reality of his dream images. He remembers the scene with Philipp and the chest (box). "I have found love of the mother and jealousy of the father in my own case too, and now believe it to be a general phenomenon of early childhood." "The gripping power of Oedipus Rex"; everyone was once "a budding Oedipus in phantasy." The same theme is found in the "hysteric Hamlet": he had entertained the idea of murdering his father out of "passion for his mother" and therefore could not punish the murderer. "His conscience is his unconscious feeling of guilt" *(ibid., 221ff.)*.

October 27: His self-analysis leads Freud to the discovery of "some sad secrets of life," which he has "traced back to their first roots." He experiences the same reactions to dreams and their analysis as his patients. He realizes that his patients' resistance is "nothing but the child's character," and that to overcome it, he must get the patient to face up to that character.

"Longing is the chief characteristic of hysteria"; it gives rise to fantasies coupled to masturbation, later making way for repression *(ibid., 225f.)*.

October 31: "My own analysis is going on, and it remains my chief interest." The most disagreeable thing about it is "one's moods, which often completely hide reality from one. Also, sexual excitation is of no more use to a person like me."

"Under the influence of the analysis, my heart-trouble is now often replaced by stomach-trouble" *(ibid., 227f.)*.

November 5: Freud's self-analysis is stagnating again, "or rather it trickles on without my understanding its progress" *(ibid., 228)*.

November 14: Freud's self-analysis still interrupted. "I can only analyse myself with objectively acquired knowledge (as if I were a stranger); self-analysis is really impossible, otherwise there would be no illness" (*ibid.*, 234f.). Freud has "often suspected that something organic played a part in repression." Infantile sexual excitation is far less important than sexual excitation during later phases of life "because the determining apparatus and the amount of secretion have increased in the meantime." Links between childhood experiences and anxiety, shame and morality. There is a "crying need" for "a prompt elucidation of common neurasthenic anxiety." Freud had a bout of migraine a few days earlier (*ibid.*, 229ff.).

November 18: Freud feels as if he has succeeded in something important but does not know what it is (*ibid.*, 235).

December 3: Freud realizes that his longing for Rome is "deeply neurotic" and connected with "his schoolboy hero-worship of the Semitic Hannibal," who also could not reach Rome. "Since I have started studying the unconscious I have become so interesting to myself. It is a pity that one always keeps one's mouth shut about the most intimate things. 'Das Beste, was Du wissen kannst, darfst Du den Buben doch nicht sagen' [After all, the best of what you know may not be told to the boys—a quotation from Goethe's *Faust*]."

Freud realizes that his anxiety about travel is connected with the move from Freiberg to Leipzig when he was three years old and when he was frightened by the gas lamps on Breslau railway station. They reminded him of "souls burning in hell" (*ibid.*, 235ff.).

December 5 and 19: Lectures on dreams to the B'nai B'rith Society (*ibid.*, 238); the date given by Jones, 1953, I, 355 is probably wrong.

December 12: There are "endopsychic myths" resulting from the "dim inner perception of one's own psychical apparatus." These are "naturally" projected outward (1950a, 237).

Freud suffers from nasal suppuration and occlusion. He looks forward to his meeting with Fliess after carrying what he calls the craziest ideas in his head for months, having had no "sensible person" around to whom he could unburden himself (Schur, 1972, 135f.).

December 22: Masturbation is the "primary addiction"; alcohol, morphine, tobacco, etc., are mere substitutes. Addiction plays a prodigious part in hysteria, hence there are grave doubts that it is curable. Perhaps analysis and therapy must be content with "transforming a hysteria into a neurasthenia." In obsessional neurosis, the verbalized ideas are of crucial importance, above all, "copro-erotic terms." Freud can hardly tell "how many things I (a new Midas) turn into—filth." Birth, miscarriage, and menstruation are all "connected with the lavatory via the word 'abort,' " which means both "abortion" and "lavatory" in German. In psychoses, "words, sentences and whole paragraphs" are blacked out, as they are with "Russian censorship" (1950a, 238ff.).

Christmas: Meeting with Fliess in Breslau (Jones, 1953, I, 301).

December 29: Back in Vienna. Freud criticizes Fliess's left-handedness theory (1950a, 241).

"I am still feeling too well for serious work." In Breslau, Freud had had his nose cauterized by Fliess: "My nose is behaving itself and conveys its thanks" (Schur, 1972, 140).

1898

January 4: Freud gives a detailed explanation of his rejection of Fliess's theory of left-handedness (1950a, 242f.). He sends Fliess his "drekkologikal reports" (the German word *Dreck* means "mud," "dirt," "filth," "feces," and Freud uses it to indicate the abundance of anal material then emerging in his self-analysis. However, he keeps back "wild dreams" that have also come up in his self-analysis. He had a few desolate days with "rotten mood and pain, displaced from the head (or heart) to my legs" (Schur, 1972, 140).

January 16: "Happiness is the deferred fulfilment of a prehistoric wish" (1950a, 244).

Freud sends Fliess further "drekkologikal reports" (Schur, 1972, 141).

Freud is depressed because he owes Breuer 2,300 gulden (Jones, 1953, I, 160).

February 9: "I am deep in the dream

book." "Self-analysis has been dropped in favour of the dream book."

"Sexuality in the Aetiology of the Neuroses" (1898a). Freud compares his sexual theory of neurasthenia and anxiety neurosis with his theory of the neuroses of defense. According to the latter, sexual experiences in childhood have a delayed effect. The paper discusses the efficacy of psychoanalysis in the treatment of the neuroses of defense.

Freud relates a dream in which his rumored investment with the title of professor is linked with "unpublishable" ideas because its deeper meaning "shuttles to and fro" between his nurse (his mother) and his wife (1950a, 244f.).

February 23: Several chapters of *The Interpretation of Dreams* are completed. "It looks promising. It takes me deeper into psychology than I intended" (Jones, 1953, I, 357).

March 5: The "best composed part" of *The Interpretation of Dreams* is completed *(ibid.).*

March 10: Theory of the origin of dreams, fantasies, and neuroses in the "prehistoric stage of life" (1–3 years).

Freud sees himself "growing older, contentedly on the whole, watching my hair rapidly growing grey and the children rapidly growing up" (1950a, 246f.).

March 15: Freud sends Fliess the second chapter of *The Interpretation of Dreams.* He is afraid that Fliess will object to "the candid remarks in the professor-dream." He plans to read more about the Oedipus legend. He feels completely disoriented over hysteria *(ibid.,* 248f.).

March 24: Freud is pleased about Fliess's comments on his "dream manuscript". He plans to continue writing before going on to study the literature. "So long as I have not finished my own work I cannot read" *(ibid.,* 249).

April 3: Freud continues working on his "dream book" *(ibid.,* 250).

Beginning of April (Easter): After Fliess has called off their meeting, Freud takes his brother Alexander to Istria for four days *(ibid.,* 251ff.).

May 1: Freud sends Fliess the third chapter of *The Interpretation of Dreams.* "I am

completely wrapped up in dreams and very dull about them." He is dissatisfied with many passages *(ibid.,* 254).

June 9: At Fliess's suggestion, Freud is prepared to delete a dream in which he has "lost the feeling of shame required," but regrets doing so very much. He asks Fliess to what parts he has taken objection. "Was it my anxiety, or Martha, or my poverty or my being without a fatherland?" He will have a substitute dream in which these things are left out, for he can have dreams like that to order (Schur, 1966, 75).

June 18: Freud spends a weekend in Aussee, where his family is already on vacation.

June 20: Freud again expresses regret at the deletion of the dream. A "substitute dream," in which "a house constructed of building blocks collapsed," could not be used because of its allusions *(ibid.,* 75).

Freud interprets C. F. Meyer's story *Die Richterin (The [female] Judge):* it is a "family romance," written as a defense against incest (1950a, 256f.).

July 7: Freud sends Fliess another consignment—either part of his *Interpretation of Dreams* (the "Psychology of the Dream-Processes"?) or else a piece on his self-analysis, which was "all written by the unconscious." It was not "written to be read."

Analysis of C. F. Meyer's *Die Hochzeit des Mönchs (The Monk's Wedding) (ibid.,* 258).

July: Meeting with Fliess in Aussee (Jones, 1953, I, 301), or:

Beginning of August (more probable): Meeting with Fliess in Munich *(ibid.,* 335).

Beginning to middle of August: Freud travels with Minna Bernays to Kufstein, Innsbruck, Landeck, Trafoi, etc., up the Stelvio Pass and over to Bormio in Italy, then back to Aussee to see his family *(ibid.,* and 1950a, 259f.).

Mid-August to August 31: In Aussee.

August 26: Freud mentions that he had repressed a name (Julius Mosen). The "analysis resolved the thing completely; unfortunately I cannot make it public any more than my big dream" (1950a, 261f.).

August 31: Freud leaves with Martha for Dalmatia. He tours without Martha to Cattaro (repression of the name Signorelli). With Martha to Spalato (Split) and Trieste. Without Martha, who goes on to Merano, he travels to Brescia and Milan (Jones, 1953, I, 335; 1950a, 262).
September 19–20: Return to Vienna (1950a, 264).
September 22: Reports his failure to recall the name of Signorelli *(ibid.)*.
September 27: "The Psychical Mechanism of Forgetfulness" (1898b). This paper deals with Freud's repression of the name Signorelli. Freud writes about a new patient who had wetted his bed as a boy and now shows hysterical symptoms. "Was it spontaneous or the result of seduction?" *(ibid.,* 265ff.).
October 9: Has ten to eleven psychotherapeutic sessions a day *(ibid.,* 268).
October 23: Freud congratulates Fliess on his "most important date of all" (Fliess's fortieth birthday).
"The dream book is irremediably at a standstill." Obstacles to finishing it include "the gap left by the thoroughly analysed example." Freud is afraid that his hope of gaining "an insight into the whole of mental activity" may never be fulfilled *(ibid.,* 269).
December 5: Freud reads the literature on dreams with great reluctance *(ibid.,* 270).
Christmas or New Year: Meeting with Fliess in Vienna *(ibid.)*.

1899

January 3: Self-analysis has shown that "phantasies are products of later periods which project themselves back from the present into earliest childhood." "The answer to the question of what happened in infancy is: Nothing, but the germ of a sexual impulse was there."
Dreams are the key to hysteria.
January 16: Freud writes about patients with various hysterical symptoms whom he can help with the "phantasy key" *(ibid.,* 272f.).
January 30: Freud makes further discoveries. "The phantasy key is substantiating itself" *(ibid.,* 274).
February 6: Freud reflects on death: "Thou owest Nature [God] a death." He

hopes that when his own time comes, he will find somebody who will treat him "with respect and tell me when to be ready." "My father knew that he was dying, did not speak about it, retained his composure to the end."
Freud thinks seriously of changing his occupation and place of residence. Longs to go to Rome *(ibid.,* 276).
February 19: "It is not only dreams that are fulfillments of wishes, but hysterical attacks as well." Freud examines this thesis in the light of case histories *(ibid.,* 277f.).
Work and gainful professional activity are eating him up like a cancer (Schur, 1972, 193).
March 2: "Rome is still far away." "I am obviously much more normal than I was four or five years ago." Freud stops lecturing for the rest of the year. "When Rome becomes possible, perhaps I shall throw up the lectureship" (1950a, 279f.).
April (Easter): Meeting with Fliess in Innsbruck (Jones, 1953, I, 335f.).
May 28: Freud sends "Screen Memories" (1899a) to the printer (see 1.3.2 above). "The dreams, however, have suddenly taken shape" and "this time for good." Freud has decided that "all the efforts at disguise will not do," nor will "giving it all up." He is still studying the literature. *The Interpretation of Dreams* is his own "dung-heap," his own "seedling" and a *"nova species mihi."*
He enjoys Schliemann's account of his childhood: "The man found happiness" because "happiness comes only from fulfillment of a childhood wish" (1950a, 281f.).
June 4: Minna and the children go to Berchtesgaden *(ibid.,* 282).
June 9: Every dream tries to fulfill the wish for sleep *(ibid.,* 283).
June 27: First proofs of *The Interpretation of Dreams* are sent to the printer. Freud dreams that he is in the "Sexta," the sixth class, and says that the only possible explanation is that Anna is his sixth child, his "Sexta" *(ibid.,* 284).
June 29–July 2: Freud joins his family in Königssee, near Berchtesgaden *(ibid.)*.
July 17: Freud chooses quotations for *The Interpretation of Dreams (ibid.,* 286).
July 22: Freud proposes to send Fliess *The*

Interpretation of Dreams for correction (*ibid.,* 287).

August 1: Freud sends Fliess proofs of the introductory chapter from Berchtesgaden. "The gap made by the big dream which you took out is to be filled by a small collection of dreams" (*ibid.,* 288).

August 6: Freud compares *The Interpretation of Dreams* to a walk: First comes the "dark wood" of the authorities; then there is "a cavernous defile" of his specimens, with its "peculiarities, its details, its indiscretions, and its bad jokes"; and then, all at once, "the high ground and the prospect."

The Interpretation of Dreams contains nothing "really private, i.e., personally sexual." Freud calls it his "Egyptian dream book" (1950a, 290f.).

August 20: Freud has now replaced the "complete dream" deleted by Fliess with "a small collection of dream-fragments" (*ibid.,* 292).

He has "a trace of writer's cramp" (*ibid.*).

His brother Alexander is to be appointed professor extraordinary, "long before me, in fact" (*ibid.*).

August 27: Freud is "completely absorbed in the dreams" and "useless for anything else." The dream book will contain "2,467 mistakes."

He proposes a meeting with Fliess in Rome at Easter (*ibid.,* 293f.).

September 6: "I am completely absorbed in the dreams, I am writing eight to ten pages a day." "I ended by putting more into it than I intended." "I have avoided sex, but 'dirt' is unavoidable." "If only someone could tell me the real worth of the whole thing" (*ibid.,* 295).

September 11: Freud finishes *The Interpretation of Dreams.* He believes that the "matter about dreams" is "unassailable." He intends to leave the psychological part entirely to Fliess's judgment—"whether I should revise it again or let it go as it is" (*ibid.,* 296f.).

September 21: Back in Vienna. Freud tells Fliess how he would like him to read the proofs.

Freud is worried about his income: "I once knew helpless poverty and have a constant fear of it" (*ibid.,* 298).

October 4: Freud has "the painful feeling of parting with something that has been your very own." "In my case it must have been even more painful because what separated itself was not ideational possessions but my very own feelings" (Schur, 1972, 198).

October 9: Freud has once again been passed over in the professorial promotions (1950a, 300).

October 11: "A sexual theory may be the immediate successor to the dream book."

About October 20: First copies of *The Interpretation of Dreams* ready (*ibid.,* 300f.).

November 5: The sexual theory makes progress, "but I am baffled by the *(absit omen!)* feminine side."

Freud realizes that he had confused the names of Hamilcar and Hasdrubal in *The Interpretation of Dreams* (*ibid.,* 302).

End of November–beginning of December: Fliess visits Vienna (*ibid.,* 303).

December 9: Thoughts about the sexual theory (*ibid.,* 303f.).

December 21: His analysis of a patient provides Freud with a solution of his own railway phobia. It was "a poverty, or rather a hunger phobia, arising out of my infantile gluttony and called up by the circumstance that my wife had no dowry (of which I am proud)" (*ibid.,* 306).

1900

January 8: The "most interesting thing" about the new century for Freud and Fliess is that "it contains the dates of our death" (*ibid.,* 307).

February 1: "I am actually not at all a man of science, not an observer, not an experimenter, not a thinker. I am by temperament nothing but a *conquistador,* an adventurer if you want to translate this term—with all the inquisitiveness, daring and tenacity characteristic of such a man. Such people are customarily valued only if they have been successful, have really discovered something; otherwise they are thrown by the wayside" (Schur, 1972, 201).

February–March: Freud continues work on his sexual theory. He notes that *The Interpretation of Dreams* has attracted little attention (1950a, 311).

March 3: Depressive mood.

March 23: Freud declines a meeting proposed by Fliess.

May 7: On the occasion of his birthday on May 6: "Well, I really am forty-four now, a rather shabby old Jew." Freud thinks that it would be a fitting punishment for him that "none of the unexplored regions of the mind in which I have been the first mortal to set foot will ever bear my name or submit to my laws. When breath threatened to fail me in the struggle I prayed the angel to desist, and that is what he has done since then. But I did not turn out to be the stronger, though since then I have been noticeably limping" (ibid., 318f.; Jacob and the angel, Genesis 32: 24–32, M.K.).

June 3 (Whitsun): Emanuel and Sam Freud visit Sigmund and his family at Bellevue (1950a, 321).

June 12: Freud wonders whether the house in Bellevue will ever boast a marble tablet commemorating the fact that it was in this house that the secret of dreams (the Irma dream) was revealed to him on 24 July 1895 (1950a, 322).

Early August: Meeting with Fliess at Achensee. The two men clash. Freud goes on with Martha through the Tyrol and then with a friend to Venice. Further tours of Corinthia and Tessin with Minna (Jones, 1953, I, 336).

Mid-September: Return to Vienna (ibid.).

October 14: Freud collects material for *The Psychopathology of Everyday Life.* He starts the analysis of an eighteen-year-old girl, probably Dora (cf. 1905e, 13) (1950a, 325).

November 25: "Being the last of one's tribe—or the first and perhaps the only one—these are quite similar situations" (Schur, 1972, 211).

1901

January 1: Freud suggests that he and Fliess stop writing to each other for a time (ibid., 212).

January 25: "Fragment of an Analysis of a Case of Hysteria" (1905e) completed (the Dora case), but not published until 1905.

May 8: Freud corrects the proofs of *The Psychopathology of Everyday Life* (1901b)

(1950a, 330; published in book form in 1904).

June 9: To Fliess: "You have reminded me of that beautiful and difficult time when I had reason to believe that I was very close to the end of my life, and it was your confidence that kept me going" (Schur, 1972, 214).

Mid-July: Freud takes his family to Thumsee, near Reichenhall (1950a, 333f.).

August 7: To Fliess: "As far as Breuer is concerned you were certainly quite right in calling him *the* brother. However, I do not share your contempt for friendship between men, probably because I am to a high degree a party to it. As you well know, in my life a woman has never been a substitute for a comrade, a friend" (Schur, 1972, 216f.).

End of August–early September: First visit to Rome with his brother, Alexander. "It was all more splendid than he could say. He had never felt so well in his life" (Jones, 1955, II, 19ff.; 1950a, 313).

Freud explains his view of their difference of opinion to Fliess (1950a, 335ff.).

Autobiographical entry in J. L. Pagel's (German) *Biographical Lexicon of Eminent Doctors of the Nineteenth Century* (1901c).

1902

March: Freud has the title of professor extraordinary conferred on him (1950a, 341).

March 8 and 11: Freud tells Fliess what steps he took to pave the way for his professorship (ibid., 342ff.).

September: Tour of Italy (Rome, Naples, Paestum, and Capri) (ibid., 345; Jones, 1955, II, 20ff.

October: Foundation of the Psychological Wednesday Society (which changed its name in April 1908 to the Vienna Psychoanalytical Society) with Alfred Adler, Wilhelm Stekel, Max Kahane, and Rudolf Reitler (Jones, 1955, II, 7ff.).

1904

July 27: Last letter to Fliess (Fliess 1906).

Eugen Bleuler starts a correspondence with Freud.

Beginning of September: Unplanned sea voyage from Trieste to Athens with brother Alexander. "A Disturbance of Memory on the Acropolis" (1936a).

The Psychopathology of Everyday Life (1901b) published in book form. "Freud's Psycho-Analytic Procedure" (1904a) published anonymously in a collective work.

1905

Publication of: *Three Essays on the Theory of Sexuality* (1905d); *Jokes and Their Relation to the Unconscious* (1905c); "Fragment of an Analysis of a Case of Hysteria" (1905e), finished by Freud as early as 1901 but withdrawn before publication); and of a paper: "On Psychotherapy" (1905a).

1906

April: Start of Freud–Jung correspondence (Freud/Jung, 1974).
September: Publication of a collection of some of his papers under the title *Sammlung kleiner Schriften zur Neurosenlehre aus den Jahren 1893–1906*, Bd. I (1906b).

1907

March: Jung visits Freud in Vienna (Freud/Jung, 1974, 24).

1908

April: First International Psychoanalytical Congress, in Salzburg (Jones, 1955, II, 39ff.).
September: Freud visits his half-brothers Emanuel and Philipp in England. Four days' stay in Zurich (*ibid.*, 51ff.).
Essay: "On the Sexual Theories of Children" (1908c).

1909

January: Foundation of the *Jahrbuch für psychosomatische und psychopathologische Forschungen*, editor C. G. Jung (Freud/Jung, 1974, 621).
February: Mathilde Freud becomes the first of Freud's children to marry (Jones, 1955, II, 54f.).
September: Visit to America with Jung and Sandor Ferenczi; Freud lectures at Clark University, Worcester, Massachusetts (*ibid.*, 55ff.).

Essays: "Analysis of a Phobia in a Five-Year-Old Boy" (1909b) and "Family Romances" (1909c).

1910

March: Second International Psychoanalytical Congress, in Nüremberg; foundation of the International Psychoanalytical Association. Jung is elected president. First disagreements between Jung and Freud (Jones, 1955, II, 67ff.; Freud/Jung 1974).
Foundation of the *Zentralblatt für Psychoanalyse*, with Stekel and Adler as editors (Jones, 1955, II, 70).
September: With Ferenczi to Paris, Rome, and Sicily (*ibid.*, 81ff.).
Publication of *Leonardo da Vinci and a Memory of His Childhood* (1910c).

1911

June: Alfred Adler resigns from the Vienna Psychoanalytical Society (Jones, 1955, II, 131ff.).
August 29: Death of Freud's half-brother Philipp in Manchester.[22]
September: Third International Psychoanalytical Congress, in Weimar (*ibid.*, 85ff.)
"Psycho-Analytic Notes on an Autobiographical Account of a Case of Paranoia (Dementia Paranoides)" (1911c).

1912

Spring: Disagreement with Stekel about the editorship of the *Zentralblatt* (Jones, 1955, II, 136).
Freud founds the periodical *Imago* (*ibid.*, 84).
Beginning of serious disagreements with Jung (Freud/Jung, 1974).
Summer: Ernest Jones sets up the "Committee." Members: Freud, Sandor Ferenczi, Otto Rank, Karl Abraham, Hanns Sachs, Ernest Jones, and, from 1919, Max Eitingon (Jones, 1955, II, 152ff.).
September: Freud visits Rome with Ferenczi (*ibid.*, 94ff.).
October: Stekel resigns from the Vienna Society (*ibid.*, 135; Stekel, 1950).
November: Decision to found the "Internationale Zeitschrift für ärztliche Psychoanalyse" at a meeting where Stekel

refuses to surrender the *Zentralblatt.* At this meeting Freud faints in the presence of Jung (Jones, 1953, I, 317; Freud/Jung, 1974, 522).
Publication of first part of *Totem and Taboo* (1912–13).

1913

January: Freud breaks off private contacts with Jung (Freud/Jung, 1974, 539).
September: Fourth International Psychoanalytical Congress, in Munich. Jung reelected president (*ibid.,* 549f.; Jones, 1955, II, 102f.).
October: Jung gives up the editorship of the *Jahrbuch.*
Publication of *Totem and Taboo* (1912–13).

1914

April: Jung resigns from the presidency of the International Psychoanalytical Association (Freud/Jung, 1974, 551).
March 13: Freud's daughter Sophie presents him with his first grandson (Jones, 1955, II, 105).
July: Jung resigns from the International Psychoanalytical Association (Freud/Abraham, 1965, 183).
July: Beginning of World War I. Freud's sons volunteer for the army (Jones, 1955, II, 173f.)
October 17: Death of Freud's half-brother Emanuel in Manchester.[21]
"The Moses of Michelangelo" (1914b); "On Narcissism: An Introduction" (1914c).

1915

March–July: Twelve papers on "Metapsychology" (of which only five have come down to us: 1915c, 1915d, 1915e, 1917d, and 1917e) (Freud/Abraham, 1965, 228; Jones, 1955, II, 185).

1915–16

Winter semester: Last series of lectures published as *Introductory Lectures on Psycho-Analysis* (1916–17).

1918

September: Fifth International Psychoanalytical Congress, in Budapest (Jones, 1955, II, 197f.).
Anton von Freund decides to dispose of his vast fortune and to devote it to the furtherance of psychoanalysis (*ibid.,* 196). Inflation erodes much of its value.
November: End of World War I.
Publication of "From the History of an Infantile Neurosis" (1918b) (case history of the "Wolf Man").

1919

January: Foundation of the International Psycho-Analytical Press with money donated by Von Freund (Jones, 1957, III, 35ff.).
Spring: Freud works on *Beyond the Pleasure Principle* and on *Group Psychology and the Analysis of the Ego* (*ibid.,* 40, 42).

1920

January: Death of Anton von Freund. Death of Freud's daughter Sophie (Jones, 1957, III, 8).
Foundation of the *International Journal of Psycho-Analysis* (*ibid.,* 37ff.).
August: Last Committee meeting, at which differences with Rank are aired (*ibid.,* 54ff.).
Summer: Last journey to Rome, accompanied by his daughter Anna (*ibid.,* 93f.).
September: Sixth International Psychoanalytical Congress, in The Hague (*ibid.,* 26f.)
Publication of *Beyond the Pleasure Principle* (1920g).
October: Radical operation on the upper part of the lower jaw and the palate. Freud is forced to wear a huge prosthesis that seriously impedes him while eating and speaking (*ibid.,* 94f.).

1924

Break between Freud and Otto Rank (*ibid.,* Chap. 2).
"The Dissolution of the Oedipus Complex" (1924d); "A Short Account of Psycho-Analysis" (1924f).

1925

An Autobiographical Study (1925d).
December: Death of Karl Abraham (Jones, 1957, III, 116).

1926

May 6: Seventieth birthday.
Inhibitions, Symptoms and Anxiety

(1926d; written in 1925); *The Question of Lay Analysis* (1926e).

1927
The Future of an Illusion (1927c).

1928
Publication of "Dostoevsky and Parricide" (1928b), written as early as 1926 or 1927 (Jones, 1957, III, 142f.).

1929
Max Schur becomes Freud's personal physician (Schur, 1972, 407f.).
Summer: *Civilization and Its Discontents* (1930a).
Autumn: Ferenczi withdraws from Freud (Jones, 1957, III, 147f.).

1930
The city of Frankfurt bestows the Goethe Prize on Freud.
September 12: Death of Freud's mother, Amalie Freud, in Vienna.
October: Further surgery (Schur, 1972, 424).

1931
Spring: Several operations (*ibid.,* 424ff.).
"Female Sexuality" (1931b).

1932
Spring: Freud starts work on the *New Introductory Lectures on Psycho-Analysis* (1933a); publication in December (Jones, 1957, III, 175f.).
Crisis at the International Psycho-Analytical Press due to the world economic depression (*ibid.,* 167ff.).
Letter to Albert Einstein: *Why War?* (1933b).

1933
January: Hitler seizes power in Germany.
May: Death of Sandor Ferenczi (Jones, 1957, III, 178).
Freud's books burned in Berlin (*ibid.,* 182).
August: Freud starts work on *Moses and Monotheism* (Schur, 1972, 454f.).
Dissolution of the German Psychoanalytical Society; many members escape to other countries (Jones, 1957, III, 185ff.).

1934
Summer: Freud writes the first version of his Moses book: "The Man Moses, an historical novel" (Freud/Zweig, 1968, 91ff.; Jones, 1957, III, 193ff.).

1936
May 6: Celebrations and tributes to Freud on the occasion of his eightieth birthday (Schur, 1972, 476ff.; Jones, 1957, III, 202ff.).
Letter to Romain Rolland: "A Disturbance of Memory on the Acropolis" (1936a).
July: Development of new lesion, and operation (Schur, 1972, 483).
Further work on Moses (Jones, 1957, III, 207).
December: Discovery of the Fliess correspondence by Marie Bonaparte (Schur, 1972, 486).

1937
Spring: Publication of "Moses, an Egyptian" (1937b) (Part I of *Moses and Monotheism*) (Jones, 1957, III, 216).
Summer: "Analysis Terminable and Interminable" (1937c) (Schur, 1972, 490).
Rewriting of Part III of the "Moses'-booz" (Jones, 1957, III, 216).
End of year: "If Moses Was an Egyptian . . ." (1937e) (Part II of *Moses and Monotheism*) (Jones, 1957, III, 216f.).

1938
January: Further cancer operation (Schur, 1972, 492).
March 11: Nazis march into Austria.
June 4: Freud emigrates via Paris to London together with: Martha, his wife; Minna Bernays, his sister-in-law; Anna, his daughter; Martin, his son; Esti, Martin's wife; Walter and Sophie, Martin's children; Ernst Halberstadt, his grandson; Mathilde, his daughter; R. Hollitscher, Mathilde's husband; Max Schur, his personal doctor; Schur's wife and two children; Paula Fichtl, housekeeper. (Jones, 1957, III, 227ff.; Schur, 1972, 501ff.).
Work on *An Outline of Psycho-Analysis* (1940a, published posthumously).
August: Publication of the German edition of *Moses and Monotheism* (1939a) in Amsterdam (Jones, 1957, III, 239).

September: Last operation (Schur, 1972, 509ff.).

Freud moves into 20, Maresfield Gardens, in Hampstead (Jones, 1957, III, 232).

1939

February: New, inoperable lesion (Schur, 1972, 570ff.).

August: Deterioration in Freud's condition (*ibid.*, 526ff.).

September 21: Freud begs Schur to put an end to his suffering (*ibid.*, 529).

September 23: Freud, having been given an injection of morphine, dies following a coma lasting one and a half days.

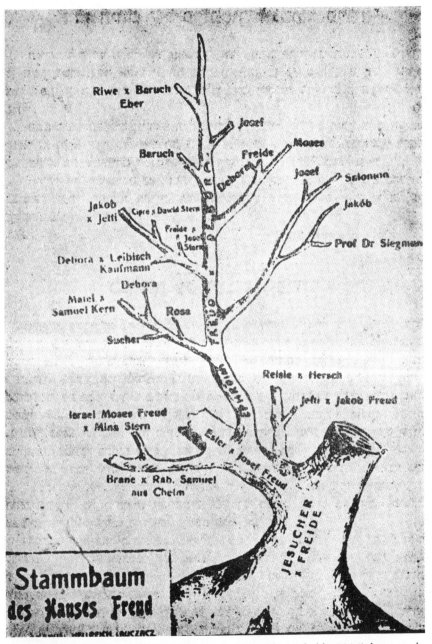

TABLE 2 Facsimile of a Freud family tree by Hellreich (probably 1914) from tombstones in the Jewish cemetery of Buczacz (in: I. Kohn, ed., *Sefer Buczacz,* Tel-Aviv, 1955)

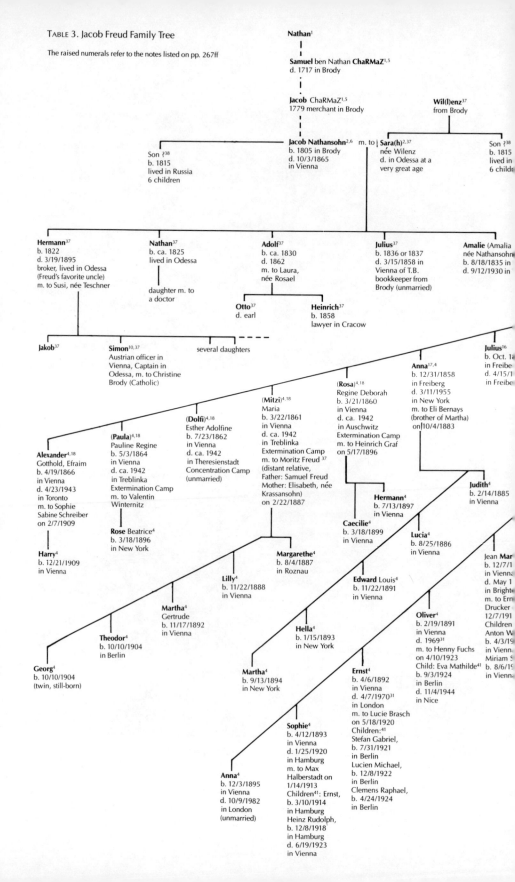

TABLE 3. Jacob Freud Family Tree

The raised numerals refer to the notes listed on pp. 267ff

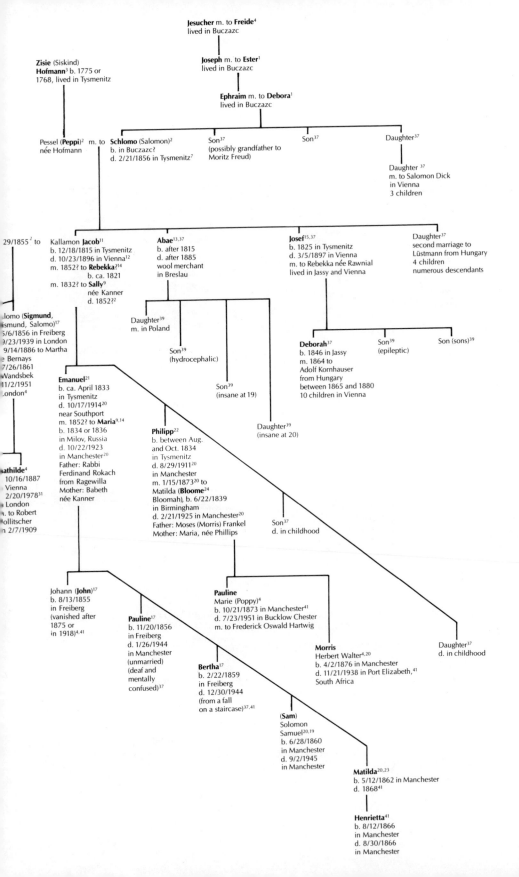

Jesucher m. to Freide[4]
lived in Buczazc

Joseph m. to Ester[1]
lived in Buczazc

Ephraim m. to Debora[1]
lived in Buczazc

Pessel (Peppi)[2] m. to
née Hofmann

Zisie (Siskind)
Hofmann[3] b. 1775 or
1768, lived in Tysmenitz

Schlomo (Salomon)[2]
b. in Buczazc?
d. 2/21/1856 in Tysmenitz[7]

Son[37]
(possibly grandfather to
Moritz Freud)

Son[37]

Daughter[37]

Daughter[37]
m. to Salomon Dick
in Vienna
3 children

29/1855[2] to

Kallamon Jacob[11]
b. 12/18/1815 in Tysmenitz
d. 10/23/1896 in Vienna[12]
m. 1852? to Rebekka?[14]
b. ca. 1821
m. 1832? to Sally[9]
née Kanner
d. 1852?[2]

Abae[13,37]
b. after 1815
d. after 1885
wool merchant
in Breslau

Josef[15,37]
b. 1825 in Tysmenitz
d. 3/5/1897 in Vienna
m. to Rebekka née Rawnial
lived in Jassy and Vienna

Daughter[37]
second marriage to
Lüstmann from Hungary
4 children
numerous descendants

lomo (Sigmund,
ismund, Salomo)[17]
5/6/1856 in Freiberg
9/23/1939 in London
9/14/1886 to Martha
e Bernays
7/26/1861
Wandsbek
11/2/1951
London[4]

Daughter[39]
m. in Poland

Son[39]
(hydrocephalic)

Deborah[37]
b. 1846 in Jassy
m. 1864 to
Adolf Kornhauser
from Hungary
between 1865 and 1880
10 children in Vienna

Son[39]
(epileptic)

Son (sons)[39]

athilde[4]
10/16/1887
Vienna
2/20/1978[31]
London
n. to Robert
ollitscher
n 2/7/1909

Emanuel[21]
b. ca. April 1833
in Tysmenitz
d. 10/17/1914[20]
near Southport
m. 1852? to Maria[9,14]
b. 1834 or 1836
in Milov, Russia
d. 10/22/1923
in Manchester[20]
Father: Rabbi
Ferdinand Rokach
from Ragewilla
Mother: Babeth
née Kanner

Philipp[22]
b. between Aug.
and Oct. 1834
in Tysmenitz
d. 8/29/1911[20]
in Manchester
m. 1/15/1873[20] to
Matilda (Bloome[24]
Bloomah), b. 6/22/1839
in Birmingham
d. 2/21/1925 in Manchester[20]
Father: Moses (Morris) Frankel
Mother: Maria, née Phillips

Son[39]
(insane at 19)

Daughter[39]
(insane at 20)

Son[37]
d. in childhood

Johann (John)[17]
b. 8/13/1855
in Freiberg
(vanished after
1875 or
in 1918)[4,41]

Pauline[17]
b. 11/20/1856
in Freiberg
d. 1/26/1944
in Manchester
(unmarried)
(deaf and
mentally
confused)[37]

Bertha[17]
b. 2/22/1859
in Freiberg
d. 12/30/1944
(from a fall
on a staircase)[37,41]

Pauline
Marie (Poppy)[4]
b. 10/21/1873 in Manchester[41]
d. 7/23/1951 in Bucklow Chester
m. to Frederick Oswald Hartwig

Morris
Herbert Walter[4,20]
b. 4/2/1876 in Manchester
d. 11/21/1938 in Port Elizabeth,[41]
South Africa

Daughter[37]
d. in childhood

(Sam)
Solomon
Samuel[20,19]
b. 6/28/1860
in Manchester
d. 9/2/1945
in Manchester

Matilda[20,23]
b. 5/12/1862 in Manchester
d. 1868[41]

Henrietta[41]
b. 8/12/1866
in Manchester
d. 8/30/1866
in Manchester

TABLE 4 Facsimile of the Register of Jews Resident in Freiberg of 1852 (District Archives, N. H]ičín, photocopy by J. Sajner)

Transcript of the entries under Jacob Freud

(Heading): The Jew/Name/Age/Family members/Name/Age/Whether a resident or a stranger./If a stranger/registered in what other municipality/whether in possession of certificate of citizenship and of what date/If he is owner of landed property in this municipality, which property/what is his occupation or what trade does he follow/ Year of his arrival/Comments/

Jakob Freud/38 yrs./ Wife Rebekka/ 32. / Sons/ Emanuel/21 yrs./ his wife/18 yrs./Filip/16 yrs./-/Kloksdorf/Certificate of citizenship issued by Kloksdorf Municipality on 31 October 1852 No. 195/None/Produce dealer/1840, only wife and sons since 1852/

TABLE 5 Facsimile of entry in Passport Register (photocopy by P. Swales)

Transcript of the entries under Emanuel, Jakob, and Rebekka Freud

194./Emanuel Freud/22/Clerk/31 Oct. 1852/4 years/in all provinces
195./Jakob Freud and/38/Merchant/ditto/ditto/ditto son Filipp

196./Rebekka Freud/31/Wife/ditto/ditto/ditto

(The entry under "Rebekka Freud" has been crossed out.)

TABLE 6 "List of Articles Imported and Weighed In by [Freiberg] Merchants in the Years 1852, 1853, 1854" (District Archives, N. Jičćin; copy by J. Sajner; italics added).[29]

	Sheep's Wool				Tallow				Honey		Aniseed	
	1852	1853	1854	To end March 1855	1852	1853	1854	To end March 1855	1852	1853	1852	1853
1. Moses Leib Horowitz	1624.99	1035.87	2348.07	482.91		4.88	11.03	6.06	8.06	3.82		
2. Berisch Kanner	614.94	1293.96	1618.18	299.56	23.06	193.86	77.15	133.42			5.10	
3. Wolf Harling	666.67	658.91	1832.05	411.69	1.65	8.10		27.03				
4. Jakob Freud	1309.—	910.86	1199.14	215.07	69.24				10.10			
5. David Frisch	521.47	699.05	1027.77	168.01								
6. Trundlich Magder	622.77	934.84	969.11	124.—		3.18				5.—		4.16
7. Barisch Meiseles	835.—		782.39	204.60					4.25			
8. Juda Mittelmann	98.82	395.20	385.91	48.75			17.72					
9. Ignaz Fluss	347.46	53.42	235.04	37.45	378.—				6.31			
10. Abrah. Perl	46.05	540.73	284.06		26.57				5.34	16.21		
11. Samueli	495.05	569.52	228.13	292.61								
12. Franz Repa	90.97	465.30	260.20	46.48								
13. Urban Knurek	450.14	251.66	88.66									
14. Nachim Kris	291.—											
15. Popper	90.97											
16. Mayer Bach			213.17	166.89								
17. Jos. Feldstein	52.32		61.40	38.31								
18. Anselm Jarosch		96.15										
Conventional coin: Florins, Kreuzers	8163.76	7905.47	11540.82	2536.30	418.51	210.—	105.90	136.51	34.40	25.30	5.10	4.16

Crauungs-Zeugniss

TABLE 7 Facsimile of marriage certificate of Jacob and Amalie Freud dated 1855 (in W. Aron: "Notes on Sigmund Freud's Ancestry and Jewish Contacts," in *Yivo Annual of Jewish Studies,* New York, 1956–57.)[33]

TABLE 8 Facsimile of the birth entries of Sigmund and Pauline Freud and of Emil Fluss in the Register of Copies of Entries of Persons of Different Faith in Freiberg (State Archives, Opava (Troppau), photograph by J. Sajner)[34]

TABLE 9 Facsimile of the birth entries of Anna and Bertha Freud in the Register of Copies of Entries of Persons of Different Faith in Freiberg (State Archives, Opava Troppau, photograph by J. Sajner)[35]

TABLE 10 Facsimile of the death entry of Julius Freud in the Register of Copies of Entries of Persons of Different Faith in Freiberg (State Archives, Opava Troppau, photograph by J. Sajner)[36]

Aus dem Gerichtssaale.

Wien, 22. Februar. [Orig. Ber.] (Creditpapier-Verfälschung.) Vorsitzender: Präsident Ritter v. Schwarz; öffentlicher Ankläger: Staatsanwalts-Substitut Mottloch; Vertheidiger: Dr. Neuda und Dr. Alfred Stern.

Auf der Anklagebank befinden sich Joseph Freud, aus Tysmienetz in Galizien gebürtig, 40 Jahre alt, Handelsmann, und Osias Weich, aus Wisnet in der Bukowina gebürtig, 40 Jahre alt, Handelsmann. Der vom Staatsanwalt gegen sie erhobenen Anklage entnehmen wir: Joseph Freud wendete sich im Mai 1865 an den Commissionär Simon Weiß mit der Anfrage, ob er ihm nicht einen Käufer für 100 Stück Fünfzig-Rubelscheine namhaft machen wolle, denn es sei Jemand da, der dieselben, weil sie falsch seien, billig verkaufen möchte. Weiß ging scheinbar auf den Antrag ein, ließ sich ein Exemplar der Falsificate ausfolgen und entfernte sich, um, wie er vorschützte, einen Käufer zu suchen. Weiß begab sich mit dem Falsificate zur Polizei, verabredete mit Freud ein Rendezvous im „Hotel Victoria", wo denn auch dem Freud 400 Stück Fünfzig-Rubelscheine abgekauft und 200 Gulden Angabe gegeben wurden. Die Auszahlung des weiteren Kaufschillings wurde bei Uebergabe der Waare (Falsificate) bedungen, und als daher Weiß die Falsificate holte und Freud mit denselben erschienen war, wurde dieser von der Sicherheitsbehörde festgenommen.

Man fand ihn im Besitze von 100 Stück Falsificaten, und bei der unter Einem in seiner Wohnung vorgenommenen Hausuchung wurden noch weitere 259 Stück Falsificate vorgefunden. Freud gab an, daß er im Sommer 1864 den Osias Weich in Galacz kennen gelernt, mit demselben öfter im „Hotel Zuckermann" gespeist habe, und eines Tages von demselben aufgefordert wurde, ob er geneigt sei, ein gutes Geschäft zu machen, worauf Weich weiters mittheilte, er habe von einem Herrn in England falsche Rubelnoten gekauft, welche ihm auf 25 Percent zu stehen kommen; er wollte nur 5 Percent verdienen und dem Freud die Verwechslung übertragen. Er, Freud, will auf den Vorschlag nicht eingegangen sein. Im September 1864 sei Weich nach Wien gekommen, habe ihn, Freud, im Café Wagner in der Leopoldstadt aufgesucht und um ein Darlehen von 300 fl. ersucht. Freud habe ihm die 300 Gulden geliehen und als Deckung die beanständeten, in einem englischen Couvert verwahrten Falsificate übernommen. Freud will auf der Messe in Leipzig wiederholt mit Weich zusammengekommen und demselben, weil es ihm schlecht gegangen, 25 fl. per Post nach Leipzig geschickt haben. In Folge dieser Angaben wurde dem Osias Weich nachgeforscht, derselbe in Leipzig ermittelt, festgenommen und hieher eingeliefert. Weich, welcher sich über keinen ordentlichen Erwerb ausweisen kann, wurde im Besitze von Adressen aus London betreten, die auf Personen lauten, welche als sehr verdächtig bezeichnet werden. (Eine im diplomatischen Wege dem Gerichte zugegangene Auskunft bezeichnet insonderheit die Adresse Mrs. Lewy als die einer Jüdin, welche sich mit dem Hausiren mit Falsificaten befaßt.) Weiters fand man bei ihm mehrere Couverts, in Größe und Form vollkommen ähnlich demjenigen, in welchem Freud die Rubelscheine verwahrt hatte, und die auch vollkommen so eingerichtet waren, daß Rubelscheine hineinpassen. Nach dem Gutachten der kaiserlich russischen Bank in Petersburg sind die dem Joseph Freud beanständeten Falsificate auf gewöhnlichem Papier in Kupferstich und durch Steindruck erzeugt, eine Sorte jener Falsificate, mit welchen alle europäischen Handelsplätze überschwemmt sind, und die bereits zu mehrfachen Verurtheilungen Veranlassung gegeben haben. Aus Leipzig liegt noch ein Bericht vor, wodurch Osias Weich verdächtig erscheint, derselbe zu sein, welcher vor mehreren Jahren in polnischer Kleidung auf der Leipziger Messe gegen ähnliche Falsificate Uhren von Schweizer Fabrikanten eingekauft hat.

Die Art und Weise, in welcher sich beide Angeklagte gegen diese Anklage vertheidigen, war mitunter eine sehr drastische. Freud war wie, in der Voruntersuchung, auch in der Schlußverhandlung geständig, und beschuldigte den Weich als denjenigen, der ihm, dem Freud, die Falsificate an Deckung übergeben hatte. Weich bezeichnet mit seltener Gereiztheit diese Angaben als lügenhaft, will nie im Besitze solcher Falsificate gewesen sein und sagt, Freud, dessen Familie in London lebt, benütze ihn, um dem Gerichte überhaupt Jemanden namhaft zu machen, von dem die Falsificate herrühren. — In der That habe die Angabe insoferne den Schein der Wahrscheinlichkeit für sich, weil Beide zusammen gereist seien, was Freud wohlweislich berechnet hatte. Doch es sei das Ganze nur ein lügenhaftes Gewebe. In Besitz der Londoner Adressen will Weich höchst wahrscheinlich dadurch gelangt sein, daß, er, was leicht möglich ist auf Reisen, im Hotel dieselben vorgefunden und mitgenommen habe. Den Besitz der englischen Couverts, welche als ähnlich mit demjenigen erkannt wurden, in welchem Freud die Falsificate verwahrt gehalten, rechtfertigt Weich damit, daß Freud auf Reisen öfters seinen, Weich's Koffer, benützt hatte, und daß so wahrscheinlich die Couverts im Koffer zurückgeblieben seien. — Die Angeklagten ergehen sich noch in gegenseitigen Beschuldigungen und Beschimpfungen, welche das Meritorische der Anklage jedoch nicht zu erschüttern vermögen.

Der Staatsanwalt beantragt für Freud eine zehn-, für Weich eine zwölfjährige schwere Kerkerstrafe.

Das in später Nachmittagsstunde erfolgte Urtheil lautet: Joseph Freud und Osias Weich sind des Verbrechens der versuchten Theilnehmung an der Fälschung öffentlicher Creditspapiere schuldig, und sollen deßhalb durch je zehn Jahre in schwerem Kerker angehalten werden. — Bei Freud beschloß der Gerichtshof, die Acten zur Strafmilderung dem Obergerichte vorzulegen. — Die Verurtheilten meldeten Berufung an.

TABLE 12 Report in the Vienna daily newspaper *Neue Freie Presse* of the trial of Josef Freud in 1866 (first published in R. Gickelhorn: *Sigmund Freud und der Onkeltraum*, Vienna, 1976)[40]

108. „ **Amalie Freud, Wollhänd-
lersgattin** mit dem Kinde Sig=
mund und dem Dienſtmädchen
Reſi Wittek v. Freiberg, Nr. 180 **3**

TABLE 13 Facsimile of entry in Roznau Register of Spa Visitors for 5 June 1857: "108. Amalie Freud, wool merchant's wife, with child Sigmund and maid Resi Wittek from Freiberg, No. 180" (photograph by J. Sajner and P. Swales)

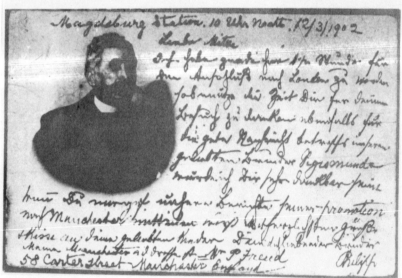

TABLE 14 Facsimile of postcard—snapshot of himself—sent by Philipp Freud to his half-sister Marie, dated March 12, 1902 (Library of Congress)

"Magdeburg Station, 10 P.M. 12/3/1902
Dear Mitzi:
I have to wait here for 1½ hours for the connection to London and use this opportunity to thank you for your visit and also for the good news about our beloved brother Sigismund, and should be very grateful if you would kindly send more news about his graduation to me in Manchester. With warmest regards and kisses to your dear children, your affectionate brother,

Philipp

My address in Manchester is Mr. P. Freud,
58 Carter Street, Manchester, England."

Notes

1. THE CRISIS IN FREUD'S LIFE AND THOUGHT

1. All quotations from Freud's works are taken (with certain amendments) from, and dated as in, the Standard Edition of the *Complete Psychological Works of Sigmund Freud*. London, The Hogarth Press, Vol. XXIV. Freud's name is not mentioned after this entry. For full bibliographical data, see the Bibliography below.

All italics in quoted material are in the original, unless otherwise specified.

2. See Jones, 1953, I, 265ff. and 324ff.; Kris, 1950, 33f.; Grubrich-Simitis, 1971, 11f.; Robert, 1975, 114ff.; Bally, 1961, 57; Schur, 1972, 114; Roazen, 1975, 92; Ellenberger, 1970, 488; Mannoni, 1971, 50; and many others.

3. "This book . . . contains . . . the most valuable of all the discoveries it has been my good fortune to make. Insight such as this falls to one's lot but once in a lifetime." Preface to the Third (Revised) English edition of 1931 (1900a, xxxii).

4. The history of these letters is highly dramatic (Jones, 1953, I, 287f.). In 1928, they were sold by Wilhelm Fliess's widow to a Berlin bookseller, who offered them for sale to Marie Bonaparte, a psychoanalyst and good friend of Freud's. She bought the letters together with Freud's various drafts, but when she told Freud of her acquisition, he asked her to destroy everything. She nevertheless deposited the material in a bank in Vienna, and when the Nazis marched in had it removed, first to Paris and then to London. In 1950, a selection of the letters was published by her in collaboration with Anna Freud, Sigmund Freud's daughter, and Ernst Kris, in abbreviated form. It is a matter for regret that these important biographical documents, though expanded since, have never been published in full without any cuts. Some biographers (Jones, Schur) were able to peruse them in the original version and have published further extracts, from which it is clear that the unpublished material must contain important information that may well call for trenchant revisions of our picture of Freud. On the other hand, it is understandable that, out of filial piety, Anna Freud should not have wished to break her father's taboo, absolute loyalty to one's father having been the leitmotif of the Freud family for several generations.

5. Ellenberger, however, states that Charcot's ideas had already filtered through to Vienna (Ellenberger, 1970, 434). For hysterical symptoms, see Table 1.

6. Mathilde, born 16 October 1887; Jean Martin, born 7 December 1889; Oliver, born 19 February 1891; Ernst, born 6 April 1892; Sophie, born 12 April 1893; and Anna, born 3 December 1895.

7. In a letter to Fliess dated 29 August 1888, Freud mentions the "very large family" he had to support, at a time when he and Martha had just one child (1954, 57).

8. Admittedly, Erikson places Freud's moratorium at an earlier phase of his life, when he was still engaged in his physiological studies (Erikson, 1958, 43). I believe,

however, that it is better, even in Erikson's sense, to date Freud's moratorium at between 1890 and 1900.

9. Freud was later able to proffer a psychological interpretation of Fliess's rather extreme theories of periodicity and nasal neurosis: "The conviction that his father, who died of erysipelas after suffering for many years from nasal suppuration, could have been saved was what made him into a doctor, and indeed into a rhinologist. The sudden death of his only sister two years later . . . led—as a consolation—to the fatalistic theory of predestined lethal dates. This piece of analysis, very unwelcome to him, was the real reason for the break between us which he engineered in such a pathological (paranoic) fashion" (Jones, 1955, II, 446f.).

10. For the rest, his ideas about the alleged differences between men and women in respect of the etiology of these neuroses in women reflect a considerable lack of empathy. The symptoms of anxiety can quite easily be understood as the woman's fear of a new pregnancy.

11. The subject of anxiety neurosis and its etiology was, moreover, the prime cause of Freud's clash with Wilhelm Stekel in about 1908, although the actual break had other, more personal, reasons. In his *Nervöse Angstzustände und ihre Behandlung* of 1908, Stekel claimed that anxiety neurosis too has psychic causes (see 4.1.2.1).

12. In 1895, Freud published a short paper entitled "Über die Bernhardt'sche Sensibilitätsstörung am Oberschenkel" (1895e). It dealt with a condition, Bernhardt's paresthesia, from which he himself had been suffering for at least seven years. He described it as follows: "A furry sensation, a feeling of having an 'alien skin' which . . . is intensified by walking and is often accompanied by painful brief stabbing pains vertically to the surface of the skin and by painful sensitivity to friction produced by clothing" (1895e, 491). Whether or not Freud considered this condition a symptom of his "neurasthenia" is not clear from the paper (see Jones, 1953, I, 170).

13. It is incomprehensible why the publishers of the Fliess letters should have removed these slips of the pen and why they failed to revert to the original even in the 1975 edition, which appeared later than Schur's biography of Freud.

14. Moreover, Richter and Beckmann quote Freud's ideas on anxiety neurosis, and also mention that Freud himself suffered from these symptoms. They do not however enter into Freud's theory of anxiety neurosis, according to which this illness results from "abnormal" sexual practices, probably because they discovered a completely different etiological nexus (Richter/Beckmann, 1969, 4).

15. It is also quite possible that Schur wanted to absolve his great teacher and revered patient from the taint of neurosis and therefore postulated an organic heart condition.

16. The German edition has "my anxiety neurosis," the English translation "the anxiety neurosis."

17. Anna's birth was, however, unwanted, as we can tell from the way in which Freud told Fliess about Martha's latest pregnancy: "If you have really solved the problem of conception [Fliess believed that his theory of periodicity helped him to tell the fertile from the infertile phases of the female cycle, M.K.], the only thing left for you to do is to make up your mind what kind of marble you prefer. For me the discovery is a few months too late, but it may come in useful next year" (1950a, 120, 25 May 1895; cf. Roazen, 1975, 51f.).

18. Martha Bernays was born on 26 July 1861.

19. There have been many allegations that Freud had an affair with Minna Bernays, Martha's unmarried sister, who lived in Freud's house from 1896 (Jones, 1953, I, 153). Roazen, for his part (1975, 62f.), has argued that if there had been a physical relationship between the two, there would have been some evidence of it in Freud's life and work, when there is none. The mere fact that his sister-in-law was a more stimulating conversational partner than his wife and that they often traveled together, is of course no proof of a liaison. However, Peter Swales's most recent research appears to

have produced fairly conclusive evidence that Freud and Minna did have an affair in 1900 that resulted in a pregnancy and abortion (Swales, 1982a).

20. See also his unchanged views some ten years later (Nunberg/Federn, 1977, II, 518ff.).

21. In the Standard Edition, this paper appears under (1895c) and (1895h), but the second entry is merely a German translation of the first published in the same year.

22. However, Freud assigned other phobic symptoms to the neuroses of defense, which neuroses he did not blame on current sexual practices and which he believed were susceptible to psychotherapy (see 1.1.2.4 and 1.1.2.5). Characteristically, these were symptoms from which he himself did not suffer.

23. Like his deliberations on masturbation, this quotation shows that Freud looked upon sexuality as a harmful force, as "one of the most dangerous activities of the human being" (cf. Roazen, 1975, 52).

One wonders therefore why Freud was also able to argue that the same sexual "chemism" had no harmful effects when expressed heterosexually, in other words, that the harmful effect was due to the absence of a suitable partner. The lack of logic in this type of reasoning is something Freud obviously failed to appreciate.

24. See Schur, 1972, 64f. It is noticeable that from 1895 on, Freud developed a touch of irony about his friend's scientific discoveries. He wrote that Fliess was an even greater "visionary than I" (1950a, 130, 31 October 1895), and criticized Fliess's paper on the relationship between the nose and the female genitals so sharply (1950a, 158f., 1 March 1896) that he obviously upset his friend badly, so much so that he felt bound to reassure Fliess about the validity of the theory of periodicity (1950a, 160, 16 March 1896).

25. None of the letters referring to the Emma episode are included in the published version of the Fliess correspondence (1950a), or in the 1975 edition, although Schur had published them by then. Emma is only mentioned in the "Project for a Scientific Psychology," in connection with a discussion of hysterical symptoms (1950a, 410ff.; see p. 00 below).

26. The "*Non-vixit*" dream, too, contains associations to the Emma episode: operations, Fliess's "unobtrusive" presence in Vienna, a warning not to discuss the matter with anyone, Freud's being "very disagreeably affected" by the veiled reproach, because it was not "wholly without justification" (1900a, 421 and 481).

27. Although Freud was not involved in Breuer's treatment of Anna O., his keen interest in that case, too, which also agreed with the above-mentioned structural scheme, might well have been due to the same childhood experience. Breuer, a friend whom Freud greatly respected, had also applied a new therapeutic method with strong sexual overtones, and under the veil of secrecy (see 1.1.1 above and 3.1.8 below).

28. It would take us too far to compare Freud's diagnostic criteria with those used by modern psychiatrists. It is however worth pointing out that many symptoms Freud described as neurotic would nowadays be considered psychotic (Schatzman, 1974, 149). At the time, Freud failed to draw a clear distinction between neurosis and psychosis, which explains why he included paranoia among the neuroses of defense.

29. The patient in question was Anna O.

30. It was this difference of opinion which led to the termination of their scientific collaboration two or three years later, though personal matters played an essential role as well (see 1893h, 38; 1925d, 22f.; Jones, 1953, I, 253ff; 1950a, 73, 30 May 1893).

31. "In answering the question of when it is that a mental process becomes pathogenic—that is, when it is that it becomes impossible for it to be dealt with normally—Breuer preferred what might be called a physiological theory: he thought that the processes which could not find a normal outcome were such as had originated during unusual, 'hypnoid,' mental states. . . . I, on the other hand, was inclined to suspect the existence of an interplay of forces and the operation of intentions and

purposes such as are to be observed in normal life. Thus it was a case of 'hypnoid hysteria' versus 'neuroses of defence.' " (1925d, 23; cf. 1950a, 94f., 22 June 1894).

32. Freud's view of neurone function had many parallels with the concept of "synapses" introduced by Foster and Sherrington in 1897 and accepted to this day (1900a, xvii; Anzieu, 1959, 15). It also bore—as has been emphasized from various quarters—striking similarities to more recent theoretical work in brain physiology (Jones, 1953, I, 369f.; Anzieu, *op. cit.*).

33. A comparison of Freud's analysis of Frau P. with the famous case of Daniel Paul Schreber, who also suffered from paranoia, provides an excellent illustration of the consequences of Freud's later renunciation of the seduction theory in favor of the Oedipus theory (see 1.3 above). In 1896, Freud attributed Frau P.'s symptoms to early childhood experiences, which he probed systematically and brought back into consciousness, thus curing the symptoms (1896b). In 1911, he considered Schreber's symptoms the direct result of his current homosexuality, which apparently needed no further probing. Freud could easily have established that Schreber's delusions, no less than his homosexuality, were due to seduction by Schreber's father, the physician and health fanatic Daniel Gottlob Moritz Schreber, but the Oedipus theory prevented him from doing so. According to that theory, the actions of the parents were far less important than the fantasies of the child, which allegedly followed a universal pattern independent of the parents' actions (cf. Schatzman, 1973, and Krüll, 1977b).

34. A remark Freud made in 1914 does suggest that his colleagues' criticism nevertheless had a marked effect on him: "I innocently addressed a meeting of the Vienna Society for Psychiatry and Neurology with Krafft-Ebing in the chair, expecting that the material losses I had willingly undergone would be made up for by the interest and recognition of my colleagues. I treated my discoveries as ordinary contributions to science and hoped they would be received in the same spirit. But the silence which my communications met with, the void which formed itself about me, the hints that were conveyed to me, gradually made me realize that assertions on the part played by sexuality in the aetiology of the neuroses cannot count upon meeting with the same kind of treatment as other communications. I understood that from now onwards I was one of those who had 'disturbed the sleep of the world,' as Hebbel says, and that I could not reckon upon objectivity and tolerance" (1914d, 21f.).

35. In this connection, mention must also be made of Freud's view that lack of "verbal consciousness" in childhood stands in the way of the conscious recall of traumatic experiences (1950a, 164ff, 30 May 1896; 142, 1 January 1896).

36. At that time, Jacob Freud lived in the immediate vicinity of his son's apartment. But he seems to have fallen ill in Baden near Vienna, for Freud wrote to Fliess that during the first few weeks of his father's illness he had to go to see him there (1950a, 168, 30 June 1896). Jacob died in Vienna in his own apartment at 14, Grüne Thorgasse (now Grünentorgasse) (Register of Deaths of the City of Vienna). Two weeks before his illness, Emanuel, Jacob's elder son of his first marriage, had arrived on a visit from England.

37. "My father knew that he was dying, did not speak about it and retained his composure to the end" (1950a, 276, 6 February 1899).

38. Freud's associations to the "No Smoking" notices in the second version of the dream in *The Interpretation of Dreams* reflect his fight against smoking in order to offset his cardiac neurosis (see p. 15 above, and Anzieu, 1959, 46) and hence, as I shall try to show below, his traumatic separation experience in childhood. The associations to the railway waiting rooms also have the same background.

39. Freud may also have been making concessions to Fliess. In the same letter, he discussed Fliess's theory of periodicity, and tried to link it to his own views. Someone with a less pronounced biogenetic orientation than Fliess's might very well have had a very different, perhaps even opposite influence on Freud. However, all such specula-

tions are idle, for Freud's views of man were firmly anchored in the scientific conceptions of his age, and especially those of the Helmholtz school (see p. 25 above).

40. I believe it was no accident that it was at just this time that Freud began to collect the antique statues that were eventually to fill his consulting rooms and studies (cf. Engelman, 1976). "I have now adorned my room with plaster casts of the Florentine statues. It was the source of extraordinary refreshment to me" (1950a, 181, 6 December 1896).

41. An allusion to a joke quoted by Freud on several occasions: An impecunious Jew boards the express train to Karlsbad without a ticket, is repeatedly caught and put off the train, repeatedly reboards, and is treated with increasing severity on each occasion. At one of the stations he meets an acquaintance, who asks him where he is traveling to. "To Karlsbad," he replies, "if my constitution can stand it" (see 1950a, 183, note 1).

42. Including Emma (see 1.1.2.3 above), as appears from part of a letter published by Schur (Schur, 1966, 83, 17 January 1897).

43. This phrase indicates that Freud was able to get one of his patients—clearly Emma once again—to remember a real childhood scene.

44. In June, Freud wrote to Fliess: "Let me confess that I have recently made a collection of deeply significant Jewish stories" (1950a, 211, 12 June 1897; according to Schur, 22 June 1897; or June 23). It is quite possible that he looked for confirmation of his theory even in that material. On the other hand, his interest may well have reflected a growing concern with Judaism, triggered off by his father's death.

45. Note the use of the term "primal scene" in the singular in later publications (1918b, 39). Here the term did not refer to the child's observation of parental coitus but to seduction or sexual violation in early childhood.

46. Kris, one of the publishers of the Fliess letters, claims that these ideas point to Freud's later theory of infantile sexual fantasies "under the pressure of the Oedipus complex" (Kris, in Freud, 1950a, 205, note 2). I believe, however, that something quite different was involved. The fantasies of a child in the grip of the Oedipus complex cannot, according to Freud, be reduced any further. They are not based on any real experiences; the parents are neutral objects of the child's fantasies, not agents. The infantile fantasies to which Freud refers *here,* on the other hand, are woven around real events. The child has been sexually abused and spins "romances" based on adult conversations to explain the terrifying experiences.

47. See Gicklhorn/Gicklhorn, 1960; Eissler, 1966; and Jones, 1953, I.

48. In this Draft, moreover, Freud includes melancholia among the obsessive neuroses, that is, among the neuroses of defense, for the first time. According to his theory, this inclusion meant that melancholia cannot be attributed to actual sexual practices but is the result of traumatic childhood experiences (1950a, 201, Draft N, 31 May 1896; see Table 1).

49. In the framework of the present study it is unfortunately impossible to compare this definition of "holiness" with that used in Freud's later works, particularly in his last book, *Moses and Monotheism* (1939a, 120ff.). It could be shown that this term had a central, symbolic meaning for Freud: it stood for Jacob's unmentionable taboo based on the Fifth Commandment. In *Moses and Monotheism,* Freud made the following assertion: "[The Latin] 'sacer' means not only 'sacred,' 'concecrated,' but also something that we can only translate as 'infamous,' 'detestable.' " The son's relationship to the father is equally ambivalent: circumcision (the symbolic substitute for castration) is a sign of the subjection of the child to the father's will. And as if Freud, now eighty-two, wanted to complete the remarks of his forty-two-year-old former self, he added that some ethical precepts are "justified rationally by the necessity for delimiting the rights of society as against the individual, the rights of the individual as against society and those of individuals as against one another. But what seems to us so *grandiose about ethics, so mysterious and, in a mystical fashion, so self-evident, owes these*

characteristics to its connection with religion, its origin from the will of the father" (1939a, 121f., italics added; cf. 4.2 below).

50. The links in this dream between Freud's cardiac neurosis and the seduction scene on the staircase can moreover be used as corroboration of my hypothesis that Freud's neurotic fear was connected to his abrupt separation from his "seductress" (see 3.2 below).

51. The family stayed on in Aussee but Freud returned to his practice in Vienna.

52. The new edition of the Fliess letters also gives the date of this letter as June 12. Schur, who was allowed to peruse the entire correspondence, states that the letter (with an illegible date) was, according to Freud, written on a Tuesday when June 12 was a Saturday (1972, 112). According to my calculation, however, 22 June 1897 was a Monday, so that Freud probably wrote this letter on June 23 or—which is unlikely —made a mistake in the weekday. In Jones (1953, I, 306), the letter is dated even more erroneously as 6 December 1897.

53. Later, after renouncing his seduction theory, Freud wrote: "I can only analyse myself with objectively acquired knowledge (as if I were a stranger); *self-analysis is really impossible, otherwise there would be no illness"* (1950a, 234f., italics added).

54. It is however possible that Martha was present even on this tour, and there-fore accompanied Freud to Orvieto, as Anzieu (1959, 267) believes she did. In any case, Freud did not see Rome on that occasion, a fact he later blamed on a neurotic inhibition.

55. Cf. Anzieu, 1959, 105.

56. Cf. p. 2, note 2.

57. The passage has not been omitted in the English edition of the Fliess letters, which Strachey included in the Standard Edition. However, in the sentence this passage is placed in a position where again the reference to Freud's father might be overlooked. See the retranslation above, p. 51.

58. This led, in a further development of the Oedipus theory, to the idea of racial heredity. Because the sons of the primal horde had killed the primal father, all sons ever since (not, mark you, all daughters) have had an Oedipal wish to murder their fathers (1912–13, Chap. IV; cf. 4.1.2.2 below).

59. Freud was wrong here. The journey from Leipzig to Vienna took place in the winter of 1859, when Freud was three.

60. There may in fact have been no mistake since, as a child, he might well have had the feeling of doing something wrong and being guilty too, even if he had not been personally involved in the theft. Elsewhere he has described this part of the dream detail as follows: "She used to insist on my dutifully handing over to her the small coins I received as presents" (1901b, 50).

61. I shall be returning to the lack of agreement about Philipp's age. (If he was sixty-three in 1897, he must have been not twenty, but twenty-two, years older than Freud, who was born in 1856—see Table 3.)

62. On a later occasion, Freud compared his daughter Anna with Antigone (Freud/Zweig, 1968, 66 and 106; cf. p. 30 above).

63. Devereux has also drawn attention to a very interesting connection between the Oedipus story and the family histories of both Laius and Pelops, with which the Greeks must have been acquainted through Sophocles' drama. Hence we may take it that the latter was not so much a "drama of inevitable fate," but rather—as modern family therapist would say—the story of a multi-generational imbalance in the "loyalty ledgers" of a family (Bozormenyi-Nagy/Spark, 1973; Devereux, 1953, 138f.).

64. In 1901, Freud distinguished between "retro-active" screen memories, an-ticipatory screen memories, and "contemporary" screen memories, thus making non-sense of what had originally been a significant concept (1901b, 44).

65. Freud produced an equally contradictory interpretation of another dream

involving his childhood—the dream of a "communication from the town council" (see p. 128, note 39, below).

66. Freud used the image of a horseman on a bucking horse many years later to illustrate the relationship between the Ego and the Id (1923b, 25).

67. The year of publication is given as 1900, although the book made its first appearance late in 1899 (1900a, xii).

68. Freud also mentioned the seduction theory in his last work, *Moses and Monotheism* (1939a, 2).

2. PREHISTORY: KALLAMON JACOB FREUD

1. Most of Freud's German-speaking biographers spell the name of his father, Jacob, with a k, although Jacob himself always wrote it with a c. Indeed, it is spelled with a c on his gravestone (E. Freud, 1977, 161). We do not know how Freud spelled his father's name, because it does not appear in any of his publications. Kallamon is sometimes rendered as Kolloman, or as Kalman.

2. This account is based on Dubnow, 1927–29, Vols. VI–IX; Dubnow, 1975; Friedmann, 1929; Ruppin, 1911; Thon, 1908; I. Friedlaender, 1915; Scholem, 1961; Gelber, 1924; Buber, 1947; Buber, 1948; Bakan, 1958; Barta, 1975; Stadtmüller, 1963; Maier, 1973; Fraenkel, 1967; and Kinder/Hilgemann, 1964.

3. Bakan's assumption that Jacob Freud named his son after this Polish king (1958, 56) is plainly incorrect. Even more improbable is the suggestion (Freud-Gesellschaft, 1975, 12) that Freud was named after "the Emperor Sigismund (1368–1437), King of Bohemia," because this king was never known as a friend of the Jews.

4. The link between Jewish number mysticism and Freud's premonitions of death has already been mentioned (see 1.1.2.1).

5. I shall however be looking at the question of whether Hasidism could really have had an incisive influence on Jacob's life (cf. 2.1 below).

6. Other sources mention 150,000 Galician Jews in 1772 (Thon, 1908; Friedmann, 1929). Dubnow bases his figure on the fact that there were many unregistered Jews. The *Encyclopedia Judaica* puts the number of Galician Jews at the time of the incorporation of Galicia into Austria at 224,980. The apparent precision of these figures is plainly deceptive, but the number is in any case larger than the figure given by Dubnow (*Encyclopaedia Judaica*, Vol. XVI, 1325).

7. It even appears as if the Enlightenment had precursors in Galicia as far back as the beginning of the eighteenth century (see pp. 83f. below).

8. It should be remembered that in 1670, just over a hundred years earlier, Leopold I, the grandfather of Maria Theresa, banished the Jews from Vienna. They were ordered to leave the city within a few months, which spelled ruin and even death to many. Reading the relevant documents—humble petitions to the emperor, hate-filled accusations by Viennese burghers, and the emperor's laconic replies—brings home the arrogance and intolerance of Christians before the Enlightenment (Pribram, 1918, Vol. I, 197ff., particularly 235ff.).

9. Scholem, for instance, argues that it is possible to find links between individual champions of the Jewish Reform movement and Sabbatean and other mystical sects (1961, 301ff.).

10. Freud's mother is said to have owned a *yikhus* letter establishing her descent from a family of famous rabbis from Brody (Aron, 1971, 170). Against the background of this tradition, Freud's association to the dream about Count Thun (1900a, 434) gains a further dimension. Freud himself wanted to be "an ancestor," that is, acquire *yikhus atsmo*, by his own efforts; he was not an "heir" to greatness and had moreover to make up for his father's—unspecified—lapses.

11. There can be no doubt that both Jacob and Sigmund Freud interiorized this particularly Jewish attitude to sexuality to such an extent that the biblical command-

ments and prohibitions seemed perfectly "natural" to them, every breach arousing feelings of guilt. In Jacob's case, we can only assume this attitude (see 2.5 below); but for Sigmund Freud, I believe, it became the basis of his theory of the neuroses, in particular of the actual neuroses, and most probably also of his personal sexual life. (see Part 4 below).

12. Most of my knowledge of Tysmenitz comes from Szlomo Blond, whose memorial (1974) describes the tragic history of the Jews in his birthplace. Szlomo Blond was also kind enough to provide me with additional information in a series of personal communications.

13. Of these 856 Jews, only 54 are said to have been children. This low figure shows that the Galician census figures were not reliable, many Jews refusing to register for a variety of reasons.

14. However, Beer Bolekhov tells us in his memoirs that adherents of Sabbateanism existed in Tysmenitz even in the early eighteenth century (1927, 18).

15. Blond writes in this connection: "The first school for Jewish children was opened in 1788. Herschl Schulmann was the teacher. His pay was 200 Rhenish [Austrian florins or guilders, M.K.]. This amount was paid from the teachers' fund established by Count Potocki in 1817. Out of this fund the Ruthenians and Ukrainians were paid 60 Rhenish, the Poles 20 and the Jews 14 Rhenish a month. The rest was contributed by the congregation" (1974, 156; translated from Hebrew into German, from German into English).

16. Blond mentions Salomo Fraenkel (1816–1894) as one of the leading *maskilim* in Tysmenitz. He helped to establish a German-language school for Jewish children in neighboring Stanislav, which was however opposed by the local Hasidim and closed. Another *maskil* from Tysmenitz was Jehuda Julius Barasch (1815–1863), who moved to Leipzig, studied medicine, and later helped to spread Haskalitic ideas in Bucharest (1974, 160).

17. This letter was a reply to Smolka's warning to the Jews to be temperate in their demands for freedom and justice lest they incite the displeasure of their non-Jewish neighbors (Blond, 1974, 144; cf. Bakan, 1958, 56). Blond stresses that the letter shows clearly how open Tysmenitz Jews were to progressive ideas. Bakan believes that this letter is an expression of the revolutionary spirit of 1848, because it asserts that all the differences between Christians and Jews stem from the political backwardness of the old system, which would have to be changed by revolution.

18. The newest research sheds doubt on Jacob's birthdate. It might be that he was born as early as 1814 (see Table 3, note 11).

19. Jones, basing his theory on Leslie Adams, states that Jesucher and Freide Freud came from Chelm. No doubt he or Adams must have consulted Hellreich's family tree, but they clearly misread its branches (Jones, 1960, I, 17, German edition).

20. Various authorities give different years for Emanuel's birth, but most mention 1832. In that case, Jacob would have become a father at the age of sixteen. Computations based on the death entry in the General Register Office, London (see Table 3) strike me as being more reliable.

21. The dates given for Philipp's birth vary a great deal as well, 1836 being the year most frequently mentioned. As in the case of Emanuel, however, computations based on the death entry in the General Register Office, London, seem to me to be the most reliable (see Table 3).

22. The railway link between Moravia and Galicia was built between the years 1856 and 1861 (dates supplied by J. Sajner).

23. It is quite possible that the copies made by J. Sajner contain a series of mistakes, since some of the original documents are in a poor state of preservation and since there were no facilities for taking photocopies and hence for checking Sajner's transcriptions.

24. The "Israelitic merchants petitioning for toleration" were Juda Simcha Mittel-

mann (Lemberg), Schmelke Brittwitz (Tysmenitz), Kallmann Jakob Freud (Tysmenitz), Abraham Berisch Czopp (Lemberg), David Frisch (Tysmenitz), Moses Laib Horowitz (Stanislav), Samuel Samuely (Tysmenitz), and Josef Goldstein (Tysmenitz) (District Archives, N. Jičín, transcript by J. Sajner). Nothing is known about Siskind Hofmann's further life. He does not seem to have died in Freiberg (research by J. Sajner). From a passport issued in 1847, we can tell that in that year Jacob spent a few days in Breslau on another three occasions (Gicklhorn, 1976, 16–17, transcript by J. Sajner).

25. It is impossible to tell whether or not "Fany" was a spelling mistake for "Sally." Since the names of Jacob Freud and of Siskind Hofmann too were spelled in many different ways, both by the officials and also by themselves, such discrepancies were quite usual. It is also possible that Sally's second name was Fany. If Jacob was indeed referring to his wife, then this letter is proof that she was still alive in 1848 (cf. pp. 92f. below).

26. Some of these rights were revoked in the 1850s. It was not until 1866 that the emancipation of the Jews became law in Austria (Kinder/Hilgemann, 1966, II, 62f.).

27. Other Jews did not miss this chance of acquiring domiciliary rights. Whereas only nine Jewish families were registered as residents of Freiberg in 1844, the figure had risen to twenty-nine by 1852, still including several "tolerated" persons.

28. Grinstein has this to say about the publisher: "Ludwig Philippson (1811–1889) was born in Dessau, Germany, and was educated at Helle and at the University of Berlin. In 1833 he became the rabbi in Magdeburg. In 1837 he founded and edited the *Allgemeine Zeitung des Judenthums,* a journal which was an organ of Reform Judaism and of the Jewish rights in Prussia. Although he was not regarded as a Reform rabbi, he advocated moderate reform in Judaism, opposing both the radical reformers and the Orthodox. The Philippson Bible was significant not only because of its scholarly commentary which included notes about ancient history, comparative religion, and culture, but also because it was illustrated" (1968, 447f.).

29. Oddly enough, Jacob's brother Josef also had a wife by the name of Rebekka. It is impossible to tell whether she was identical with the assumed wife of Jakob (see Table 3).

30. Berisch Kanner (51 years), Feige Kanner (23 years) with child Rahel (2 years), and Gitat Kanner (22 years) (Register of Jews in Freiberg, 1852, District Archives, Novẏ Jičín, after Sajner; see 3.1.5 below).

31. In the marriage certificate his address is given as Leopoldstadt 476, which corresponds to a house in Circusgasse (see Table 7, note 2).

32. It is not certain whether the house Gicklhorn inspected shortly before it was pulled down in 1950 was in fact the Nathansohns' residence, because "Donaulände 17" was not their address. Jakob Nathansohn always lived at 45, Untere Donaustrasse, which was 726, Untere Donau before the streets of Vienna were renamed in 1860 (Lehmann, 1859, 1861, and subsequent years; cf. marriage certificate in Table 7, and Fig. 14).

33. Gicklhorn states that the quantities involved were metric hundred weights *(Zentners)* (1969, 41). Clearly, this is a mistake, as can be seen from J. Sajner's careful copy. Moreover, Gicklhorn's claim that Jacob's business declined in 1855 is incorrect, for the sales figures entered for that year cover the first three months only.

34. A sign of the change might be that Jacob altered the date of his birth: "After his marriage he and his wife changed from the Jewish to the Gregorian calendar, and he chose April 1 for his birthday" (Jones, 1953, I, 2, note 210). According to information supplied by Ernst Freud, Jacob chose that date because it was the birthday of Otto Bismarck, whom he admired. Oddly enough, Freud invariably calculated the age at which his father died from this arbitrarily chosen birthday, and so always declared it to have been eighty-one and a half. On Jacob Freud's gravestone itself we can read that

he died on 23 October 1896 in the eighty-second year of his life, which is only correct if his birthday was on 1 April 1815 (E. Freud, 1977, 161). But see note 17 above.

35. Freud himself could not break this taboo either, for although he made a profound study of sexuality, he felt unable to discuss it openly with his children (see Part, 4).

3. THE TRAUMA: SIGMUND FREUD'S CHILDHOOD AND YOUTH

1. Many authors, especially those with a psychoanalytical background, have tried in more or less detective style to reconstruct Freud's childhood from his dreams. I can therefore base my presentation on a great number of such dream analyses. However, it would be a near impossibility to have read all the secondary literature on the subject, so that some important contributions are bound to have escaped me. Alternatively, I may be proffering interpretations as my own that others have published before me.

2. For that reason, all official documents that have been discovered in the archives were written in German.

3. The Freuds also seem to have lived, at least temporarily, in house No. 417 in the immediate vicinity, for in Julius Freud's death record that address is given as his residence (see Table 9).

4. There has been much speculation about Freud's first name. Bakan (1958, 56) contends that Jacob named his son after three Polish kings (see 2.1 above) renowned as protectors of the Jews (see Bernfeld, 1951, 125). Such practice was, however, absolutely unthinkable to nineteenth-century Jews, however un-Orthodox. According to information provided by Szlomo Blond, who grew up in Tysmenitz, enlightened nineteenth-century Jews were in the habit of giving their children a German as well as a Hebrew name, the first name bearing some resemblance to the second, e.g., Abraham —Adolf; Paysach—Paul; Chaim—Wilhelm; Hirsch—Heinrich. Szlomo Blond himself used to be called "Siegmund" in his youth (written communication).

Not too much importance should therefore be attached to the fact that Freud altered his name from Sigismund to Sigmund at the end of his schooldays (1969a; editor's note, 109f.). True, this even greater Germanization of his name may have been a (conscious or unconscious) symbolic act, but equally Jones's assumption that Freud objected to the repeated s's might be correct (Jones, 1960, I, 40; German edition). Nor can Stanescu's hypothesis that Freud changed his first name because there was another Sigismund Freud in the family be rejected out of hand (1965, 127).

5. Schmuel (Samuel) Samueli and Lippe Hurwitz (Laib Horowitz) were Galician merchants, as we know from the register of "Israelitic merchants petitioning for toleration" of 1847 (see p. 91, note 23, above). Laib Horowitz came from Stanislav and Samuel Samueli from Tysmenitz.

6. He explained why he nevertheless kept many things back, again quoting Goethe's "After all, the best of what you know cannot be told to the boys" (1900a, 142, 453f.).

7. The remark that something had to be "carefully fished out" moreover provides a link with the Emma–Anna episode (see 1.1.2.3 above). There is also a possible link to the defloration scene in "Screen Memories" by way of Louise N., whose name resembles that of Pauline Freud both rhythmically and also phonetically, as is the case with the names of Emma, Irma, and Anna.

8. In his further associations, Freud stated that the theme of seduction played a role in this dream. Thus he explained that some dream images were taken from novels in which "the guide is a woman." These novels also involved "perilous journeys," and in them, "the guide, instead of finding immortality for herself and the others, perishes in the mysterious subterranean fire." A fear of that kind, Freud contended, was "unmistakably active in the dream-thoughts" (1900a, 454). These remarks point clearly to his nursemaid Resi, who appeared as a seductress in other of Freud's dreams as well (see

3.1.3 below; cf. Grinstein, 1968, Chap. 17). The main themes of this dream, accordingly, were seduction by a father figure and by a mysterious woman.

9. A disease of the eye from which Freud's father suffered in 1885 and for which he underwent surgery by one of Freud's colleagues, who applied cocaine as a local anesthetic (Jones, 1953, I, 87).

10. In this connection, it is worth mentioning that *shtetl* children who had a fright were told either to say a prayer or else to urinate. "One invokes divine aid, or else one eliminates the poison bred by fear. In either case, the typical *shtetl* attitude is: get rid of it" (Zborowski/Herzog, 1952, 345). Does it not seem reasonable to conclude that Jacob had kept the habit of urinating in panic situations, and perhaps had advised his son to act likewise? Fear and urination—possibly also masturbation—would then have become inseparably associated during Freud's earliest childhood, which would also throw fresh light on some of the more far-fetched assumptions of his sexual theory of actual neuroses (cf. 1.1.2.2 above). According to S. Blond (written communication), the prohibition against undressing was not absolute. For example, on Friday nights father and son would go to the ritual bath together and undress.

11. See also the series of dreams in Freud's brief "On Dreams" (1901a), where a father figure appears with a hat in the shape of a glass cylinder with plainly sexual connotations (cf. p. 133 below).

12. Particularly revealing are Freud's associations to the dream of Goethe and Herr M. (1900a, 439f.; 1901a, 662ff.). However, dreams about his own father looking like Garibaldi (1900a, 447f.), or about the hall with infernal machines (1900a, 364ff.) also reflect his ambivalent relationship to his father (see Grinstein, 1968).

13. It is possible that Freud himself had a similar dream, for he wrote to Fliess: "I had a fascinating dream . . . unfortunately it is unpublishable, because its background, its deeper meaning, shuttles to and from between my nurse (my mother) and my wife. . . . Well, the best that you know, etc." (1950a, 245, 9 February 1898, second ellipsis in original).

14. One could go even further and claim that Freud always needed to have three "mothers" round him. In his later years they were his wife Martha, her sister Minna, and his unmarried daughter Anna. Whether the peculiar similarity in the sound of the names—Amalie was also known as Malka—is incidental is impossible to say.

15. When Freud later compared himself to his mother, he was probably referring to the traits mentioned by Martin Freud: boldness, fearlessness, "burning passion", "all the defiance and all the passions with which our ancestors defended their Temple." Unlike his mother, however, he hid these qualities under a "surface of timidity" (Letter to Martha Bernays, 2 February 1886, 1960a, 215).

16. It is not clear whether the piano was taken away before the Freuds moved to Kaiser-Josef-Strasse in about 1875, by which time Sigmund Freud was already a student (see 3.3.1 below). In her memoirs, Anna Freud Bernays mentions an even more telling episode. An uncle of Amalie's came to Vienna from Russia in about 1874 and wanted to marry sixteen-year-old Anna. He promised her a horse, the most splendid wardrobe, enthused about the beauties of Russia, and assured her that his six married children would receive her with open arms. After a sleepless night she went to her mother and told her everything. "She was extremely surprised and could already see me radiant in my happiness, but wanted first to speak to her counsellor, my brother, without whom she would make no decision. My brother was far less delighted and, horrified, made it clear to my mother what it meant for a fifty-nine-year-old man to marry a blooming girl of not yet sixteen, and I was thrown out of my seventh heaven with a few fraternal slaps across the face" (Bernays, 1930, 13; translated from the German). The reader must remember that Freud himself was just eighteen at the time!

17. In 1915, he wrote to Lou Andreas-Salomé: "I cannot be an optimist, and I believe I differ from the pessimists only in that wicked, stupid, senseless things don't upset me because I have accepted them from the beginning as part of what the world

is made of" (Freud/Andreas-Salomé, 1966, 33). This is, moreover, a typically Jewish attitude; pessimism about the immediate future but optimism in the long term (Simon, 1957, 299).

18. See also Freud's undoubtedly autobiographical remark in his last book: "If one is the declared favourite of the dreaded father, one need not be surprised at the jealousy of one's brothers and sisters, and the Jewish legend of Joseph and his brethren shows very well where this jealousy can lead" (1939a, 106). Here he is not the darling of his mother but of his father.

19. Unless otherwise stated, I shall base all my following remarks on Freud's letters to Fliess of May 31, October 3, October 4 and 15 October 1897 (see pp. 48f. and 56ff. above).

20. The "Register of Servants Resident in Freiberg" for the first quarter of 1857 lists under house No. 42, as employees of Maria Freud, the servants Monika Zajíc, maid, and Magdalena Kabat, wet-nurse (Sajner, 1968, 174; Gicklhorn, 1969, 42, with additions from the original document by Sajner). That was the reason why it was first believed that Monika Zajíc had been the nursemaid of Amalia's child, too.

21. In *The Psychopathology of Everyday Life,* Freud mentions a slip by which his subconscious helped him to break a promise he had made to his brother Emanuel. Consciously, he had been too afraid to break that promise—to travel to England by the shortest route. But because he inadvertently missed the train, he was able to fulfill a long-cherished wish and see the Rembrandt paintings in The Hague and in Amsterdam (1901b, 227). It is worth recalling that Freud was fifty-two at the time (Jones, 1955, II, 51f.). Freud's children also seem to have deferred to Emanuel. When Martin Freud was twenty-four and paid a visit to England, his eighty-year-old uncle did not want him to take a rowing boat, and after a long argument had his way (M. Freud, 1957, 13). From unpublished family letters, P. Swales has concluded that Emanuel was an extremely authoritarian person. It is impossible to tell whether that trait was responsible for the disappearance of his oldest son or for the fact that none of his children married.

22. In the birth certificates of the two children of Emanuel and Maria who were born in Manchester, Maria's maiden name is given as Rookach (General Register Office, London). Remarkably, both Maria's mother and Emanuel's had the maiden name of Kanner, which suggests that Emanuel may have married one of his mother's relatives. From the documents J. Sajner discovered in Nový Jičín, it appears that several persons with the name of Kanner lived in Freiberg in 1852–55 (see p. 93 above). It is therefore quite possible that Maria had relatives in Freiberg who were also relatives of her mother-in-law.

23. Freud may well have concealed his brother Philipp in the *"Non-vixit"* dream and also in the "dream of the uncle with the yellow beard" (1900a, 421ff., 137ff.), but since he does not say so explicitly, we can do no more than speculate on the matter. If we knew whether Philipp had a fair beard like so many other members of Freud's family but above all Jacob Freud, (cf. p. 101 above), then our speculation would of course gain greatly in credibility. From records of applications for exit permits by Jacob and his family which J. Sajner and P. Swales have discovered in Freiberg archives, it appears that Philipp might have had a blond beard, for although some entries give "brown" for the color of his hair, others give "blond." In contrast to Jacob and Emanuel, whose height is given as "medium," Philipp is invariably described as "short." There is a photograph of Philipp, taken in 1902, but now in a very bad state of preservation. The original also seems to have been of poor quality because it apparently came from a photographic booth and was printed on a postcard that Philipp sent to his half-sister Marie (see Table 13).

24. In a letter to Martha Bernays, Freud referred to his half-brother Philipp as "Mr. Robinson," without stating where this nickname came from (1960a, 94).

25. He states that he had had this dream at the age of seven or eight in Vienna, which cannot be correct because of the content. The dream refers to the death of his

grandfather, and that grandfather could only have been Amalie's father, who died on 3 October 1865 in Vienna (see 3.3.5 below). In other words, Freud was nine and a half years old at the time. He did not interpret this dream until some thirty years later, at the time of his self-analysis. The reason why he believed he had dreamed the dream earlier than he actually did may be that it involves Philippson's Bible, which in fact had fascinated Freud at an earlier age.

26. The fact that it was Philipp who caught the nursemaid in the act of stealing could, against this background, have had yet another significance. Perhaps Resi Wittek had an inkling of Amalie's relationship with Philipp, so that Philipp had her dismissed quickly not only in order to protect his small brother but also in his own interests. It is relevant, too, that Anna was conceived at about the time of the death of Amalie's brother Julius, and that soon afterward, Amalie's second son, whom she had also called Julius, died at the age of six months (see Table 3 and 3.1.2 above).

27. Emanuel and Alexander, the names of his two other brothers, were much more "unusual" than Philipp at that time.

28. Amalia is the niece of an old count whose son Karl, a heroic robber, she loves. Franz, the wicked second son of the count, ill-treats his father and intrigues against Karl in the hope of being made the sole heir and winning Amalia. The drama ends with the death of all except Karl, who prepares to surrender to his pursuers.

The play includes a poem based on a dialogue between Brutus and Caesar. At the age of fourteen Freud recited that dialogue with his nephew John in the family circle, a certain sign that it had made a strong impression on him (1900a, 423f., 483). The poem tells of the return of the beaten Brutus from the Battle of Philippi, only to be accused of murder by Caesar's ghost. Though Brutus justifies himself with "Where Brutus lives, Caesar must die," the "son" is made to pay for the murder of his "Caesar-father" with his own death: "No world for Brutus left!" (Schiller: *The Robbers,* IV, v).

29. Freud's detailed account of the sexual development of boys and their Oedipal fantasies, incidentally, also incriminates Amalie. Thus he asserted that, to a boy, "phantasies of his mother's unfaithfulness" are by far the most preferred; that the "lover with whom she commits her act of infidelity almost always exhibits the features of the boy's own ego"; and that the "precondition of the loved one's being like a prostitute" derives "directly from the mother complex" (1910h, 171f.). Elsewhere we read: "The child, having learned about sexual processes, tends to picture to himself erotic situations and relations, the motive force behind this being his desire to bring his mother (who is the subject of the most intense sexual curiosity) into situations of secret infidelity and into secret love-affairs. In this way the child's phantasies, which started by being, as it were, asexual, are brought up to the level of his later knowledge. . . . *A younger child is very specially inclined* to use imaginative stories such as these in order *to rob those born before him of their prerogatives*—in a way which reminds one of historical intrigues; and *he often has no hesitation in attributing to his mother as many fictitious love-affairs* as he himself has competitors" (1909c, 239f., italics added; cf. Freud's "The 'Uncanny,' " 1919h).

30. In a different context, he mentioned the fact that he had had a fight with John and explained that adolescents often used *wichsen* for *schlagen* (to hit). Without knowing whether Freud knew that *wichsen* also means "masturbating" in vulgar slang, we cannot tell whether or not he was alluding to a homosexual episode in his relationship with John (1900a, 425).

31. I suspect that his other male friendships too, which were structured in a similar way and ended just as abruptly, foundered for the same reason (see 4.1.2 below).

32. If I am right in thinking that "Screen Memories" is part of the "big" dream left out by Freud (see pp. 64ff. above), then the dream mentioned here might have been another part.

33. Many of his female patients, too, must have been "Paulines" for him. To what

extent veiled memories of his experiences with Pauline also affected his pubertal love for Gisela Fluss at the age of sixteen can be gleaned from "Screen Memories" (see 3.2 below). A series of associations in the "Irma" dream, in the dream of the "botanical monograph," and in many others also makes it seem likely that Freud was unable to overcome his Pauline complex even in his marital relations. Anna, Freud's youngest daughter, whom he named after Anna Hammerschlag-Lichtheim, could have been a Pauline for him as well. Perhaps he expected her to help him solve the great problem of human sexuality, which had so acutely bothered him at the time of her birth on 3 December 1895, but which was really the same problem that had vexed him in Freiberg. Is that why he once dreamed that she was his "Sexta" (1950a, 284, 27 June 1899)? Did Anna Freud become a child analyst the better to answer little Sigmund's questions?

34. He might, however, have retained unconscious memory traces of the events surrounding his sister Anna's birth, which were thrown up in his dream of Frau Doni: "I was going to the hospital . . . through a district in which there were houses and gardens. . . . There I asked for Frau Doni and was told that she lived at the back in a small room with three children. . . ." (1900a, 446). In his association, Freud explains that a Frau "Dona A . . . y," who had died in childbirth, had been looked after by the same midwife as had attended his wife. Was there perhaps a connection between "Doni" and "Resi"? Was it perhaps to her home that he was taken when his mother was in labor?

35. In connection with his views on the son's fantasies about his mother's unfaithfulness (see p. 120, note 29, above), Freud explained: "An interesting variant of the family romance may then appear, in which the hero and author returns to legitimacy himself while his brothers and sisters are eliminated by being bastardized. . . . In this way, for instance, the young phantasy-builder can get rid of his . . . kinship with one of his sisters if he finds himself sexually attracted by her" (1909c, 240). Here too there is a hint that Freud did not consider his sister Anna "legitimate." It is probable that she aroused his sexual interest, at least at times (see p. 143f below).

36. See pp. 144. below. Anna Freud's subsequent life was both turbulent and fulfilling. She became a teacher, worked for several years as a governess, married Eli Bernays, the brother of Sigmund Freud's wife Martha, emigrated with him to America, and brought up five children (Bernays, 1930).

37. Julius does not seem to have been born in Freiberg, for no record of his birth could be found there (from information supplied by J. Sajner).

38. It is however possible that he was nevertheless affected by his brother's death. We may take it that Julius was treated by a doctor before his death. Was he the same "one-eyed" man, "of short stature, stout, and with his head sunk deep in his shoulders" (1916–17, 201; 1900a, 17, 560; 1950a, 222), who treated Freud when he cut his chin at a time when he was "more than two and not yet three years old"? This man, whom J. Sajner has identified as Dr. Josef Pur, was a temporary mayor of Freiberg (Sajner, 1968, 175), and also appeared in Freud's dreams. He made a marked impression on little Sigmund, possibly because he was connected with Julius's illness and death.

39. As in "Screen Memories" (see pp. 62f. above), Freud did not trace the dream back to childhood experiences, but reversed the relationship: "Whereas normally a dream deals with rebellion against someone else, behind whom the dreamer's father is concealed, the opposite was true here. My father was made into a man of straw, in order to screen someone else; and the dream was allowed to handle in this undisguised way a figure who was as a rule treated as sacred, because at the same time I knew with certainty that it was not he who was really meant" (1900a, 436). Here Freud was asserting nothing less than that the basic principle of dream formation did not apply to him personally. In his case the dream was *not* the royal road to the unconscious, to repressed childhood experiences, but childhood memories became a "screen" for impermissible thoughts in the present! I believe that in this example, too, the Oedipus theory was imposed on the dream as a censor (see 1.3, 1.4 above). Thoughts that

besmirched the "sacred" figure of his father could be admitted into his dreams because Freud no longer sought reasons for his accusations against his father. Had he still upheld the seduction theory, he would not have been able to dream this dream so freely, for then he would have had to search for his father's misconduct.

40. It is not known whether the persons with the name of Freud listed in the Vienna address directory (Lehmann) were relatives of Jacob. They were: the carpenter Vincenz Freud, a merchant in flour, Arnold Freud, the salesman Josef Freud, the brandy-maker Selig Freud, and the "Master of Obstetrics" Dr. David Freud. Josef Freud could have been Jacob's brother, who lived in Vienna from 1861 on. Selig Freud might have been a relative too, since Jacob lived in his house in 1860 (see 3.3.1 below). It would be most interesting to know if Dr. David Freud was a close relative who might have had an influence on Sigmund Freud's decision to study medicine.

41. Several Viennese residents by the name of Nathansohn might also have been related to Amalie. From entries in the Vienna address directory (Lehmann), we know that in the 1860s Nathan Nathansohn, wholesaler in Turkish goods and exporter, lived in Leopoldstadt. There was also Nachim or Noachim Nathansohn, merchant, and Adolf Nathansohn, merchant, who even came from Brody like Amalie's parents. From his age at death, as recorded in the Vienna death protocols of 27 October 1879, we can tell that he was born in 1807, so that he could have been a brother of Jacob Nathansohn, who was born in 1805 (see Table 3).

42. Birth registration in the record books of the Israelitic Congregation of Vienna: Regina Debora Freud, daughter of Jakob Freud, wool merchant, and of Amalia, born Nathansohn, 3, Weissgärber (now 1, Obere Weissgärberstrasse, in the Third District; see Fig. 13). Anna Freud Bernays states that she was taken to Leipzig with her father and her eldest brother when she was six weeks old: "There in the hotel I had scarlet fever which was not recognized as such, and as a consequence I feel ill with hydrophilia" (Bernays, 1930, 3). The Freuds' exodus to Leipzig would accordingly have taken place as early as February 1859. I suspect, however, that Freud's sister was mistaken about her age.

43. In the English edition of his Freud biography, Jones states that Jacob, Emanuel, and Philipp traveled from Freiberg to Saxony in about June 1859, and that Amalie, Sigmund, and Anna arrived in Leipzig in October of the same year (1953, I, Chronology). I do not know where Jones obtained this information; in the German edition these dates are missing.

44. It is a great pity that the editors of the Fliess correspondence cut the letter at just this point, for it is possible that Freud gave even clearer indications of the background to his train phobia and hence of what had happened during the journey from Freiberg. The curtailed explanation of his panic on the train simply mentions "hunger" and "infantile gluttony," but we may take it that the portion cut by the editors concerned less innocuous matters.

45. From the Fliess letters it appears that though the *Three Essays on the Theory of Sexuality* was only published in 1905, Freud had been collecting material for a sexual theory from early 1899 or 1900 (1905d, 129, editor's note).

46. The reference to the glass hat might also be a pointer to the "dream of Count Thun" (1900a, 209ff.), in which Freud hands his father a "male glass urinal" and sees Jacob's penis "in plastic form." As I pointed out earlier, the dream symbol might have referred to masturbation by Freud's father or by Freud himself (pp. 105f.). It is even conceivable that he actually observed his father masturbating/urinating during the train journey, which terrified him because of his earlier experiences.

47. Because Freud knew that *ausreissen* (pulling out) and *abreissen* (pulling off) were vulgar references to masturbation, it is conceivable that as a child he associated the near-homophonous *ausreisen* (emigrate) or *abreisen* (depart) with masturbation (see 1899a, 319; 1916–17, 164).

48. It is quite possible that this hypothesis is based on Freud's own remarks in

"Screen Memories," in which he has his "patient" say: "When I was about three, the branch of industry in which my father was concerned met with a catastrophe. He lost all his means and he was forced to leave the place and move to a large town" (1899a, 312). Just as he "embellished" his age in this essay—the "patient" was said to be "a man of university education, aged thirty-eight" while Freud himself was forty-three in 1899—so he also probably "embellished" the reasons for his family's departure from Freiberg, thus vindicating his father.

49. In a letter Freud sent to Emil Fluss, the son of Ignaz Fluss, in 1873, he wrote: "Today I want to tell you a story that is now two years old. . . . You will remember that during my first visit to Freiberg . . . I was accompanied by my friend Silberstein. . . . When we inspected the weaving mill my friend absentmindedly ran his hand over one of your machines" (1969a, 113; translated from the German).So Ignaz Fluss owned machines in 1871.

50. In the Vienna address directory of 1875, Ignaz Fluss is listed as a "manufacturer," residing at 23, Herminengasse, in the Second District (Leopoldstadt). From 1888 on, the entry reads: "Fluss, Ignaz, 23F II Herminengasse. Cloth and hat manufacturer in Freiberg, Moravia, under Royal Warrant. Branch at 72, VII Mariahilfergasse" (according to Lehmann, this branch opened in 1884). Ignaz Fluss, unlike Jacob Freud, was therefore a successful businessman even in Vienna.

51. A Leipzig connection was discovered as well when an accomplice of Josef Freud was arrested in that city, and charged with using forged rouble notes to pay for goods bought at the Leipzig Easter Fair in 1863. It was established that Josef Freud was frequently seen in the company of the accused (Memorandum by Minister of Police, Sections IV and V of *Haus-, Hof- und Staatsarchiv,* Vienna, 16 October 1865; see Table 11, and Gicklhorn, 1976, 8).

52. Anna Freud Bernays writes: "Every Easter, Mother started to cough, and would then go to recuperate for three months in Roznau, a health resort in Moravia, invariably taking her weakest child with her, leaving me, the rest of the children and Father in town for the summer" (1930, 8). From the list of patients taking the cure in Roznau, J. Sajner and P. Swales were able to establish precisely when and in which guest houses Amalie and her children stayed in Roznau. After her visit in June 1857 with Sigmund and Resi Wittek, she was back in Roznau "with family" in 1868 and 1869, in 1870 "with 2 children," in 1871 "with 6 children and 1 maid," in 1872 "with 2 children," and in 1875 "with 3 children." She stayed in various guest houses in the vicinity of the Kurhaus. It is not known how these fairly expensive stays were financed.

53. Jacob Freud also moved house on many subsequent occasions, but did not leave Leopoldstadt until a few years before his death, long after Sigmund Freud had married and opened his practice at 19, Berggasse, in the Ninth District, one of the best parts of Vienna. In 1892, Jacob Freud is listed by Lehmann under 14, Grüne Thorgasse (now Grünenthorgasse), in the Ninth District, near Berggasse. It was here that Jacob Freud died (death registered on 23 October 1896, Vienna City Archives). The reasons for Jacob's last move are unknown, but Sigmund may well have fetched his parents from the Jewish quarter as a sign of filial affection.

54. In the marriage certificate, Amalie's address is given as 726, Leopoldstadt, which became 45, Untere Donaustrasse in 1860 when the old system of numbering the houses was given up (see Table 7 and Fig. 13).

55. In a letter to Martha, Freud wrote: "Well, today I heard from Simon (Nathanson) that the uncle had instructed his bank to remit to Anna [Freud's sister, M.K.] 100 fl. to buy herself something for the wedding. It is none of my business, but this really isn't much from a rich uncle, nor is it very delicately given. If we ever get rich, sweetheart, we will do things differently" (1960a, 56f., 22 August 1883). (As a result of the latest investigations by P. Swales, it appears that Simon Nathanson was not Freud's uncle but his cousin—he was the son of Amalie's brother Hermann; (see Table 3). From Anna Freud Bernays's reminiscences, it seems that Amalie's parents helped

the family out by taking the children for holidays and during Amalie's visits to Roznau (1930, 4).

56. Cf. 1900a, 191ff., 216ff., 468ff., and Chapter VI(C) on absurd dreams, which is almost entirely made up of dreams in which disparagement of the father is associated with the son's ambition (see 3.1.1 above).

57. In her memoirs, Anna Freud Bernays tells us that Freud was taught by his mother. "My oldest brother was altogether the pride of the family. My mother taught him at home throughout the primary school years, so that, when he entered the Gymnasium at the age of ten, he set foot in a school for the first time in his life" (1930, 7; translated from the German). Freud's mother had gone to the same elementary school to which she later sent her daughters, on Karmeliterplatz, in the Second District (*ibid.*, 4).

58. According to Rosenfeld, Freud was only given the second volume of the three-volume edition (1956, 110).

59. Translation and notes by K. E. Grözinger. The translation by Jones of this dedication is obviously incorrect and incomplete (Jones, 1953, I, 21f.; cf. Aron, 1956–57, 289).

60. It should also be mentioned that King Solomon, the son of David, with whom Freud certainly identified himself as well because he was his namesake (cf. 1901b 199), broke the Second Commandment, worshipping Phoenician and other gods. Solomon was not punished for his transgression, but his successors were (1 Kings 11).

61. The memorandum and related documents on this and further forgeries are filed under "Admin. F. 21 Kart, Fälschungen 5 und 6" in the Haus-, Hof- und Staatsarchiv, Vienna.

62. After the death of Jacob Nathansohn, his widow Sarah, née Wilenz, lived at 30, Glockengasse (Lehmann, 1870). Since Freud's sister Anna claims that her father and his family had also lived in Glockengasse for some time (Bernays, 1940, 335), Sarah Nathansohn may well have moved in with her son-in-law, although Jacob Freud's official address during these years was 1, Pfeffergasse. From the Phiebig family tree (see Table 3), we know that she died at the home of one of her sons in Odessa.

63. As I mentioned earlier, it is also possible that Sigmund became the intentional or accidental observer of sexual intercourse between his parents shortly before he had this dream, so that that experience too may have been a "day residue" onto which he could associate his childhood memories (see p. 117 above).

64. It is even possible that the same differences also occurred a generation before, in the brothers Jacob and Josef. And their age difference was the same as that between Sigmund and Alexander—ten years.

65. Gicklhorn's statement that he enrolled in 1866–67 (1965, 18) is mistaken, as we can tell from the annual report of the Gymnasium in 1873, when Freud took his final examination (E. Freud, 1977, 74). When Freud attended this school, it was not yet called the "Sperlgymnasium," as Jones states (1953, I, 20), for it was not until 1877, when Freud had long since been a university student, that the school moved from 24, Taborstrasse to Sperlgasse (Gicklhorn, 1965, 18; Artner, 1937, 340, 156).

66. The staff record book of 1869, discovered by Gicklhorn, states that three pupils in the fourth class had been found guilty of "disorderly behaviour" inside school and of having had contacts with "loose harlots" outside. It goes on to say that "Freud mentioned a disreputable bar in the vicinity of Rotenthurmstrasse which they frequent" (Gicklhorn, 1965, 21).

67. This must have been an allusion to their second name, Fluss ("river"), as Gedo and Wolf (1970, 787) believe it was. But Freud might very well have also been familiar with a student song by Victor von Scheffel in which an "Ichthyosaurus" swims in the sea alongside a forest of horse-tail plants, and complains bitterly that times are getting worse and worse, an "Iguanadon" having had the effrontery to kiss his "Ichthyosaura." The song was written in 1854 (Scheffel, 1916, 10; information supplied by J. Stagl).

68. The friends seem also to have indulged in other adolescent pranks in Freiberg. From Freud's letter to Emil Fluss, it appears that they promenaded through the streets of Freiberg in fancy dress: "I would beg you in due course to uncover our masked jest to high-born Freiberg society (hats off!). Lift the mysterious veil over the 8–16 Russians, Turks and Tartars and show the cream of Freiberg our well-known faces. If it gives you pleasure, embellish the story further; tell them that things happened which would never have occurred to us in our wildest dreams—so long as you give the public cause to find *us* entertaining" (1969a, 111, 28 September 1872; translated from the German).

69. My surmise that "Screen Memories" was, in fact, the "big dream" left out from *The Interpretation of Dreams* would be corroborated further if these assumptions are valid.

70. The letter also throws interesting light on Freud's close relationship to his friends: "The reason why I am not writing in Spanish is because of a resolution I have made. Since I am heartily ashamed of not owning a diccionario, I have decided to purchase one. Once I have one, things will be much easier and I shall write frequently in Spanish; therefore why write in Spanish today when I have not yet acquired the dictionary? As you can see, this is sound idler's logic. I am delighted that you recently had occasion to use the noble lengua Castellana, and once again managed to exercise your verbal skills at some length, and I am longing for the hours and walks next year in which, after a twelve months' separation interrupted by a three days' meeting, we shall be able to exchange words for words and, God willing, thoughts for thoughts as well. I honestly believe that we shall never be rid of each other; although we became friends by free choice we are now as attached to one another as if nature had put us on this earth as blood relatives; I believe that we have come so far that the one loves the very person of the other and not, as before, merely his good qualities, and I am afraid that were you, by an unworthy act, to prove quite different tomorrow from the image I keep of you, I could still not cease to wish you well. That is a weakness, and I have taken myself to task for it several times. . . ." (letter transcribed and translated by A. J. Pomerans).

71. Emanuel was never one of the poorest inhabitants, because the census returns of 1861 and of 1871 show that he employed a maidservant.

72. At 21, Albert Road (W. H. Pollick, Manchester).

73. Emanuel, incidentally, died in 1914 as the result of a fall from a train traveling between Manchester and Southport. The death certificate reads: "Cause of death: accidental injuries received through falling from Manchester to Southport Express in which he was a passenger whilst in motion on date of death" (General Register Office, London).

4. The Fulfillment of the Mandate

1. M. Freud, 1957; Jones, 1953, I, 1955, II, 1957, III, *passim;* Freeman, 1971; Roazen, 1975; and Emma Jung in Freud/Jung, 1974, 504.

2. It was Anna who tended Freud during his long illness, although Martha was still fit. And when Freud could no longer bear the pain and asked his personal physician to put him out of his misery, it was apparently Anna alone who was informed of that fact (Schur, 1972, 529). Jacob Freud too had been tended during his fatal illness by his unmarried daughter, although his wife Amalie had also been fit and well (*ibid.,* 105f.). (Letter to Fliess of 15 July 1896; cf. Puner, 1949, 208ff.)

3. This attachment to her father, Roazen believes, was further strengthened by Freud's analysis of her: "Freud's motives may have been the very best, but medically and humanly the situation was bizarre. As her analyst, he would inevitably mobilize her feelings of overevaluation, while at the same time invading the privacy of her soul; he added new transference emotions to their relationship, without the possibility of ever really dissolving them. A genius who was also naturally an immense figure in his

daughter's fantasy life, as her analyst he tied her permanently to him" (Roazen, 1975, 440).

4. Any student of Freud must guard against attributing "Victorian" ideas to him. Even though the bourgeois London of Queen Victoria was not unlike the bourgeois Vienna of the emperor Franz-Joseph, where sexual prudery was concerned, there were considerable differences. At the turn of the nineteenth century, Vienna was considered a city of rather high moral permissiveness.

5. Cf. Jones, 1955, II, 1957, III; Freud/Abraham, 1965; Freeman, 1971; Sachs, 1945; and Nunberg/Federn, 1976.

6. See, Roazen 1969, and 1975; Freud/Andreas-Salomé, 1966; and Nunberg/Federn, 1976. But cf. Eissler, 1971.

7. Anton von Freund had died of cancer in January 1920. During the many months of his illness, Freud was deeply concerned about him and developed the idea of a death instinct at that time. After the sudden death of his daughter Sophie, in March 1920, he continued work on *Beyond the Pleasure Principle* (1920g), in which he presented his theory of the death instinct, so that this event too, if it did not actually contribute to the development of the idea, may nevertheless have contributed to its final formulation (Schur, 1972, 328ff.; Jones, 1957, III, 40f.).

8. Lorenzer, 1973a, 1972, 1973b, 1973c, 1977, 1971; Ricoeur, 1974; Schülein, 1975; Wehler, 1972; Dahmer, 1973; and many others.

9. Exodus 32; 7–11, 14–20, 30–35. Moreover, Freud does not quote from Philippson's version but, as he himself put it, "in an anachronistic manner" from Luther's translation (1914b, 230).

10. As Freud has explained, once he had surmounted his inhibition against traveling to Rome, he was able to use many of his connections in Vienna to obtain a professorship (Jones, 1953, I, 339f.; 1950a, 342ff.).

11. In my view, Stekel's theory and the idea of "active analysis" based on it deserve greater attention than has been paid to them. Even if his ideas have been superseded —for instance, his view that psychoses are incurable—his theoretical studies contain surprisingly clear insights into the socio-psychological nexus, and his therapeutic work reflects his great powers of empathy. I believe that the man, his work, and his "school" have mistakenly been allowed to be overshadowed by orthodox psychoanalysis.

12. From the Freud–Jung correspondence, which was published only a few years ago without abbreviations (1974), it is possible to retrace the dramatic course of their relationship until the break in 1913. A close analysis of the Freud–Jung controversy in the light of this correspondence, and of the works of both authors written during that period, would probably reveal that the theoretical concepts of both men were mirrors of their changing relationship. On the one hand they supported or challenged each other in their writings, and on the other hand their writings helped each to come to grips with his ambivalent feelings for the other.

13. During the first period of their relationship, admittedly, Freud relived the Fliess episode, which in turn was a revival of his childhood experiences with his nephew John (see 1.1.2.1 and 3.1.7 above). This happened, among other reasons, because Eugen Bleuler was an authoritarian father figure for Jung as well as for Freud, one whom both men were determined to subdue. Once Bleuler had withdrawn from the psychoanalytical movement, the controversy between Jung and Freud grew apace (Freud/Jung, 1974, 468ff., 30 November 1911). Here too there are obvious parallels with the Freud–Fliess relationship, at a time when Breuer had represented the father figure (cf. Wallace, 1978, 46f.).

14. Jones claims that these fainting spells were also connected with Freud's quarrel with Fliess. Their final break took place in the same hotel, probably even in the same room (Jones, 1953, I, 317).

15. In 1901, in Bremen, the fainting spell had similarly been preceded by a discussion of death, and on that occasion too Freud had successfully warded off a personal

attack by Jung. Jung recalled that Freud said, after recovering, that he was convinced Jung wished him dead (Jung, 1962, 161). According to Jones, Freud explained that this and similar incidents could be traced back to the effect the death of his brother Julius had had on him (1955, II, 146). One would need more details about his feelings to understand what he meant by this. Freud also thought that "there is some piece of unruly homosexual feeling at the root of the matter" (Jones, 1953, I, 317).

16. "Even Adler's cronies do not regard me as one of yours [instead of "one of theirs," M.K.]" (Freud/Jung, 1974, 533, 11–14 December 1912).

17. According to Schur, quoting from an unpublished letter to Arnold Zweig of 18 August 1933 (1972, 448).

18. See Robert (1975, 38), who quotes Buber's criticism of *Moses and Monotheism*. According to Buber, Freud's writings in this field are at best the work of a dilettante and at worst of an ignoramus who dares to venture into unchartered territory with which he is totally unfamiliar.

19. One might add that "The Moses of Michelangelo" (1914b) could be considered as a testimonial of the intermediate phase, when Freud started out to fulfill his father's mandate, which he had first unconsciously acknowledged in *The Interpretation of Dreams* (1900a).

20. In this connection, the reader is referred to Freud's "Family Romances" (1909c), which also contains important autobiographical material.

21. Freud might have been referring to his own study of Moses when he wrote about the Bible: "The text, however, as we possess it today, will tell us enough about its own vicissitudes. Two mutually opposed treatments have left their traces on it. On the one hand it has been subjected to revisions which have falsified it in the sense of their secret aims, have mutilated and amplified it and have even changed it into its reverse; on the other hand a solicitous piety has presided over it and has sought to preserve everything as it was, no matter whether it was consistent or contradicted itself. Thus almost everywhere noticeable gaps, disturbing repetitions and obvious contradictions have come about—indications which reveal things to us which it was not intended to communicate. In its implications the distortion of a text resembles a murder: the difficulty is not in perpetrating the deed, but in getting rid of its traces. . . . Accordingly, in many instances of textual distortion, we may nevertheless count upon finding what has been suppressed and disavowed hidden away somewhere else, though changed and torn from its context. Only it will not always be easy to recognize it" (1939a, 43; cf. Bakan, 1958, 162ff.).

Incidentally, Freud completely failed to mention in his book the study of Akhenaten written in 1912 by his disciple, Karl Abraham. The omission is the more surprising as this essay and its bibliography undoubtedly served as the basis of his own reconstruction, in which he made Akhenaten the spiritual father of Moses. The omission might have been an unconscious stratagem on Freud's part, for Abraham's essay went at length into Akhenaten's special relationship with his parents, whereas Freud ignored this relationship in his own book, which moreover brings out many parallels with Freud's own family. Freud possibly forgot Abraham's study because Jacob's taboo prevented him from probing into Akhenaten's prehistory, much as—and I believe for the same reason—he also stripped Oedipus of his prehistory, in which similar events were involved.

22. Corroboration of this interpretation was provided by Freud himself in a footnote on the etymological connection between God's name, Yahweh, and the name of Jochanan, in the forms of Johann, John, and Hannibal (1939a, 45). This reference to his partner in childish games of war in Freiberg and to his own militant phase (see pp. 120ff. above) is proof that the plane of Freud's confrontation with his own childhood was involved in this representation, and also of the fact that the militant Yahweh was his antagonist as well as his idol—that he felt himself to be as ambivalent a person as he had portrayed Moses to be.

23. The fact that Freud used not only the structure theory of the psyche (Id, Ego, Superego) from the 1920s (1939a, 96, 116f.) here but also concepts and ideas derived from the seduction theory (*ibid.*, 73ff., 95f., 126f.) is also stressed by the editors of the German *Studienausgabe* of Freud's works. This might be an indication that in his last book he wished to square accounts with his father even in this respect. The theory he had renounced out of filial piety was belatedly restored to honor.

24. There follows a short paragraph, in which he does no more than stress the flaws of his arguments once again.

25. This seems to have been the main reason why Freud turned the earlier version of his third essay into Part II of *Moses and Monotheism:* its symbolic language is easily seen to be coded autobiography. Chapter A is an account of Freud himself; B is an account of his father; C attributes Freud's intellectual interests to his having been chosen by his father; D describes Freud's fight against his instincts and against the resulting guilt feelings; E is an analysis of his search for the true background of his personality; F deals with the rediscovery of his Freiberg childhood; G describes the search for Jacob's "prehistory"; and H describes the ineluctable course his life had to take in the execution of his mandate. Moreover, Freud might also have wanted to retain the earlier version because of its sweeping finale. While the revised version (Part I of III) ends with reservations, apologies, and qualifications, the end of Part II is an apotheosis of the entire book and—if you like—of Freud's biography.

26. "Freud may therefore be said to have been a revolutionary inasmuch as he was a Jew of the Old Testament, but a conservative inasmuch as he was a semibourgeois modern Jew. He is modest and wary, having largely adopted the moral and intellectual norms of an adopted culture, but remorseless and capable of great boldness as he continues to dream the dreams of an unyielding people who stick to their own path and to what they believe is the truth with dogged determination" (Robert, 1975, 51; translated from the German).

TABLES AND CHRONOLOGY

Note that proper names and place names are spelled differently in the different documents, e.g., Nathansohn, Nathanson; Wilenz, Willenz; Hoffmann, Hofman; Rockach, Kokach; Amalie, Amalia; Jakob, Jacob; Kallamon, Kolloman, Kalman; Soloman, Samuel; Maria, Marie; Ragewilla, Ragewitza.

1. Freud family tree, probably drawn up in 1914 by Hellreich from inscriptions on gravestones in Buczacz cemetery, after Kohn (1955, 8); cf. Table 2.

2. Marriage certificate of Jacob and Amalie Freud (Table 7). The official marriage certificate of the Vienna Israelitic Congregation (No. 390/1855/I of 28 March 1977) also states that Jacob Freud had been a "widower since 1852," that he resided in Vienna at 476, Leopoldstadt, and that Amalie resided at 726, Leopoldstadt (see Fig. 10).

3. Documents from the District Archives of Nový Jičín (Neu Titschein), Moravia; cf. Sajner (1968), Gicklhorn (1969), and 2.5.1, 2.5.2, and 2.5.3 above.

4. Family tree (unpublished, S. Freud Archives, New York).

5. Aron (1956–57, 291) from information supplied by N. M. Gelber, who has collected gravestone inscriptions from the Jewish cemetery, Brody. "ChaRMaZ" is probably an abbreviation for "sagacious teacher of uprightness" (Hebrew: *charif, more, zedek*), which was later turned into family names. In 1800, the descendants of the first Nathan called themselves "Nathansohn."

6. Stadt-und Landesarchiv, Vienna, death records.

7. Entry in the family Bible.

8. Freud's comment: "An old aunt of my own, who had married into the Heine family," leaves it an open question whether she was a sister of Jacob or of Amalie (1905c, 141).

9. Record of the birth of Pauline and of Bertha Freud in the "Register of Persons of Different Faiths in Freiberg" (Opava State Archives), after Sajner (1968); see Table 4. The year of Maria's birth is computed from the "Register of Freiberg Jews of 1852" (Table 4), which also tallies with Freud's own statement (1922a, 198), but not with her age of eighty-seven at the time of her death in 1923, according to which she would have been born in 1836 (General Register Office, London).

10. Freud (1960a, 56f.). According to Ernst Freud (1977, 81), however, Simon Nathansohn was Amalie's cousin.

11. Jones (1953, I, 2f.). The date of Jacob Freud's birth has been put in question by the recent research of J. Sajner and P. Swales, and also by declarations of his age at various points of his life. It now seems more likely that he was born in 1814.

12. Freud (1950 a, 170); Stadt- und Landesarchiv, Vienna, death records.

13. Freud (1960a, 222): "He is a younger brother of my father."

14. Document in the District Archives of Nový Jičín (Neu Titschein) of 1852; cf. Sajner (1968), Gicklhorn (1969), and Table 4.

15. Memorandum by Belcredi, minister of police, dated 16 October 1865 (Vienna, Haus-, Hof- und Staatsarchiv); cf. Gicklhorn (1976, 39), 3.3.4 above, and Table 12.

16. Record of the death of Julius in the "Register of Persons of Different Faiths in Freiberg" (Opava State Archives), after Sajner (see Table 8).

17. Record of births in the "Register of Persons of Different Faiths in Freiberg" (Opava State Archives), after Sajner (see Tables 8 and 9).

18. Record of births in the register of the Vienna Israelitic Congregation.

19. Census, 1861, Lower Broughton, Manchester (personal information from B. Williams, Manchester).

20. General Register Office, London, Register of Births, Deaths and Marriages.

21. References to the year of Emanuel Freud's birth differ considerably: 1. The official death record in the General Register Office, London, states that he died on 17 October 1914 at the age of eighty-one. 2. In a letter to Sandor Ferenczi dated 11 November 1914, Sigmund Freud wrote that his brother had "just died" at the age of eighty-one and a half (Jones, 1955, II, 174; cf. Freud/Abraham, 1965, 226). Emanuel would accordingly have been born in about *April 1833* (plus or minus one or two months). This date differs from that given in most biographies, which is 1832. Freud also mentions various age differences between him and his half-brothers. 3. In the recently discovered Freud–Silberstein correspondence of 1875, Freud states that Emanuel was twenty-two years his senior (see p. 158 above). This does not tally with my own surmise that Emanuel was born in 1833, which would make him twenty-three years older than Sigmund. Together with other age references in the passport register discovered by J. Sajner and P. Swales, Freud's statement indicates that Emanuel must have been born toward the end of 1833. In that case, Freud's claim that his brother died at the age of eighty-one and a half must have been mistaken.

22. References to the year of Philipp Freud's birth differ considerably. The most reliable seem to be: 1. The official death entry in the General Register Office, London, according to which he was seventy-six years old when he died on 29 August 1911. The information comes from his daughter Pauline Hartwig. 2. In a letter to Fliess dated 15 October 1897, Freud remarked that his brother Philipp was "now sixty-three" (1950a, 223). From these two references it is possible to put the date of Philipp's birth at some time between the end of August and the middle of October 1834. This date differs from that of 1836 given by most biographers, and also does not tally with Freud's remark to Silberstein (see p. 158) that Philipp was two years younger than Emanuel and twenty years older than Sigmund. Taking these and other references in the passport register into account, Philipp might also have been born toward the end of 1835, which does not agree with the conclusions mentioned above. This question has to remain open, just as in the case of Jacob's and Emanuel's dates of birth.

23. Previously unknown daughter of Emanuel and Maria, also not listed in the

family tree held by the Sigmund Freud Archives, New York. The child seems to have died before 1871, because she is not listed in the census of 1871 (research by B. Williams, Manchester).

24. It is not entirely clear who Bloome Frankel was. On 22 June 1839, a daughter by the name of Matilda was born to Morris Frankel, "gilt toymaker," and Maria, née Phillips, in Birmingham. We must presume that this daughter was Bloome, for Morris Frankel had no other daughters (research in General Register Office, London, by E. Kuhne), and her marriage certificate states that she is the daughter of Morris Frankel, or rather of Moses Frankel, "Morris" being a common translation of Moses; furthermore, one of the witnesses at the wedding was called Jacob Phillips, and may thus have been a relative of her mother. However, the ages given at various periods in the life of Bloome/Matilda do not agree. At her marriage in 1873, she is said to have been twenty-eight; yet according to the birth register, she must have been thirty-four at the time (on this marriage certificate, admittedly, Philipp too had been "rejuvenated"; he was not thirty-four as stated, but thirty-nine). On her death in 1925 she is said to have been eighty-seven, when she could not have been more than eighty-six according to the Register of Birth (all figures taken from the General Register Office, London).

25. Adolf Lehmann, ed.: General Advertiser of Addresses and Trades in the Royal and Imperial Residence of Vienna of 1876.

26. Jones, 1953, I, 100ff.

27. Sigmund-Freud-Gesellschaft, ed.: Sigmund Freud House Catalogue, Vienna, 1975, 13.

28. Lists of guests taking the cure in Roznau (from the latest research by J. Sajner and P. Swales; see Table 13). Cf. Sajner (1981).

29. It is impossible to tell how the many obvious mistakes have crept into the tables. They might have been added in error to the original, or be due to mistakes in the copy. The style of recording dates and sums of money has been adapted to present-day usage.

30. Information kindly supplied by W. Ernest Freud and Hans Walter Lange.

31. Information kindly supplied by H. Lobner, Sigmund Freud House, Vienna.

32. Jones, 1955, II, 105; 1957, III, 91, 102, 105.

33. Translation: Marriage certificate. The undersigned hereby certifies that on the nine-and-twentieth day of the month of July in the year One thousand eight hundred and fifty-five (29 July 1855) the couple: Herr Jacob Freud, produce merchant, legitimate son of Herr Salomon Freud and his wife Pessel, née Hofmann, born in Tysmenitz, Galicia, and domiciled in Klogsdorf near Freiberg in Moravia, forty years old and being the bridegroom, and the virgin Amalia or Malka Nathanson, daughter of Herr Jacob Nathanson and Frau Sara née Willenz, born in Brody, nineteen years old and being the bride, were married in accordance with Israelitic customs and laws and had their marriage blessed in the presence of the witnesses Herr Jacob Nathanson and Osias Rosin after due authorization by the Royal and Imperial District Authorities in Zloczow on 12 June 1855 (Z. 11722 Municipal Council, District Commissariat Freyberg, Moravia, 12 April/21 June 1855 Z 91) by the undersigned Minister, the Reverend Mannheimer of Vienna, in the Israelitic Prayer House, No. 794. Which act of marriage has also been entered under the same date in the Marriage Records of the Israelitic Congregation, Vienna, Littera 4, No. 390. In confirmation the signature in his own hand of the undersigned together with the office seal. Vienna, 15 February 1859. Ministry of the Israelitic Congregation in Vienna. Signed: Mannheimer, Minister.

34. Translation of the entries under Sigmund Freud, Emil Fluss, and Paulina Freud: [Headings]: Time of birth/Place of birth/House Number/Name of Child/Israelitic Religion/Male/Female/ Legitimate/Illegitimate/Name and Occupation of Father/Name of Mother/Name of Circumciser and of Godparents or Witnesses//

1856 6 May/Freiberg/117/Sigismund/ √ / √ /-/ √ /-/Jakob Freud, merchant in Freiberg, son of Salomon Freud, merchant, and of Pepi, née Hoffmann of Tysmenitz

/Amalia, daughter of Jacob Nathansohn, commercial agent in Vienna and Sara, née Wilenz from Brody/on 13 May circumcised by Samson Frankel from Ostrau. Lipe Horowitz and his sister Fräulein Mina from Cernowitz/[Entry across the columns]: Midwife Cäcilie Smolka from Freiberg, No. 114/

1856 8 October/Freiberg/20/Emil/ √ / √ /-/ √ /-/ Ignaz Fluss, merchant in Freiberg, son of Emanuel Fluss, merchant from Tysmenitz and his wife Getzi(?), née Maydan (?) from Tysmenitz, Galicia/Eleonora, daughter of Lazar Moser,(?) of Karlsbad and his wife Henrietta, née Becher from (?) in Bohemia/15 October Moses Leib Siebenschein, leaseholder from Weisskirchen./[Entry across the columns]: Midwife Veronika Schubert from Freiberg No. 371//

1856 20 November/Freiberg/42/Paulina/ √ /-/ √ / √ /-/ Emanuel Freudt, merchant in Freiberg, son of Jakob Freudt, merchant in Freiberg and Saly, née Kanner from Tysmenitz/Marie, daughter of Ferdinand Rokach, Rabbi in Ragewilla and Babette Kanner from Milow in Russia/-/[Entry across the columns]: Midwife Cäcilie Smolka from Fberg No. 114//

M. Balmary's assumption that Sigmund Freud was conceived outside marriage is not tenable. The facsimile shows clearly that he was born on May 6, not March 6 as Balmary claims. This is borne out by a comparison of the y's in that entry with those in the old German spelling of "Freyberg," "Tysmenitz," etc. (cf. Balmary, 1979, 65ff.).

Apart from this difference, Balmary's study, which was published at about the same time as my book and was therefore unknown to me, contains surprisingly similar ideas to those formulated here.

35. Translation of entries under Anna Freud and Bertha Freud [Headings]: Time of Birth/Place of Birth/House Number/Name of Child/Israelitic Religion/Boy/Girl /Legitimate/Illegitimate/Name and Occupation of Father/Name of Mother/Name of Circumciser and Witnesses// . . .

1858 December 31/Freiberg/117/Anna/ √ /-/ √ / √ /-/Jacob Freud, merchant in Freiberg, son of Salomon Freud, merchant and Peppi, née Hoffmann, from Tysmenitz /Amalia, daughter of Jakob Nathansohn, commercial agent in Vienna and Sara, née Wilenz from Brody/-/[Entry across the columns]: Midwife Cäcilia Smolka from Freiberg No. 114//

1859 February 22/Freiberg/42/Bertha/ √ /-/ √ / √ /-/ Emanuel Freudt, merchant in Freiberg, son of Jakob Freudt, merchant in Freiberg, and Saly, née Kanner from Tysmenitz/Marie, daughter of Ferdinand Kokach, Rabbi in Ragewilla and of Babeth Kanner from Milow in Russia/-/[Entry across the columns]: Midwife Cäcilia Smolka from Freiberg, No. 114//

36. Translation of entry under Julius Freud: [Headings]: Grave(?) and Time of Burial/Residence (?) Place of Death/Place of Burial/Number/Name and Occupation of Deceased/Jewish/Male/Female/Age/Illness and Nature of Death(?)// . . .

1858 April 15/Freiberg/Weisskirchen/417/Julius, son of Jakob Freud, merchant in Freiberg/ √ / √ /-/6 months/infection of the intestines//

37. This information was kindly provided by Peter J. Swales after my book was first published. It is the result of searches he and his wife Julia made in various archives in the years 1980 and 1981. The essential source is a forgotten Freud–Nathanson family tree which was compiled by Albert J. Phiebig of White Plains, N.Y., probably in the 1930s, and which is now kept in the Sigmund Freud Archives of the Library of Congress, Washington, D.C. Additional information was obtained from the Siegfried Bernfeld Collection, which is also kept in the Library of Congress and contains letters from children and relatives of Freud to Bernfeld, who was collecting material for a Freud biography. Some years before his death, Bernfeld made some of the material available to Ernest Jones, who was working on his own Freud biography. Bernfeld generally provided no information other than that Jones had explicitly asked for, with the result that a large amount of the important data Bernfeld collected has never been published. Moreover, the Bernfeld Collection itself is not freely accessible. P. Swales

has, as far as possible, checked all the information with documents held by the Vienna Israelitic Congregation, if necessary correcting and expanding it using his further genealogical research. He and Josef Sajner also checked the information concerning Freud's uncle Abae in Breslan against various Breslau address books.

38. According to Anna Freud Bernays (1930, 13).

39. Freud, 1960a, 222f.

40. Translation of Table 12: From the Courtroom

Vienna, 22 February (orig. rep.) (Forgery of Banknotes). Presiding Judge: Ritter von Schwartz; Prosecution: Acting Public Prosecutor Mottloch; Defense: Dr. Neuda and Dr. Alfred Stern.

In the dock were Joseph Freud from Tysmenitz, Galicia, forty years old, merchant, and Osias Weich from Wisnek, Bukovina, forty years old, merchant. From the indictment it appears that in May 1865, Joseph Freud enquired of the commission agent, Simon Weiss, whether he knew of a buyer for 100 fifty-rouble notes from someone willing to let them go cheaply because they were forged. Weiss appeared to be willing and took receipt of a specimen forged note ostensibly in order to find a buyer but, in fact, to take the forgery to the police. He also arranged to meet Freud in the "Hotel Victoria," where he agreed to purchase from him 400 fifty-rouble notes, and handed over a deposit of 200 guilders. Payment of the rest of the money was to be made on presentation of the goods (forgeries), and when Weiss accordingly came to fetch the forged notes and Freud handed them over, he was arrested by the police.

Freud was found to be in possession of 100 forged notes and a search of his house brought to light a further 259 forged notes. Freud declared that he had met Osias Weich in Galacz in the summer of 1864 and that he had frequently dined with him in the "Hotel Zuckermann," and that one day Weich had asked him if he was interested in a bargain, Weich further informing him that he had bought forged rouble notes from a gentleman in England, which had cost him 25 percent of the nominal value, but that he only wanted 5 percent for himself provided he could leave the transaction to Freud. He, Freud claims, did not accept the proposal. In September 1864, Weich came to Vienna and sought him, Freud, out in the Café Wagner in Leopoldstadt and asked him for a loan of 300 guilders. Freud claims that he lent him that sum and that he took the forgeries, which were in an English envelope, as security. Freud also claims that he met Weich on several occasions at the Leipzig Fair and that he sent the latter, who was in financial difficulties, 25 guilders to Leipzig by post. As a result of this information, Osias Weich was traced in Leipzig, arrested and brought here. Weich, who cannot prove that he has any fixed employment, was found in possession of addresses in London of persons described as highly suspicious characters (information, which reached the court by diplomatic channels, mentioned in particular a Mrs. Lewy, who was a Jewess engaged in peddling forgeries). Moreover, several envelopes similar in size and shape to those in which Freud had kept the rouble notes and constructed in such a way that the rouble notes fitted into them, were discovered in his possession. In the expert opinion of the Imperial Russian Bank in Petersburg the forgeries in Joseph Freud's possession were produced by copperplate engraving and lithography on ordinary paper, and are of a kind with the many forgeries with which all European trading centers are flooded and which have already led to the sentencing of several persons. From Leipzig there is yet another report casting suspicion on Osias Weich. He could be the same person, dressed in Polish garb, who several years ago purchased watches of Swiss manufacture, with similar forgeries at the Leipzig Fair.

Both of the accused offered a vigorous defense. Freud pleaded guilty to the offense both at the preliminary investigation and also at the trial, but claimed that Weich had left the forgeries with him as security. Weich, with unusual vehemence, called this charge a lie, claimed that he had never been in possession of the forgeries, and alleged that Freud, whose family lives in London, was simply using his name to proffer a spurious source of the forgeries to the court.—Freud's charge had a semblance of truth because the two of them had traveled together, a fact Freud had shrewdly taken into account. However, the whole story was a tissue of lies. Weich claimed that he came into possession of the London addresses simply because, as happens to many travelers, he had found them in a hotel and had taken them. His possession of the English envelopes, which were identified as being similar to those in which Freud had kept the forgeries, was explained by Weich as resulting from the fact that, during their travels, Freud frequently used Weich's suitcase, and that the envelopes had probably been left inside.—The accused continued their mutual recriminations and insults but were unable to shake the merit of the case of the prosecution.

The prosecutor demanded a prison sentence of ten years for Freud and of twelve years for Weich.

The sentences, passed late in the afternoon, were: Josef Freud and Osias Weich, having both been found guilty of attempted circulation of forged banknotes, were sentenced to ten years' penal servitude each.—In the case of Freud the court decided to refer the documents to a higher court for mitigation of sentence.—The accused gave notice of their intention to appeal.

41. Information given by Hans Walter Lange.

Translated by A. J. Pomerans

Bibliography

The works of Sigmund Freud are listed in accordance with the Bibliography in the Standard Edition of the *Complete Psychological Works of Sigmund Freud,* translated from the German under the general editorship of James Strachey (24 vols.). The Institute of Psycho-Analysis, The Hogarth Press, London, 1953–74.

Abraham, Karl (1912): "Amenhotep IV. (Echnaton). Psychoanalytische Beiträge zum Verständnis seiner Persönlichkeit und des monotheistischen Aton-Kultes." *Imago,* I, 334–360.
——— (1969): *Psychoanalytische Studien zur Charakterbildung. Und andere Schriften.* Edited and introduced by Johannes Cremerius. Frankfurt.
Adams, Leslie (1953–54): "A New Look at Freud's Dream 'The Breakfast Ship.' " *The American Journal of Psychiatry,* 110, 381–384.
———(1954): "Sigmund Freud's Correct Birthday: Misunderstanding and Solution." *Psychoanalytic Review,* 41, 359–362.
Adler, H. G. (1960): *Die Juden in Deutschland. Von der Aufklärung bis zum Nationalsozialismus.* Munich.
Aleichem, Sholem (1964): *Menachem Mendel, der Spekulant.* Munich and Zurich.
———(1965): *Der Sohn des Kantors.* Berlin/GDR (first published in Yiddish as *Motl Peisse dem Khazns,* 1907).
———(1972): *Marienbad. Kein Roman in 36 Briefen, 13 Billets-doux und 47 Telegrammen.* Munich (first published in Yiddish in 1911).
Alexander, Franz, and Sheldon T. Selesnick (1965): "Freud–Bleuler Correspondence." *Archives of General Psychiatry,* 12, 1–9.
Anzieu, Didier (1959): *L'auto analyse. Son rôle dans la découverte de la psychoanalyse par Freud. Sa fonction en psychoanalyse.* Paris.
———(1978): "Inwiefern die Psychoanalyse von ihren Ursprüngen geprägt ist." In Janine Chasseguet-Smirgel, ed. (1978): *Wege des Anti-Ödipus.* Frankfurt, Berlin, and Vienna, 127–135.
Aron, Willy (1956–57): "Notes on Sigmund Freud's Ancestry and Jewish Contacts." *Yivo Annual of Jewish Social Studies,* 11, 286–295.
———(1971): "Fartsaykhnungen vegen opshtam fun Sigmund Freud un vegen zein yiddishkeit." *Yivo Bleter,* 40, 166–174.
Artner, Karl, Otto Guth, and Emil Nekovar (1937): *Die Leopoldstadt. Ein Heimatbuch.* Vienna.
Baeck, Leo (1958): *Aus drei Jahrtausenden. Wissenschaftliche Untersuchungen und Abhandlungen zur Geschichte des jüdischen Glaubens.* Tübingen (first published 1938).

————(1960): *Das Wesen des Judentums.* Cologne (first published 1906).

Bakan, David (1958): *Sigmund Freud and the Jewish Mystical Tradition.* New York.

Balaban, Majer (1914): *Dzieje Zydow w Galiciyi w rzeczypospolitej Krakowskiej 1772–1868.* Lvov (in Polish).

Bally, Gustav (1961): *Einführung in die Psychoanalyse Sigmund Freuds.* Reinbek.

Balmary, Marie (1979): *L'homme aux statues. Freud et al faute cachée du père.* Paris.

Barta, Johannes (1975): *Jüdische Familienerziehung. Das jüdische Erziehungswesen im 19. und 20. Jahrhundert.* Zurich, Einsiedeln, and Cologne.

Baruk, H. (1959): "Freud et le Judaïsme." *Revue d'histoire et de la médecine hébraïque,* 12, 29–49.

Beer Bolechow (Dob Beer Bolechower; Bolechower, Beer; Bär) (1922): *Zikronot (Memoirs),* edited with introduction and explanations by M. Wischnitzer. Berlin (in Yiddish).

Bergmann, Martin S. (1976): "Moses and the Evolution of Freud's Jewish Identity." *Israel Annals of Psychiatry and Related Disciplines,* 3–26. Jerusalem.

Bernays, Anna Freud (*ca.* 1930): *Erlebtes.* Vienna.

————(1940) "My Brother Sigmund Freud." *American Mercury,* 335–342.

Bernfeld, Siegfried (1944): "Freud's Earliest Theories and the School of Helmholtz." *Psychoanalytic Quarterly,* 13, 341–362.

————(1946): "An Unknown Autobiographical Fragment by Freud." *The American Imago,* 4, 3–19.

————(1949): "Freud's Scientific Beginnings." *The American Imago,* 6, 163–196.

————(1951): "Sigmund Freud, M.D., 1882–1885." *International Journal of Psycho-Analysis,* 32, 204–217.

————, and *Suzanne Cassirer Bernfeld* (1944): "Freud's Early Childhood." *Bulletin of the Menninger Clinic,* 8, 107–113.

Bernfeld, Suzanne Cassirer (1951): "Freud and Archeology." *The American Imago,* 8, 107–128.

Besançon, Alain (1978): "Freud, Abraham, Laios." In Janine Chasseguet-Smirgel, ed.: *Wege des Anti-Ödipus.* Frankfurt, Berlin, and Vienna, 17–29.

Birnbaum, Solomon A. (1946): "The Cultural Structure of East Ashkenazic Jewry." *Slavonic East European Review,* 25, 73–92.

Bittner, Günther (1974): *Das andere Ich. Rekonstruktionen zu Freud.* Munich.

Blond, Szlomo, ed. (1974): *Tysmienica. A Memorial Book.* Tel-Aviv (in Hebrew and Yiddish).

Blum, Ernst (1956): "Über Sigmund Freuds: Der Mann Moses und die monotheistische Religion." *Psyche,* 25, 367–390.

Börne, Ludwig (1862): *Gesammelte Schriften,* Vols. 1 and 2. Hamburg and Frankfurt.

Boszormenyi-Nagy, Ivan (1976): "Loyalität und Übertragung." *Familiendynamik,* 1, 153–171.

————, and Geraldine Spark (1973): *Invisible Loyalties. Reciprocity in Intergenerational Family Therapy.* Hagerstown, New York.

————, and James L. Framo, eds. (1965): *Intensive Family Therapy, Theoretical and Practical Aspects.* New York.

Brenner, Charles (1955): *An Elementary Textbook of Psychoanalysis.* New York.

Breuer, Josef (1895): "Frl. Anna O. . . . " In Freud (1895d), 20–29.

Buber, Martin (1974): *The Tales of Rabbi Nachman.* London.

————(1947): *Tales of the Hasidim. The Early Masters.* New York.

————(1948): *Tales of the Hasidim. The Late Masters.* New York.

Buxbaum, Edith (1951): "Freud's Dream Interpretation in the Light of His Letters to Fliess." *Bulletin of the Menninger Clinic,* 15.

Chasseguet-Smirgel, Janine, ed. (1978): *Wege des Anti-Ödipus.* Frankfurt, Berlin, and Vienna (first publication as *Les Chemins de l'Anti-Oedipe.* Toulouse, 1974).

Chertok, Leon (1973): "Freud in Paris (1885–86). Eine Psychologische Studie." *Psyche,* 27, 431–448.

Chirowski, Dominik (1938): *Dzieje Miasta Tysmienicy.* Lvov (in Polish).

Clark, Ronald W. (1980): *Freud, the Man and the Cause.* London.

Dahmer, Helmut (1973): *Libido und Gesellschaft. Studien über Freud und die Freudsche Linke.* Frankfurt.

————, and Thomas Leithäuser, Alfred Lorenzer, et. al. (1973): *Das Elend der Psychoanalyse-Kritik* (Beispiel Kursbuch 29). Subjektverleugnung als politische Magie, Frankfurt.

Devereux, George (1953): "Why Oedipus Killed Laius. A Note on the Complementary Oedipus Complex in Greek Drama." *International Journal of Psycho-Analysis,* 34, 132–141.

————(1976): *Angst und Methode in den Verhaltenswissenschaften,* Frankfurt, Berlin, and Vienna (first publication 1973 as *From Anxiety to Method in the Behavioural Sciences.* Paris, 1967).

Dubnow, Simon (1927): *Weltgeschichte des jüdischen Volkes. Von seinen Uranfängen bis zur Gegenwart,* Berlin (first publication in Russian 1920–23). English translation: *History of the Jews;* S. Brunswick, N.J. 1967. Vol. 6: *Die Geschichte des jüdisches Volkes in der Neuzeit. Erste Periode. Das 16. und die erste Hälfte des 17. Jahrhunderts.*

————(1928): *Weltgeschichte . . .* Vol. 7: *Die Geschichte des jüdischen Volkes in der Neuzeit. Die zweite Hälfte des 17. und das 18. Jahrhunderts.*

————(1928a): *Weltgeschichte . . .* Vol. 8: *Die neueste Geschichte des jüdischen Volkes. Das Zeitalter der ersten Emanzipation 1789–1815.*

————(1929): *Weltgeschichte . . .* Vol. 9: *Die neueste Geschichte des jüdischen Volkes. Das Zeitalter der ersten Reaktion und der zweiten Emanzipation 1815–1881.*

————(1975): *History of the Jews in Russia and Poland from the Earliest Times until the Present Day.* With a Biographical Essay, new Introduction, and Outline of the History of Russian and Soviet Jewry, 1912–1974, by Leon Shapiro. 2 vols., Philadelphia (first publication 1916 and 1920).

Dussler, Luitpold, ed. (1927): *Luca Signorelli. Des Meisters Gemälde.* Berlin and Leipzig.

Eissler, Kurt R. (1964): "Mankind at Its Best." *Journal of the American Psychoanalytic Association,* 12, 187–222.

————(1966): *Sigmund Freud und die Wiener Universität. Über die Pseudo-Wissenschaftlichkeit der jüngsten Wiener Freud-Biographik.* Bern and Stuttgart.

————(1971): *Talent and Genius. The Fictitious Case of Tausk Contra Freud.* New York.

————(1977): "Biographische Skizze." In Ernst Freud, *et al.* (1977).

Ellenberger, Henry F. (1970): *The Discovery of the Unconscious. The History and Evolution of Dynamic Psychiatry.* New York.

d'Elvert, Christian (1970): *Zur Cultur-Geschichte Mährens.* Brünn (Brno).

Encyclopaedia Judaica (1971). 16 vols., Jerusalem, 1971–72.

Engelman, Edmund (1976): *Berggasse 19. Sigmund Freud's Home and Offices, Vienna, 1938.* New York.

Erikson, Erik H. (1954): "The Dream Specimen of Psychoanalysis." *Journal of the American Psychoanalytical Association,* 2.

————(1959): *Young Man Luther, a Study in Psychoanalysis and History.* London.

————(1964): *Insight and Responsibility.* New York.

————(1975): *Life History and the Historical Moment,* New York.

Falk, Avner (1977): "Freud and Herzl." *Midstream,* 3–24.

————(1978): "Freud and Herzl." *Contemporary Psychoanalysis,* 14, 357–387.

Fliess, Wilhelm (1906): *In eigener Sache, Gegen Otto Weininger und Hermann Swoboda.* Berlin.

Fraenkel, Josef, ed. (1967): *The Jews of Austria. Essays on Their Life, History and Destruction.* London.

Freeman, Erika (1971): *Insights. Conversations with Theodor Reik.* Englewood Cliffs, N.J.

Freeman, Lucy (1972): *The Story of Anna O.* New York.

Freud, Anna (1936): *Das Ich und die Abwehrmechanismen.* Munich (English translation: *The Ego and the Mechanisms of Defense.* London, 1937).

Freud, Ernst, Lucie Freud, and Ilse Grubrich-Simitis, eds. (1977): *Sigmund Freud, His Life in Pictures and Words.* London.

Freud, Martin (1957): *Glory Reflected. Sigmund Freud—Man and Father.* London.

————(1967): "Who Was Freud?" In Josef Fraenkel, ed.: *The Jews of Austria.* London, 197–211.

Freud, Sigmund (1872–74): see Freud (1969a).

————(1873–1939): see Freud (1961).

————(1884e): "On Coca." In S. Freud: *The Cocaine Papers.* Vienna and Zurich, 1963.

————(1885): see Freud (1960b).

————(1886f): Translation of J.-M. Charcot's Leçons sur les maladies du système nerveux. Vol. III, Paris, 1887, into German. Preface translated into English: Preface to the translation of Charcot's *Lectures on the Diseases of the Nervous System. Standard Ed.,* I, 19.

————(1886): see Freud (1956a).

————(1887–1902): see Freud (1950a).

————(1888b): "Hysteria" and "Hystero-Epilepsy." *Standard Ed.,* I, 39 and 58. Published in German in A. Villaret, ed.: *Handwörterbuch der gesamten Medizin.* Vol. I, Stuttgart. (authorship merely assumed because the articles are not signed; possibly Freud is also the author of the articles on "Aphasia," "Coca," and "Brain," M.K.)

————(1888–89) Translation of H. Bernheim's *De la suggestion et de ses applications à la thérapeutique,* Paris, 1886, into German. Preface translated into English: Preface to the translation of Bernheim's *Suggestion, Standard Ed.,* I, 73.

————(1890a): "Psychical (or Mental) Treatment." *Standard Ed.,* VII, 283.

————(1891b): *On Aphasia.* London and New York, 1953.

————(1891c): "Kinderlähmung" and "Lähmung." In L. A. Villaret, ed.: *Handwörterbuch der gesamten Medizin.* Vol. 2, Stuttgart (unsigned, authorship uncertain).

————(1891d) "Hypnosis." *Standard Ed.,* I, 105.

————(1892a): Translation of H. Bernheim's *Hypnotisme, suggestion et psychothérapie; études nouvelles,* Paris, 1891, into German.

————(1892): see Freud (1940d), (1941a), (1941b).

————(1892–93): "A Case of Successful Treatment by Hypnotism," *Standard Ed.,* I, 117.

————(1892–94): Translation of J.-M. Charcot's *Leçons du mardi à la Salpêtrière,* Paris, 1888, into German. Preface and footnotes translated into English: Preface and Footnotes to the translation of Charcot's *Tuesday Lectures. Standard Ed.,* I, 131.

————(1893a) with J. Breuer: "On the Psychical Mechanism of Hysterical Phenomena: Preliminary Communications," *Standard Ed.,* II, 3.

————(1893b): "Zur Kenntniss der cerebralen Diplegien des Kindesalters (im Anschluss an die Little'sche Krankheit)." In von Kassowitz, ed.: *Neue Folge der Beiträge zur Kinderheilkunde.* Vienna.

————(1893c) [1888]: "Some Points for a Comparative Study of Organic and Hysterical Motor Paralyses." *Standard Ed.,* I, 157.

————(1893d): "Über familiäre Formen von cerebralen Diplegien." *Neurologisches Zentralblatt,* 12, 512–515 and 542–547.

————(1893f): "Charcot" [Epitaph]. *Standard Ed.,* III, 9.

————(1893g): "Über ein Symptom, das häufig die Enuresis nocturna der Kinder begleitet." *Neurologisches Zentralblatt,* 12, 735–737.

————(1893h): Lecture "On the Psychical Mechanism of Hysterical Phenomena." *Standard Ed.,* III, 27.

————(1894a): "The Neuro-Psychoses of Defence," *Standard Ed.,* III, 43.

————(1895b) [1894]: "On the Grounds for Detaching a Particular Syndrome from Neurasthenia under the Description 'Anxiety Neurosis.' " *Standard Ed.,* III, 87.

————(1895c) [1894]: "Obsessions and Phobias," *Standard Ed.,* III, 71.

————(1895d) with J. Breuer: *Studies on Hysteria. Standard Ed.,* II.

————(1895e): "Über die Bernhardt'sche Sensibilitätsstorung am Oberschenkel." *Neurologisches Zentralblatt,* 14, 491–492.

————(1895f): "A Reply to Criticism of My Paper on "Anxiety Neurosis." *Standard Ed.,* III, 121.

————(1895g): "Über Hysterie. Zusammenfassung von drei Vorträgen vor dem Wiener medicinischen Doctorencollegium" (author A-r). *Wiener klinische Rundschau,* 9, nos. 42–44 (research M.K.).

————(1895h): "Zwangsvorstellungen und Phobien. Ihr psychischer Mechanismus und ihre Ätiologie." *Wiener klinische Rundschau* 8, nos. 17, 18 (Translation into German by A. Schiff of the French article under 1895c (research M.K.)

————(1895): see Freud, 1950a.

————(1896a): "Heredity and the Aetiology of the Neuroses." *Standard Ed.,* III, 143.

————(1896b): "Further Remarks on the Neuro-Psychoses of Defence," *Standard Ed.,* III, 159.

————(1896c): "The Aetiology of Hysteria," *Standard Ed.,* III, 189.

————(1897a): "Die infantile Cerebrallähmung," Part II, Section II of Nothnagel's *Specielle Pathologie und Therapie,* 9. Vienna.

————(1897b): *Abstracts of the Scientific Writings of Dr. Sigm.* Freud (1877–1897). *Standard Ed.,* II, 225.

————(1898a): "Sexuality in the Aetiology of the Neuroses," *Standard Ed.,* III, 261.

————(1896b): "The Psychical Mechanism of Forgetfulness." *Standard Ed.,* III, 289.

————(1899): see Freud (1941c).

————(1899a): "Screen Memories." *Standard Ed.,* III, 301.

————(1900a) [1898–99]: *The Interpretation of Dreams. Standard Ed.,* IV–V.

————(1901a): *On Dreams. Standard Ed.,* V, 633.

————(1901b): *The Psychopathology of Everyday Life. Standard Ed.,* VI.

————(1901c) [1899]: "Autobiographical Note." *Standard Ed.,* III, 325.

————(1904a) [1903]: "Freud's Psycho-Analytic Procedure," *Standard Ed.,* VII, 249.

————(1905a): "On Psychotherapy." *Standard Ed.,* VII, 257.

————(1905c): *Jokes and Their Relation to the Unconscious. Standard Ed.,* VIII.

————(1905d): *Three Essays on the Theory of Sexuality. Standard Ed.,* VII, 125.

————(1905e) [1901]: "Fragment of an Analysis of a Case of Hysteria," *Standard Ed.,* VII, 3.

————(1906a): "My Views on the Part Played by Sexuality in the Aetiology of Neurosis," *Standard Ed.,* VII, 271.

————(1906b) Collection of articles under the title *Sammlung kleiner Schriften zur Neurosenlehre aus den Jahren 1893–1906.* Preface translated into English as Preface to *Freud's Shorter Writings, 1893–1906. Standard Ed.,* III, 3.

————(1906–23): see Freud/Jung (1974).

————(1906–31): see Freud (1955b).

———(1907a) [1906]: *Delusions and Dreams in Jensen's "Gradiva."* Standard Ed., IX, 3.

———(1907b): "Obssessive Actions and Religious Practices," *Standard Ed.*, IX, 116.

———(1907c): "The Sexual Enlightenment of Children." *Standard Ed.*, IX, 131.

———(1907–26): see Freud/Abraham (1965a).

———(1908a): "Hysterical Phantasies and Their Relation to Bisexuality." *Standard Ed.*, IX, 157.

———(1908b): "Character and Anal Erotism." *Standard Ed.*, IX, 169.

———(1908c): "On the Sexual Theories of Children." *Standard Ed.*, IX, 207.

———(1908d): " 'Civilized' Sexual Morality and Modern Nervous Illness." *Standard Ed.*, IX, 179.

———(1909a) [1908]: "Some General Remarks on Hysterical Attacks." *Standard Ed.*, IX, 229.

———(1909b): "Analysis of a Phobia in a Five-Year-Old Boy." *Standard Ed.*, X, 3.

———(1909c) [1908]: "Family Romances." *Standard Ed.*, IX, 237.

———(1909d): "Notes upon a Case of Obsessional Neurosis." *Standard Ed.*, X, 155.

———(1909–16): see Freud/Putnam (1971).

———(1909–39): see Freud/Pfister (1963a).

———(1910a) [1909]: "Five Lectures on Psycho-Analysis." *Standard Ed.*, XI, 3.

———(1910c): *Leonardo da Vinci and a Memory of His Childhood, Standard Ed.*, XI, 59.

———(1910d): "The Future Prospects of Psycho-Analytic Therapy." *Standard Ed.*, XI, 141.

———(1910e): ' "The Antithetical Meaning of Primal Words.' " *Standard Ed.*, XI, 155.

———(1910h): "A Special Type of Choice of Object Made by Men." *Standard Ed.*, XI, 165.

———(1910k): " 'Wild' Psycho-Analysis." *Standard Ed.*, XI, 221.

———(1911c) [1910]: "Psycho-Analytic Notes on an Autobiographical Account of a Case of Panaranoia (Dementia Paranoides)." *Standard Ed.*, XII, 3.

———(1912b): "The Dynamics of Transference." *Standard Ed.*, XII, 99.

———(1912c): "Types of Onset of Neurosis." *Standard Ed.*, XII, 229.

———(1912d): "On the Universal Tendency to Debasement in the Sphere of Love." *Standard Ed.*, XI, 179.

———(1912e): "Recommendations to Physicians Practising Psycho-Analysis." *Standard Ed.*, XII, 111.

———(1912–13): *Totem and Taboo. Standard Ed.*, XIII, 1.

———(1912–36): see Freud/Andreas-Salomé (1972).

———(1913f): "The Theme of the Three Caskets." *Standard Ed.*, XII, 291.

———(1913g): "Two Lies Told by Children." *Standard Ed.*, XII, 305.

———(1913i): "The Disposition to Obsessional Neurosis." *Standard Ed.*, XII, 313.

———(1913–38): see Reik (1956).

———(1914b): "The Moses of Michelangelo." *Standard Ed.*, XIII, 211.

———(1914c): "On Narcissism: an Introduction." *Standard Ed.*, XIV, 69.

———(1914d): "On the History of the Psycho-Analytic Movement." *Standard Ed.*, XIV, 3.

———(1914f): "Some Reflections on Schoolboy Psychology," *Standard Ed.*, XIII, 241.

———(1915b): "Thoughts for the Times on War and Death," *Standard Ed.*, XIV, 275.

———(1915c): "Instincts and Their Vicissitudes," *Standard Ed.*, XIV, 111.

———(1915d): "Repression." *Standard Ed.*, XIV, 143.

———(1915e): "The Unconscious," *Standard Ed.*, XIV, 161

———(1916–17) [1915–16]: *Introductory Lectures on Psycho-Analysis. Standard Ed.*, XV–XVI.

———(1917b): "A Childhood Recollection from *Dichtung und Wahrheit.*" *Standard Ed.,* XVII, 147.

———(1917d) [1915]: "A Metapsychological Supplement to the Theory of Dreams." *Standard Ed.,* XIV, 219.

———(1917e) [1915]: "Mourning and Melancholia." *Standard Ed.,* XIV, 239.

———(1917–34): see Groddeck/Freud (1974).

———(1918a) [1917]: "The Taboo of Virginity." *Standard Ed.,* XI, 193.

———(1918b) [1914]: "From the History of an Infantile Neurosis," *Standard Ed.,* XVII, 3.

———(1919h): "The 'Uncanny.' " *Standard Ed.,* XVII, 219.

———(1920a): "The Psychogenesis of a Case of Female Homosexuality." *Standard Ed.,* XVIII, 147.

———(1920b): "A Note on the Prehistory of the Technique of Analysis." *Standard Ed.,* XVIII, 263.

———(1920g): *Beyond the Pleasure Principle. Standard Ed.,* XVIII, 7.

———(1921c): *Group Psychology and the Analysis of the Ego. Standard Ed.,* XVIII, 69.

———(1922a) [1921]: "Dreams and Telepathy." *Standard Ed.,* XIII, 197.

———(1923b): *The Ego and the Id. Standard Ed.,* XIX, 3.

———(1923d) [1922]: "A Seventeenth-Century Demonological Neurosis." *Standard Ed.,* XIX, 69.

———(1923e): "The Infantile Genital Organization." *Standard Ed.,* XIX, 141.

———(1924b) [1923]: "Neurosis and Psychosis." *Standard Ed.,* XIX, 149.

———(1924c): "The Economic Problem of Masochism." *Standard Ed.,* XIX, 157.

———(1924d): "The Dissolution of the Oedipus Complex." *Standard Ed.,* XIX, 173.

———(1924f) [1923]: "A Short Account of Psycho-Analysis." *Standard Ed.,* XIX, 191. (First published as "Psycho-Analysis: Exploring the Hidden Recesses of the Mind.")

———(1925a) [1924]: "A Note upon the 'Mystic Writing-Pad.' " *Standard Ed.,* XIX, 227.

———(1925d) [1924]: *An Autobiographical Study. Standard Ed.,* XX, 3. [Postscriptum of 1935.]

———(1925j): "Some Psychical Consequences of the Anatomical Distinction between the Sexes." *Standard Ed.,* XIX, 243.

———(1926d) [1925]: *Inhibitions, Symptoms and Anxiety. Standard Ed.,* XX, 77.

———(1926e): *The Question of Lay Analysis. Standard Ed.,* XX, 179.

———(1927c): *The Future of an Illusion. Standard Ed.,* XXI, 3.

———(1927–1939): see Freud/A. Zweig (1970).

———(1928b) [1927]: "Dostoevsky and Parricide," *Standard Ed.,* XXI, 175.

———(1930a) [1929]: *Civilization and Its Discontents. Standard Ed.,* XXI, 59.

———(1930e): Address delivered in the Goethe House at Frankfurt. *Standard Ed.,* XXI, 208.

———(1931b): "Female Sexuality." *Standard Ed.,* XXI, 223.

———(1931e): Letter to the Burgomaster of Příbor. *Standard Ed.,* XXI, 259.

———(1933a) [1932]: *New Introductory Lectures on Psycho-Analysis. Standard Ed.,* XXII, 3.

———(1933b) [1932]: *Why War? Standard Ed.,* XXII, 197.

———(1934b) [1930]: Preface to the Hebrew Translation of *Totem and Taboo. Standard Ed.,* XIII, xv.

———(1936a): Letter to Romain Rolland, "A Disturbance of Memory on the Acropolis." *Standard Ed.,* XXII, 239.

———(1937b): see Freud (1939a).

———(1937c): "Analysis Terminable and Interminable." *Standard Ed.,* XXIII, 211.

———(1937e): see Freud (1939a).

————(1939a) [1934–39]: *Moses and Monotheism. Standard Ed.,* XXIII, 3. (The first two essays were published in 1937.)

————(1940a) [1938]: *An Outline of Psycho-Analysis. Standard Ed.,* XXIII, 141.

————(1940b) [1938]: "Some Elementary Lessons in Psycho-Analysis." *Standard Ed.,* XXIII, 281.

————(1940d) [1892] with J. Breuer: "On the Theory of Hysterical Attacks." *Standard Ed.,* I, 151.

————(1940e) [1938]: "Splitting of the Ego in the Process of Defence," *Standard Ed.,* XXIII, 273.

————(1941a) [1892]: Letter to Josef Breuer. *Standard Ed.,* I, 147.

————(1941b) [1892]: "III," *Standard Ed.,* I, 149.

————(1941c) [1899]: "A Premonitory Dream Fulfilled," *Standard Ed.,* V, 623.

————(1941e) [1926]: Address to the Members of the *B'nai B'rith. Standard Ed.,* XX, 273.

————(1941f) [1938]: "Findings, Ideas, Problems." *Standard Ed.,* XXIII, 299.

————(1950a) [1887–1902]: *Aus den Anfängen der Psychoanalyse:* see (1954).

————(1954): *The Origins of Psycho-Analysis* (Letters to Wilhelm Fliess, Draft and Notes, 1887–1902), ed. Marie Bonaparte, Anna Freud, and Ernst Kris. London.

————(1955b) [1906–31]: "Zehn Briefe an Arthur Schnitzler." *Die Neue Rundschau,* 66, no. 1.

————(1956a) [1886]: "Report on My Studies in Paris and Berlin, on a Travelling Bursary Granted from the University Jubilee Fund, 1885–6." *Standard Ed.,* I, 3.

————(1960a): *Letters 1873–1939,* ed. Ernst and Lucie Freud. London.

————(1960b) [1885]: *Curriculum Vitae,* in Freud (1971b), 124–126.

————(1963a): see Freud/Pfister (1963).

————(1965a): see Freud/Abraham (1965).

————(1966a): see Freud/Andreas-Salomé (1966).

————(1966b) [1938]: Introduction to S. Freud and W. C. Bullitt: *Thomas Woodrow Wilson, Twenty-Eighth President of the United States: A Psychological Study.* Boston and London, 1967.

————(1968a): see Freud/Zweig (1970).

————(1969a) [1872–74]: "Sieben Briefe und zwei Postkarten an Emil Fluss." In Freud (1971b), 103–123. (First published in *Die Neue Rundschau,* 1969; also in *Psyche,* 24, 1970, 766–784.)

————(1971a): see Freud/Putnam (1971).

————(1971b): *Selbstdarstellung. Schriften zur Geschichte der Psychoanalyse.* Edited and introduced by Ilse Grubrich-Simitis. Frankfurt.

————, and Karl Abraham (1965): *Letters, 1907–1926,* ed. Hilda C. Abraham and Ernst L. Freud. London.

————, and Lou Andreas-Salomé (1972): *Letters* (1912–36), ed. E. Pfeiffer. London.

————, and Josef Breuer (1892): see Freud (1940d).

————, and Josef Breuer (1893): see Freud (1893a).

————, and Josef Breuer (1895): see Freud (1895d).

————, and Sandor Ferenczi (1969): "Briefwechsel aus dem Jahre 1908." *Psyche,* 23, 349–353.

————, and Georg Groddeck (1974): see Groddeck/Freud (1974) (Letters, 1917–1934).

————, and Carl Gustav Jung (1974): *Letters* (1906–1923), ed. William McGuire and Wolfgang Sauerländer. London.

————, and Oskar Pfister (1963): *Letters, 1909–1939,* ed. Ernst L. Freud and Heinrich Meng. London.

————, and James Jackson Putnam (1971): see Hale (1971 (Letters, 1909–1916).

————, and Theodor Reik (1976): see Reik (1976) (Letters, 1913–1938).

————and Arthur Schnitzler (1955): see Freud (1955b) (Letters, 1906–1931).

————and Arnold Zweig (1970): *Letters* (1927–1939), ed. Ernst L. Freud. London.

Freud-Gesellschaft (1975): see Sigmund-Freud-Gesellschaft (1975).

Friedlaender, Israel (1915): *The Jews of Russia and Poland. A Bird's-eye View of Their History and Culture.* New York and London.

Friedlaender, Michael (1890): *The Jewish Religion.*

Friedmann, Filip (1929): *Die galizischen Juden im Kampfe um ihre Gleichberechtigung, 1848–1868.* Frankfurt.

Fromm, Erich (1963): *Sigmund Freud's Mission. An Analysis of His Personality and Influence.* New York (first published 1959).

Gardiner, Muriel, ed. (1971): *The Wolf-Man.* New York.

Gartner, Lloyd P. (1960): *The Jewish Immigrant in England, 1870–1914.* London.

Gay, Peter (1976): "Sigmund Freud: A German and His Discontents." In Edmund Engelman: *Berggasse 19.* New York.

Gedo, John E., and Ernest Wolf (1970): "Die Ichthyosaurusbriefe." *Psyche,* 24, 785–797.

Gelber, N. M. (1924): *Aus zwei Jahrhunderten—Beiträge zur neueren Geschichte der Juden.* Vienna and Leipzig.

Gicklhorn, Josef, and Renée Gicklhorn (1960): *Sigmund Freuds akademische Laufbahn im Lichte der Dokumente.* Vienna and Innsbruck.

Gicklhorn, Renée (1965): "Eine Episode aus Sigmund Freuds Mittelschulzeit." *Unsere Heimat,* 36, 18–24.

————(1969): "The Freiberg Period of the Freud Family." *Journal of the History of Medicine,* 24, 37–43.

————(1976): *Sigmund Freud und der Onkeltraum. Dichtung und Wahrheit.* Vienna.

Gicklhornová, Renée, František Kalivoda, and Josef Sajner (1967): "Nové archívní nálezy o dětství Sigmunda Freuda v Příboře." *Čs psychiatrie,* 63, 131–136 (in Czech).

Gorion, Emanuel bin (1966): *Geschichten aus dem Talmud.* Frankfurt.

Graf, Max (1942): "Reminiscences of Professor Sigmund Freud." *Psychoanalytic Quarterly,* 2, 465–477.

Grinstein, Alexander (1968): *On Sigmund Freud's Dreams.* Detroit.

Groddeck, Georg, and Sigmund Freud (1974): *Briefe über das Es.* Munich. (Letters, 1917–1934).

Grubrich-Simitis, Ilse (1971): "Sigmund Freuds Lebensgeschichte und die Anfänge der Psychoanalyse." In Freud (1971b), 7–33.

————ed.: see Freud (1971b).

Grünwald, Max (1941): "Meetings with Sigmund Freud." *Haaretz,* 21 September 1941, 120–122 (in Hebrew).

Güdemann, Moritz (1968): *Quellenschriften zur Geschichte des Unterrichts und der Erziehung bei den deutschen Juden von den ältesten Zeiten bis auf Mendelssohn.* Amsterdam (reprint of the Berlin edition of 1891).

Haas, Theodor (1908): *Die Juden in Mähren. Darstellung der Rechtsgeschichte und Statistik unter besonderer Berücksichtigung des 19. Jahrhunderts.* Brünn (Brno).

Hale, Nathan G., ed. (1971): *James Jackson Putnam and Psychoanalysis. Letters between Putnam and Sigmund Freud, Ernest Jones, William James, Sandor Ferenczi and Morton Prince, 1877–1917.* Cambridge, Mass.

Hall, Calvin S., and Bill Domhoff (1968): "The Dreams of Freud and Jung." *Psychology Today.*

Heller, Judith Bernays (1956): "Freud's Mother and Father." *Commentary,* 21, 418–421.

Henle, Ilse (1977): "Die Tragödie der Labdakiden. Unentrinnbares Schicksal einer Alkoholikerfamilie?" *Praxis der Kinderpsychologie und Kinderpsychiatrie,* 26, 46–52.

Hilburg, Erwin K. J. (1968): "Der Chassidismus." *Germania Judaica,* 7, 1–32.

Jones, Ernest (1953, I): *The Life and Work of Sigmund Freud.* Vol. 1: *The Formative Years and the Great Discoveries, 1856–1900.* New York.
——(1955, II): *The Life and Work of Sigmund Freud.* Vol. 2: *The Years of Maturity, 1901–1919.* New York.
——(1957, III): *The Life and Work of Sigmund Freud.* Vol. 3: *The Last Phase, 1919–1939.* New York.
Jordan, František (1959): "Beginnings and Development of Capitalism, 1850–1914." In *Brno: From the Beginnings to Today.* Brünn (in Czech).
Jung, Carl Gustav (1912): see Jung (1952).
——(1952): *Symbole der Wandlung, Analyse des Vorspiels zur einer Schizophrenie.* Zurich (revised 4th edn. of *Wandlungen und Symbole der Libido,* 1912). (English translation: *Symbols of Transformation,* in *The Collected Works of C. G. Jung.* London.)
——(1962): *Erinnerungen, Träume, Gedanken,* recorded and edited by Aniela Jaffé. Zurich and Stuttgart. (English translation: *Memories, Dreams, Reflections.* New York, 1962.)
Kinder, Hermann, and Werner Hilgemann (1964): *dtv-Atlas zur Weltgeschichte.* Vol. 1: *Von der Anfängen bis zur Französischen Revolution.* Munich.
——(1966): *dtv-Atlas zur Weltgeschichte.* Vol. 2: *Von der Französischen Revolution bis zur Gegenwart.* Munich.
Kohn, Israel, ed. (1955): *Sefer Buczacz.* Tel-Aviv (in Hebrew).
Kobler, Franz (1962): "Die Mutter Sigmund Freuds." *Bulletin des Leo Baeck Instituts,* 5, 149–171.
Kolb, G. F. (1875): *Handbuch der vergleichenden Statistik der Völkerzustands- und Staatenkunde.* Leipzig.
Kris, Ernst (1950): "Introduction to the Letters to Wilhelm Fliess." In Freud (1950a), 3–47.
Krüll, Marianne (1977a): *Schizophrenie und Gesellschaft. Zum Menschenbild in Psychiatrie und Soziologie.* Munich.
——(1977b): "Adolf Hitler—Daniel Paul Schreber. Zwei familiendynamische Studien im Vergleich." *Familiendynamik,* 2, 229–242.
——(1978): "Freuds Absage an die Verführungstheorie im Lichte seiner eigenen Familiendynamik." *Familiendynamik,* 3, 102–129.
Kutter, Peter, ed. (1977): *Psychoanalyse im Wandel.* Frankfurt.
Landes, Ruth, and Mark Zborowski (1950): "Hypotheses Concerning the Eastern Jewish Family." *Psychiatry,* 13, 447–464.
Landmann, Salcia, ed. (1965): *Jüdische Anekdoten und Sprichwörter.* Munich.
Langer, Georg (1959): *Neun Tore. Das Geheimnis der Chassidim,* Munich and Planegg (first published in Czech).
Lehmann, Adolf (since 1859): *Allgemeiner Wohnungs-Anzeiger nebst Gewerbe-Adressbuch der kk. Reichshaupt- und Residenzstadt Wien.* Vienna. (Published annually since 1859, with a few exceptions.)
Lehmann, Herbert (1966): "Two Dreams and a Childhood Memory of Freud." *Journal of the American Psychoanalytical Association,* 13, 388–405.
Loewenberg, Peter (1970): "A Hidden Zionist Theme in Freud's 'My Son, the Myops . . .' Dream." *Journal of the History of Ideas,* 31, 129–132.
Loewenstein, R.M. et. al. eds.: (1966) Psychoanalysis. A General Psychology, New York.
——(1971): " 'Sigmund Freud as a Jew': A Study in Ambivalence and Courage." *Journal of the History of the Behavioral Sciences,* 7, 363–369.
Lorenzer, Alfred (1971): "Symbol, Interaktion und Praxis." In Lorenzer, *et al.: Psychoanalyse als Sozialwissenschaft.* Frankfurt, 9–59.
——(1972): *Kritik des Psychoanalytischen Symbolbegriffs.* Frankfurt.
——(1973a): *Über den Gegenstand der Psychoanalyse. Oder: Sprache und Interaktion.* Frankfurt.

————(1973b): *Sprachzerstörung und Rekonstruktion. Vorarbeiten zu einer Metatheorie der Psychoanalyse.* Frankfurt (first publication 1970).

————(1973c): *Zur Begründung einer materialistischen Sozialisationstheorie.* Frankfurt (first publication 1972).

————(1976): *Die Wahrheit der psychoanalytischen Erkenntnis. Ein historisch-materialistischer Entwurf.* Frankfurt (first publication 1974).

————(1977): *Sprachspiel und Interaktionsformen. Vorträge und Aufsätze zu Psychoanalyse, Sprache und Praxis.* Frankfurt.

————, Helmut Dahmer, Klaus Horn, Karola Brede, *et al.* (1971): *Psychoanalyse als Sozialwissenschaft.* Frankfurt.

————Ludwig, Emil (1956): *Erinnerungen an Sigmund Freud.* Bern.

————(1973): *Doctor Freud.* New York (first publication 1947).

Lynkeus (Josef Popper-Lynkeus) (1900): *Phantasieen eines Realisten.* Dresden and Leipzig.

MacIntyre, Alasdair C. (1958): *The Unconscious. A Conceptual Analysis.* London.

Mahler, Raphael (1942): *Haskole un khsides in galitsie in der ershter helft 19tn jorhundert.* New York (in Yiddish).

Maier, Johann (1973): *Das Judentum von der biblischen Zeit bis zur Moderne.* Munich.

Majer Balaban (1914): see Balaban.

Mannoni, Octave (1971): *Sigmund Freud in Selbstzeugnissen und Bilddokumenten.* Reinbek (first publication as *Freud par lui-même,* Paris, n.d.).

Marcuse, Ludwig (1964): *Sigmund Freud. Sein Bild vom Menschen.* Munich.

Mayer, Sigmund (1911): *Ein jüdischer Kaufmann 1831 bis 1911. Lebenserinnerungen.* Leipzig.

Maylan, Charles E. (1929): *Freuds tragischer Komplex. Eine Analyse der Psychanalyse.* Munich.

Meerwein, F. (1965): *Psychiatrie und Psychoanalyse in der psychiatrischen Klinik* (including *Freud, der Moses des Michelangelo und die "statistische" Psychiatrie*). Basel and New York.

Meyer-Palmedo, Ingeborg, ed. (1975): *Sigmund Freud-Konkordanz und -Gesamtbibliographie.* Frankfurt.

Michael, Moshe (1971): "The Jewish Attitude of Freud." Korot, 5, 484–498 and 67–71.

Mitscherlich, Alexander (1969): "Über mögliche Missverständnisse bei der Lekture der Werke Sigmund Freuds." In *Studienausgabe der Werke Sigmund Freuds.* Vol. 1, 19–25.

Niederland, William G. (1959): "The 'Miracled-up' World of Schreber's Childhood." *The Psychoanalytic Study of the Child,* 14.

Nunberg, Herman, and Ernst Federn, eds. (1962): *Minutes of the Vienna Psychoanalytic Society,* Vol. 1: *1906–1908.* New York.

————(1967) *Minutes of the Vienna Psychoanalytic Society,* Vol.2: *1908–1910.* New York.

Philippson, Ludwig, ed. (1858–59): *Die Israelitische Bibel. Enthaltend: Den heiligen Urtext, die deutsche Übertragung, die allgemeine ausführliche Erläuterung mit mehr als 500 englischen Holzschnitten.* 2nd corrected ed., 3 vols., Leipzig (1st ed, 4 vols., 1838–54).

Politzer, Heinz (1974): "Freud als Deuter seiner eigenen Träume." In Jürgen vom Scheidt, ed.: *Der unbekannte Freud.* Munich, 56–71 (first publication in *Merkur,* 24, 1970, 34–48).

Popper-Lynkeus, Josef (1900): see Lynkeus.

Pribram A. F., ed. (1918): *Urkunden und Akten zur Geschichte der Juden in Wien. Allgemeiner Teil 1526–1847* (1849), Vols. 1 and 2. Vienna and Leipzig. (Series: Quellen und Forschungen zur Geschichte der Juden in Deutsch-Österreich. Edited by the Historical Commission of the Israelitic Congregation in Vienna.)

Puner, Helen Walker (1949): *Freud, His Life and His Mind. A Biography.* London.

Rank, Otto (1922): *Der Mythus von der Geburt des Helden.* Leipzig and Vienna (2nd revised edn; first published 1908).

———(1926): *Das Inzest-Motiv in Dichtung und Sage, Grundzüge einer Psychologie des dichterischen Schaffens.* Leipzig and Vienna (2nd revised edn.; first publication 1912).

Reik, Theodor (1956): The search within. *The Inner Experience of a Psychoanalyst.* New York. (With letters by Sigmund Freud from the years 1913–1938.)

Richter, Horst-Eberhard (1963): *Eltern, Kind und Neurose. Psychoanalyse der kindlichen Rolle.* Stuttgart.

———(1970): *Patient Familie. Entstehung, Struktur und Therapie von Konflikten in Ehe und Familie.* Reinbek.

———, and Dieter Beckmann (1969): *Herzneurose.* Stuttgart.

———, Hans Strotzka, and Jürg Willi, eds. (1976): *Familie und seseelische Krankheit. Eine neue Perspektive der Psychologischen Medizin und der Sozialtherapie.* Reinbek.

Ricoeur, Paul (1974): *Die Interpretation. Ein Versuch über Freud.* Frankfurt (first publication as *De l'interprétation. Essai sur Freud.* Paris, 1965).

Riesman, David (1954): *Individualism Reconsidered.* Chicago.

Riviere, Joan (1959): "A Character Trait of Freud's." In John D. Sutherland, ed.: *Psychoanalysis and Contemporary Thought.* New York, 145–149.

Roazen, Paul (1968): *Freud: Political and Social Thought.* New York.

———(1969): *Brother Animal. The Story of Freud and Tausk.* New York.

———(1975): *Freud and His Followers.* New York.

Roback, A. A. (1957): *Freudiana,* including unpublished letters from Freud, *et al.* Cambridge, Mass.

Robert, Marthe (1975): *Sigmund Freud zwischen Moses und Ödipus. Die jüdischen Wurzeln der Psychoanalyse.* Munich (first publication as *D'Oedipe à Moise. Freud et a l conscience juive.* Paris, 1974).

Rosenfeld, Eva M. (1956): "Dream and Vision. Some Remarks on Freud's Egyptian Bird Dream." *International Journal of Psycho-Analysis,* 37, 97–105.

Rosenkötter, Lutz (1974): "Freud and Brücke. Neue Aspekte des Traumes 'Non vixit.' " In Jürgen vom Scheidt, ed: *Der unbekannte Freud.* Munich, 171–178 (first publication in *Psyche,* 25, 1971, 948–955).

Rosenthal, Celia Stopnicka

———(1953): "Social Stratification of the Jewish Community in a Small Polish Town." *American Journal of Sociology,* 50, 1–10.

———(1954): "Deviation and Social Change in the Jewish Community of a Small Polish Town." *American Journal of Sociology,* 60, 177–181.

Roskies, Diane, and David G. (1975): *The Shtetl Book.* New York.

Rutschky, Katharina, ed. (1977): *Schwarze Pädagogik. Quellen zur Naturgeschichte der bürgerlichen Erziehung.* Frankfurt, Berlin, and Vienna.

Rubinstein, Aryeh, ed. (1975): *Hasidism.* Jerusalem.

Rudy, Zvi (1965): *Soziologie des jüdischen Volkes.* Reinbek.

Ruppin, Arthur (1911): *Die Juden der Gegenwart. Eine sozialwissenschaftliche Studie.* Cologne and Leipzig (2nd revised edn; first publication 1904).

Sachs, Hanns (1945): *Freud, Master and Friend.* London.

Sajner, Josef (1968): "Sigmund Freuds Beziehungen zu seinem Geburtsort Freiberg (Příbor) und zu Mähren." *Clio Medica,* 3, 167–180.

———(1981): "Drei do kumentarische Beiträge zur Sigmund Freud-Biographik aus Böhmen und Mähren." *Jahrbuch der Psychoanalyse,* 13, 143–152, Stuttgart.

Salber, Wilhelm (1973): *Entwicklungen der Psychologie Sigmund Freuds.* 3 vols., Bonn.

Schachter, M. (1959): "Psychanalyse et interprétations de rêves dans le Talmud." *Revue d'histoire et de la médecine hébraïque,* 12, 57–60.

Schatzman, Morton (1971): "Paranoia or Persecution: The Case of Schreber." *Family Process,* 10, 177–207.

———(1973): *Soul Murder. Persecution in the Family*. London.

———(1976): Book review of W. G. Niederland's *The Schreber Case*. In *Familien-dynamik*, I, 172–176.

Scheffel, Joseph Victor von (1916): *Collected Works*, Vols. 4–6. Leipzig: Johannes Franke.

Scheidt, Jürgen vom (1973): "Sigmund Freud und das Kokain." *Psych*, 27, 385–430.

———, ed. (1974): *Der unbekannte Freud. Neue Interpretationen seiner Träume durch E. H. Erikson, A. Grinstein, H. Politzer, L. Rosenkötter, M. Schur, et al.* Munich.

Scholem, Gershom (1961): *Major Trends in Jewish Mysticism*. Jerusalem.

———(1969): *On the Kabbalah and Its Symbolism*. New York.

Schorske, Carl E. (1973): "Politics and Patricide in Freud's Interpretation of Dreams." *American Historical Review*, 78, 328–347.

Schreber, Daniel Paul (1973): *Denkwürdigkeiten eines Nervenkranken*. Edited and introduced by Samuel M. Weber. Frankfurt, Berlin, and Vienna (first publication 1903).

Schülein, Johann August (1975): *Das Gesellschaftsbild der Freudschen Theorie*. Frankfurt and New York.

Schur, Max (1966): "Some Additional 'Day Residues' of the 'Specimen Dream of Psychoanalysis.' " In R. M. Loewenstein, *et. al.*, eds.: *Psychoanalysis. A General Psychology*. New York.

———(1972): *Freud, Living and Dying*. New York.

Schwab, Gustav (1975): *Sagen des klassischen Altertums*. 3 vols., Frankfurt. (Reprint of the 1932 edn. First publication 1838–40.)

Sigmund-Freud-Gesellschaft, ed. (1975): *Sigmund Freud-Haus Katalog*. Vienna.

Simon, Ernst (1957): "Sigmund Freud, the Jew." In *Leo Baeck Institute Year Book II*, edited by Robert Weltsch. London.

Simon, I. (1959):"La biographie de Sigmund Freud." *Revue d'histoire et de la médecine hébraïque*, 12, 7–26.

Slipp, Samuel (1978): "Interpersonelle Faktoren der Hysterie: Freuds Verführungs-theorie und der Fall Dora." *Familiendynamik*, 3, 130–147.

Smith, W. Robertson (1956): *The Religion of the Semites*. New York (first publication 1889).

Somogyi, Tamar (1982): *Die Schejnen und die Prosten. Untersuchungen zum Schönheits-ideal der Ostjuden in Bezug auf Körper und Kleidung unter besonderer Berücksichtigung des Chassidismus*. Berlin.

Stadtmüller, Georg (1963): *Geschichtliche Ostkunde*. Vol. I: *Die Zeit bis zum Jahre 1914*, 2nd, expanded edn. Munich and Stuttgart (first publication ca. 1955).

Stănescu, Heinz (1965): "Unbekannte Briefe des jungen Sigmund Freud an einen rumänischen Freund." *Neue Literatur. Zeitschrift des Schriftstellerverbandes der RVR*, 123–177.

Stekel, Wilhelm (1908): see Stekel (1921a).

———(1909): *Dichtung und Neurose, Bausteine zur Psychologie des Künstlers und des Kunstwerks*. Wiesbaden.

———(1921a): *Nervöse Angstzustände und ihre Behandlung*. 3rd revised edn of Vol. 1 of the 10-volume series *Störungen des Trieb- und Affektlebens* (first publication 1908 with a Foreword by Sigmund Freud).

———(1921b): *Onanie und Homosexualität. Die homosexuelle Neurose*. 2nd revised edn. of Vol. 2 of the 10-volume series *Störungen des Trieb- und Affektlebens*.

———(1931–32): "Die Technik der Psychoanalyse." In *Psychoanalytische Praxis. Vier-teljahresschrift für die aktive Methode der Psychoanalyse*, 1 and 2.

———(1938): *Die Technik der analytischen Psychotherapie. Eine zusammenfassende Darstellung auf Grund dreissigjähriger Erfahrung*. Bern.

———(1950): *The Autobiography of Wilhelm Stekel. The Life Story of a Pioneer*

Psychoanalyst. Edited by Emil A. Gutheil with an Introduction by Hilda Stekel. New York.

———(1972): *Wege zum Ich. Psychologische Orientierungshilfe im Alltag.* Edited by Friedrich Scheidt. Munich.

Stern, Paul J. (1976): *C. G. Jung, The Haunted Prophet.* New York.

Stierlin, Helm (1971): *Das Tun des Einen ist das Tun des Anderen. Versuch einer Dynamik menschlicher Beziehungen.* Frankfurt.

———(1974): *Separating Parents and Adolescents.* New York.

———(1976a: *Adolf Hitler—A Family Perspective.* New York. (First publication 1975 as *Adolf Hitler, Familienperspektiven.* Frankfurt.)

———(1976b): "The Dynamics of Owning and Disowning: Psychoanalytic and Family Perspectives." *Family Process,* 15. (First publication 1975 as "Innerer Besitz und Zwang zur Wahrheit." *Ehe,* 12, 132–147.)

———(1978): *Delegation und Familie. Beiträge zum Heidelberger familiendynamischen Konzept.* Frankfurt.

———(1979): *Psychoanalysis and Family Therapy.* New York. (First publication 1975 as *Von der Psychoanalyse zur Familientherapie.* Stuttgart.)

Strachey, James (1969): "Sigmund Freud. Eine Skizze seines Lebens und Denkens." *Sigmund Freud Studienausgabe,* I, Frankfurt, 7–18.

Sutherland, John D., ed. (1959): *Psychoanalysis and Contemporary Thought.* New York.

Swales, Peter J. (1982a): "Freud, Minna Bernays and the Conquest of Rome." *New American Review,* I.

———(1982b): *Freud, Johann Weier, and the Status of Seduction; the Role of the Witch in the Conception of Fantasy.* New York.

Thon, Jakob (1908): *Die Juden in Österreich.* Edited by the Bureau für Statistik der Juden, Berlin.

Trachtenberg, Joshua (1939): *Jewish Magic and Superstition. A Study in Folk Religion.* New York.

Velikovsky, Immanuel (1941): "The Dreams Freud Dreamed." *Psychoanalytic Review,* 30, 487–511.

Vogel, Paul (1953/54): "Eine erste, unbekannt gebliebene Darstellung der Hysterie von Sigmund Freud." *Psyche,* 7, 481–500.

Waelder, Robert (1963): *Die Grundlagen der Psychoanalyse.* Bern and Stuttgart.

Wallace, Edwin R., IV (1977): "The Psychodynamic Determinants of *Moses and Monotheism.*" *Psychiatry,* 40, 79–87.

———(1978): "Freud's Father Conflict: The History of a Dynamic." *Psychiatry,* 41, 33–56.

Wehler, Hans-Ulrich, ed. (1972): *Soziologie und Psychoanalyse.* Stuttgart and Berlin.

Wilhelm, Kurt, ed. (n.d.): *Jüdischer Glaube. Eine Auswahl aus zwei Jahrtausenden.* Birsfelden-Basel.

Williams, Bill (1976): *The Making of Manchester Jewry, 1740–1875.* Manchester and New York.

Wittels, Fritz (1924): *Sigmund Freud. Der Mann, die Lehre, die Schule.* Leipzig, Vienna, and Zurich.

———(1931): *Freud and His Time. The Influence of the Master Psychologist on the Emotional Problems in Our Lives.* New York.

Wolf, G., ed. (1880): *Die alten Statuten der jüdischen Gemeinden in Mähren sammt den nachfolgenden Synodalbeschlüssen.* Vienna.

Zborowski, Mark (1966): "The Place of Book-Learning in Traditional Jewish Culture." In M. Mead and M. Wolfenstein, eds.: *Childhood in Contemporary Cultures.* Chicago and London (first publication 1955).

———, and Elizabeth Herzog (1952): *Life Is with People. The Jewish Little-Town of Eastern Europe.* New York.

Index

Abraham, Karl, 21, 182
actual neuroses, sexual theory of, 35, 38
and rejection of seduction theory, 14–20,
57
Adler, Alfred, 189
Adler, H. G., 70
Aeneid (Virgil), 67
agoraphobia, 48
amentia, acute hallucinatory, 39
seduction theory of, 32
Anna O., 1, 6–7, 26, 249n
anti-Semitism:
in Galicia, 76
in Moravia, 91–92, 143–44, 147
anxiety, types of, 34
anxiety neurosis, 11, 38
Anzieu, Didier, 21
Ashkenazim, 72

Bakan, David, 74, 77, 187
Balaban, Majer, 85
Barta, Johannes, 160
Bathsheba, 127
Beckmann, Dieter, 14, 16, 122,
248n
Berr of Bolekhov, 86
Bergmann, Martin S., 147
Bernays, Anna, 149, 156, 160, 167
Bernays, Martha, 215
birth of, 214, 248n
Freud engaged to, 5, 10, 176 216
marries Freud, 7
moves to Vienna, 5–6
see also Freud, Martha
Bernays, Minna:
and Freud, 248–49n
view of theory of child sexuality, 46
Bernfeld, Siegfried, 26, 66, 131
Bernfeld, Suzanne, 167
Besht, 74
Blond, Szlomo, 89
Borgia, Lucrezia, 114

Breuer, Josef, 33
catharsis, 6–7
end of Freud's friendship with, 8
and Freud's heart troubles, 15–16
"On the Psychical Mechanism of
Hysterical Phenomena: Preliminary
Communication" (with Freud), 1,
24–25
specific hypnoid state theory of hysteria,
25
Studies on Hysteria (with Freud), 26
treatment of Anna O., 1, 6–7, 215,
249n
Breuer, Mathilde, 21
Brody, Galicia, 77
Brücke, Ernest, 5, 26

cardiac neurosis, 13–14
castration, fear of, 110–11
catharsis and cathartic method, 6–7, 24
Charcot, Jean-Martin, 1, 6
Chmielnicki, Bogdan, 72, 73
Christianity, 205–8
circumcision, and castration, 110–11
cocaine, anaesthetic effects of, 113
counterfeit money affair, 164–66
contraceptive practices, and neurasthenia, 12

David (King), 126–27
defense, neuroses of:
and actual neuroses, 35
and repression, 26–27
seduction theory of, 31–40
see also seduction theory
defense mechanisms, 25
see also repression
Devereux, George, 62
Dora, 182
dreams and dream interpretation, 64–68
Bismark's, 188
castration, 111–12
and rejection of seduction theory, 57

dreams and dream (*continued*)
    as wish fulfillment, 49
    see also Interpretation of Dreams, The

Eckstein, Emma, 21–24, 134
Ego, 183
Elizabeth von R., 217
Elizer, Israel ben, 74
Emma episode, 21–24, 29, 134
    and Semitic sex cult, 46
Emmy von N., 7, 216
Encyclopaedia Judaica, 86
Erickson, Erik H., 8
exorcism, medieval theories of, 45

family life, in *shtetl* 82–84
fantasies and fantasy theory, 57
    origin of fantasies, 46–48
    prostitution fantasy, 48–49
    sexual, 171
female sexuality, 183
Ferenozi, 182
Fliess, Wilhelm, 5, 8–10, 248n, 249n
    friendship with Freud, 10, 130
    meeting with Freud in Nuremberg, 46
    nasal operation for Emma Eckstein,
        21–22
    not interested in Freud's self-analysis, 64
    rejects seduction theory, 32
    visit from Freud in Berlin, 58
Fluss, Emil, 138, 160, 169, 170, 172
    letters, 169
Fluss, Gisella, 170
Fluss, Ignaz, 143
Fluss family, 104, 138, 215
fragmentation, process of, 48
Frank, Jacob, 73–74
Frankel, Bloome, 173
Frankism, 73–74
Frau P., 35, 249n
Freiberg, Moravia, 92–95, 103–8
    in castration dream, 111
    departure of Freud family from, 140–47
Freud, Abae (uncle), 89–90, 104, 139
Freud, Adolfine (sister), 104, 134 153, 215
Freud, Alexander, (brother), 40, 53, 166–67,
    215
Freud, Amalie (mother), 71, 104, 115–19,
    151, 153, 154, 215
    and birth of Alexander Freud, 166–67
    birthplace of, 77
    character of, 116–17
    confirms memory of nursemaid, 59–60
    departs Frieberg, 140
    marries Jacob Freud, 97–99, 214
    and Philipp Freud, 60, 116, 124–28
    relatives of, 139–40
    tuberculosis, 148
Freud, Anna (sister), 104, 110, 132, 134–35,
    214
    see also Bernays, Anna

Freud, Anna (daughter), 17, 31, 46, 219,
    247n, 248n, 260n
    observes Jacob Freud's taboo, 56
Freud, Bertha (niece), 104, 132, 214
Freud, Bloome (sister-in-law), 173
Freud, Emanuel (half-brother), 15, 90, 96,
    97, 98, 104, 108, 110, 122–23, 145,
    151, 167, 213, 214, 258n
    connection with counterfeiting affair, 165,
        166
    emigrates to England, 145–46, 214
    in England, 173–76
Freud, Ernest (son), 247n
Freud, Jacob (father), 3, 71, 138, 151, *152,*
    249n
    autodidactic, 160
    birth of, 88–89, 213
    birthplace of, 85–88, 90
    character and disposition, 109–10
    children, 91
    death of, 4, 9, 40–43, 220
    departs Freiberg, 143–45, 214
    father's death, 99
    feelings of guilt, 99, 100–101
    financial and physical condition on
        marriage to Amalie Nathansohn,
        98–99
    in Freiberg, 92–95, 104, 108
    and Freud's education in Jewish tradition,
        160–61
    grandparents, 89, 90
    Judaic tradition, 74–78, 90
    mandate to Freud, 178–80
    marriage to Amalie Nathansohn, 97–99,
        214
    marriage to Rebekka, 96–97, 101, 135,
        214
    marriage to Sally Kanner, 90–91, 96, 213
    present of Bible to Freud, 160–61
    relationship with Freud, 108–14
    travels with grandfather, 91–95, 213–14
    taboo, 43, 63, 68, 70, 100–101, 155, 178
    in Vienna, 147–51, 154
Freud, Jean Martin (son), 247n
Freud, John (nephew), 104, 109, 111, 123,
    124, 126, 128–130, 156, 214
    and Pauline Freud, 131–33, 214
Freud, Josef (uncle), 90, 104, 139, 213
    counterfeiting affair, 164–66 215
Freud, Juluis (brother), 104, 116, 135,
    214
Freud, Maria (aunt), 104
Freud, Maria (sister), 214
Freud, Maria (sister-in-law), 96, 115, 123,
    151, 173, 214
Freud, Martha (wife):
    menopause, 18
    in Orvieto, 53, 252n
    relationship with Freud, 18–19, 181–82
    and "Screen Memories," 65
    view of theory of child sexuality, 46

Freud, Martin (son), 109, 110, 116, 117, 151,
    175–76
  book about Freud, 181
Freud, Mathilde (daughter), 216, 247n
  Freud's dream about, 51
Freud, Matilda (niece), 173, 215
Freud, Oliver (son), 216, 247n
Freud, Pauline (niece), 104, 111, 123, 124,
    126, 129, 130–34, 135, 142, 156,
    214
Freud, Pauline (niece), 173
Freud, Pauline (sister), 215
Freud, Peppi (grandmother), 89, 97, 104,
    138, 139
Freud, Philipp (half-brother), 91, 96, 98,
    104, 108, 110, 122, 123, 124–28,
    144–45 151, 166–67, 213, 258n
  and Amalie Freud, 60, 116, 124–28
  catches Resi Wittek stealing, 121, 124,
    214, 259n
  connection with counterfeiting affair, 165,
    166
  emigrates to England, 145–46, 214
  in England, 173–78
Freud, Rebekka (father's second wife),
    96–97, 104, 135–37, 214
Freud, Rebekka (aunt), 104, 255n
Freud, Rosa (sister), 15, 128, 134, 151, 153,
    214
Freud, Sally (father's first wife), 90–91, 96,
    104, 123, 138–39
Freud, Sam (nephew) 214
Freud, Schlomo (grandfather), 89, 90, 95, 97,
    104, 138, 139, 179
  death of, 99, 214
Freud, Selig (relative), 148
Freud, Sigmund, *3, 152, 153, 209, 210*
  PERSONAL AND PROFESSIONAL
    LIFE
    alienates colleagues, 7–8, 249n
    ambitiousness of, 44, 154
    application for associate professorship
      denied, 49
    appointed *Privatdozent,* 5, 216
    birth of, 95, 103
    and birth of Anna Freud, 248n
    and birth of Sophie Freud, 17
    and Breuer, 8, 217, 218
    at Brücke's Physiological Institute, 5,
      215
    cancer, 194
    cardiac symptoms, 15–17, 21, 122, 217,
      218, 219, 252n
    children of, 7, 181, 247n
    considers study of his children, 46
    correspondence with Martha Bernays, 6
    critical reception of essay on
      neurasthenia and anxiety neurosis,
      20
    dates of crisis, 5
    death fantasies, 9, 20

and death of Jacob Freud, 4, 40–43, 220
departs Freiberg with family, 140–48
desire to explore father's past, 44
Dora case, 182
education in Jewish tradition, 156,
    160–63
and Emanuel Freud, 123, 124
Emma episode, 21–24, 29, 31, 134, 177,
    218, 249n, 251n, 256n
emotional ambivalence of, 187–88
engaged to Martha Bernays, 10, 176,
    216
examines evidence of seduction in
    paternal family, 46
father's taboo as mandate, 178–80, 181,
    183
  see also taboo, Jacob's
and Fliess, 8, 10, 23–24, 130
followers of, 70, 182, 189–94
and Frankism, 74
Frau P. case, 35, 249n
and Gisela Fluss, 170–71, 177
at Gymnasium, 168–69, 215
icy reception for "The Aetiology of
    Hysteria," 36
"intellectual paralysis," 53–54, 220,
    247–48n
interest in archeology, 44
interest in Bible, 161–62
interpretation of Michelangelo's Moses,
    184–87
interprets his own symptoms as hysteria,
    53
and John Freud, 128–30
and Jung, 190–93
last hours of, 211, 232
lectures before Viennese College of
    Physicians, 30–31
"longing" for philosophical knowledge,
    40, 220
marries Martha Bernays, 7, 216
meeting with Fliess in Nuremberg, 46,
    220
"militaristic" phase, 167
as Moses, 194–208
  see also Moses, Biblical
named for grandfather, 99, 108,
    256n
number mysticism, 9–10
nursemaid, 52, 58–60, 116, 118
  see also Wittek, Resi
as patriarch, 188–94
and Pauline Freud, 130–34
and Philipp Freud, 124–28
railway phobia, 20, 63, 216
and Rebekka Freud, 135–37
relationship with father, 4, 50, 54,
    108–14, 147, 155–56, 178–80,
    220–21
relationship with Martha Freud, 18–19,
    181–82

Freud (*continued*)
    relationship with mother, 115–19
    relevance of theories today, 211–12
    and Rome, 120, 146
    Schreber case, 182
    secrecy of, 4
    self-analysis, 50–54, 58, 63, 68–69,
        220–21
    smoking, 15, 16, 17, 216, 249n
    travels to Orvieto, 53–54
    tripartition of mother figure, 115–16,
        123, 151, 256n
    Vienna childhood, 147–51, 152, 154–56
    visits half–brothers in England, 173–76,
        215
    visits Charcot, 1
    visits Fliess, 58, 217
    visits Freiberg, 169–72, 215
    "Wolf Man" case, 182
DREAMS
    "botanical monograph," 156
    castration, 111–12, 141–42
    Count Thun, 109, 112–13, 253n
    farewell dream, 146
    of incest, 156
    Irma dream, 21–24, 218
    early childhood, 58
    Jacob Freud's funeral, 41–43, 220
    nursemaid, 58–59, 122, 124, 256–57n
    "people with bird's beaks," 162, 166
    relationship between Amalie and Philipp
        Freud, 124–28
    staircase dream, 51–52, 122, 252n
    Uncle Josef, 164–66
    urination scenes in, 112–14
PUBLICATIONS, DRAFTS, AND
        LECTURES
    "The Aetiology of Hysteria," 36, 220
    "The Aetiology of Neuroses," 217
    "Aphasia," 216
    Autobiographical Study, 70, 89, 118–19,
        161, 230
    "Brain," 216
    "A Case of Successful Treatment by
        Hypnotism," 217
    "Charcot," 217
    " 'Civilized' Sexual Morality and
        Modern Nervous Illness," 18
    "Coca," 216
    *Collection of Shorter Writings on the
        Theory of Neuroses,* 66
    draft of theory of origins of anxiety,
        17–18
    Drekkologikal reports, 64
    "Female Sexuality," 183
    "Further Remarks on the
        Neuro-Psychoses of Defence," 32,
        34, 219
    "L'héréité et l'étilogique des névroses,"
        32–33

    "How Anxiety Originates," 218
    "Hysteria," 216
    "Hysteroepilepsy," 216
    "Infantile Paralysis," 216
    The Interpretation of Dreams: see *The
        Interpretation of Dreams*
    Melancholia, 218
    Migraine, 218
    Moses and Monotheism, 101, 122, 163,
        194–208, 251n
      see also *Moses and Monotheism*
    "The Moses of Michelangelo," 183,
        184–87
    "The Neuropsychoses of Defence," 26,
        217
    "Obsessions and Phobias," 20
    "On Aphasia," 217
    "On the Grounds for Detaching a
        Particular Syndrome from
        Neurasthenia under the description
        'Anxiety Neurosis,' " 17
    "On the Psychical Mechanism of
        Hysterical Phenomena: Preliminary
        Communication" (with Breuer), 1,
        24–25, 218
    Outline of Psychoanalysis, 194
    papers on anatomy of brain, 5
    "Papers on Metapsychology," 182
    Paranoia, 218
    "Physical (or Mental) Treatment,"
        217
    "Project for a Scientific Psychology,"
        10, 27–30, 182, 218
    The Psychology of Everyday Life, 54
    The Psychopathology of Everyday Life,
        10, 229
    "Quelques considerations pour une
        étude comparative des paralyses
        motrices organiques et hysteriques,"
        216
    "Report on My Studies in Paris and
        Berlin," 6, 7
    "Screen Memories," 23, 65–66, 115,
        131, 132, 134, 140–41, 142, 156,
        169, 170, 171, 252n
    Studies on Hysteria (with Breuer), 26
    "The Theme of the Three Fates," 115
    "Three Essays on the Theory of
        Sexuality," 141–42, 229
    Totem and Taboo, 191, 193, 203
    *Zur Kenntriss der cerebralen Diplegien
        des Kindesalters,* 217
SEDUCTION AND
        PSYCHOANALYTIC THEORIES
    advocates Charcot's theory of hysteria,
        7
    analysis of Emma, and seduction theory,
        32
    death and sexuality as two great themes,
        54

development of seduction theory, 24–31
discovery of Oedipus theory, 2
  see also Oedipus theory
on masturbation, see masturbation
mother confirms seduction theory, 59
reductionism, 26, 27
renunciation of seduction, theory, 1–2,
  54–58, 220
sexual theory of actual neuroses, 10–14
struggles to save seduction theory,
  43–49
symptoms of actual neuroses, 20
writes retraction letter, 54–56
Freud, Solomon (nephew), 173
Freud, Sophie (daughter), 17, 217 247n
Freud family tree, 89
Freud–Fliess correspondence, 5, 8, 247n
calls *The Interpretation of Dreams* "my
  Egyptian dream book," 161
"Christmas fairy tale" outline of seduction
  theory, 31–32
on death of Freud's father, 40, 41
"drekkological" statements, 112
Emma incident, 22–24
on explanation of defense, 27, 30
first hint of Oedipus theory in, 50
Fliess's letters destroyed, 5
Freud complains of heart trouble, 15,
  16
on John Freud, 128
on leaving Freiberg, 140
"libido towards matrem," 128
no overt reference to Freud's sexual
  problems in, 18
nursemaid dream, 52, 59–60
on Orvieto visit, 53
"Project for a Scientific Psychology," 10
on rejection of Freud for associate
  professorship, 49
retraction letter, 54–56
Semitic sex cult mentioned, 45–46
sexual theory of actual neuroses, 1–12, 13
time frame of seduction, 37
Friedman, Filip, 77

Galicia, 72, 85
Gattl, Dr., 53
General Hospital of Vienna, 5
Gicklhorn, Renée, 71, 90, 92, 96, 97, 98,
  108, 119, 144, 149, 151, 164–66,
  168
Goethe, Johann Wolfgang von, 64, 118, 135
Graf, Cecelia, 117
Graf, Rosa, 117
  see also Freud, Rosa
Grinstein, Alexander, 65, 114, 120, 122, 125,
  126, 127, 135, 146, 156
Grubrich-Simitis, Ilse, 169
Grunwald, Max, 151
guilt, theory of hereditary, 204–5

Haas, Theodor, 95
Hamlet (Shakespeare), 63, 127
Hammerschlag, Samuel, 21
Hammerschlag-Lichtheim, Ann, 21, 31
Hasidism, 74–76, 86, 90
Haskalah, 76, 77, 78, 86, 87, 90, 161,
  199
heart symptoms, neurotic, 11, 13–14,
  38
Hebrew, Freud's ignorance of, 161
Heller, Judith Bernays, 110, 116, 117,
  160
Helmholtz, 26, 27
heredity, and neurotic symptoms, 57, 252n
  theory of acquired characters, 204–5
Herzl, Theodor, 147
Herzog, Elizabeth, 78
Hofmann, Peppi, 89, 97, 104, 213
Hofmann, Siskind, 89, 90, 91–95, 104, 139,
  199, 213
"holiness," 50–51, 251n
Homberg, Naphtali Herz, 76, 86
homosexuality, 13, 37, 130
Hungary, Jews in, 75
hypnosis, 6, 7
hysteria, 39
  Charcot's treatment for, 6
  multigenerational theory of, 44
  as "neurosis of defence," 24–25
  seduction theory of, 32, 33
  sexual etiology of, 25–26, 39
  symptoms of, 24, 25, 39

Id, 183
incest, 50–51
  see also seduction theory
infantile sexuality, 2, 121
International Psychoanalytical Association,
  189, 191
Interpretation of Dreams, The (Freud),
  64–68, 70, 195
  allusion to Rebekka Freud in, 136
  and Amalie Freud, 115, 118
  Bismark's dream, 187–88
  "botanical monograph" dream," 65–66
  censored "big dream," 65
  as "Egyptian dream book," 161
  as end of Freud's crisis, 5
  epigraph, 67
  farewell dream in, 146
  inaccessibility of Rome, 120
  as interpretation of relationship with Jacob
    Freud, 4
  and Pauline Freud, 132–33
  preface to second edition, 4
  and "Project for a Scientific Psychology,"
    27
  staircase dream, 51–52
Irma dream, 21–24
Israelitic Congregation (Vienna), 116

Jacob, Biblical, 161
Jews, Eastern European:
  Galician, 71–78
  and March Revolution, 95
  piety, 79–80
  shtetl, life in, 78–85
Jones, Ernest, 1, 40, 45, 53, 118–19, 124–25,
    143, 160, 182, 188–89
  on Freud's intellectual paralysis, 52
  on Freud's need for a censor, 64
Josef II (king of Austria), 75, 76,
    86
Joseph, Biblical, 161–62
Judaism:
  mystical strain in, 10, 72–73, 77,
    84
  and piety, 50–51
  Semitic sex cult, 45–46
  taboos of, 51, 91, 100–101, 110–11
  see also Moses and Monotheism
Jung, Carl Gustav, 190–93
  correspondence with Freud, 10
  criticism of Freud's self-censoring, 70
  Freud's "unruly" homosexual feelings for,
    130

Kabbalah, 72–73
Kanner, Babath, 123
Kanner, Berisch, 138
Kanner, Moises, 144–45
Kanner, Sally, 90–91
  see also Freud, Sally
Kanner family, 104
Kokach, Ferdinand, 123
kosher, 80
Krafft-Ebing, Professor, 36
Kris, Ernst, 50, 65, 247n

Landes, Ruth, 78, 83–84
Last Judgment, The (Signorelli), 53–54
Leopoldstadter Communales Realund
    Obergymnasium, 168–69
libido, 69
  theory of, 183

Making of Manchester Jewry, The
    (Williams), 175
Malleus Maleficarum, 45
Maria Teresa (queen of Austria), 75
maskilim, 77
masturbation, 121
  castration threat, 65, 110, 132, 141–42
  in dreams, 111–14
  Judaic ban on, 91, 100–101, 110–11
melancholia, 20, 38
  periodic, 34–35
Mendelssohn, Moses, 76, 86
Meynert, Theodor, 7
Michelangelo, 184–87
migraine, 38
  sexual theory of, 20

Mitnaggedim, 86
moratorium, intellectual, 8
  Freud's, 8, 52–54
Moravian Jews, 91–92
Moses, Biblical, 163, 184–85, 187–88
  introduction of circumcision by, 200
  Freud as, 193–94
  historical reconstruction of, 197–201
  and Michelangelo's *Moses,* 184–87,
    193–94
  as patriarch, 188–89
Moses (Michelangelo), 184–87
Moses and Monotheism (Freud):
  as coded confession, 196–97, 267n
  historical reconstruction of Biblical Moses,
    197–200, 266n
  Moses as murdered "primal father," 203–5
  Paul and Christianity, 205–8
  writing of, 194–95, 202–3

Nathansohn, Amalie, 97–98
  brothers and sisters of, 139
  see also Freud, Amalie
Nathansohn, Jacob, 97–98, 104, 138 139,
    149, 213
Nathansohn, Julius, 104, 115
Nathansohn, Sarah, 104, 139,
    149
Nervous States and Their Treatment (Stekel),
    189–90
neurasthenia, 38
  in males, 11, 12
  melancholia as, 35
  periodic, 34–35
  symptoms of, 10–11, 38
  in women, 11–12
Neurologisches Zentralblatt, 32
neuroses:
  sexual theory of, 8
  see also specific neuroses, e.g.: actual
    neuroses
New Ghetto, The (Herzl), 147
Nunberg, Herman, 182

obsessional neurosis, 24, 31, 34, 38
Oedipus theory:
  first presentation as compromise, 61
  as inner censor, 69
  as redemption from guilt, 207–8
  and renunciation of seduction theory, 2,
    50
  and "Screen Memories," 66
  as theory of patricide, 183, 193
Oedipus legend, 61–63, 127
Orvieto, Italy, 53–54

Paneth, Sophie, 21
Pappenheim, Bertha, 6
  see also Anna O.
paranoia, 39
  as defensive psychosis, 35

and repressed fantasies, 48–49
seduction theory of, 32, 34, 39
paresthesias, 11
Paul, biblical, 205–8
Pentateuch, the, 73, 80, 81
periodicity theory (Fliess), 8–9, 249n
personality theory, 196
Philippson, Ludwig, 95, 255n
Bible, 95, 126–27, 157–59, 162, 198
phobias, 24
piety, 50–51
Poland, Jews in, 72–75, 78
possession, medieval theories of, 45
Potocki, Count, 85
psychoanalysis, starting point of, 1, 54–56
psychoses, extension of seduction theory to, 35
Pur, Josef *137*, 138

Rabbinism, 75, 76
Rank, Otto, 182
Räuber, Die, 127
Rebecca joke, 57, 136–37
Reiger, Dr., 35
Reik, Theodor, 182
repression, 26–27
in "The Aetiology of Hysteria," 36–37
of fantasies, 48
and female sexuality, 183
hermeneutic approach to, 43–44
of hostile impulses against parents, 50
mechanism of, 33
and nursemaid dream, 60
and piety, 50–51, 251n
and seduction theory, 29–30
shame and morality as forces, 32
time frame of, 30–31
Revue neurologique, 32
Richter, Horst-Eberhard, 14, 15, 122, 248n
Roazen, Paul, 18, 19, 117, 248n
Ricouer, Paul, 26, 28
Robert, Marthe, 4, 41, 42, 161, 196, 208
Rokach, Ferdinand, 123
Rokach, Maria, 123, 213

Sabbateanism, 73
sexual mystery cult, 73–74
Sachs, Hanns, 182, 187–88
Sagen des klassischen Altertums (Myths of Classical Antiquity) (Schwab), 61–63
Sajner, Josef, 71, 85, 92, 96, 108, 109, 119, 122, 138, 144
Sâlpetrière (Paris), 6
Schiller, 127
Schreber, Daniel Paul, 182, 249n
Schur, Max:
on censored "big dream," 65
on connection between Emma episode and conception of Anna Freud, 31

on Emma incident, 22–23
on Freud's death expectations, 9–10
on Freud's heart troubles, 15, 16–17, 243n
on Freud's last hours, 211
on Rebecca joke, 57, 136–37
on Rebekka Freud, 135–36
on Semitic sex cult, 45
Schwab, Gustav, 61–63
seduction theory:
age at which seduction occurs, 44–45
consequences of renunciation of, 56–57
development of, 24–31
and fantasies, 46–48
and medieval theories of exorcism and possession, 45
and Oedipus theory, 61
outline of, 31–32
perversity of seducers, 43, 44, 56
proofs of, 45
renunciation of, 1–2, 3, 54–58
and sexual theory of actual neuroses, 14
and Stekel, 190
and true psychoanalytic theory, 69–70
self-analysis, 50–54
Semitic sex cult, 45–46
Shakespeare, William, 63
shtetl, life in, 78–85
ban on extramarital intercourse and masturbation in, 91, 100–101
Sigmund Freud, the Jew (Simon), 18–19
Signorelli, Luca, 53–54
Silberstein, Eduard, 168–69, 170, 173
Simon, Ernst, 18–19, 181
Smolka, Franciszek, 88
Society of Psychiatry and Neurology, 36
sociogenetic theory, 35, 205–6
Solomon (king), 127
Stanescu, Heinz, 169
Stekel, Wilhelm, 70, 189–90, 248n
Stierlin, Helm, 70, 180, 212
structural theory, 183, 196
sublimation, fantasies as, 47
Superego, 183
Swales, Peter J., 21, 91, 109, 116, 119, 122, 139
Symbols of Transformation (Jung), 191

taboo, Jacob's, 63, 68, 70, 100–101, 155, 178
dream of Jacob's funeral, 42–43
Freud's ambition and, 44, 154
and Jung, 192
and *Moses and Monotheism,* 194–208
role in Freud's creation of Oedipus theory, 61, 69, 212
Talmud, *see* Pentateuch, the
Tausk, 70, 182
Torah, the, 72–73, 80, 81, 84, 86
Tov, Baal Shem, 74
Tysmenitz, Galicia, 75, 76, 78, 85–88
Freud never visited, 138

unconscious, 60
urination, and masturbation, 112–14

Vienna Psychoanalytic Association,
    188–89
Viennese College of Physicians, 30–31
Virgil, 67

Weich, Osias, 165
Weiss, E., 184
Williams, Bill, 175
Wischnitzer, M., 86
witches, and seduction theory, 45

Wittek, Resi, 104, 119–22, 151, 177, 214
"Wolf Man" case, 182

Yiddish, 72, 138

Zaddiks and Zaddikim, 74–75
Zajíc, Johann, 138
Zajíc, Monika, 104, 108, 119, 138
Zajíc family, 104, 108, 119, 138
Zborowski, Mark, 78, 83–84
Zentralblatt für Psychoanalyse, 189
Zevi, Shabbetai, 73, 74
Zweig, Arnold, 195